THE ROMAN POTTERY OF KENT

Monograph Series
of the
Kent Archaeological Society

(General Editor: A.P. Detsicas, B.A., M.A., D.Litt., F.S.A.)

No. V

THE ROMAN POTTERY OF KENT

By

R.J. Pollard, B.A., Ph.D., M.I.F.A.

Published by the
Kent Archaeological Society
Maidstone
1988

Front Cover: Lullingstone Roman Villa. Roman Tableware, Second Century A.D.
(Crown Copyright. Courtesy of English Heritage)

Published with the aid of grants from the British Academy, the Marc Fitch Fund
and the Twenty-seven Foundation Awards

© 1988 Kent Archaeological Society

ISBN 0 906746 12 4

Produced in England and distributed by
Alan Sutton Publishing Ltd.,
30 Brunswick Road, Gloucester GL1 1JJ.

CONTENTS

LIST OF FIGURES

A NOTE ON THE POTTERY ILLUSTRATIONS

The 215 illustrations depict a selection of the products of the various known and postulated industries operating in Kent during the first to early fifth century A.D., together with some of the imports from other parts of Roman Britain and the Continent that have been recorded in the county. The dating appended to each figure caption refers to the *floruit* of the type in Kent alone, unless otherwise specified, and to the form-fabric association figured. These dates are only broad approximations, with speculative wider ranges quoted in brackets. There exist too few well-stratified, closely-dated recorded sites in Kent, as yet, for the more precise dating of the kind quoted by Gillam (1957, 1970), for example, to be attempted.

ACKNOWLEDGEMENTS

The author would like to thank the many individuals and institutions consulted, for their advice and assistance. They are too numerous to list here, but are named either in the body of the study or in Appendices 1 and 5. However, the staff of the Canterbury Archaeological Trust merit especial mention for their hospitality and patience: the pottery analysts, Miss Marion Green and Mr Nigel Macpherson-Grant, may be singled out for their endeavours in this field of study. The following permitted unpublished items to be drawn for inclusion in this work, and the author is particularly indebted to them on this account: Mr J. Bradshaw; the late Mr S. Harker; Dr F. Jenkins; Mr T.A. Jones; the Department of the Environment; the British Museum; Maidstone Museum.

It is a pleasure to acknowledge the constant advice and encouragement offered by Dr M. G. Fulford, whose guidance has been invaluable; to Dr Fulford, and indeed to all of the staff of the Department of Archaeology, University of Reading, the author is deeply indebted. Misses J. Pulliblank and J. Fanshaw and Mrs. J. King are to be warmly congratulated on producing typescripts from my cramped manuscripts with the greatest patience. Thanks are due to the Kent Archaeological Society, and in particular to the Society's Honorary Editor, Dr A. P. Detsicas, for the opportunity to publish my doctoral thesis in an abridged form. Finally, I would like to thank my parents, Mr and Mrs. J. A. Pollard, and my friends, in particular Ms W. Owen and Ms R. Wales, for their tolerance and encouragement during the years of struggle.

The thesis was completed towards the end of 1982 and, but for minor revisions made in early 1985, remains unamended. Account should, therefore, be taken of the passage of time between writing and publication, particularly with regard to references to work in progress in the 1980s, and the sources of certain wares (e.g. 'North Gaulish' colour-coated ware, whose sources seem less assured in 1988 than they did in 1982 – R. Symonds, pers. comm.)

ABBREVIATIONS

Antiq. J.	*The Antiquaries Journal*
Arch. Aeliana	*Archaeologia Aeliana*
Arch. Cant.	*Archaeologia Cantiana*
Arch. Canterbury	The Archaeology of Canterbury Monograph Series
Arch. Excavs.	H.M. Stationery Office Annual Report on Archaeological Excavations
Arch. J.	*The Archaeological Journal*
BAR(B)	British Archaeological Reports, British Series
BAR(I)	British Archaeological Reports, Supplementary/International Series
CBA Res. Reps.	Research Reports of the Council for British Archaeology
Essex Arch. Hist.	*Essex Archaeology and History*
Essex J.	*The Essex Journal*
Herts. Arch.	*Hertfordshire Archaeology*
JBAA	*The Journal of the British Archaeological Association*
JRS	*The Journal of Roman Studies*
KAR	*Kent Archaeological Review*
KARN	*Kent Archaeological Research Groups' Council Newsletter*
London Arch.	*The London Archaeologist*
PPS	*Proceedings of the Prehistoric Society*
Soc. Antiq. Res. Reps.	Reports of the Research Committee of the Society of Antiquaries of London
Surrey Arch. Coll.	*Surrey Archaeological Collections*
Sussex Arch. Coll.	*Sussex Archaeological Collections*
TEAS	*Transactions of the Essex Archaeological Society*
TLMAS	*Transactions of the London and Middlesex Archaeological Society*
World Arch.	*World Archaeology*

BIBLIOGRAPHY

Alcock 1971   L. Alcock, *Arthur's Britain*, London, 1971.

Allen 1954   A.F. Allen, 'Roman and other Remains from Chalk near Gravesend', *Arch. Cant.*, lxviii (1954), 144–58.

Allen 1959   A.F. Allen, 'Further Discoveries of Roman Kilns and Remains at Chalk near Gravesend', *Arch. Cant.*, lxxiii (1959), 270–3.

Allen 1970   A.F. Allen, 'Chalk and Shorne', *Arch. Cant.*, lxxxv (1970), 184–7.

Allen 1961   D.F. Allen, 'The Origins of Coinage in Britain: A Reappraisal', in Frere 1961, 97–308.

Allen 1971   D.F. Allen, 'British Potin Coins: A Review', in Jesson and Hill 1971, 127–54.

Allen 1976   D.F. Allen, 'Wealth, Money and Coinage in a Celtic Society', in (Ed.) J.V.S. Megaw, *To illustrate the Monuments*, London, 1976, 199–208.

Anderson 1980   A.C. Anderson, *A Guide to Roman Fine Wares*, VORDA Research Series no. 1, Highworth, 1980.

Anderson *et al.* 1982 A.C. Anderson, M.G. Fulford, H. Hatcher and A.M. Pollard, 'Chemical Analysis of Hunt Cups and allied Wares from Britain', *Britannia*, xiii (1982), 229–38.

Anderson 1978   A.S. Anderson, 'Wiltshire Fine Wares', in Arthur and Marsh 1978, 373–92.

Anon 1924   Anon, 'Rare Pottery from Kent', *Antiq. J.*, iv (1924), 158–9.

Anthony 1968   I.E. Anthony, 'Excavations in Verulam Hill Field, St. Albans, 1963–4', *Herts. Arch.*, i (1968), 9–50.

Arthur 1978   P.A. Arthur, 'The lead-glazed Wares of Roman Britain', in Arthur and Marsh 1978, 293–356.

Arthur 1986   P.A. Arthur, 'Roman Amphorae from Canterbury', *Britannia*, xvii (1986), 239–58.

Arthur forthcoming P.A. Arthur, 'The Amphorae', in N.C. Macpherson-Grant, *Excavations at Highstead, near Chislet, 1975–1977*, forthcoming.

Arthur and Marsh 1978 (Eds.) P.A. Arthur and G. Marsh, *Early Fine Wares in Roman Britain*, BAR (B), no. 57, Oxford, 1978.

Atkinson 1970   D. Atkinson, *Report on Excavations at Wroxeter in the County of Salop, 1923–7*, Oxford, reprinted 1970.

Balls 1958   H.J. Balls, 'Dartford and Crayford', *Arch. Cant.*, lxxii (1958), p. xlvii-xlviii.

Baxter and Mills 1978 R. Baxter and R. Mills, 'The Romano-British Site at Radfield, Sittingbourne', *Arch. Cant.*, xciv (1978), 239–48.

Bedwin 1978   O. Bedwin, 'The Excavation of a Romano-British Site at Ranscombe Hill, South Malling, 1976', *Sussex Arch. Coll.*, cxvi (1978), 241–56.

Bell 1976   (Ed.) M. Bell, 'The Excavation of an early Romano-British Site and Pleistocene Landforms at Newhaven', *Sussex Arch. Coll.*, cxiv (1976), 218–305.

Bell 1977   M. Bell, 'Excavations at Bishopstone', *Sussex Arch. Coll.*, cxv (1977).

Bennett *et al.* 1978	P. Bennett, P. Garrard and N.C. Macpherson-Grant, 'Excavations at 16–21 North Lane, Canterbury', *Arch. Cant.*, xciv (1978), 165–91.
Bennett *et al.* 1980	P. Bennett, N.C. Macpherson-Grant and P. Blockley, 'Four minor Sites excavated by the Canterbury Archaeological Trust, 1978–79', *Arch. Cant.*, xcvi (1980), 267–304.
Bennett *et al.* 1982	P. Bennett, S.S. Frere and S. Stow, *Excavations at Canterbury Castle*, Arch. Canterbury, Vol. I, Maidstone, 1982.
Bennett forthcoming	P. Bennett, 'Excavations on the Site of the Almonry Chapel', in (Ed.) P. Bennett, *Excavations in the Cathedral Precincts: (i) The 'Aula Nova', Almonry Chapel and Lanfranc's Dormitory*, Arch. Canterbury, Vol. III, forthcoming.
Bidwell 1977	P. Bidwell, 'Early Black-burnished Ware at Exeter', in Dore and Greene 1977, 189–98.
Birchall 1965	A. Birchall, 'The Aylesford-Swarling Culture: The Problem of the Belgae reconsidered', *PPS*, xxxi (1965), 241–367.
Bird 1977	J. Bird, 'African Red Slip Ware in Roman Britain', in Dore and Greene 1977, 269–78.
Bird 1981	J. Bird, 'German(?) Flagons from Roman Sites', *KAR*, 63 (1981), 55.
Bird 1982a	J. Bird, 'Imports from Germany', in Bennett *et al.* 1982, 133.
Bird 1982b	J. Bird, 'The Samian Ware', in Bennett *et al.*, 1982, 158–9.
Bird forthcoming	J. Bird, 'The Samian Ware', in (Eds.) K. Blockley and M. Day, forthcoming.
Bird *et al.* 1978a	(Eds.) J. Bird, H. Chapman and J. Clark, *Collectanea Londiniensia*, London and Middlesex Archaeological Society Special Paper no. 2, London, 1978.
Bird *et al.* 1978b	(Eds.) J. Bird, A.H. Graham, H.L. Sheldon and P. Townend, *Southwark Excavations 1972–74*, London and Middlesex Archaeological Society and Surrey Archaeological Society Joint Publication no. 1, London, 1978.
Bird *et al.* 1978c	J. Bird, M.J. Hammerson and C. Murray, 'The other imported Pottery', in Bird *et al.* 1978b, 529–32.
Bird and Marsh 1978	J. Bird and G. Marsh, 'The Samian Ware', in Bird *et al.* 1978b, 527–9.
Bird and Marsh 1981	J. Bird and G. Marsh, 'The Samian Ware', in Philp 1981, 178–202.
Bird and Williams 1983	J. Bird and D.F. Williams, 'German Marbled Flagons in Roman Britain', *Britannia*, xiv (1983), 247–52.
Birley 1979	A. Birley, *The People of Roman Britain*, London, 1979.
Blockley and Day 1978	K. Blockley and M. Day, '16 Watling Street, Canterbury', *Arch. Cant.*, xciv (1978), 273–5.
Blockley and Day 1979	K. Blockley and M. Day, 'Marlowe Car Park Excavations', *Arch. Cant.*, xcv (1979), 267–70.
Blockley and Day 1980	K. Blockley and M. Day, 'The Marlowe Car Park Excavations', *Arch. Cant.*, xcvi (1980), 402–5.
Blockley and Day forthcoming	K. Blockley and M. Day, *The Marlowe Car Park and associated Excavations*, Arch. Canterbury, Vol. V, forthcoming.
Blumstein 1956	M. Blumstein, 'Roman Pottery from Hoo', *Arch. Cant.*, lxx (1956), 273–7.
Blurton 1977	(Ed.) T.R. Blurton, 'Excavations at Angel Court, Walbrook', *TLMAS*, xxviii (1977), 14–100.
Boon 1974a	G.C. Boon, *Silchester: The Roman Town of Calleva*, London, 1974.
Boon 1974b	G.C. Boon, 'Counterfeit Coins in Roman Britain', in Casey and Reece 1974, 95–172.
Bradley 1978	R.J. Bradley, *The Prehistoric Settlement of Britain*, London, 1978.
Bradshaw 1970	J. Bradshaw, 'Wye', *Arch. Cant.*, lxxxv (1970), 177–8.
Bradshaw 1972	J. Bradshaw, 'Wye', *Arch. Cant.*, lxxxvii (1972), 233.
Branigan 1976	K. Branigan, *The Roman Villa in south-west Britain*, Bradford-on-Avon, 1976.
Breeze 1977	D.J. Breeze, 'The Fort at Bearsden and the Supply of Pottery to the Roman Army', in Dore and Greene 1977, 133–46.

Breeze and Dobson 1978   D.J. Breeze and B. Dobson, *Hadrian's Wall*, London, 1978.

Brent 1861   J. Brent (Jnr.), 'Roman Cemeteries in Canterbury, with some Conjectures concerning its earliest Inhabitants', *Arch. Cant.*, iv (1861), 27–43.

Brewster 1972   N.H. Brewster, 'Corbridge: Its Significance for the Study of Rhenish Ware', *Arch. Aeliana* (4th series), 1 (1972), 205–16.

Brinson 1944   J.G.S. Brinson, 'Two Burial Groups of Belgic Age, Hothfield Common, near Ashford', *Arch. Cant.*, lvi (1944), 41–7.

de Brisay and Evans 1975   (Eds.) K.W. de Brisay and K.A. Evans, *Salt: The Study of an ancient Industry*, Colchester Archaeological Group Monograph, Colchester, 1975.

Brodribb 1969   G. Brodribb, 'Stamped Tiles of the "Classis Britannica"', *Sussex Arch. Coll.*, cvii (1969), 102–25.

Brodribb 1979   G. Brodribb, 'Tile from the Roman Bath House at Beauport Park', *Britannia*, x (1979), 139–56.

Brown and Sheldon 1974   A.E. Brown and H.L. Sheldon, 'Highgate Wood; The Pottery and its Production', *London Arch.*, 2, no. 9 (1974), 222–31.

Bryant 1973   G.F. Bryant, 'Experimental Romano-British Kiln Firings', in Detsicas 1973, 149–60.

Burkitt 1849   O.O. Burkitt, 'Researches at Higham, Kent', *JBAA* iv (1849), 393–4.

Burnham and Johnson 1979   (Eds.) B.C. Burnham and H.B. Johnson, *Invasion and Response: The Case of Roman Britain*, BAR(B), no. 73, Oxford, 1979.

Bushe-Fox 1913   J.P. Bushe-Fox, *First Report on the Excavations on the Site of the Roman Town at Wroxeter, Shropshire 1912*, Soc. Antiq. Res. Reps., i, Oxford, 1913.

Bushe-Fox 1914   J.P. Bushe-Fox, *Second Report on the Excavations on the Site of the Roman Town at Wroxeter, Shropshire*, Soc. Antiq. Res. Reps., ii, Oxford, 1914.

Bushe-Fox 1916   J.P. Bushe-Fox, *Third Report on the Excavations on the Site of the Roman Town at Wroxeter, Shropshire*, Soc. Antiq. Res. Reps., iv, Oxford, 1916.

Bushe-Fox 1925   J.P. Bushe-Fox, *Excavation of the Late-Celtic Urnfield at Swarling, Kent*, Soc. Antiq. Res. Reps., v, Oxford, 1925.

Bushe-Fox 1926   J.P. Bushe-Fox, *First Report on the Excavation of the Roman Fort at Richborough, Kent*, Soc. Antiq. Res. Reps., vi, Oxford, 1926.

Bushe-Fox 1928   J.P. Bushe-Fox, *Second Report on the Excavation of the Roman Fort at Richborough, Kent*, Soc. Antiq. Res. Reps., vii, Oxford, 1928.

Bushe-Fox 1932   J.P. Bushe-Fox, *Third Report on the Excavation of the Roman Fort at Richborough, Kent*, Soc. Antiq. Res. Reps., x, Oxford, 1932.

Bushe-Fox 1949   J.P. Bushe-Fox, *Fourth Report on the Excavation of the Roman Fort at Richborough, Kent*, Soc. Antiq. Res. Reps., xvi, Oxford, 1949.

Caiger 1958   J.E.L. Caiger, 'A Belgic Site at Bexley', *Arch. Cant.*, lxxii (1958), 186–9.

Callender 1965   M.H. Callender, *Roman Amphorae*, Oxford, 1965.

Callender 1968   M.H. Callender, 'The Amphora Stamps', in Cunliffe 1968, 162–71.

Casey 1974   P.J. Casey, 'The Interpretation of Romano-British Site Finds', in Casey and Reece 1974, 37–51.

Casey 1979   (Ed.) P.J. Casey, *The End of Roman Britain*, BAR(B), no. 71, Oxford, 1979.

Casey 1980   P.J. Casey, *Roman Coinage in Britain*, Shire Archaeology, no. 12, Aylesbury, 1980.

Casey and Reece 1974   (Eds.) P.J. Casey and R. Reece, *Coins and the Archaeologist*, BAR(B), no. 4, Oxford, 1974.

Castle 1972   S.A. Castle, 'A Kiln of the Potter Doinus', *Arch. J.*, cxxix (1972), 69–88.

Castle 1973a   S.A. Castle, 'Trial Excavations in Field 410, Brockley Hill, Part 1', *London Arch.*, 2, no. 2 (1973), 36–9.

Castle 1973b   S.A. Castle, 'Trial Excavations at Brockley Hill, Part 2', *London Arch.*, 2, no. 4 (1973), 78–83.

Castle 1974   S.A. Castle, 'Excavations at Brockley Hill, Middlesex, March-May, 1972',
                           TLMAS, xxv (1974), 251–63.

Castle 1974/76   S.A. Castle, 'Roman Pottery from Radlett, 1959', *Herts. Arch.*, iv (1976),
                           149–52.

Castle 1976   S.A. Castle, 'Roman Pottery from Brockley Hill, Middlesex, 1966 and
                           1972–1974', *TLMAS*, xxvii (1976), 206–27.

Castle 1978   S.A. Castle, 'Amphorae from Brockley Hill', *Britannia*, ix (1978), 383–92.

Castle and Warbis 1973   S.A. Castle and J.B. Warbis, 'Excavations on Field no. 157, Brockley Hill
                           (Sulloniacae?), Middlesex', *TLMAS*, xxiv (1973), 85–110.

Catherall 1983   P.D. Catherall, 'A Romano-British Pottery Manufacturing Site at Oakleigh
                           Farm, Higham, Kent', *Britannia*, xiv (1983), 103–41.

Cawood 1986   T. Cawood, 'The Pottery', in Rudling 1986, 213–8.

Champion 1976   T.C. Champion, *The Earlier Iron Age in the Region of the Lower Thames:
                           Insular and external Factors*, unpublished D.Phil. thesis, Institute of Archaeolo-
                           gy, Oxford.

Chaplin 1962   R.E. Chaplin, 'Excavations in Rochester, Winter 1961–62', *Arch. Cant.*,
                           lxxvii (1962), pp. l-li.

Chaplin and Brooks 1966   R.E. Chaplin and R.T. Brooks, 'Excavation of a Romano-British Site at South
                           Ockendon', TEAS (3rd series), ii (1966), 83–94.

Chaplin and Coy 1961   R.E. Chaplin and J.P Coy, 'Cliffe 1961', *Arch. Cant.*, lxxvi (1961), 205–6.
Chaplin and Coy 1962   R.E. Chaplin and J.P. Coy, 'Cliffe, Kent 1962', *Arch. Cant.*, lxxvii (1962), p. l.
Chapman and Johnson 1973   H. Chapman and T. Johnson, 'Excavations at Aldgate and Bush Lane House in
                           the City of London, 1972', *TLMAS*, xxiv (1973), 1–73.

Charles 1847   T. Charles, 'Excavation of the Roman Villa at the Mount near Maidstone',
                           JBAA, ii (1847), 86–8.

Cherry *et al.* 1978   (Eds.) J.F. Cherry, C. Gamble and S. Shennan, *Sampling in contemporary
                           British Archaeology*, BAR(B), no. 50, Oxford, 1978.

Clark 1949   A.J. Clark, 'Fourth Century Romano-British Pottery Kilns at Overwey, Til-
                           ford', *Surrey Arch. Coll.*, li (1949), 29–56.

Clarke 1977   (Ed.) D.L. Clarke, *Spatial Archaeology*, London, 1977.
Clarke 1979   G. Clarke, *The Roman Cemetery at Lankhills*, Winchester Studies, 3ii, Oxford,
                           1979.

Cleere 1970   H. Cleere, 'The Romano-British industrial Site at Bardown, Wadhurst', Sussex
                           Arch. Soc. Occasional Paper 1, 1970.

Cleere 1974   H. Cleere, 'The Roman Iron Industry of the Weald and its Connexions with the
                           Classis Britannica', *Arch. J.*, cxxxi (1974), 171–99.

Cleere 1977   H. Cleere, '*The Classis Britannica*', in Johnston 1977, 16–19.
Cockett 1976   R.A.C. Cockett, 'Ash', *Arch. Cant.*, xcii (1976), 249.
Collis 1974   J. Collis, 'A functionalist Approach to pre-Roman Coinage', in Casey and
                           Reece 1974, 1–11.

Cook 1928   N.C. Cook, 'A Roman Site in the Church Field at Snodland', *Arch. Cant.*,
                           xl (1928), 79–84.

Cook and McCarthy 1933   N.C. Cook and M.J. McCarthy, 'A Roman Cemetery at West Wickham, Kent',
                           Arch. Cant., xlv (1933), 188–92.

Corder 1941   P. Corder, 'A Roman Pottery of the Hadrian-Antonine Period at Verulamium',
                           Antiq. J., xxi (1941), 271–98.

Corder 1957   P. Corder, 'The Structure of Romano-British Pottery Kilns', *Arch. J.*,
                           cxiv (1957), 10–27.

Cotton 1958   M.A. Cotton, 'The coarse Roman Pottery', in Cotton and Gathercole 1958, 59–90.
Cotton and Gathercole 1958 M.A. Cotton and P.W. Gathercole, *Excavations at Clausentum, Southampton,
                           1951–54*, Ministry of Works Archaeological Reports, no. 2, London, 1958.

Cotton and Richardson 1941 M.A. Cotton and K.M. Richardson, 'A Belgic Cremation Site at Stone, Kent',
                           PPS, vii (1941), 134–41.

Cotton and Richardson 1949	M.A. Cotton and K.M. Richardson, 'A Romano-British Cremation Cemetery at Stone, Kent', *Arch. J.*, cvi (1949), 46–50.
Couchman 1924	J.E. Couchman, 'Recent Discoveries at Ramsgate', *Antiq. J.*, iv (1924), 53–4.
Couchman 1925	J.E. Couchman, 'A Roman Cemetery at Hassocks', *Sussex Arch. Coll.*, lxvi (1925), 34–61.
Cunliffe 1965	B.W. Cunliffe, 'The Pottery', in F.A. Hastings, 'Excavation of an Iron Age Farmstead at Hawks Hill, Leatherhead', *Surrey Arch. Coll.*, lxii (1965), 13–39.
Cunliffe 1968	(Ed.) B.W. Cunliffe, *Fifth Report on the Excavation of the Roman Fort at Richborough, Kent*, Soc. Antiq. Res. Reps., xxiii, Oxford, 1968.
Cunliffe 1971	B.W. Cunliffe, *Excavations at Fishbourne 1961–1969, Volume II: The Finds*, Soc. Antiq. Res. Reps., xxvii, London, 1971.
Cunliffe 1973	B.W. Cunliffe, *The Regni*, London, 1973.
Cunliffe 1977	B.W. Cunliffe, 'The Saxon Shore – Some Problems and Misconceptions', in Johnston 1977, 1–6.
Cunliffe 1978	B.W. Cunliffe, *Iron Age Communities in Britain*, 2nd edition, London, 1978.
Cunliffe 1980	B.W. Cunliffe, 'Excavations at the Roman Fort at Lympne', *Britannia*, xi (1980), 227–88.
Cunliffe and Rowley 1976	(Eds.) B.W. Cunliffe and T. Rowley, *Oppida in barbarian Europe*, BAR(I), no. 11, Oxford, 1976.
Cunliffe and Rowley 1978	(Eds.) B.W. Cunliffe and T. Rowley, *Lowland Iron Age Communities in Europe*, BAR(I), no. 48, Oxford, 1978.
Dale 1971	L.C. Dale, 'Belgic and Roman Pottery from Dartford', *Arch. Cant.*, lxxxvi (1971), 210–15.
Dannell 1973	G.B. Dannell, 'The Potter Indixivixus', in Detsicas 1973, 139–42.
Dannell 1979	G.B. Dannell, 'Eating and drinking in pre-Conquest Britain', in Burnham and Johnson 1979, 177–84.
Darling 1977	M.J. Darling, 'Pottery from early military Sites in western Britain', in Dore and Greene 1977, 57–100.
Day 1980	M. Day, 'The Roman Period in the Parishes of St. Martin and St. Paul', in (Ed.) M. Sparks, *The Parish of St. Martin and St. Paul: Historical Essays in Memory of James Hobbs*, Canterbury, 1980, 5–11.
Detsicas 1966	A.P. Detsicas, 'An Iron Age and Romano-British Site at Stone Castle Quarry, Greenhithe', *Arch. Cant.*, lxxxi (1966), 136–90.
Detsicas 1967	A.P. Detsicas, 'Excavations at Eccles, 1966: I. Fifth Interim Report. II. The Tilery', *Arch. Cant.*, lxxxii (1967), 162–78.
Detsicas 1973	(Ed.) A.P. Detsicas, *Current Research in Romano-British Coarse Pottery*, CBA Res. Reps., no. 10, London, 1973.
Detsicas 1974	A.P. Detsicas, 'Excavations at Eccles, 1973: Twelfth Interim Report', *Arch. Cant.*, lxxxix (1974), 119–34.
Detsicas 1975	A.P. Detsicas, 'A Romano-British Building at Charing', *Arch. Cant.*, xci (1975), 107–10.
Detsicas 1976	A.P. Detsicas, 'Excavations at Eccles: Fourteenth Interim Report', *Arch. Cant.*, xcii (1976), 157–64.
Detsicas 1977a	A.P. Detsicas, 'First Century Pottery Manufacture at Eccles, Kent', in Dore and Greene 1977, 19–36.
Detsicas 1977b	A.P. Detsicas, Review of (Ed.) D.P.S. Peacock, *Pottery and early Commerce* [Peacock 1977f], *Arch. Cant.*, xciii (1977), 237–40.
Detsicas 1983	A.P. Detsicas, *The Cantiaci*, Gloucester, 1983.
Doran and Hodson 1975	J.E. Doran and F.R. Hodson, *Mathematics and Computers in Archaeology*, Edinburgh, 1975.
Dore and Greene 1977	(Eds.) J. Dore and K.T. Greene, *Roman Pottery Studies in Britain and beyond*, BAR(I), no. 30, Oxford, 1977.

Dowker 1878   G. Dowker, 'Roman Remains at Preston near Wingham', *Arch. Cant.*, xii (1878), 47–8.

Dowker 1882   G. Dowker, 'A Roman Villa at Wingham', *Arch. Cant.*, xiv (1882), 134–9.

Dowker 1883   G. Dowker, 'The Roman Villa at Wingham. Part II', *Arch. Cant.*, xv (1883), 351–7.

Dowker 1893   G. Dowker, 'On "Romano-British" fictile Vessels from Preston near Wingham', *Arch. Cant.*, xx (1893), 49–53.

Down 1974   A. Down, *Chichester Excavations II*, Chichester, 1974.

Down 1978   A. Down, *Chichester Excavations III*, Chichester, 1978.

Down 1981   A. Down, *Chichester Excavations V*, Chichester, 1981.

Down and Rule 1971   A. Down and M. Rule, *Chichester Excavations I*, Chichester, 1971.

Drewett 1978   (Ed.) P.L. Drewett, *Archaeology in Sussex to AD 1500*, CBA Res. Reps., no. 29, London, 1978.

Drury 1973   P.J. Drury, 'Observation of Roadworks in Thurrock 1969–70', *Essex Arch. Hist.*, (3rd series), v (1973), 113–22.

Drury 1976a   P.J. Drury, 'Braintree: Excavations and Research, 1971–76', *Essex Arch. Hist.*, (3rd series), viii (1976), 1–143.

Drury 1976b   P.J. Drury, ' "Rettendon" Ware Kiln Debris and other Materials from Sandon', *Essex Arch. Hist.*, (3rd series), viii (1976), 253–8.

Drury 1977   P.J. Drury, 'Excavations at Rawreth, 1968', *Essex Arch. Hist.*, (3rd series), ix (1977), 20–47.

Drury 1978   P.J. Drury, *Excavations at Little Waltham, 1970–71*, CBA Res. Reps., no. 26, London, 1978.

Drury and Rodwell 1973 P.J. Drury and W.R. Rodwell, 'Excavations at Gun Hill, West Tilbury', *Essex Arch. Hist.*, (3rd series), v (1973), 48–112.

Drury and Rodwell 1980 P.J. Drury and W.R. Rodwell, 'Settlement in the later Iron Age and Roman Periods', in (Ed.) D.G. Buckley, *Archaeology in Essex to AD 1500*, CBA Res. Reps., no. 34, London, 1980, 59–75.

Duncan-Jones 1974   R.P. Duncan-Jones, *The Economy of the Roman Empire*, Cambridge, 1974.

Dunnett 1966   B.R.K. Dunnett, 'Excavations on North Hill, Colchester', *Arch. J.*, cxxiii (1966), 27–61.

Dunnett 1971   (Ed.) B.R.K. Dunnett, 'Excavations in Colchester, 1964–68', *TEAS*, (3rd series), iii (1971), 1–130.

Dunnett 1975   B.R.K. Dunnett, *The Trinovantes*, London, 1975.

Eames 1957   J. Eames, 'A Roman Bath-house at Little Chart, Kent', *Arch. Cant.*, lxxii (1957), 130–46.

Edwards and Green 1977 D.A. Edwards and C.J.S. Green, 'The Saxon Shore Fort and Settlement at Brancaster, Norfolk', in Johnston 1977, 21–9.

Elliston Erwood 1916   F.C. Elliston Erwood, 'The Earthworks at Charlton, London, S.E.', *JBAA*, (New series), xxii (1916), 125–91.

Elliston Erwood 1923   F.C. Elliston Erwood, 'A further Report on the Earthworks at Charlton, London, S.E.', *JBAA*, (New series), xxix (1923), 227–39.

Elliston Erwood 1951   F.C. Elliston Erwood, 'Further Excavations on the Site of the Earthworks at Charlton', *Arch. Cant.*, lxiv (1951), 158–60.

Elsdon 1975   S.M. Elsdon, *Stamp and Roulette decorated Pottery of the La Tène Period in eastern England: A Study in geometric Designs*, BAR(B), no. 10, Oxford, 1975.

Ettlinger 1977   E. Ettlinger, 'Cooking Pots at Vindonissa', in Dore and Greene 1977, 47–56.

Evans 1890   A.J. Evans, 'On a Late-Celtic Urnfield at Aylesford, Kent', *Archaeologia*, lii (1890), 317–88.

Evans 1949   J.H. Evans, 'Roman Remains from the Upchurch Marshes', *Arch. Cant.*, lxii (1949), 146–7.

Evans 1950   J.H. Evans, 'Report for the Year ended 31st December, 1949', *Arch. Cant.*, lxiii (1950), pp. xliv-xlv.

Evans 1953   J.H. Evans, 'Archaeological Horizons in the north Kent Marshes', *Arch. Cant.*, lxvi (1953), 103–46.

Evans 1974   K.J. Evans, 'Excavations on a Romano-British Site, Wiggonholt, 1964', *Sussex Arch. Coll.*, cxii (1974), 97–151.

Farrar 1973   R.A.H. Farrar, 'The Techniques and Sources of Romano-British Black-burnished Ware', in Detsicas 1973, 67–103.

Fletcher and Meates 1969   E. Fletcher and G.W. Meates, 'The ruined Church of Stone-by-Faversham', *Antiq. J.*, xlix (1969), 273–94.

Fletcher and Meates 1977   E. Fletcher and G.W. Meates, 'The ruined Church of Stone-by-Faversham: Second Report', *Antiq. J.*, lvii (1977), 67–72.

Flight and Harrison 1978   C. Flight and A.C. Harrison, 'Rochester Castle, 1976', *Arch. Cant.*, xciv (1978), 27–60.

Fox 1943   C. Fox, *The Personality of Britain*, revised edition, Cardiff, 1943.

Frere 1942/43   S.S. Frere, 'A Roman Ditch at Ewell Council School', *Surrey Arch. Coll.*, xlviii (1943), 45–60.

Frere 1944   S.S. Frere, 'An Iron Age Site at West Clandon, Surrey, and some Aspects of Iron Age and Romano-British Culture in the Wealden Area', *Arch. J.*, ci (1944), 50–67.

Frere 1954   S.S. Frere, 'Canterbury Excavations, Summer 1946', *Arch. Cant.*, lxviii (1954), 101–43.

Frere 1961   (Ed.) S.S. Frere, *Problems of the Iron Age in southern Britain*, Institute of Archaeology Occasional Paper no. 11, London, 1961.

Frere 1966   S.S. Frere, 'The End of Towns in Roman Britain', in (Ed.) J.S. Wacher, *The Civitas Capitals of Roman Britain*, Leicester, 1966, 87–100.

Frere 1970   S.S. Frere, 'The Roman Theatre at Canterbury', *Britannia*, i (1970), 83–113.

Frere 1972   S.S. Frere, *Verulamium Excavations I*, Soc. Antiq. Res. Reps., no. xxviii, Oxford, 1972.

Frere 1974   S.S. Frere, *Britannia: A History of Roman Britain*, London, 1974.

Frere 1977   S.S. Frere, 'Roman Britain in 1976', *Britannia*, viii (1977), 355–425.

Frere 1981   S.S. Frere, 'Verulamium in the late second and third Centuries', in (Eds.) A. King and M. Henig, *The Roman West in the third Century*, BAR(I), no. 109, Oxford, 1981, 383–92.

Frere 1984   S.S. Frere, 'Roman Britain in 1983', *Britannia*, xv (1983), 265–356.

Frere and St. Joseph 1974   S.S. Frere and J.K. St. Joseph, 'The Roman Fortress at Longthorpe', *Britannia*, v (1974), 1–129.

Frere *et al.* 1982   S.S. Frere, S. Stow and P. Bennett, *Excavations on the Roman and medieval Defences of Canterbury*, Arch. Canterbury, Vol. II, Maidstone, 1982.

Fulford 1973a   M.G. Fulford, 'A fourth Century colour-coated Fabric and its Types in south-east England', *Sussex Arch. Coll.*, cxi (1973), 41–4.

Fulford 1973b   M.G. Fulford, 'The Distribution and Dating of New Forest Roman Pottery', *Britannia*, iv (1973), 160–78.

Fulford 1975a   M.G. Fulford, *New Forest Roman Pottery*, BAR(B), no. 17, Oxford, 1975.

Fulford 1975b   M.G. Fulford, 'The Pottery', in B.W. Cunliffe, *Excavations at Portchester Castle, Vol. I: Roman*, Soc. Antiq. Res. Reps., xxxii, Leeds, 1975, 270–367.

Fulford 1977a   M.G. Fulford, 'Pottery and Britain's foreign Trade in the later Roman Period', in Peacock 1977f, 35–84.

Fulford 1977b   M.G. Fulford, 'The Location of Romano-British Pottery Kilns: Institutional Trade and the Market', in Dore and Greene 1977, 301–16.

Fulford 1978a   M.G. Fulford, 'Coin Circulation and Mint Activity in the Late Roman Empire: Some economic Implications', *Arch. J.*, cxxxv (1978), 67–114.

xxii R. J. POLLARD

Fulford 1978b   M.G. Fulford, 'The Romano-British Pottery', in Hartridge 1978, 119–31.

Fulford 1978c   M.G. Fulford, 'The Interpretation of Britain's late Roman Trade: The Scope of medieval historical and archaeological Analogy', in du Plat Taylor and Cleere 1978, 59–69.

Fulford 1979   M.G. Fulford, 'Pottery Production and Trade at the end of Roman Britain: The Case against Continuity', in Casey 1979, 120–32.

Fulford 1981   M.G. Fulford, 'Roman Pottery: Towards the Investigation of economic and social Change?', in (Eds.) H. Howard and E.L. Morris, *Production and Distribution: A ceramic Viewpoint*, BAR(I), no. 120, Oxford, 1981, 195–208.

Fulford and Bird 1975   M.G. Fulford and J. Bird, 'Imported Pottery from Germany in late Roman Britain', *Britannia*, vi (1975), 171–81.

Fulford and Hodder 1974   M.G. Fulford and I. Hodder, 'A Regression Analysis of some late Romano-British Pottery: A Case Study', *Oxoniensia*, xxxix (1974), 26–33.

Galliou *et al.* 1980   P. Galliou, M.G. Fulford and M. Clément, 'La Diffusion de la Céramique "A l'Eponge" dans le Nord-ouest de l'Empire romain', *Gallia*, xxxviii (1980), fasc. 2, 265–78.

Gallois 1965   R.W. Gallois, *British regional Geology: The Wealden District*, 4th Edition, London, 1965.

Gaunt 1974   J. Gaunt, 'Roman Burial at Hothfield, near Ashford', *KAR*, 38 (1974), 230–1.

Gentry *et al.* 1977   A. Gentry, J. Ivens and H. McClean, 'Excavations at Lincoln Road, London Borough of Enfield, Nov. 1974 – March 1976', *TLMAS*, xxviii (1977), 101–89.

Gillam 1939   J.P. Gillam, 'Romano-British Derbyshire Ware', *Antiq. J.*, xix (1939), 429–37.

Gillam 1957   J.P. Gillam, 'Types of Roman Coarse Pottery Vessels in northern Britain', *Arch. Aeliana* (4th series), xxxv (1957), 180–251.

Gillam 1960   J.P. Gillam, 'The Coarse Pottery', in K.A. Steer, 'Excavations at Mumrills Roman Fort 1958–1960', *Proceedings of the Society of Antiquaries of Scotland*, xciv (1961), 113–29.

Gillam 1970   J.P. Gillam, *Types of Roman Coarse Pottery Vessels in northern Britain*, 3rd edition, Newcastle-upon-Tyne, 1970.

Gillam 1973   J.P. Gillam, 'Sources of Pottery found on northern military Sites', in Detsicas 1973, 53–62.

Gillam 1979   J.P. Gillam, 'Romano-Saxon Pottery: An alternative Interpretation', in Casey 1979, 103–18.

Gillam and Mann 1970   J.P. Gillam and J.C. Mann, 'The northern British Frontier from Antoninus Pius to Caracalla', *Arch. Aeliana*, (4th series), xlviii (1970), 1–44.

Godwin 1931   F. Godwin, 'Report for the Year ending 31st December 1930', *Arch. Cant.*, xliii (1931), pp. xlviii-xlix.

Goodburn 1978   R. Goodburn, 'Roman Britain in 1977', *Britannia*, ix (1978), 403–72.

Goodburn 1979   R. Goodburn, 'Roman Britain in 1978', *Britannia*, x (1979), 268–338.

Gose 1950   E. Gose, *Gefässtypen der römischen Keramik im Rheinland*, Bonner Jahrbuch, Beiheft 1, Kevelaer, 1950.

Graham 1936   J. Graham, 'A Romano-Celtic Temple at Titsey, and the Roman Road', *Surrey Arch. Coll.*, xliv (1936), 84–101.

Green 1976   C.M. Green, 'The Coarse Pottery', in Bell 1976, 256–87.

Green 1977   C.M. Green, 'The Roman Pottery', in Bell 1977, 152–78.

Green 1978a   C.M. Green, 'The Pottery', in Bedwin 1978, 245–53.

Green 1978b   C.M. Green, 'Flavian "Ring-and-dot" Beakers from Londinium: Verulamium Form 130 and allied Types', in Arthur and Marsh 1978, 109–18.

Green 1980   C.M. Green, 'Hand-made Pottery and Society in late Iron Age and Roman East Sussex', *Sussex Arch. Coll.*, cxviii (1980), 69–86.

Green 1981   M.J. Green, 'Romano-British "Streak-burnished" Ware', *KAR*, 66 (1981), 128–30.

Green forthcoming	M.J. Green, 'The Fine Wares from fourth Century Deposits', in Blockley and Day forthcoming.
Greene 1973	K.T. Greene, 'The Pottery from Usk', in Detsicas 1973, 25–37.
Greene 1978a	K.T. Greene, 'Imported Fine Wares in Britain to AD 250: A Guide to Identification', in Arthur and Marsh 1978, 15–30.
Greene 1978b	K.T. Greene, 'Mould-decorated Central Gaulish glazed Ware in Britain', in Arthur and Marsh 1978, 31–60.
Greene 1978c	K.T. Greene, 'Roman Trade between Britain and the Rhine Provinces: The Evidence of Pottery to c. AD 250', in du Plat Taylor and Cleere 1978, 52–8.
Greene 1979a	K.T. Greene, *Usk: The pre-Flavian Fine Wares*, Reports on the Excavations at Usk 1965–1976, Vol. I, Cardiff, 1979.
Greene 1979b	K.T. Greene, 'Invasion and Response: Pottery and the Roman Army', in Burnham and Johnson 1979, 99–106.
Greenfield *et al.* 1948	E. Greenfield, G.W. Meates and E. Birchenough, 'Darent Valley archaeological Research', *Arch. Cant.*, lxi (1948), 180–3.
Greenwood 1979	P.A. Greenwood, *The Excavation at Church Road, Leyton, 1978*, Passmore Edwards Museum Monograph, London, 1979.
Grew 1980	F.O. Grew, 'Roman Britain in 1979', *Britannia*, xi (1980), 346–402.
Grimes 1930	W.F. Grimes, *Holt, Denbighshire: The Works Depot of the XX Legion at Castle Lyons, Y Cymrodor*, xli, London, 1930.
Hamilton 1977	S. Hamilton, 'The Iron Age Pottery', in Bell 1977, 83–117.
Hammerson 1978	M.J. Hammerson, 'The Coins', in Bird *et al.* 1978b, 587–99.
Hammerson and Coxshall 1977	M.J. Hammerson and R. Coxshall, 'The Coins', in Gentry *et al.* 1977, 161–8.
Hammerson and Murray 1978	M.J. Hammerson and C. Murray, '8 Union Street; Other Roman Pottery', in Bird *et al.* 1978b, 225–30.
Hanworth 1968	R. Hanworth, 'The Roman Villa at Rapsley, Ewhurst', *Surrey Arch. Coll.*, lxv (1968), 1–70.
Harden and Green 1978	D.B. Harden and C.M. Green, 'A late Roman Grave-group from the Minories, Aldgate', in Bird *et al.* 1978a, 163–75.
Hardy and Curwen 1937	H.R. Hardy and E.C. Curwen, 'An Iron Age Pottery Site near Horsted Keynes', *Sussex Arch. Coll.*, lxxviii (1937), 252–65.
Harker 1970	S.R. Harker, 'Springhead – The Well, F.19', *Arch. Cant.*, lxxxv (1970), 139–48.
Harker 1975	S.R. Harker, 'Excavations at Chalk', *KAR*, 40 (1975), 282–5.
Harker 1980	S.R. Harker, 'Springhead: A brief Reappraisal', in (Ed.) W.R. Rodwell, *Temples, Churches and Religion in Roman Britain*, BAR(B), no. 77, Oxford, 1980, 285–8.
Harrison 1970	A.C. Harrison, 'Excavations in Rochester', *Arch. Cant.*, lxxxv (1970), 95–112.
Harrison 1972	A.C. Harrison, 'Rochester East Gate, 1969', *Arch. Cant.*, lxxxvii (1972), 121–58.
Harrison and Flight 1968	A.C. Harrison and C. Flight, 'The Roman and medieval Defences of Rochester in the Light of recent Excavations', *Arch. Cant.*, lxxxiii (1968), 55–104.
Harrison 1961	E.E. Harrison, 'A pre-Roman and Romano-British Site at Charterhouse, Godalming', *Surrey Arch. Coll.*, lviii (1961), 21–34.
Hartley 1960	B.R. Hartley, *Notes on the Roman Pottery Industry in the Nene Valley*, Peterborough Museum Society Occasional Paper no. 2, Peterborough, 1960.
Hartley 1969	B.R. Hartley, 'Samian Ware or Terra Sigillata', in R.G. Collingwood and I. Richmond, *The Archaeology of Roman Britain*, 2nd edition, London, 1969, 235–51.
Hartley 1972	B.R. Hartley, 'The Roman Occupation of Scotland: The Evidence of Samian Ware', *Britannia*, iii (1972), 1–55.
Hartley 1963	K.F. Hartley, 'The Distribution of stamped Mortaria from the Colchester Potteries', in Hull 1963, 114–16.

Hartley 1968   K.F. Hartley, 'The Mortaria', in Cunliffe 1968, 172–82.

Hartley 1972   K.F. Hartley, 'Mortaria', in Harrison 1972, 134–9.

Hartley 1973a   K.F. Hartley, 'The Marketing and Distribution of Mortaria', in Detsicas 1973, 39–51.

Hartley 1973b   K.F. Hartley, 'The Kilns at Mancetter and Hartshill, Warwickshire', in Detsicas 1973, 143–7.

Hartley 1976   K.F. Hartley, 'The Mortarium Stamps', in Castle 1976, 211–23.

Hartley 1977   K.F. Hartley, 'Two major Potteries producing Mortaria in the first Century AD', in Dore and Greene 1977, 5–18.

Hartley 1981   K.F. Hartley, 'The Mortaria', in Philp 1981, 203–7.

Hartley 1982   K.F. Hartley, 'The Mortaria', in Bennett et al. 1982, 150–8.

Hartley forthcoming   K.F. Hartley, 'The Mortaria', in N.C. Macpherson-Grant, Excavations at Highstead, near Chislet, 1975–1977, forthcoming.

Hartley and Richards 1965   K.F. Hartley and E.E. Richards, 'Spectrographic Analysis of some Romano-British Mortaria', Institute of Archaeology Bulletin no. 5, London, 25–44.

Hartridge 1978   R. Hartridge, 'Excavations at the prehistoric and Romano-British Site on Slonk Hill, Shoreham', Sussex Arch. Coll., cxvi (1978), 69–142.

Haselgrove 1979   C.C. Haselgrove, 'The Significance of Coinage in pre-Conquest Britain', in Burnham and Johnson 1979, 197–209.

Hassall 1977   M.W.C. Hassall, 'The historical Background and military Units of the Saxon Shore', in Johnston 1977, 7–10.

Hassall 1978   M.W.C. Hassall, 'Britain and the Rhine Provinces: Epigraphic Evidence for Roman Trade', in du Plat Taylor and Cleere 1978, 41–8.

Hawkes 1931   C.F.C. Hawkes, 'Hill Forts', Antiquity, v (1931), 60–97.

Hawkes 1939   C.F.C. Hawkes, 'The Caburn Pottery and its Implications', Sussex Arch. Coll., lxxx (1939), 217–62.

Hawkes and Hull 1947   C.F.C. Hawkes and M.R. Hull, Camulodunum, Soc. Antiq. Res. Reps., xiv, Oxford, 1947.

Hayter and Whiting 1929   G.C.F. Hayter and W. Whiting, 'Durolevum, the Evidence of the Coins', Arch. Cant., xli (1929), 197–206.

Hinton 1977   D.A. Hinton, '"Rudely made earthen Vessels" of the twelfth to fifteenth Centuries', in Peacock 1977f, 221–38.

Hodder 1974a   I. Hodder, 'The Distribution of two Types of Romano-British Coarse Pottery in the West Sussex Region', Sussex Arch. Coll., cxii (1974), 86–96.

Hodder 1974b   I. Hodder, 'Some marketing Models for Romano-British Coarse Pottery', Britannia, v (1974), 340–59.

Hodder 1974c   I. Hodder, 'The Distribution of Savernake Ware', Wiltshire Archaeology and Natural History Magazine, lxix (1974), 67–84.

Hodder 1974d   I. Hodder, 'A Regression Analysis of some Trade and marketing Patterns', World Arch., 6 (1974), 172–89.

Hodder 1979   I. Hodder, 'Pre-Roman and Romano-British Tribal Economies', in Burnham and Johnson 1979, 189–96.

Hodder and Orton 1976   I. Hodder and C. Orton, Spatial Analysis in Archaeology, Cambridge, 1976.

Hoffman 1975   B. Hoffman, 'Les Matérieux de Construction antiques en Terre cuite', Céramique en Gaule romaine, Dossier archéologique, no. 9 (Dijon), 118.

Hogarth 1974   A.C. Hogarth, 'Barham Downs', Arch. Excavs. 1973, London, 1974, 47.

Holden 1979   E.W. Holden, 'A Romano-British Pottery Kiln at Polhill's Farm, Arlington', Sussex Arch. Coll., cxvii (1979), 58–62.

Holmes 1949   J.M. Holmes, 'Romano-British Cemeteries at Haslemere and Charterhouse', Surrey Arch. Coll., li (1949), 1–28.

Holmes 1979   J.M. Holmes, 'The Pottery', in Holden 1979, 60–1.

Hopkins 1980   K. Hopkins, 'Taxes and Trade in the Roman Empire (200 BC – AD 400)', JRS, lxx (1980), 101–25.

Horner 1965	G.K. Horner, 'Crayford Archaeological Research Group', *KARN*, 1 (1965), 14–15.
Horner 1966	G.K. Horner, 'Romano-British Site at Lullingstone Park', *KARN*, 3 (1966), 9–10.
Horner 1967	G.K. Horner, 'Further Excavations at Lullingstone', *KAR*, 8 (1967), 5–6.
Howe *et al.* 1980	M.D. Howe, J.R. Perrin and D.F. Mackreth, *Roman Pottery from the Nene Valley: A Guide*, Peterborough City Museum Occasional Paper no. 2, Peterborough, 1980.
Huggins 1978	R.M. Huggins, 'Excavation of a late Roman Site at Sewardstone Hamlet, Waltham Holy Cross, Essex, 1968–1975', *Essex Arch. Hist.*, (3rd series), x (1978), 174–86.
Hull 1958	M.R. Hull, *Roman Colchester*, Soc. Antiq. Res. Reps., xx, Oxford, 1958.
Hull 1963	M.R. Hull, *The Roman Potters' Kilns at Colchester*, Soc. Antiq. Res. Reps., xxi, Oxford, 1963.
Hurst 1976	J.G. Hurst, 'The Pottery', in (Ed.) D.M. Wilson, *The Archaeology of Anglo-Saxon England*, London, 1976, 283–321.
Hutchings 1966	R.F. Hutchings, 'Cliffe', *Arch. Cant.*, lxxxi (1966), pp. liv-lvi.
Jackson and Ambrose 1978	D.A. Jackson and T.M. Ambrose, 'Excavations at Wakerley, Northants., 1972–75', *Britannia*, ix (1978), 115–242.
Jackson 1962	I. Jackson, 'Upchurch: Two Roman Pottery Kilns', *Arch. Cant.*, lxxvii (1962), 190–5.
Jackson 1972/73	I. Jackson, 'Romano-British Pottery Kiln on the Upchurch Marshes', *KAR*, 30 (1973), 288–90.
James and James 1977	D.J. James and H.R. James, 'Little Shelford, Roman Site', *Essex Arch. Hist.*, (3rd series), ix (1977), 100–1.
James and James 1978	D.A. James and H.R. James, 'Roman Burials at Little Shelford, Foulness, Essex, 1972', *Essex Arch. Hist.*, (3rd series), x (1978), 227–30.
Jenkins 1950	F. Jenkins, 'Canterbury Excavations in Burgate Street, 1946–8', *Arch. Cant.*, lxiii (1950), 82–118.
Jenkins 1951	F. Jenkins, 'Archaeological Notebook, Canterbury, 1949–1951', *Arch. Cant.*, lxiv (1951), 63–73.
Jenkins 1952	F. Jenkins, 'Canterbury Excavations, June-December 1947', *Arch. Cant.*, lxv (1952), 114–36.
Jenkins 1956a	F. Jenkins, 'A Roman Tilery and two Pottery Kilns at Durovernum (Canterbury)', *Antiq. J.*, xxxvi (1956), 40–56.
Jenkins 1956b	F. Jenkins, 'Canterbury and District', *Arch. Cant.*, lxx (1956), 248.
Jenkins 1960	F. Jenkins, 'Two Pottery Kilns and a Tilery of the Roman Period at Canterbury', *Arch. Cant.*, lxxiv (1960), 151–62.
Jenkins 1962	F. Jenkins, *Men of Kent before the Romans: Cantium in the Early Iron Age*, Canterbury Archaeological Society Occasional Paper no. 3, Canterbury, 1962.
Jenkins 1965	F. Jenkins, 'Wingham', *Arch. Cant.*, lxxx (1965), pp. lviii-lix.
Jenkins 1966a	F. Jenkins, *Roman Kent: Cantium in Roman Times*, Canterbury Archaeological Society Occasional Paper no. 5, Canterbury, 1966.
Jenkins 1966b	F. Jenkins, 'Wingham', *Arch. Cant.*, lxxxi (1966), p. lxvi.
Jenkins 1967	F. Jenkins, 'Wingham – The Roman Villa', *Arch. Cant.*, lxxxii (1967), p. lx.
Jenkins 1973	F. Jenkins, 'Brenley Corner, Boughton', Arch. Excavs. 1972, London, 1973, 56–7.
Jenkins 1974	F. Jenkins 'Brenley Corner', Arch. Excavs. 1973, London, 1974, 47–8.
Jesson and Hill 1971	(Eds.) D. Jesson and M. Hill, *The Iron Age and its Hillforts*, University of Southampton Monograph Series no. 1, Southampton, 1971.
Jessup 1928	R.F. Jessup, 'A Romano-British Settlement at Springhead, Kent', *Antiq. J.*, viii (1928), 337–43.

Jessup 1932	R.F. Jessup, 'Bigberry Camp, Harbledown, Kent', *Arch. J.*, lxxxix (1932), 87–115.
Jessup 1935	R.F. Jessup, 'Roman Cemetery near Sittingbourne', *Antiq. J.*, xv (1935), 208–13.
Jessup 1939	R.F. Jessup, 'Further Excavations at Julliberrie's Grave, Chilham', *Antiq. J.*, xix (1939), 260–81.
Jessup 1956	R.F. Jessup, 'The "Temple of Mithras" at Burham', *Arch. Cant.*, lxx (1956), 168–71.
Jessup 1959	R.F. Jessup, 'Barrows and walled Cemeteries in Roman Britain', *JBAA*, (3rd series), xxii (1959), 1–32.
Jessup and Cook 1936	R.F. Jessup and N.C. Cook, 'Excavations at Bigberry Camp, Harbledown', *Arch. Cant.*, xlviii (1936), 151–68.
Jessup and Taylor 1932	R.F. Jessup and M.V. Taylor, 'Part VII: Topographical Index', in (Ed.) W. Page, *Victoria County History, Kent*, iii, London, 1932.
Jessup *et al.* 1954	R.F. Jessup, N.C. Cook and J.M.C. Toynbee, 'Excavation of a Roman Barrow at Holborough, Snodland', *Arch. Cant.*, lxviii (1954), 1–61.
Johns 1971	C. Johns, *Arretine and Samian Pottery*, London, 1971.
Johnson 1975	S. Johnson, 'Vici in Lowland Britain', in Rodwell and Rowley 1975, 75–84.
Johnson 1976	S. Johnson, *The Roman Forts of the Saxon Shore*, London, 1976.
Johnson 1980	S. Johnson, *Later Roman Britain*, London, 1980.
Johnston 1969	D.E. Johnston, 'Romano-British Pottery Kilns near Northampton', *Antiq. J.*, xlix (1969), 75–97.
Johnston 1972	D.E. Johnston, 'A Roman Building at Chalk', *Britannia* iii (1972), 112–48.
Johnston 1977	(Ed.) D.E. Johnston, *The Saxon Shore*, CBA Res. Reps., no. 18, London, 1977.
Johnston and Williams 1979	D.E. Johnston and D.F. Williams, 'Relief-patterned Tiles: A Re-appraisal', in McWhirr 1979b, 375–93.
Jones 1974	A.H.M. Jones, *The Roman Economy: Studies in ancient economic and administrative History* (Ed. P.A. Brunt), Oxford, 1974.
Jones 1968	M.U. Jones, 'Crop-mark Sites at Mucking, Essex', *Antiq. J.*, xlviii (1968), 210–30.
Jones 1972	M.U. Jones, 'Potters' Graffiti from Mucking, Essex', *Antiq. J.*, lii (1972), 335–8.
Jones 1973	M.U. Jones, 'An ancient Landscape Palimpsest at Mucking', *Essex Arch. Hist.*, (3rd series), v (1973) 6–12.
Jones 1974	M.U. Jones, 'Excavations at Mucking, Essex', *Antiq. J.*, liv (1974), 183–99.
Jones and Rodwell	M.U. Jones and W.J. Rodwell, 'The Romano-British Pottery Kilns at Mucking', *Essex Arch. Hist.*, (3rd series), v (1973), 13–47.
Karslake 1926	J.B.P. Karslake, 'Discovery of a Roman Brickfield near Silchester', *Antiq. J.*, vi (1926), 75–6.
Kaye 1914	W. Kaye, *Roman (and other) triple Vases*, London, 1914.
Kelly 1962	D.B. Kelly, 'Lyminge', *Arch. Cant.*, lxxvii (1962), 205.
Kelly 1964	D.B. Kelly, 'Borden. Group of Roman Bronzes', *Arch. Cant.* lxxix (1964), 213–8.
Kelly 1968	D.B. Kelly, 'Snargate', *Arch. Cant.*, lxxxiii (1968), 265–6.
Kelly 1971	D.B. Kelly, 'Quarry Wood Camp, Loose: A Belgic *Oppidum*', *Arch. Cant.*, lxxxvi (1971), 55–84.
Kelly 1978	D.B. Kelly, 'Sittingbourne', *Arch. Cant.*, xciv (1978), 267.
Kelly and Myres 1973	D.B. Kelly and J.N.L. Myres, 'A fifth-century Anglo-Saxon Pot from Canterbury', *Antiq. J.*, liii (1973), 77–8.
Kent 1978	J.P.C. Kent, 'The London Area in the Late Iron Age: An Interpretation of the earliest Coins', in Bird et al. 1978a, 53–8.

Kent 1979	J.P.C. Kent, 'The End of Roman Britain: The literary and numismatic Evidence reviewed', in Casey 1979, 15–27.
Kenyon 1948	K.M. Kenyon, *Excavations at the Jewry Wall Site, Leicester*, Soc. Antiq. Res. Reps., xv, Oxford, 1948.
Keulemanns 1963	M. Keulemanns, 'New Light on the Roman Bath Building and Villa at Beddington', *Surrey Arch. Coll.*, lx (1963), 37–44.
King 1981	A. King, 'Samian Production in the third Century', in (Eds.) A. King and M. Henig, *The Roman West in the third Century*, BAR(I), no. 109, Oxford, 1981, 55–78.
Kirkman 1940	J.S. Kirkman, 'Canterbury Kilnsite – The Pottery, *Arch. Cant.*, liii (1940), 118–33.
Klein 1928	W.G. Klein, 'The Roman Temple at Worth, Kent', *Antiq. J.*, viii (1928), 76–86.
de Laet *et al.* 1970	S.J. de Laet, H. Thoen and A. van Doorselaer', 'La Tombe collective de la Nécropole gallo-romaine de Destelbergen-lez-Gand', *Helinium*, x, 1 (1970), 3–30.
Lambrick 1978	G. Lambrick, 'Iron Age Settlements in the Upper Thames Valley', in Cunliffe and Rowley 1978, 103–20.
Laws 1976	A. Laws, 'Excavations at Northumberland Wharf, Brentford', *TLMAS*, xxvii (1976), 179–205.
van der Leeuw 1977	S.E. van der Leeuw, 'Towards a Study of the Economics of Pottery Making', in (Eds.) B.L. van Beek, R.W. Brandt and W. Groenman-van-Waateringe, *Ex Horreo*, Amsterdam, 1977, 68–76.
Lemmon and Hill 1966	C.H. Lemmon and J. Hill, 'The Romano-British Site at Bodiam', *Sussex Arch. Coll.*, civ (1966), 88–102.
Little 1961	R.I. Little, 'The Excavation of a Romano-British Settlement in King's Wood, Sanderstead', *Surrey Arch. Coll.*, lviii (1961), 35–46.
Little 1964	R.I. Little, 'The Atwood Iron Age and Romano-British Site, Sanderstead, 1960', *Surrey Arch. Coll.*, lxi (1964), 29–38.
Loughlin 1977	N. Loughlin, 'Dales Ware: A Contribution to the Study of Roman Coarse Pottery', in Peacock 1977f, 85–146.
Lowther 1927	A.W.G. Lowther, 'Excavations at Ashtead, Surrey, first Report', *Surrey Arch. Coll.*, xxxvii (1927), 144–63.
Lowther 1929	A.W.G. Lowther, 'Excavations at Ashtead, Surrey, second Report', *Surrey Arch. Coll.*, xxxviii (1929), 1–17.
Lowther 1930	A.W.G. Lowther, 'Excavations at Ashtead, Surrey, third Report', *Surrey Arch. Coll.*, xxxviii (1930), 132–48.
Lowther 1946/47	A.W.G. Lowther, 'Excavations at Purberry Shot, Ewell, Surrey', *Surrey Arch. Coll.*, l (1947), 9–46.
Lowther 1948	A.W.G. Lowther, *A Study of the Patterns of Roman Flue Tiles and their Distribution*, Surrey Archaeological Society Res. Rep. no. 1, Guildford, 1948.
Lyne and Jefferies 1979	M.A.B. Lyne and R.S. Jefferies, *The Alice Holt/Farnham Roman Pottery Industry*, CBA Res. Reps. no. 30, London, 1979.
Macpherson-Grant 1980	N.C. Macpherson-Grant, 'Archaeological Work along the A2: 1966–1974', *Arch. Cant.*, xcvi (1980), 133–83.
Macpherson-Grant 1982	N.C. Macpherson-Grant, 'The Coarse Wares', in Bennett *et al.* 1982, 97–123, 133–49.
Mainman forthcoming	A. Mainman, 'The Saxon Pottery', in Blockley and Day, forthcoming.
Manning 1962	W.H. Manning, 'Excavation of an Iron Age and Roman Site at Chadwell St. Mary, Essex', *TEAS* (3rd series), i (1962), 127–40.
Margary 1939	I.D. Margary, 'Roman Roads from Pevensey', *Sussex Arch. Coll.*, lxxx (1939), 29–62.

Margary 1947   I.D. Margary, 'Roman Communications between Kent and the East Sussex Ironworks', *Sussex Arch. Coll.*, lxxxvi (1947), 22–41.

Margary 1973   I.D. Margary, *Roman Roads in Britain*, 3rd edition, London, 1973.

Marsden 1966   P.R.V. Marsden, *A Roman Ship from Blackfriars, London*, London, 1966.

Marsden 1975   P.R.V. Marsden, 'Excavation of a Roman Palace Site in London, 1961–1972', *TLMAS*, xxvi (1975), 1–102.

Marsh 1978   G. Marsh, 'Early second Century Fine Wares in the London Area', in Arthur and Marsh 1978, 119–24.

Marsh and Tyers 1976 G. Marsh and P.A. Tyers, 'Roman Pottery from the City of London', *TLMAS*, xxvii (1976), 228–44.

Marshall 1963   K. Marshall, 'The Excavation of a ditched Enclosure Site at Corbets Tey, Hornchurch', *Essex Naturalist*, 31 (1963), 118–31.

May 1916   T. May, *Pottery found at Silchester*, Reading, 1916.

McIsaac et al. 1979   W. McIsaac, I. Schwab and H.L. Sheldon, 'Excavations at Old Ford, 1972–1975', *TLMAS*, xxx (1979), 39–96.

McWhirr 1979a   A.D. McWhirr, 'Tile Kilns in Roman Britain', in McWhirr 1979b, 97–190.

McWhirr 1979b   A.D. McWhirr, *Roman Brick and Tile*, BAR(I), no. 68, Oxford, 1979.

McWhirr and Viner 1978 A.D. McWhirr and D. Viner, 'Production and Distribution of Tiles', *Britannia*, ix (1978), 357–76.

Meates 1953   G.W. Meates, 'The Lullingstone Roman Villa', *Arch. Cant.*, lxvi (1953), 15–36.

Meates 1954   G.W. Meates, 'Otford', *Arch. Cant.*, lxviii (1954), pp. xliv-xlv.

Meates 1973   G.W. Meates, 'Farningham Roman Villa II', *Arch. Cant.*, lxxxviii (1973), 1–22.

Meates 1979   G.W. Meates, *The Roman Villa at Lullingstone, Kent. I. The Site*, Monograph Series of the Kent Archaeological Society, Vol. I, Maidstone, 1979.

Meates 1987   G.W. Meates, *The Roman Villa at Lullingstone, Kent. II. The Wall Paintings and Finds*, Monograph Series of the Kent Archaeological Society, Vol. III, Maidstone, 1987.

Meates et al. 1950   G.W. Meates, E. Greenfield and E. Birchenough, 'The Lullingstone Roman Villa', *Arch. Cant.*, lxiii (1950), 1–49.

Meates et al. 1952   G.W. Meates, E. Greenfield and E. Birchenough, 'The Lullingstone Roman Villa', *Arch. Cant.*, lxv (1952), 130–49.

Merrifield 1965   R. Merrifield, *The Roman City of London*, London, 1965.

Mertens and van Impe 1971 J. Mertens and L. van Impe, 'Het Laat-Romeins Grafveld van Oudenburg', *Archaeologia Belgica*, cxxxv (1971), Deel I: Tekst; Deel II: Platen.

Middleton 1979   P.S. Middleton, 'Army Supply in Roman Gaul: An Hypothesis for Roman Britain', in Burnham and Johnson 1979, 81–98.

Miles 1972   A. Miles, 'Romano-British Building at the Mount, Maidstone', *Arch. Cant.*, lxxxvii (1972), 217–9.

Miles 1973   A. Miles, 'Cooling Romano-British Site', *Arch. Cant.*, lxxxviii (1973), 207–8.

Miles 1975   A. Miles, 'Salt-panning in Romano-British Kent', in de Brisay and Evans 1975, 26–31.

Miles and Syddell 1967 A. Miles and M.J.E. Syddell, 'Cooling, near Rochester, a Romano-British industrial Site', *KAR*, 10 (1967), 5–6.

Millett 1979   M. Millett, 'The Dating of Farnham Pottery', *Britannia*, x (1979), 121–38.

Monaghan 1982   J. Monaghan, 'An Investigation of the Romano-British Pottery Industry on the Upchurch Marshes', *Arch. Cant.*, xcviii (1982), 27–50.

Monaghan 1983   J. Monaghan, 'The Woodruff Collection', *Arch. Cant.*, xcix (1983), 199–217.

Monaghan 1987   J. Monaghan, *Upchurch and Thameside Roman Pottery: A ceramic Typology, first to third Centuries A.D.*, BAR(B), no. 173, Oxford, 1987.

Money 1968   J.H. Money, 'Excavations in the Iron Age Hill-fort at High Rocks, near Tunbridge Wells, 1957–1961', *Sussex Arch. Coll.*, cvi (1968), 158–205.

Money 1974	J.H. Money, 'Iron Age and Romano-British Iron Working Site in Minepit Wood, Rotherfield, Sussex', *Bulletin of the Historical Metallurgy Group*, 8, no. 1 (1974), 1–20.
Money 1975	J.H. Money, 'Excavations in the Iron Age Hill-Forts on Castle Hill, Capel, near Tonbridge, 1965 and 1969–71', *Arch. Cant.*, xci (1975), 61–85.
Money 1977	J.H. Money, 'Garden Hill, Sussex: Interim Report', *Britannia*, viii (1977), 339–50.
Money 1978	J.H. Money, 'Aspects of the Iron Age in the Weald', in Drewett 1978, 38–40.
Morris 1975	J. Morris, 'London's Decline AD 150–250', *London Arch.*, 2, no. 13 (1975), 343–4.
Munby 1975	J. Munby, 'Some moulded Face-flagons from the Oxford Kilns', *Britannia*, vi (1975), 182–8.
Murray Threipland 1957	L. Murray Threipland, 'Excavations in Dover', *Arch. Cant.*, lxxi (1957), 14–37.
Murray Threipland and Steer 1951	L. Murray Threipland and K.A. Steer, 'Excavations at Dover, 1945–1947', *Arch. Cant.*, lxiv (1951), 130–49.
Mynott 1973	E. Mynott, 'Horton Kirby', *Arch. Cant.*, lxxxviii (1973), 215.
Mynott 1977	E. Mynott, 'The Roman Villa Site at Keston', *KAR*, 49 (1977), 215–8.
Myres 1944	J.N.L. Myres, 'Wingham Villa and Romano-Saxon Pottery in Kent', *Antiquity*, xviii (1944), 52–5.
Myres 1956	J.N.L. Myres, 'Romano-Saxon Pottery', in (Ed.) D.B. Harden, *Dark Age Britain*, London, 1956, 16–39.
Myres *et al.* 1974	J.N.L. Myres, S.G.P. Weller and B. Westley, 'A late fourth Century Cremation from Billericay, Essex', *Antiq. J.*, liv (1974), 282–5.
Nicklin 1971	K. Nicklin, 'Stability and Innovation in Pottery Manufactory', *World Arch.*, 3 (1971), 13–48.
Noël Hume 1954	I. Noël Hume, 'Romano-British Potteries on the Upchurch Marshes', *Arch. Cant.*, lxviii (1954), 72–90.
Noël Hume 1956	I. Noël Hume, 'Ritual Burials on the Upchurch Marshes', *Arch. Cant.*, lxx (1956), 160–7.
Noël Hume and Noël Hume 1951	I. and A. Noël Hume, 'Roman Pottery from the Upchurch Marshes', *Arch. Cant.*, lxiv (1951), 168–71.
Norris 1956	N.E.S. Norris, 'Romano-British Cremations at Herstmonceux', *Sussex Arch. Coll.*, xciv (1956), 4–5.
Ocock 1966	M.A. Ocock, 'Lower Medway Archaeological Group Report', *Arch. Cant.*, lxxxi (1966), p. lix.
Ocock 1974	M.A. Ocock, 'Late-Belgic Pottery from Court Lodge Farm, Teston', *Arch. Cant.*, lxxxix (1974), 206–7.
Ocock and Syddell 1967	M.A. Ocock and M.J.E. Syddell, 'The Romano-British Buildings in Church Field, Snodland', *Arch. Cant.*, lxxxii (1967), 192–217.
Ogilvie 1982	J.D. Ogilvie, 'The Hammill Ritual Shaft', *Arch. Cant.*, xcviii (1982), 145–66.
Ordnance Survey 1956	*Map of Roman Britain*, 3rd edition, Chessington, 1956.
Ordnance Survey 1965	'Cliffe', *Arch. Cant.*, lxxx (1965), 278.
Ordnance Survey 1978	*Map of Roman Britain*, 4th edition, Southampton, 1978.
Orton 1975	C.J. Orton, 'Quantitative Pottery Studies. Some Progress, Problems and Prospects', *Science and Archaeology*, 16 (1975), 30–5.
Orton 1977a	C.J. Orton, 'Introduction to the Pottery Reports', in Blurton 1977, 28–30.
Orton 1977b	C.J. Orton, 'Roman Pottery (excluding Samian)', in Blurton 1977, 30–53.
Orton 1978	C.J. Orton, 'Is Pottery a Sample?', in Cherry *et al.* 1978, 399–411.
Orton 1980	C.J. Orton, *Mathematics in Archaeology*, London, 1980.
Orton and Orton 1975	C.J. and J. Orton, 'It's later than you think: A statistical Look at an archaeological Problem', *London Arch.*, 2, no. 17 (1975), 285–7.

| Palmer 1975 | S. Palmer, 'Orpington: Poverest, Interim Report; May Avenue Burials', *Arch. Cant.*, xci (1975), 206–7. |

Parsons 1957 — A.J.J. Parsons, 'Orpington Historical Records Society Report, 1956', *Arch. Cant.*, lxxi (1957), 239–40.

Partridge 1977 — C. Partridge, 'Excavations and Fieldwork at Braughing, 1968–73', *Herts. Arch.*, v (1977), 22–108.

Partridge 1981 — C. Partridge, *Skeleton Green: A late Iron Age and Romano-British Site*, *Britannia* Monograph Series no. 2, London, 1981.

Payne 1874 — G. Payne, 'Roman Coffins, of Lead, from Bex Hill, Milton-next-Sittingbourne', *Arch. Cant.*, ix (1874), 164–73.

Payne 1876 — G. Payne, 'Remains of Roman Interments from East Hall, near Sittingbourne', *Arch. Cant.*, x (1876), 178–83.

Payne 1877 — G. Payne, 'Roman Interment discovered at Sittingbourne', *Arch. Cant.*, xi (1877), 47–8.

Payne 1897 — G. Payne, 'Fort Borstal, Rochester', *Arch. Cant.*, xxii (1897), p. xlix.

Payne 1898a — G. Payne, 'Roman Discoveries. III. Roman Interments discovered at "The Brook", Chatham', *Arch. Cant.*, xxiii (1898), 14–21.

Payne 1898b — G. Payne, 'Roman Discoveries. V. Traces of a Roman Pottery at Higham', *Arch. Cant.*, xxiii (1898), 22–3.

Payne 1900 — G. Payne, 'Researches and Discoveries in Kent', *Arch. Cant.*, xxiv (1900), pp. li-lx.

Payne 1902 — G. Payne, 'Researches and Discoveries in Kent', *Arch. Cant.*, xxv (1902), pp. lix-lxxii.

Payne 1911 — G. Payne, 'Researches and Discoveries in Kent', *Arch. Cant.*, xxix (1911), pp. lxxvi-lxxxiv.

Peacock 1967 — D.P.S. Peacock, 'The Heavy Mineral Analysis of Pottery: A preliminary Report', *Archaeometry*, 10 (1967), 97–100.

Peacock 1968 — D.P.S. Peacock, 'A petrological Study of certain Iron Age Pottery from western England', *PPS*, xxxiv (1968), 414–27.

Peacock 1969 — D.P.S. Peacock, 'A Contribution to the Study of Glastonbury Ware from south-western Britain', *Antiq. J.*, xlix (1969), 41–61.

Peacock 1970 — D.P.S. Peacock, 'Scientific Analysis of ancient Ceramics: A Review', *World Arch.*, 1 (1970), 375–89.

Peacock 1971 — D.P.S. Peacock, 'Roman Amphorae in pre-Roman Britain', in Jesson and Hill 1971, 161–88.

Peacock 1977a — D.P.S. Peacock, 'Ceramics in Roman and medieval Archaeology', in Peacock 1977f, 21–34.

Peacock 1977b — D.P.S. Peacock, 'Bricks of the *Classis Britannica*', *Britannia*, viii (1977), 235–46.

Peacock 1977c — D.P.S. Peacock, 'Pompeian Red Ware', in Peacock 1977f, 147–62.

Peacock 1977d — D.P.S. Peacock, 'Late Roman Amphorae from Chalk, near Gravesend, Kent', in Dore and Greene 1977, 295–300.

Peacock 1977e — D.P.S. Peacock, 'Roman Amphorae: Typology, Fabric and Origin', *Collections de l'Ecole française de Rome*, xxxii (1977), 261–78.

Peacock 1977f — (Ed.) D.P.S. Peacock, *Pottery and early Commerce*, London, 1977.

Peacock 1978 — D.P.S. Peacock, 'The Rhine and the Problem of Gaulish Wine in Roman Britain', in du Plat Taylor and Cleere 1978, 49–51.

Peacock 1982 — D.P.S. Peacock, *Pottery in the Roman World: An ethnoarchaeological Approach*, London, 1982.

Pearce 1927 — B.W. Pearce, 'Roman Site at Otford', *Arch. Cant.*, xxxix (1927), 153–8.

Pearce 1930 — B.W. Pearce, 'The Roman Site at Otford', *Arch. Cant.*, xlii (1930), 157–72.

Pemberton 1973 — F. Pemberton, 'A Romano-British Settlement on Stane Street, Ewell, Surrey', *Surrey Arch. Coll.*, lxix (1973), 1–26.

Penn 1957	W.S. Penn, 'The Romano-British Settlement at Springhead. Excavation of the Bakery, Site A', *Arch. Cant.*, lxxi (1957), 53–105.
Penn 1958	W.S. Penn, 'The Romano-British Settlement at Springhead. Excavation of the Watling Street, Shop and Pedestal, Site B', *Arch. Cant.*, lxxii (1958), 77–110.
Penn 1959	W.S. Penn, 'The Romano-British Settlement at Springhead. Excavation of Temple I, Site C1', *Arch. Cant.*, lxxiii (1959), 1–61.
Penn 1960	W.S. Penn, 'Springhead: Temples III and IV', *Arch. Cant.*, lxxiv (1960), 113–40.
Penn 1962	W.S. Penn, 'Springhead: Temples II and V', *Arch. Cant.*, lxxvii (1962), 110–32.
Penn 1964	W.S. Penn, 'Springhead: The Temple Ditch Site', *Arch. Cant.*, lxxix (1964), 170–89.
Penn 1965	W.S. Penn, 'Springhead: Map of Discoveries', *Arch. Cant.*, lxxx (1965), 107–17.
Penn 1967	W.S. Penn, 'Springhead: Temple VI/Gateway', *Arch. Cant.*, lxxxii (1967), 105–23.
Penn 1968	W.S. Penn, 'Springhead: Miscellaneous Excavations', *Arch. Cant.*, lxxxiii (1968), 163–92.
Percival 1976	J. Percival, *The Roman Villa*, London, 1976.
Philp 1957	B.J. Philp, 'Discoveries at Reculver', *Arch. Cant.*, lxxi (1957), 167–84.
Philp 1958	B.J. Philp, 'Discoveries at Reculver, 1955', *Arch. Cant.*, lxxii (1958), 160–6.
Philp 1959	B.J. Philp, 'Reculver: Excavations on the Roman Fort in 1957', *Arch. Cant.*, lxxiii (1959), 96–115.
Philp 1963a	B.J. Philp, 'The Romano-British Farmstead at Eastwood, Fawkham', *Arch. Cant.*, lxxviii (1963), 55–73.
Philp 1963b	B.J. Philp, 'Romano-British West Kent', *Arch. Cant.*, lxxviii (1963), 74–82.
Philp 1968	B.J. Philp, *Excavations at Faversham, 1965*, Kent Archaeological Research Groups' Council, Res. Rep. no. 1, 1968.
Philp 1969	B.J. Philp, 'Keston', *Current Archaeology*, 14 (1969), 73–5.
Philp 1970	B.J. Philp, *The Roman Fort at Reculver*, Dover, 1970.
Philp 1973	B.J. Philp, *Excavations in West Kent, 1960–1970*, Kent Archaeological Research Groups' Council, Res. Rep. no. 2. Dover, 1973.
Philp 1975	B.J. Philp, 'A Romano-British Site at Wrotham Road, Meopham', *KAR*, 39 (1975), 260–6.
Philp 1977	B.J. Philp, 'The British Evidence: Dover', in Johnston 1977, 20–1.
Philp 1978	B.J. Philp, 'A Romano-British Cemetery at Northbourne, Kent', *KAR*, 52 (1978), 30–49.
Philp 1980	B.J. Philp, 'London-Essex Stamped Ware from Kent', *KAR*, 61 (1980), 21–3.
Philp 1981	B.J. Philp, *The Excavation of the Roman Forts of the Classis Britannica at Dover 1970–1977*, Kent Monograph Series, Res. Rep. no. 3, Dover, 1981.
Philp (n.d.)	B.J. Philp, *The Roman Painted House at Dover*, Dover.
Philp and Philp 1974	B.J. and E. Philp, 'A Romano-British Site near Halfway House, Barham, Kent', *KAR*, 37 (1974), 206–10.
Piercy-Fox 1955	N. Piercy-Fox, 'Warbank, Keston – A Romano-British Site', *Arch. Cant.*, lxix (1955), 96–116.
Piercy-Fox 1969	N. Piercy-Fox, 'Caesar's Camp, Keston', *Arch. Cant.*, lxxxiv (1969), 185–99.
Pirie 1960	E. Pirie, 'Thurnham Roman Villa', *Arch. Cant.*, lxxiv (1960), 162–70.
du Plat Taylor and Cleere 1978	(Eds.) J. du Plat Taylor and H. Cleere, *Roman Shipping and Trade: Britain and the Rhine Provinces*, CBA Res. Reps., no. 24, London, 1978.
Polanyi *et al.* 1957	(Eds.) K. Polanyi, C.M. Arensburg and H.W. Pearson, *Trade and Market in the early Empires*, New York, 1957.
Pollard 1977	R.J. Pollard, *Cantium*, unpublished B.A. dissertation, University of Reading, 1977.
Pollard 1981a	R.J. Pollard, 'Roman Coarse Pottery', in A.C. Harrison, 'Rochester 1974–75', *Arch. Cant.*, xcvii (1981), 95–136.

Pollard 1981b   R.J. Pollard, 'Two Cremations of the Roman Period from St. Augustine's College, Canterbury', *Arch. Cant.*, xcvii (1981), 318–24.

Pollard 1982   R.J. Pollard, 'The Pottery, excluding Samian', in Ogilvie 1982, 160–6.

Pollard 1983a   R.J. Pollard, *The Roman Pottery of Kent*, unpublished Ph.D. thesis, University of Reading, 1983.

Pollard 1983b   R.J. Pollard, 'The Coarse Pottery, including the Kiln Products', in Catherall 1983, 121–38.

Pollard 1987   R.J. Pollard, 'The Pottery, excluding Samian', in Meates 1987, 164–302.

Pollard forthcoming, a   R.J. Pollard, 'Charity Field, Wye: A fourth Century Pottery Group from east Kent', forthcoming.

Pollard forthcoming, b   R.J. Pollard, 'Iron Age, Romano-British and later Pottery from Cooling, Kent', forthcoming.

Pollard forthcoming, c   R.J. Pollard, 'The Pottery', in J.H. Money and A.D.F. Streeten, 'Excavations at Garden Hill, Hartfield', *Sussex Arch. Coll.*, forthcoming.

Pollard forthcoming, d   R.J. Pollard, 'The Late Iron Age and Roman Pottery from the Marlowe Car Park Excavations', in Blockley and Day, forthcoming.

Pollard forthcoming, e   R.J. Pollard, 'The Belgic and Roman Pottery', in Rady forthcoming.

Pollard forthcoming, f   R.J. Pollard, 'The Iron Age and Roman Pottery', in P. Clay, *Excavations in the West Bridge Area, Leicester*, Leicestershire Museums, Art Galleries and Records Service, Archaeological Reports Series, forthcoming.

Powell Cotton and Pinfold 1939   P.H.G. Powell Cotton and G.F. Pinfold, 'The Beck Find. Prehistoric and Roman Site on the Foreshore at Minnis Bay', *Arch. Cant.*, li (1939), 191–203.

Price 1978   J. Price, 'Trade in Glass', in du Plat Taylor and Cleere 1978, 70–8.

Pryce 1949   T.D. Pryce, 'Decorated Samian', in Bushe-Fox 1949, 160–83.

Pyke 1974   J. Pyke, 'Romano-British Site (Rye Lane), near Otford', *KAR*, 38 (1974), 233–40.

Rady forthcoming   J. Rady, 'Excavations around St. Gabriel's Chapel, Canterbury Cathedral', in (Eds.) J. Driver, J. Rady and M. Sparks, *Excavations in the Cathedral Precincts: (ii) 'Meister Omers', Linacre Garden and St. Gabriel's Chapel*, Arch. Canterbury, Vol. IV, forthcoming.

Rae and Rae 1974   A. and V. Rae, 'The Roman Fort at Cramond, Edinburgh: Excavations 1954–66', *Britannia*, v (1974), 163–224.

Rahtz 1958   P.A. Rahtz, 'Dover: Stembrook and St. Martin-le-Grand, 1956', *Arch. Cant.*, lxxii (1958), 111–37.

Rashleigh 1803   P. Rashleigh, 'Accounts of Antiquities discovered at Southfleet in Kent', *Archaeologia*, xiv (1803), 37–9, 221–3.

Redfern 1978   E.H. Redfern, 'The Roman Coins', in Flight and Harrison 1978, 44–54.

Redman 1979   C.L. Redman, 'Description and Inference with the Late Medieval Pottery from Qsar es-Seghir, Morocco', *Medieval Ceramics*, 3 (1979), 63–80.

Reece 1968   R. Reece, 'Summary of the Roman Coins from Richborough', in Cunliffe 1968, 200–16.

Reece 1972   R. Reece, 'A short Survey of the Roman Coins found on fourteen Sites in Britain', *Britannia*, iii (1972), 269–76.

Reece 1973   R. Reece, 'Roman Coinage in Britain and the Western Empire', *Britannia*, iv (1973), 227–52.

Reece 1979   R. Reece, 'Roman monetary Impact', in Burnham and Johnson 1979, 211–7.

Renfrew 1977   A.C. Renfrew, 'Introduction: Production and Exchange in early State Societies, The Evidence of Pottery', in Peacock 1977f, 1–20.

Richardson and Tyers 1984   B. Richardson and P.A. Tyers, 'North Gaulish Pottery in Britain', *Britannia*, xv (1984), 133–42.

Richardson 1948   K.M. Richardson, 'Report on the Excavations at Brockley Hill, Middlesex, August and September 1947', *TLMAS*, x (1948), 1–23.

Rigby 1973	V. Rigby, 'Potters' Stamps on Terra Nigra and Terra Rubra found in Britain', in Detsicas 1973, 7–24.
Rigby 1981	V. Rigby, 'The Gallo-Belgic Wares', in Partridge 1981, 159–95.
Rigby 1982	V. Rigby, 'The Gallo-Belgic Imports', in Bennett *et al.* 1982, 94–5, 131–2.
Rigden 1974	R. Rigden, *The Romans in the Greenwich District*, Greenwich, 1974.
Rigold 1972	S.E. Rigold, 'Roman Folkestone reconsidered', *Arch. Cant.*, lxxxvii (1972), 31–42.
Rigold 1979	S.E. Rigold, 'Coins and Jettons', in G.H. Smith, 'The Excavation of the Hospital of St. Mary at Ospringe, commonly called Maison Dieu', *Arch. Cant.*, xcv (1979), 127.
Rivet 1964	A.L.F. Rivet, *Town and Country in Roman Britain*, 2nd edition, London, 1964.
Rivet 1969	A.L.F. Rivet, 'Social and economic Aspects', in (Ed.) A.L.F. Rivet, *The Roman Villa in Britain*, London, 1969, 173–216.
Rivet 1970	A.L.F. Rivet, 'The British Section of the Antonine Itinerary', *Britannia*, i (1970), 34–82.
Rivet 1975	A.L.F. Rivet, 'Summing up: The Classification of minor Towns and related Settlements', in Rodwell and Rowley 1975, 111–14.
Rivet and Smith 1979	A.L.F. Rivet and C. Smith, *The Place-names of Roman Britain*, London, 1979.
Roach Smith 1842	C. Roach Smith, 'Notices of recent Discoveries of Roman Antiquities at Strood, Bapchild, Oare and Upchurch', *Archaeologia*, xxix (1842), 217–26.
Roach Smith 1847	C. Roach Smith, 'On Roman Pottery discovered on the Banks of the Medway, near Upchurch, Kent', *JBAA*, ii (1847), 133–40.
Roach Smith 1852	C. Roach Smith, 'The Excavation of a Roman Villa at Hartlip, Kent', *Collectanea Antiqua*, ii (1852), 1–24.
Roach Smith 1868	C. Roach Smith, 'Remains of Roman Potteries on the Banks of the Medway and the Nen and in London', *Collectanea Antiqua*, vi (1868), 173–9.
Roach Smith 1877	C. Roach Smith, 'On Mr Teanby's Collection of Romano-British, and Romano-Gaulish, Pottery at Gravesend', *Arch. Cant.*, xi (1877), 113–20.
Robertson 1974	A.S. Robertson, 'Romano-British Coin Hoards: Their numismatic, archaeological and historical Significance', in Casey and Reece 1974, 12–36.
Robertson 1883	W.A. Scott Robertson, 'Traces of Roman Occupation in and near Maidstone', *Arch. Cant.*, xv (1883), 68–80.
Rodwell 1966a	W.J. Rodwell, 'The Excavation of a "Red Hill" on Canvey Island', *TEAS*, (3rd series), ii (1966), pt. i, 34–46.
Rodwell 1966b	W.J. Rodwell, 'Wickford: Interim Report', *TEAS*, (3rd series), ii (1966), 96.
Rodwell 1968	W.J. Rodwell, 'Wickford: Second Interim Report', *TEAS*, (3rd series), ii (1968), 159.
Rodwell 1970a	W.J. Rodwell, 'Some Romano-Saxon Pottery from Essex', *Antiq. J.*, l (1970), 262–76.
Rodwell 1970b	W.J. Rodwell, 'Wickford: Third and fourth Interim Reports', *TEAS*, (3rd series), ii (1970), 330–2.
Rodwell 1974	W.J. Rodwell, 'The Orsett "Cock" Cropmark Site', *Essex Arch. Hist.*, (3rd series), vi (1974), 13–39.
Rodwell 1975	W.J. Rodwell, 'Trinovantian Towns and their Setting', in Rodwell and Rowley 1975, 85–102.
Rodwell 1976a	W.J. Rodwell, 'Coinage, Oppida and the Rise of Belgic Power in south-east Britain', in Cunliffe and Rowley 1976, 181–366.
Rodwell 1976b	W.J. Rodwell, 'Roman and medieval Finds from South Benfleet', *Essex Arch. Hist.*, (3rd series), viii (1976), 259–63.
Rodwell 1978	W.J. Rodwell, 'Stamp-decorated Pottery of the early Roman Period in eastern England', in Arthur and Marsh 1978, 225–92.
Rodwell 1979	W.J. Rodwell, 'Iron Age and Roman Salt-winning on the Essex Coast', in Burnham and Johnson 1979, 133–76.

Rodwell and Rowley 1975   (Eds.) W.J. Rodwell and T. Rowley, *The 'Small Towns' of Roman Britain*, BAR(B), no. 15, Oxford, 1975.

Rose 1967   J.A. Rose, 'Report – Faversham Archaeological Research Group', *KAR*, 10 (1967), 4–5.

Roskams and Watson 1981   S. Roskams and L. Watson, 'The Hadrianic Fire of London – A Re-assessment of the Evidence', *London Arch.*, 4, no. 3 (1981), 60–5.

Ross 1968   A. Ross, 'Shafts, Pits, Wells – Sanctuaries of the Belgic Britons?', in (Eds.) J.M. Coles and D.D.A. Simpson, *Studies in ancient Europe*, Leicester, 1968, 235–85.

Rudling 1979   D.R. Rudling, 'Invasion and Response: Downland Settlement in East Sussex', in Burnham and Johnson 1979, 339–56.

Rudling 1986   D.R. Rudling, 'The Excavation of a Roman Tilery on Great Cansiron Farm, Hartfield, East Sussex', *Britannia*, xvii (1986), 191–230.

Sahlins 1965   M.D. Sahlins, 'On the Sociology of primitive Exchange', ASA Monograph I, 1965, 139–236.

Salzmann 1908   L.F. Salzmann, 'Excavations at Pevensey, 1907–8', *Sussex Arch. Coll.*, lii (1908), 83–95.

Sanders 1973   J. Sanders, *Late Roman Shell-gritted Ware in southern Britain*, unpublished B.A. dissertation, Institute of Archaeology, London, 1973.

Saunders and Havercroft 1977   C. Saunders and A.B. Havercroft, 'A Kiln of the Potter Oastrius and related Excavations at Little Munden Farm, Bricket Wood', *Herts. Arch.*, v (1977), 109–56.

Seillier and Thoen 1978   C. Seillier and H. Thoen, 'Céramique d'une Fosse-dépôtoir du Camp de la *Classis Britannica* à Boulogne-sur-Mer', *Septentrion*, 8 (1978), 62–75.

Sheldon 1971   H.L. Sheldon, 'Excavations at Lefevre Road, Old Ford, E.3, September 1969–June 1970', *TLMAS*, xxiii (1971), 42–77.

Sheldon 1972   H.L. Sheldon, 'Excavations at Parnell Road, and Appian Road, Old Ford, E.3, February-April 1971', *TLMAS*, xxiii (1972), 101–47.

Sheldon 1974   H.L. Sheldon, 'Excavations at Toppings and Sun Wharves, Southwark, 1970–1972', *TLMAS*, xxv (1974), 1–116.

Sheldon 1975a   H.L. Sheldon, 'A Decline in the London Settlement AD 150–250?', *London Arch.*, 2, no. 11 (1975), 278–84.

Sheldon 1975b   H.L. Sheldon, 'London's Decline AD 150–250: Reply to John Morris', *London Arch.*, 2, no. 13 (1975), 344.

Sheldon and Schaaf 1978   H.L. Sheldon and L. Schaaf, 'A Survey of Roman Sites in Greater London', in Bird *et al.* 1978a, 59–88.

Shiel 1977   N. Shiel, *The Episode of Carausius and Allectus: The literary and numismatic Evidence*, BAR(B), no. 40, Oxford, 1977.

Simpson 1970   G. Simpson, 'The decorated Samian Ware and Potters' Stamps', in Frere 1970, 111–12.

Smith 1977   C. Smith, 'A Romano-British Site at Binscombe, Godalming', *Surrey Arch. Coll.*, lxxi (1977), 13–42.

Smith 1978   D.J. Smith, 'Regional Aspects of the Winged Corridor Villa', in Todd 1978b, 117–47.

Smith 1978   J.T. Smith, 'Villas as a Key to social Structure', in Todd 1978, 149–86.

Smith 1979   V. Smith, 'Excavations at Northfleet', *KAR*, 56 (1979), 140–1.

Smythe 1883   C.T. Smythe, 'A walled Roman Cemetery in Joy Wood, Lockham, near Maidstone', *Arch. Cant.*, xv (1883), 81–8.

Stead 1969   I.M. Stead, 'Verulamium, 1966–8', *Antiquity*, xliii (1969), 45–51.

Stead 1971   I.M. Stead, 'The Reconstruction of Iron Age Buckets from Aylesford and Baldock', *British Museum Quarterly*, 35, no. 4 (1971), 250–82.

Stead 1976   I.M. Stead, 'The earliest Burials of the Aylesford Culture', in (Eds.)

G. Sieveking, I. Longworth and K. Wilson, *Problems of economic and social Archaeology*, London, 1976, 401–16.

Stebbing 1937
W.P.D. Stebbing, 'Pre-Roman, Roman and post-Roman Pottery from Burials at Worth, East Kent', *Antiq. J.*, xvii (1937), 311–13.

Swan 1975a
V.G. Swan, *Pottery in Roman Britain*, Shire Archaeology no. 3, Aylesbury, 1975.

Swan 1975b
V.G. Swan, 'Oare reconsidered and the Origins of Savernake Ware in Wiltshire', *Britannia*, vi (1975), 37–61.

Swan 1984
V.G. Swan, *The Pottery Kilns of Roman Britain*, Royal Commission for Historical Monuments (England), Supplementary Series, no. 5, London, 1984.

Tatton-Brown 1974
T.W.T. Tatton-Brown, 'Excavations at The Custom House Site, City of London, 1973', *TLMAS*, xxv (1974), 117–219.

Tatton-Brown 1976
T.W.T. Tatton-Brown, 'Excavations in 1976 by the Canterbury Archaeological Trust: Highstead, near Chislet', *Arch. Cant.*, xcii (1976), 236–8.

Tatton-Brown 1980
T.W.T. Tatton-Brown, 'Camelon, Arthur's O'on and the main Supply Base for the Antonine Wall', *Britannia*, xi (1980), 340–3.

Taylor 1933
M.V. Taylor, 'Roman Britain in 1932', *JRS*, xxiii (1933), 190–216.

Tebbutt 1972
C.F. Tebbutt, 'A Roman Bloomery at Great Cansiron, near Holtye', *Sussex Arch. Coll.*, cx (1972), 10–13.

Tebbutt and Cleere 1973
C.F. Tebbutt and H. Cleere, 'A Romano-British Bloomery at Pippingford, Hartfield', *Sussex Arch. Coll.*, cxi (1973), 27–40.

Tebbutt and Norris 1968
C.F. Tebbutt and N.E.S. Norris, 'A first Century Corn drying Kiln at Uckfield', *Sussex Notes and Queries*, 17, no. 1 (1968), 25–6.

Tester 1956a
P.J. Tester, 'An Anglo-Saxon Occupation Site at Dartford', *Arch. Cant.*, lxx (1956), 256–9.

Tester 1956b
P.J. Tester, 'First Century Pottery from Temple Hill, Dartford', *Arch. Cant.*, lxx (1956), 253–4.

Tester 1961
P.J. Tester, 'The Roman Villa in Cobham Park, near Rochester', *Arch. Cant.*, lxxvi (1961), 88–109.

Tester 1963
P.J. Tester, 'A Roman Settlement between Bexley and Crayford', *Arch. Cant.*, lxxviii (1963), 179–80.

Tester 1969
P.J. Tester, 'Excavations at Fordcroft, Orpington', *Arch. Cant.*, lxxxiv (1969), 39–78.

Tester and Bing 1949
P.J. Tester and H.F. Bing, 'A first Century Urnfield at Cheriton, near Folkestone', *Arch. Cant.*, lxii (1949), 21–36.

Tester and Caiger 1954
P.J. Tester and J.E.L. Caiger, 'Excavations on the Site of a Romano-British Settlement in Joyden's Wood, near Bexley', *Arch. Cant.*, lxviii (1954), 167–83.

Thompson 1977
E.A. Thompson, 'Britain AD 406–410', *Britannia*, viii (1977), 303–18.

Thompson 1953
F.H. Thompson, 'Excavations at Reculver, Kent, 1951', *Arch. Cant.*, lxvi (1953), 52–9.

Thompson 1979
F.H. Thompson, 'Three Surrey Hillforts: Excavations at Anstiebury, Holmbury and Hascombe, 1972–1977', *Antiq. J.*, lix (1979), 245–318.

Thompson 1978
I. Thompson, 'The "Belgic" Cemetery at Allington', *Arch. Cant.*, xciv (1978), 127–39.

Thompson 1982
I. Thompson, *Grog-tempered 'Belgic' Pottery of south-eastern England*, BAR(B), no. 108, Oxford, 1982.

Thornhill and Payne 1980
P. Thornhill and P. Payne, 'Some Sites in North Kent', *Arch. Cant.*, xcvi (1980), 378–82.

Tildesley 1971
J. Tildesley, 'Roman Pottery Kilns at Rettendon', *Essex J.*, vi (1971), 35–50.

Todd 1970
M. Todd, 'The small Towns of Roman Britain', *Britannia*, i (1970), 114–30.

Todd 1978a
M. Todd, 'Villas and Romano-British Society', in Todd 1978b, 197–208.

Todd 1978b
(Ed.) M. Todd, *Studies in the Romano-British Villa*, Leicester, 1978.

Todd 1981   M. Todd, *Roman Britain (55 BC–AD 400)*, Glasgow, 1981.

Toller 1977   H.S. Toller, *Roman Lead Coffins and Ossuaria in Britain*, BAR(B), no. 38, Oxford, 1977.

Toller 1980   H.S. Toller, 'Excavation of the Orsett "Cock" Enclosure, Essex', *Britannia*, xi (1980), 35–42.

Toynbee 1964   J.M.C. Toynbee, *Art in Britain under the Romans*, Oxford, 1964.

Tuffreau-Libre 1980a M. Tuffreau-Libre, *La Céramique commune gallo-romaine dans le Nord de la France*, Lille, 1980.

Tuffreau-Libre 1980b M. Tuffreau-Libre, 'Un Four gallo-romain à Labuissière (Pas-de-Calais)', *Gallia*, xxxviii (1980), 291–309.

Tyers 1977a   P.A. Tyers, *The Highgate Wood Roman Pottery Industry and its Origins*, unpublished B.Sc. dissertation, University College of Wales, Cardiff, 1977.

Tyers 1977b   P.A. Tyers, 'The Roman Coarse Pottery', in Gentry *et al.* 1977, 135–54.

Tyers 1978   P.A. Tyers, 'The Poppyhead Beakers of Britain and their Relationship to the Barbotine decorated Vessels of the Rhineland and Switzerland', in Arthur and Marsh 1978, 61–108.

Tyers 1980   P.A. Tyers, 'Correspondances entre la Céramique commune La Tène III du Sud-est de l'Angletere et du Nord de la France', *Septentrion*, 10 (1980), 61–70.

Tyers 1981   P.A. Tyers, *Aspects of the Development of the Late La Tène and early Roman Pottery Industry of Britain and Gaul*, unpublished Ph.D. thesis, University College of Wales, Cardiff, 1981.

Tyers and Marsh 1978 P.A. Tyers and G. Marsh, 'The Roman Pottery from Southwark', in Bird *et al.* 1978b, 533–82.

Vince 1977a   A.G. Vince, 'The medieval and post-medieval Ceramic Industry of the Malvern Region', in Peacock 1977f, 257–306.

Vince 1977b   A.G. Vince, 'Some Aspects of Pottery Quantification', *Medieval Ceramics*, 1 (1977), 63–74.

Wacher 1965   A. Wacher, 'East Malling, 1965', *Arch. Cant.*, lxxx (1965), 257–8.

Wacher 1969   J.S. Wacher, *Excavations at Brough-on-Humber, 1958–1961*, Soc. Antiq. Res. Reps., xxv, Leeds, 1969.

Wacher 1975   J.S. Wacher, *The Towns of Roman Britain*, London, 1975.

Walsh 1970   R.M. Walsh, 'Ash Romano-British Villa', *KAR*, 20 (1970), 13–20.

Walsh 1980   R.M. Walsh, 'Recent Investigations at the Anglo-Saxon Cemetery, Darenth Park Hospital, Dartford', *Arch. Cant.*, xcvi (1980), 305–20.

Walthew 1975   C.V. Walthew, 'The Town House and Villa House in Roman Britain', *Britannia*, vi (1975), 189–205.

Ward 1968   C.P. Ward, 'Report – Otford Historical Society Archaeological Group', *KAR*, 13 (1968), 4–6.

Ward-Perkins 1938   J.B. Ward-Perkins, 'An Early Iron Age Site at Crayford, Kent', *PPS*, iv (1938), 151–68.

Ward-Perkins 1939   J.B. Ward-Perkins, 'Excavations on Oldbury Hill, Ightham', *Arch. Cant.*, li (1939), 137–81.

Ward-Perkins 1944   J.B. Ward-Perkins, 'Excavations on the Iron Age Hill-fort at Oldbury, near Ightham, Kent', *Archaeologia*, xc (1944), 127–76.

Warhurst 1953   A. Warhurst, 'A Belgic Burial from Borough Green', *Arch. Cant.*, lxiv (1953), 157–60.

Watson 1963   M.B. Watson, 'Iron Age Site on Bridge Hill', *Arch. Cant.*, lxxviii (1963), 185–8.

Webster 1940   G.A. Webster, 'A Roman Pottery Kiln at Canterbury', *Arch. Cant.*, liii (1940), 109–36.

Webster 1976   (Ed.) G. Webster, *Romano-British Coarse Pottery: A Student's Guide*, CBA Res. Reps., no. 6, 3rd edition, London, 1976.

Webster 1977	P.V. Webster, 'Severn Valley Ware on the Antonine Frontier', in Dore and Greene 1977, 163–76.
Wheeler 1932	R.E.M. Wheeler, 'Part III: The Towns of Roman Kent', in (Ed.) W. Page, *Victoria County History, Kent*, iii, London, 1932.
Whiting 1921	W. Whiting, 'A Roman Cemetery discovered at Ospringe in 1920', *Arch. Cant.*, xxxv (1921), 1–16.
Whiting 1923	W. Whiting, 'A Roman Cemetery discovered at Ospringe in 1920', *Arch. Cant.*, xxxvi (1923), 65–80.
Whiting 1924	W. Whiting, 'Further Roman Finds in Kent', *Antiq. J.*, iv (1924), 22–5.
Whiting 1925	W. Whiting, 'Roman Cemeteries at Ospringe', *Arch. Cant.*, xxxvii (1925), 83–96.
Whiting 1926	W. Whiting, 'The Roman Cemeteries at Ospringe', *Arch. Cant.*, xxxviii (1926), 123–52.
Whiting 1927a	W. Whiting, 'Pottery from Tong and Murston, Sittingbourne', *Arch. Cant.*, xxxix (1927), 40–4.
Whiting 1927b	W. Whiting, 'Six Grave Groups found in Syndale Valley, 1913', *Arch. Cant.*, xxxix (1927), 37–41.
Whiting 1927c	W. Whiting, 'A Romano-British Burial discovered at Crismill Farm, near Bearsted, November 1926', *Arch. Cant.*, xxxix (1927), 44–5.
Whiting 1927d	W. Whiting, 'A Find at St. Mary's Street, Canterbury', *Arch. Cant.*, xxxix (1927), 44–6.
Whiting 1927e	W. Whiting, 'A Roman Cemetery at St. Dunstan's, Canterbury', *Arch. Cant.*, xxxix (1927), 46–54.
Whiting *et al.* 1931	W. Whiting, W. Hawley and T. May, *Excavation of the Roman Cemetery at Ospringe, Kent*, Soc. Antiq. Res. Reps., viii, Oxford, 1931.
Whiting and Mead 1928	W. Whiting and H.T. Mead, 'A Roman Cemetery at St. Martin's Hill, Canterbury', *Arch. Cant.*, xl (1928), 67–78.
Wilkinson 1977	P. Wilkinson, 'The Pottery', in R.T. Brooks, 'The Roman Villa at Hill Farm, Abridge', *Essex J.*, xii (1977), 51–61.
Williams 1946	A. Williams, 'Canterbury Excavations: September-October, 1944', *Arch. Cant.*, lix (1946), 64–81.
Williams 1947	A. Williams, 'Canterbury Excavations in 1945', *Arch. Cant.*, lx (1947), 68–100.
Williams and Frere 1948	A. Williams and S.S. Frere, 'Canterbury Excavations, Christmas 1945 and Easter 1946', *Arch. Cant.*, lxi (1948), 1–45.
Williams 1977	D.F. Williams, 'The Romano-British Black-Burnished Industry: An Essay on Characterization by Heavy Mineral Analysis', in Peacock 1977, 163–238.
Williams 1971	J.H. Williams, 'Roman Building Materials in south-east England', *Britannia*, ii (1971), 166–95.
Williams 1975	J.H. Williams, 'Excavations at Gravel Walk, Canterbury, 1967', *Arch. Cant.*, xci (1975), 119–44.
Willson 1981	J. Willson, 'The Coarse Pottery', in Philp 1981, 207–48.
Wilson 1966	D.R. Wilson, 'Roman Britain in 1965', *JRS*, lvi (1966), 196–216.
Wilson 1970	D.R. Wilson, 'Roman Britain in 1969', *Britannia*, i (1970), 269–305.
Wilson 1971	D.R. Wilson, 'Roman Britain in 1970', *Britannia*, ii (1971), 242–88.
Wilson 1972	D.R. Wilson, 'Roman Britain in 1971', *Britannia*, iii (1972), 298–351.
Wilson 1973	D.R. Wilson, 'Roman Britain in 1972', *Britannia*, iv (1973), 270–323.
Wilson 1975	D.R. Wilson, 'Roman Britain in 1974', *Britannia*, vi (1975), 220–83.
Wilson and Taylor 1961	D.R. Wilson and M.V. Taylor, 'Roman Britain in 1960', *JRS*, li (1961), 157–90.
Wilson 1972	M.G. Wilson, 'The other Pottery', in Frere 1972, 263–370.
Winbolt 1925a	S.E. Winbolt, *Roman Folkestone*, London, 1925.
Winbolt 1925b	S.E. Winbolt, 'Pre-Roman Finds at Folkestone', *Antiq. J.*, v (1925), 63–7.
Wood 1883	H. Wood, 'Roman Urns found near Rainham Creek, on the Medway', *Arch. Cant.*, xv (1883), 108–10.

Worsfold 1948   F.H. Worsfold, 'An Early Iron Age Site at Borden', *Arch. Cant.*, lxi (1948), 148–55.

Wright 1974   R.P. Wright, 'Carpow and Caracalla', *Britannia*, v (1974), 289–92.

Wright 1852   T. Wright, 'The Roman Potteries on the Banks of the Medway', *Gentleman's Magazine*, xxxviii (1852), 364–7.

Young 1975   C.J. Young, 'Excavations at Ickham', *Arch. Cant.*, xci (1975), 190–1.

Young 1977a   C.J. Young, *Oxfordshire Roman Pottery*, BAR(B), no. 43, Oxford, 1977.

Young 1977b   C.J. Young, 'Oxford Ware and the Roman Army', in Dore and Greene 1977, 289–94.

Young 1980   C.J. Young, 'The Pottery', in Cunliffe 1980, 274–83.

Young 1981   C.J. Young, 'The late Roman Water-mill at Ickham, Kent, and the Saxon Shore', in (Ed.) A.P. Detsicas, *Collectanea Historica: Essays in Memory of Stuart Rigold*, Maidstone, 1981.

Young and Bird 1982   C.J. Young and J. Bird, 'The Late Roman Fine Wares – Summary', in Bennett *et al.* 1982, 159–63.

CHAPTER 1

OBJECTIVES

I. THE STUDY OF ROMANO-BRITISH POTTERY: BACKGROUND

It is a truism of Romano-British archaeology that pottery is by far the most common type of artefact encountered in most field-work and excavations. This material has rarely been wholly ignored, even by those whose interests centred on structural finds such as walls and mosaics, as was often the case with the early antiquarians. However, a bias towards brightly-coloured and decorated wares such as *Terra Sigillata* (samian ware) and 'Castor ware' (colour-coated vessels with zoomorphic, anthropomorphic, or vegetal decoration) is apparent in most early pottery reports, with the far more numerous 'grey wares' receiving little or no attention. The strong sense of aesthetics shown by the antiquarians inevitably produced some invaluable pieces of research, particularly into the figure-types and forms exhibited by samian ware. The studies of ancient trade, belief and entertainment have benefited immensely from such work as, of course, has the establishment of chronologies. The latter field of investigation, invoking the undoubted worth of both the imported and indigenous pottery of Roman Britain as a dating medium, has tended to overshadow the potential of this material as an index of socio-economic matters such as trade and exchange systems and industrial organisations. The developing interest in 'grey wares' and other coarse wares in the early twentieth century, reflected in, for example, the reports by Bushe-Fox on the excavations at Wroxeter (Bushe-Fox 1913, 1914, 1916), was channelled primarily to the elucidation of chronology and stylistic affinity.

In general, the 'tribal' approach of culture-definition that was for long the cornerstone of prehistoric archaeology has not been applied to Romano-British studies, except where these involve the interaction of Roman and barbarian; for example, in the study of the Germanic infiltration of the provinces in the late period. 'Romano-Saxon' pottery styles have been alleged to reflect the influence of Germanic taste on Roman pottery (see, for example, Hurst 1976; this claim has been disputed by Gillam (1979)). It is true to say, as a general statement, that the single most striking feature of Romano-British pottery is not its diversity, but the overall similarity in the range of form and decoration over space and time, particularly with regard to coarse or 'kitchen' wares.

The last thirty years have witnessed the flowering of the study of the pottery of Roman Britain, both in its own right and as an index of broader socio-economic patterns. Research has tended to be conducted along the lines either of the study of a single 'industry' or of the pottery of a single settlement (usually a town or a fort, for these tend to provide both the greatest quantity and the widest diversity of material) in both cases involving analysis of supply and demand: the industry's 'marketing area' and the settlement's 'industry catchment area' (i.e. the range of industries represented in the settlement's pottery assemblage.) The bias towards fine 'table' wares has been overcome, and these are now studied in conjunction with the coarsest wares and those of modest quality. These developments have been greatly facilitated by the advance made in petrological analysis (e.g. Peacock 1970, 1977a) and the application of techniques of spatial analysis (Hodder and Orton 1976; Clarke 1977) of sites and artefacts. However, the pioneering studies of John Gillam into the pottery of the northern military zone (Gillam 1957, 1960) were achieved without such aids.

Gillam's approach was basically one of painstaking visual comparison of forms and fabrics, and this method, if pursued with the diligence and common-sense that are hall-marks of Gillam's work, can still pay valuable dividends (Peacock 1977a, 25). If Gillam's seminal papers on Roman pottery in northern Britain (1957, 3rd edition 1970; 1973) have provided the inspiration for the present author's research, then the detailed investigations into specific industries and pottery types that have been conducted over the last two decades provide the indispensable framework. In this context acknowledgement must be recorded of the value of the work of Farrar (1973), Fulford (1973a, 1975a), Greene (1979a), K.F. Hartley (1963, 1968, 1973a, 1977), Hull (1963), Lyne and Jefferies (1979), D.F. Williams (1977), and Young (1977a) to the study of the ceramics of south-east Britain. The debt owed to many other authors will be apparent in the body of the present study.

II. THE AIMS OF THE STUDY

In a recent review of the objectives of ceramic studies in Roman and medieval archaeology (Peacock 1977a), special emphasis was placed on 'the use of pottery as a tool for studying early economics and commerce'. The author expresses with enthusiasm the potential of investigating 'such humble yet fundamental matters on the organisation of production and distribution' of locally-produced wares (*ibid.*). Two papers in the same volume as this review (Loughlin 1977; D.F. Williams 1977) serve to illustrate this potential in the field of Romano-British studies, while Vince (1977a) focuses upon the medieval period with equal effectiveness.

The overall objective of the study is the elucidation of the whole network of pottery production, importation and distribution within a spatially defined area over the whole of the Roman period, in so far as the available data allow this. The study of continuity and change over time has been an integral part of the research, and to this end the periods of the late Iron Age and the fifth century have also been taken account of; in the main, it is the period from the mid-first century to the early fifth century A.D. that has been the focus of attention.

The extraction of the information that pottery can provide on the economic practices of Roman Britain leaves a considerable residue of information on other aspects of the study of this period; the fields of art history, religion, diet and technology have barely been touched on. The relationship between pottery assemblage variation and the differing functions, social status and prosperity of areas within settlements has not been pursued in depth.

The major portion of this study is devoted to the description of the pottery itself and of the industries that produced it within the study region. The aim of the descriptive chapters is to present a generalised pattern of spatial variation and temporal development in pottery forms and fabrics, and in the composition of assemblages as a whole.

It was not the intention of the research conducted for the study to provide firm dating for individual vessel types, and indeed the trend in ceramic studies is a departure from the belief that such dating can be established at least for coarse 'kitchen' wares. The exceptional quality of the site dating evidence in the northern military zone, provided by a high recovery rate of building inscriptions and intensive research into the historical record and its reflections in the material remains (e.g. Breeze and Dobson 1978), enabled Gillam (1957) to suggest quite precise dating for his types, although these have undergone revision in subsequent editions of the paper (cf. Gillam 1957 with Gillam 1970). The south-east generally does not provide a significant body of data relating to absolute chronology; however, stratigraphic sequences and the limited inscriptional and numismatic evidence do allow a relative chronology to be established from which ceramic 'phases' may be deduced. The study was thus designed to discern these phases and describe them at assemblage level, stressing the typical components of such assemblages, whenever possible in a quantified form (see Chapter 2). The calculation of a date, or more properly a date-range, for an assemblage or a site relies less on individual elements than on the assessment of the proportional representation of the whole range of forms and fabrics that comprise the pottery assemblage.

The dating method outlined above ideally requires a rigorously quantified data basis, enabling the proportions of fabrics or forms in an assemblage to be expressed as percentage figures, and thus providing a basis for intra- and inter-assemblage comparison at the level of relative-frequency assessment (Orton 1975, 30; 1980, 156–67). Analysis of this kind, has, until recent years, generally been neglected in Romano-British pottery studies; it has thus been an objective of the research to create such a data base for the benefit of both the present and future programmes.

The value of 'industry' studies has been emphasised above. Of the three major pottery industries known to have been founded within the study area only one has previously been studied in depth, and even then only a portion of the products has been discussed. This industry is the coarse or 'kitchen' ware industry centred around the Cliffe Peninsula between the Thames and Medway estuaries, and it produced both slipped and unslipped reduced wares. The former ware, generally known as BB2, has been the subject of intensive research in the past twenty years (Gillam 1960; Farrar 1983; Williams 1977). Its significance as a ware exported over long distances has tended to overshadow the more localised aspects of its distribution within the south-east and its relationship to the unslipped ware alongside which it was manufactured. The second industry in question has been known since the early nineteenth century thanks to the energies of antiquarians on the Medway estuary; referred to as 'Upchurch' ware after one of the larger villages that overlook the estuary, this industry remains something of an enigma. The litoral situation of the apparent production area, and the poorly recorded attentions of many generations of antiquaries and treasure hunters have led to the devastation of that area with little gain in knowledge (Noël Hume 1954; Monaghan 1982, 1983, 1987). Kilns of the Roman period do still occasionally come to light (e.g. Jackson 1962, 1972/3; Ocock 1966), but there is little doubt that the overwhelming bulk of the structural evidence has been lost.

The town-based industry that is represented by at least seven known pottery kiln sites around Canterbury has been generally neglected except for the publication of most of the kilns themselves (Bennett et al. 1978, 1980; Jenkins 1956a, 1960; Webster 1940). The industry is of

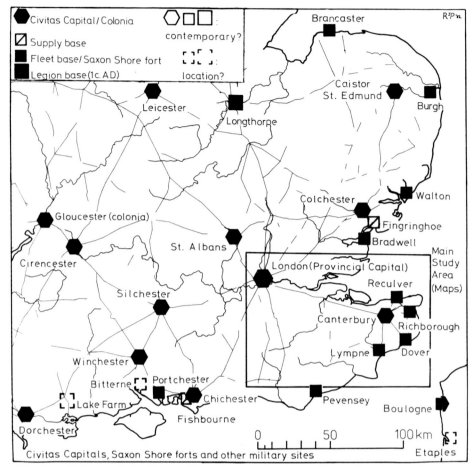

Fig. 1. *Civitas* capitals, Saxon Shore forts and other military sites in south-eastern
England.

great significance for local pottery studies in general, providing a classic example of the urban potteries that were a feature of the first two centuries of Roman Britain (Fulford 1977b). These three industries are each discussed in their own right (Chapters 5 and 6).

Consideration of production and retail costs has led to the abridgement of the original thesis (Pollard 1983a) for the purpose of the publication of the evidence therein presented. The descriptive chapters have been retained or reworked, whilst discursive treatises have, with regret, been omitted for the most part (excepting the present Chapter 6, a reworking of the original Chapter 9). The four original chapters that are not published herein in one form or another cover the following ground:

Chapter 5. An analysis of the Kent pottery and its relationship to material from neighbouring counties, based upon the construction of a series of spatial and temporal style-zones, degrees of similarity within which and between which are measured by Jaccard's correlation coefficients (see Chapter 2 below);

Chapter 8. A comparative study of three urban nucleated pottery industries in south-east Britain: Canterbury, Colchester, and the Verulamium region (including Brockley Hill and its 'satellites');

Chapter 10. An analysis of patterns of pottery distribution observed in Roman Kent, set against a classification of hypothetical distributions and discussed with reference to potential influences ('bias factors') such as communications, classes of site and of vessel, and topographical constraints, and

Chapter 11. An analysis of developments in fiscal regimes and of settlement patterns in Kent in order to assess the degrees of correlation between contemporaneous agrarian and industrial developments, and thus the extent to which pottery might be a valid index of the condition of the Romano-British economy in general.

CHAPTER 2

PROBLEMS AND METHODS

I. THE SELECTION OF A STUDY REGION

The region to be studied must satisfy two criteria, if it is to justify the research conducted on it. The first, and obvious, criterion is that there must be available sufficient material to provide wide and fairly even coverage of the spatial and temporal parameters defined. The second criterion is that the region must have well-defined boundaries, provided by topography or settlement pattern; without such boundaries it is difficult to decide upon the spatial limits of the area within which data are to be collected, for settlement zones will tend to merge with one another at their peripheries. Local artefact dispersal patterns are most easily discernible within a self-contained region, which suffers comparatively little interference from neighbouring regions. Modern political boundaries are rarely meaningful in terms of the topography or the ancient settlement pattern; they cut across the boundaries of these features more often than they respect them. The historic borders of the county of Kent are an exception to this generalisation. The Thames Estuary and the English Channel wash the north, east, and south-east shores of the county, and the sparsely populated High Weald provides the southern boundary. To the north-west the London Clay of what is now south-east London was apparently thinly inhabited also (Pollard 1977; Sheldon and Schaaf 1978). The lower Thames is a less satisfactory boundary as the Essex and Kent sides are part of the same topographic zone. In consequence a selection of sites in south Essex was included in the research programme. The same can be said of the Surrey border, which cuts across the chalk and clay-with-flints of the North Downs. However, few major excavations have been conducted inside Surrey east of the roadside settlement at Ewell, over 15 km. inside the Surrey border (Graham 1936; Keulemans 1963; Little 1961, 1964 are published exceptions); a convenient, albeit false, settlement zone boundary can thus be drawn between the Roman roads from London to Brighton and Lewes (Margary 1973, routes 150 and 14 respectively).

The region thus defined comprises somewhat more than 400 km.^{2} of land, of which a large proportion was apparently only thinly settled in the Roman period (Ordnance Survey 1978). Within the more populous areas – the river valleys through the North Downs, the Thames and Medway lowlands at the foot of the Downs, and the area between the Thames Estuary and the Straits of Dover – a large quantity of archaeological evidence has been recorded, including much pottery of all four centuries of the Roman occupation. A wide range of settlement types is present, providing the opportunity to investigate the relationship of settlement hierarchy to ceramic distribution patterning. Moreover, this material has been subjected to little synthesised study by comparison with, say, central southern England (e.g. Fulford 1975a; Hodder 1974a; Lyne and Jefferies 1979) and the south Midlands (Young 1977a) although site reports on pottery are abundant. Many of the exotic fine wares of the region have been studied in depth (e.g. Arthur 1978; Fulford 1977a; Greene 1979a; Rigby 1973; Young 1977a) as have certain of the exotic coarse wares (e.g. Hartley 1963; Lyne and Jefferies 1979; Williams 1977; Young 1977a). These studies have tended to be focused upon the fortunes of individual industries with little attempt being made to relate single industries to the broad spectrum of ceramics of the appropriate period (Greene 1979a provides a notable exception). All of these factors make the study of the pottery of Roman Kent one that is full of untapped potential.

II. THE SELECTION OF SITES AND ASSEMBLAGES FOR ANALYSIS

The number of sites within the study region for which published information exists is considerable, but the quality and extent of reports are inevitably variable. The study region contains two walled towns – Canterbury (*Durovernum Cantiacorum*) and Rochester (*Durobrivae*) – four major military bases – *Regulbium, Rutupiae, Dubris* and *Lemanis* – and three other named sites along Watling Street – *Noviomagus, Vagniacae*, and *Durolevum*. The status of these latter sites is not certain, but they may all be thought of as 'small towns' – the name of the first may imply a trading function, while *Vagniacae* (Springhead) incorporated a temple complex and a number of other buildings (Penn 1965; Harker 1980) and the large cemetery at Ospringe (Whiting *et al.* 1931) may well be related to the *Durolevum* community (cf. Rivet 1970). The Ordnance Survey (1978) lists 21 sites of 'villa' status revealed by excavations, 32 'other substantial buildings' and four rural temples and shrines. In addition a large number of cemeteries and individual burials have been recorded and a smaller number of occupation sites and deposits devoid of structures of 'villa' or other buildings status (cf. Jessup and Taylor 1932; Pollard 1977; Sheldon and Schaaf 1978, for surveys of portions of the evidence). The iron-working sites of the Weald must also be taken into account in any survey of the study region, for the road system and the presence of stamped tiles of the *Classis Britannica* alone are sufficient evidence to imply strong links between these sites and Roman Kent (e.g. see Cleere 1974, 1977; Peacock 1977b). The classification of sites is discussed below.

The pottery reports that accompany published accounts of excavations are as varied in quality as the excavations themselves. The selection of sites for examination at first hand was in the first instance dictated by the existence of a published pottery report with details of stratigraphic relationships. These sites give an uneven spread over space, time and functional ranges, and some were rejected to minimise duplication; for example, of the two villas fully published in the middle Darent valley – Lullingstone (Meates 1979) and Farningham Manor House (Meates 1973) – the former alone was examined, although the material from both was accessible. Sites with published, but unstratified pottery provided some infilling of the framework established with the stratified sites. In many cases the amount of pottery recorded suggested that further investigations of the assemblages would not be worthwhile. Consultation with museum authorities and excavators revealed a considerable body of unpublished material, some of it destined for future reports. It was not always possible to ascertain the quantity of material represented, and the research strategy was thus subjected to frequent revision as fresh material came to light which, on the grounds of the spatial and temporal co-ordinates and (where hypotheses could be formed) functions of the sites concerned could not be overlooked. The site list, Appendix 1, and the site distribution maps (Figs. 2–9) record the quality and location of the material examined, with a list of published reports which were utilised without examining the pottery at first hand. The number of major sites examined for which useful published information on the pottery was available prior to the commencement of museum research comprised slightly under half of the total of major sites that were included in that research. In the cases of the most extensive sites, such as Canterbury, Rochester, Springhead and Richborough, only a portion of the material taken account of in the overall research programme was available in published form.

The sites that have been the subjects of extensive excavations presented a problem of assemblage selection. The response to this problem varied according to various factors of publication, stratification and the accessibility of the material. The numerous pits excavated at Richborough provide most of the stratified, or at least context relateable, pottery from that site, and a selection was made of those with comparatively large assemblages in storage. The excavations of the Canterbury Archaeological Trust, which were under way during the research period, provided a data base for the city, and this base was supplemented by material from earlier excavation programmes that was available in both publications and the Canterbury Royal Museum. Much of this material was securely stratified, but it was not always possible to ascertain the retention strategies that had dictated the nature of the surviving assemblage; full quantification of all periods of the Roman city was thus not achieved. The imperfections of the resultant coverage should be overcome during future research to be conducted on the Roman pottery recovered by the Canterbury Archaeological Trust. The site at Springhead presented a different pattern again, as most of the pottery from the early seasons was discarded by the excavator, the late Mr W.S. Penn, after summary publication (S. Harker, pers. comm.). The pottery reports of this period of excavation employ an over-generalised type series (Penn 1957; 1958; 1959; 1960; 1962; 1964; 1967; 1968) deemed unsuitable by Mr Penn's successor, the late Mr S. Harker and this author as a basis for analysis of this lost material. The Springhead research has thus been confined to Mr Harker's recent series of excavations (summaries in Frere 1977; Goodburn 1978; Wilson 1970; 1971; 1972; 1973), which have produced sufficient material accessible at the time of research to provide full temporal coverage, including quantified stratified assemblages for most of the Roman period.

The material from two sites in Rochester was loaned to the present author by the excavator, Mr A.C. Harrison, for the writing of specialist reports. This material covered the late first/early second to late fourth/early fifth century overall, and was quantified, rendering personal examination of the material published from two other sites (Harrison and Flight 1968; Harrison 1972) superfluous within the terms of the research design. The published material has been taken account of, nevertheless. Examination of the pottery from the Lullingstone villa and the *Classis Britannica* fort at Dover was confined to the material selected for publication, as this was considered by the excavators (Lt.-Col. G.W. Meates and Mr B.J. Philp, respectively) to provide a full range of vessel types over the whole of the periods of occupation. Subsequently, the pottery from the former site has been re-analysed by the present author (Pollard 1987). In other instances where a larger volume of material exists than it proved possible to examine, assemblage selection was based upon a precursory study of most or all of the collection, resulting in the extraction of groups which appeared to provide full temporal coverage; in some cases this could only be ascertained by comparison of the pottery with stratified material previously studied, as site plans had not been archived with the material (e.g. Brenley Corner, Kent, and Pevensey, Sussex).

The major museum collections within the study area were studied in depth, and several of the local professional and part-time excavation groups visited, in the course of data collection. Some of the more important site collections, as judged by site function or the extent of excavation, could not be examined owing to the constraints of space and time experienced by the excavators, thus the villa at Eccles and the Saxon Shore forts at Reculver and Dover have had to be overlooked, except for the analysis of publications.

III. SITE CLASSIFICATION

There are two approaches to classification that may be entertained here, by the application of titles documented in classical sources such as '*urbs*, '*oppidum*', '*villa*' or '*vicus*', and by the description of the archaeological evidence alone. A system employing the latter approach is less evocative and more verbose than one employing the former, and most classifications adopt a compromise whereby the more ordered sites, where planning is apparent in the street-grid or the design of a house and its associated structures, are given titles of a classical nature, whilst the remaining sites are described in terms of their location, structures, or induced function (cf. Ordnance Survey 1956; 1978). Thus the titles of 'civitas capital', 'villa' and 'town' are entrenched in the archaeological literature despite the extreme rarity of a classical warrant for their application to specific sites. Discussion over just what kind of site merits these titles is frequent, and rarely conclusive (e.g. Johnson 1975; Percival 1976; Todd 1970; and Wacher 1975), as the functional interpretation of structural remains is rarely unequivocal. The classification adopted by the Ordnance Survey for its most recent 'Map of Roman Britain' (1978) is not explained in detail in the text that accompanies the maps; thus, a villa is defined as a 'rural building of substance' which has 'at least wall foundations of stone' with additional unspecified attributes that distinguish villas from other buildings of stone-based construction 'where the villa character is suggested but not finally proved' (*ibid.*, 8) (cf. Loughlin 1977, 104). Nevertheless the provision of a gazetteer, albeit without bibliographic references, enables the researcher to ascertain which sites are grouped under each major class.

The Ordnance Survey's most recent scheme is favoured by the present author as being comprehensive, if occasionally contentious; several of the classes of site defined by the Ordnance Survey are not present in the study region, notably all but one of the military categories (forts are the exception), and certain of the civilian 'communal settlements' – coloniae, spas, and burgi. Three types of site grouped by the Ordnance Survey under 'Other finds of Roman material' have been extracted by the present author for the purpose of providing a fuller description of the context of ceramic finds. These are listed in the following scheme as Classes VII – IX. The following system of classification is thus arrived at:

I.   Major towns (i.e. communal civilian settlements: civitas capitals and 'towns' – Ordnance Survey 1978);

II.   Forts and associated settlements;

III. Other communal settlements (cf. Ordnance Survey's 'Major' and 'Minor' settlements – 1978, 8);
IV. Temples and shrines;
V. Villas;
VI. Other substantial buildings (including isolated bath-houses and 'farm outbuildings');
VII. Rural occupation sites (including ditches, pits, isolated timber buildings, and surface scatters);
VIII. Cemeteries, comprising ten or more burials *in toto*;
IX. Cemeteries of less than ten burials, and individual interments;
X. Industrial sites (including iron extracting and smelting sites and salt extracting sites);
XI. Potteries;
XII. Tileries.

Chance finds of non-ceramic material have been omitted, it will be noted, as this system is designed specifically to enable the contexts of ceramic finds to be summarised. On the site distribution maps (Figs. 2–9) all sites of Classes I to V and X to XII have been plotted, according to whether they have been the subject of personal examination by the present author, examination of publications only, or have not been examined in either form. Sites of Classes VI to IX are only plotted if the present author has looked at the material in publication, or at first hand. Temples and shrines associated with sites of Classes I and II are not plotted, as it is assumed that they functioned as an adjunct of these sites rather than as sites in their own right or as a predominant feature of the site. The temple complex at Springhead, and the 'shrine' at Brenley Corner have been plotted as the former may well have dominated the life of the settlement while the latter appears to have outlived the settlement itself (Jenkins 1973; 1974).

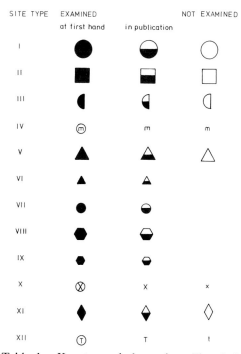

Table 1. Key to symbols used on Figs. 2–9.

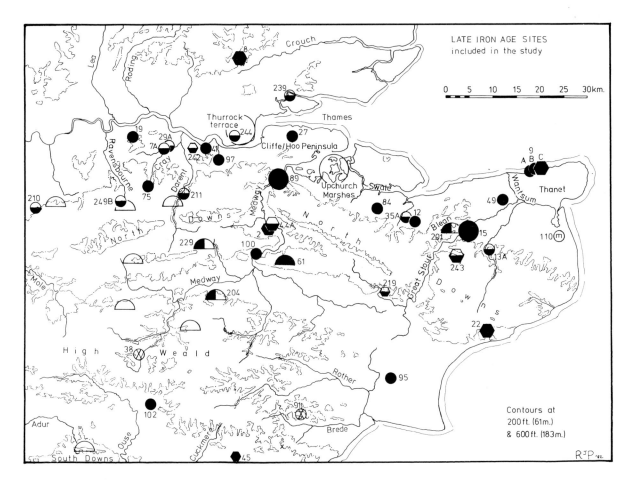

Fig. 2. Late Iron Age sites.

IV. ANALYSIS OF THE POTTERY

1. *Fabric Analysis*

The analysis of ceramic fabrics has been revolutionised by the adoption of petrological techniques (cf. for example Peacock 1970; 1977a). These enable visually similar wares to be differentiated, for example by the recording of the quantities of certain 'heavy minerals' present in the clay, or by the counting of grains of specified minerals present in a thin section. The allocation of fabrics to sources may be achieved by comparison with kiln-associated fabrics, or with geological samples (e.g. Drury 1978, 58; Williams 1977). A major disadvantage of petrological analysis is its cost in terms of time and money, which effectively restricts its application in projects of the kind undertaken by the present author. Furthermore, the differentiation of visibly-similar wares is not always successful (cf. Fulford 1975b). It would be difficult to justify the use of petrological techniques to differentiate visibly dissimilar wares, and

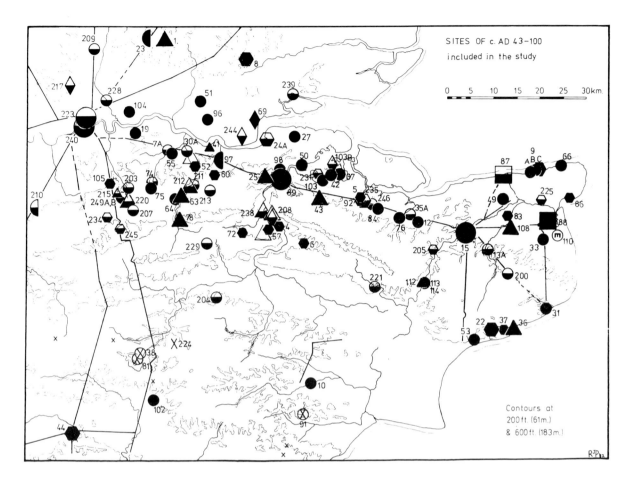

Fig. 3.   Sites of *c.* A.D. 43–100.

the use of visual techniques is a necessary prelude to the use of these techniques. The present author has adopted the approach of the Department of Urban Archaeology of the Museum of London (Orton 1977a), which involves the use of a x20 hand-lens for visual fabric characterisation. In combination with the analysis of hardness (by fingernail and penknife), and general 'feel' and appearance, the hand-lens technique can satisfactorily ascribe most wares to a fabric group which may subsequently be analysed petrologically, if the aims of the research demand this. The identification of fabric inclusions by the present author follows the guidelines laid down by the Department of Urban Archaeology (Orton 1977a, b).

A small number of characterisation projects involving petrological analysis have been conducted by other researchers which have included material from the study region (e.g. Drury 1978, 58; Peacock 1977c, d; Williams 1977). The results of these analyses have been taken into account by the present author, but no original petrological analysis has been conducted specifically for this study. Projects on fine wares found in Roman Britain, by Anderson *et al.*

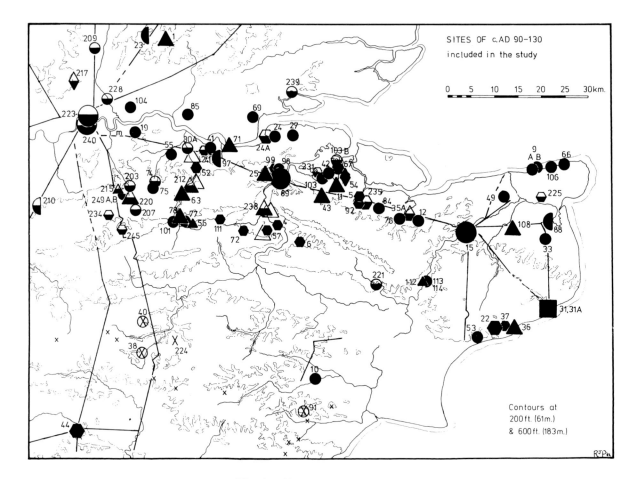

Fig. 4. Sites of *c*. A.D. 90–130.

(1982) (white-fabric colour-coated bag-beakers) and Dr Jane Timby (Gallo-Belgic wares), have been undertaken that have coincided with the present author's research, and the results of this work will hopefully clarify some of the issues that remain unresolved in the present account of pottery in Kent.

The appendix of fabrics (Appendix 2) has been abbreviated by restricting description to a summary of the visual and physical characteristics most appreciable in the hand specimen. The better-known wares have not been dealt with in detail, as description is readily available in recent publications. However, some wares have a wide range of fabric details, for example Colchester and Nene Valley colour-coated wares, and Much Hadham oxidised ware. In such cases, those fabrics which the present author has deemed most diagnostic of the ware in question are described in detail. Conversely, wares which may have been falsely attributed to a source are briefly described under the heading of that source, for example buff sandy wares under 'Brockley Hill/Verulamium'.

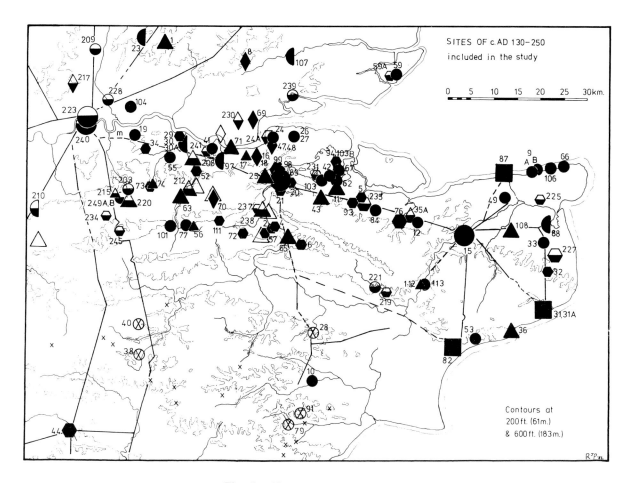

Fig. 5. Sites of *c.* A.D. 130–250.

2. *Formal Analysis*

The formal description of Roman pottery revolves around three methods: references to widely-used numbered type-series such as those constructed by Dragendorff and others for samian ware and Dressel for amphorae, the application of evocative terms such as 'poppyhead beaker' or 'pie-dish' that allude to a physical resemblance to an object or an induced function, and description of the individual features of the rim, body, and other attributes. The first and second methods are unsatisfactory, for the former may imply a similarity to a samian (for example) form which is fortuitous rather than the result of copying, while the latter is subject to the corruption of the terminology so that the terms mean different things to different people. The third method can also suffer from such corruption, but is perhaps less prone to it, the terms used being more specific. It is perhaps unfortunate that the evocative terminology of the second method is firmly entrenched in the archaeological literature, but the use of illustrations to clarify the terms overcomes the major shortcoming of corruption.

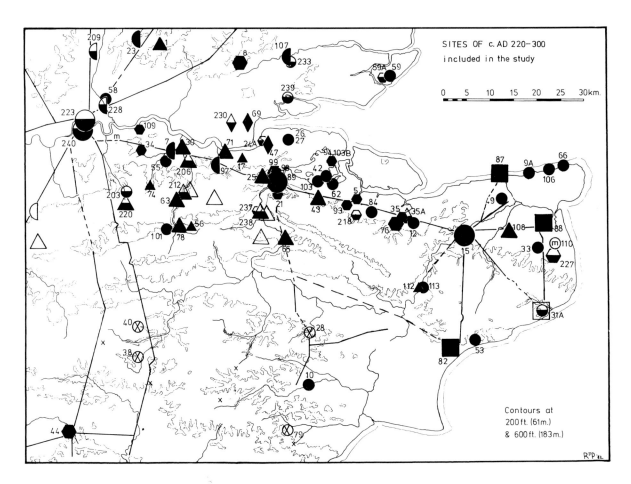

Fig. 6.   Sites of *c*. A.D. 220–300.

The construction of a type-series of forms found within the study region may be considered a desirable objective, and a working model has been established by the present author for use in the synthesis of material from Canterbury. This model follows the lines laid down by Tyers and Marsh (1978) for the Southwark Roman pottery, with some revision in the classification hierarchy involving the separation of body shapes from rim-and-neck forms, in order to facilitate the allocation of significant body sherds (such as folded or decorated pieces) to a standard type without assuming a specific rim to have been present. The method devised by Tyers and Marsh has the advantage of being 'open-ended', enabling forms unknown at the time of compilation to be inserted in a logical progression. This facility was afforded by Kenyon's type-series of the Leicester Jewry Wall assemblage (1948), and by Cotton's type-series of Southampton material (1958), but the use of a continuous numerical sequence for each form (e.g. flagons) irrespective of type (e.g. dish rim) by the former, and the inconsistent hierarchy of the latter have restricted their value. Other type-series have opted for a simple numerical

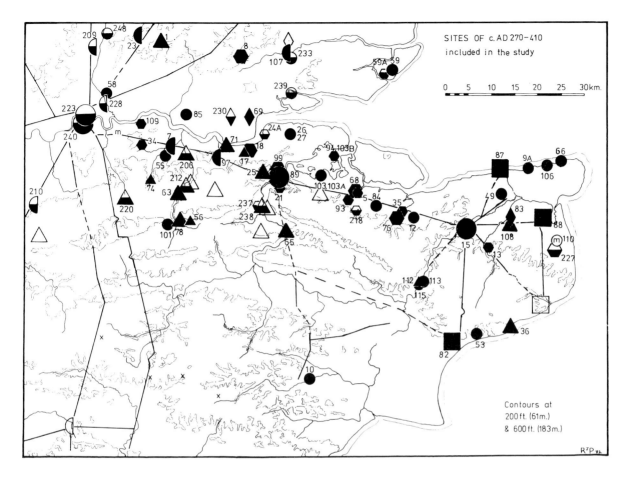

Fig. 7. Sites of *c*. A.D. 270–410.

sequence covering all vessels, allocating number-blocks to form groupings (e.g. Gillam 1957; 1970; Cunliffe 1971; Fulford 1975b), sometimes with short parts of the sequence left open for the insertion of future types (e.g. Hawkes and Hull 1947; Hull 1958). The inflexibility of these methods is a clear disadvantage. The pottery reports from most major sites have opted for less synthesised systems, illustrating a representation of the assemblage as a whole or by contexts with some repetition of forms (e.g. Bushe-Fox 1913; 1914; 1916; 1926; 1928; 1932; 1949; Cunliffe 1968; Frere 1972; Orton 1977b; Whiting *et al*. 1931).

The type-series developed by researchers studying a particular industry have used a combination of major divisions of fabric and continuous numerical sequences (e.g. Fulford 1975a; Young 1977a) or a single numerical sequence covering all fabrics (e.g. Lyne and Jefferies 1979). The present author has adopted the latter approach for the illustrations of the major wares, known or suspected to have been produced in the study region, and of other vessels of particular significance, that accompany this study. The illustrations have been selected as

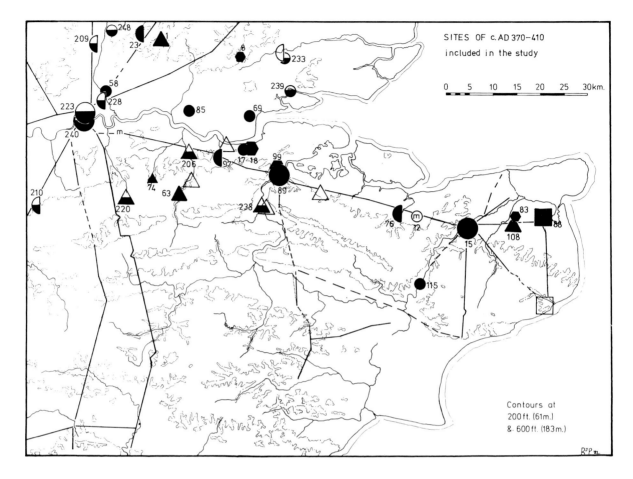

Fig. 8.   Sites of *c*. A.D. 370–410.

representative of the more common forms produced in each ware, and are grouped by wares rather than by formal similarities. The study is to a large extent concerned with production units rather than the development of individual forms. It has been considered appropriate, therefore, to publish these representative groups rather than to incorporate a full type-series of all wares irrespective of their source.

3.   *Quantification*

The value of a quantified data base lies in providing a basis for intra- and inter-assemblage comparison at the level of relative-frequency assessment (Orton 1975, 30; 1980, 156–67). This approach allows discussion of distributional aspects of ceramics such as the extent of areas within which industries were able to achieve a predominant share of the market, and the

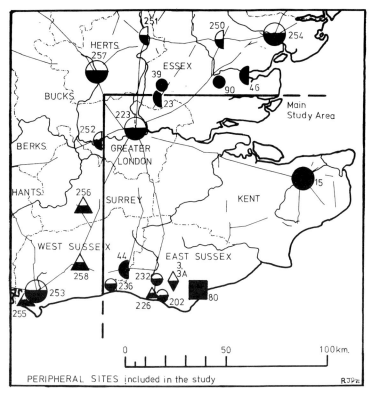

Fig. 9.   Peripheral sites included in the study.

occurrence of secondary dispersal centres (see for example Hodder and Orton 1976). These phenomena may be recognisable in simple point-distribution maps wherein the presence or absence of the artefacts under discussion is plotted (e.g. the distribution of Colchester mortaria – Hartley 1973a, fig. 7), but the facility of discussing relative quantities of artefacts enables a greater depth of discussion of such phenomena to take place.

Four measures of quantity were considered by Orton (1975; cf. 1980, 156–67) in a paper aimed at assessing the merits and demerits of each measure. Two criteria for assessment were proposed: (i) the measure should give a 'good' estimate of the relative proportions of different types in one context, and more importantly (ii) it should be such that valid comparisons of these proportions can be made between one context and another'. The four measures are subsequently ordered in decreasing merit: equivalent number of vessels; weight of sherds; number of sherds; number of vessels represented (often expressed as a minimum). The present author consequently elected to employ the first method; rim sherds only were analysed, as these provide information about the form, size and function of vessels that is rarely discernible from base sherds, which tend to exhibit a high degree of formal conservatism and less variety in size than rims. The method has the incidental advantage that only a small proportion of an assemblage need be studied in detail, featureless body sherds need not be fabric-sorted except to facilitate the search for clearly-defined wares. Rim sherds are placed on a chart with concentric arcs of preset radii divided into degrees of a circle, so that the portion of a complete circular vessel represented by each sherd is expressed as a percentage figure. In practice it is difficult to measure the diameter of sherds of less than 18° (5 per cent) of the rim; these are consequently omitted from the quantification.

It will be obvious that either the full assemblage recovered or a random sample drawn from that assemblage (Orton 1978; Redman 1979; Vince 1977b) is required for quantified techniques to produce results that reflect accurately the recovered material. These conditions can be ascertained to occur only rarely in museum collections, owing to the lack of archived notes by the excavators and receiving curators. Hodder (1974b) faced this problem when he sought to deduce marketing patterns from pottery collections; he argued that whilst collection and retention procedures might favour visibly attractive sherds, producing a bias in assemblage proportions towards fine wares, there was no evidence to suggest that these procedures treated one coarse or 'grey' ware differently to another (Hodder 1974c). It was legitimate, therefore, to use sherd-counts of coarse wares to provide data from which their marketing patterns might be hypothesised. These counts are translated into percentage expressions of relative frequency to produce comparable figures for inter-site analysis.

The present author has not favoured Hodder's method, as it is not compatible with the vessel rim equivalence analysis (Orton 1975; 1980, 156–67) conducted on suitable assemblages, and the assumptions that it makes concerning collection and retention would seem to represent a fundamental weakness that could not justify the application of the method on a large scale. The number of assemblages that have been analysed by the 'equivalent number of vessels' technique is not large, and it is unfortunate that this technique has only recently received publicity, for as a consequence of this there are few published analyses available for comparison with the present author's data. Those that have been consulted are listed in Appendix One. The 'minimum numbers of vessels represented' technique has been applied to a small number of assemblages from the north-west of Kent and Greater London (e.g. Philp 1973; Tyers 1977; Tyers and Marsh 1978). Orton's statement (1975, 31) that the results of this method cannot be compared with one another severely undermines the usefulness of these publications. However, in some instances sherd counts have also been published (e.g. Philp 1963a; 1973) providing a basis for inter-site and intra-site comparison particularly within the north-west.

4. 'Fine' and 'Coarse' wares

Something must be said concerning the division of Roman pottery into 'fine' and 'coarse' categories. These terms are widely used in both specialist reports and articles of a more general nature, without reference to a standard definition. Ironically, one of the prime examples of this malpractice is the Council for British Archaeology handbook (Webster, 1976), which claimed to represent an 'attempt to establish a consistent method of describing Romano-British coarse pottery . . . as a move towards the clarification of the terms in use for types of fabric, decoration and vessel' (*ibid.*, 3). The title and foreword (from which this quotation is taken) of the volume imply that discussion is restricted to 'coarse' pottery; the introduction states that 'the local pottery of Roman Britain. . . consists of a wide variety of fabrics both coarse and fine' (*ibid.*, 4). Fabrics described include a wide range from the hand-made, calcite-gritted Huntcliff ware to colour-coated and 'Eggshell' wares; the term 'coarse' is used solely in the cases of Dales ware and Romano-Saxon ware, whilst 'fine' is restricted to the paint on Rhenish ware, and to the general description of St. Rémy ware. The description of the heterogeneous 'Romano-Saxon wares' includes the inference that colour-coated wares are not considered to be coarse (*ibid.*, 15), in which case the reader is left to reflect upon why they are discussed in detail in a volume entitled 'Romano-British coarse pottery'. Swan's guide to *Pottery in Roman Britain* (1975a) also fails to define the terms 'fine' and 'coarse', although this may be partially excused on the grounds that they play only a small part in her discussion; the latter term is confined to the description of, as in the C.B.A. guide, Dales ware (Swan 1975a, 21).

The terms are currently used in two senses, firstly to define size ranges of inclusions in the fabric of vessels (Orton 1977a; Peacock 1977a), and secondly as generalised divisions of pottery as a whole. It is widely understood that 'fine' includes samian, colour-coated wares, and wares with no visible inclusions and a delicacy of form, whilst 'coarse' includes heavily-tempered fabrics with a surface that is harsh to the touch. This implicit convention is adhered to in the present work. The obvious problem is where to draw the line, and how this division can be justified. It has been argued elsewhere (Pollard forthcoming, a) that the grey sand-tempered Alice Holt dishes, with their glossy black, grey and white slips and tooled-decorated interiors, could have been 'fine' wares to those purchasing and handling them, on a par with the dark-slip Nene Valley and Oxfordshire ware products of the same forms (Lyne and Jefferies 1979, Classes 5B. 10, 6A. 8–10 (note); Howe *et al.* 1980, nos. 79, 87; Young 1977a, Types C93, C94). This is not merely a matter of a ceramicist's niceties; discussion of site hierarchy and prosperity may invoke the proportions of 'fine' to 'coarse' pottery, placing those sites which used slipped greyware rather than colour-coated wares at a disadvantage, if the former are implicitly taken as 'coarse'. The effect on the 'fine' ware proportion of a later fourth-century group from Wye (Pollard forthcoming, a) of re-allocating certain explicitly defined grey wares from the 'coarse' category was to raise it from under 12 per cent of the assemblage to over 16 per cent. The effect upon the 'fine' ware assemblage taken in isolation was far more dramatic: the 'fine' grey ware represented the second most common fine ware at over 27 per cent, reducing the Oxfordshire red colour-coated ware proportion from over 42 per cent to some 31 per cent, and the Nene Valley colour-coated ware from just under 18 per cent to just over 13 per cent (i.e. roughly half the 'fine' grey ware proportion). Clearly, these recalculations could have a marked influence upon the discussion of 'fine ware' marketing in late Roman Britain, suggesting that the massive colour-coated ware industries were less successful in dominating the market for fine pottery than might otherwise be thought.

The pottery of late Iron Age and early Romano-British Kent also presents a problem of defining 'fine' and 'coarse'. 'Aylesford-Swarling' pottery includes a large number of wheel-thrown, often decorated, vessels of quite complex form, such as pedestal-urns (cf. no. 124 here), biconical bowls (no. 22), platters (nos. 32, 33) and flagons (nos. 35–38). The fabrics are coarse in comparison to Gallo-Belgic imports, being tempered with large ('coarse' to 'very coarse' in grain size terms, i.e. greater than 0.5 mm. diameter) grog and organic inclusions, and of heavy build. However, in the later first century B.C. and possibly well into the first century A.D. these 'Aylesford-Swarling' wares represented the most delicate pottery available, and must surely have been thought of as 'fine', so far as pottery was concerned, to their users. The relegation of these wares to the 'coarse' category as a result of comparison with later material appears gratuitous.

The term 'fine' in the present study includes the following wares: samian; colour-coated wares; glazed wares; 'Parchment wares'; mica-dusted wares; wares with sparse (cf. Orton 1977a) inclusions/temper, whether slipped or unslipped; wares in which the only inclusions present in more than sparse quantities are minerals not thought to have been used as temper, e.g. mica and fine iron ores; Hadham oxidised wares; Gallo-Belgic slipped wares including those with abundant quartz sand.

'Coarse' wares include reduced, oxidised and white fabrics with moderate or abundant inclusions possibly used as temper, whether unslipped or coated in a white, grey or black slip. This definition thus includes BB2, Highgate Wood type wares, and Alice Holt wares, (but cf. the reservations expressed above). The inclusion of Hadham oxidised wares in the 'fine' category is contentious; the similarity of the bowl forms to late colour-coated ware types and the variety of decorative motifs employed have been considered to outweigh the presence of abundant quartz sand in the fabric as determinants of classification. The 'Aylesford-Swarling' grog-tempered forms discussed above are also included in the 'coarse ware' category for the purposes of description and quantification of Romano-British assemblages, along with the simpler forms such as bead-rim neckless jars (no. 25 here) and neck-cordoned jars (nos. 26–29). The apparently homogeneous late Iron Age assemblages have not been divided into 'fine' and 'coarse' wares.

V. INTERPRETATION

1. Single Assemblages

It is not a primary objective of this study to elucidate the nature of contexts through the study of their ceramic assemblages, although a hierarchy of sites could be constructed on the basis of, for example, the proportion of fine to coarse wares or exotic to local wares, which might be meaningful in terms of the prosperity or range of contacts of the inhabitants. Nevertheless, the quantified assemblages have been divided up into four categories of pottery: fine wares, coarse wares, mortaria, and amphorae. The purpose of this approach is to facilitate the comparison of wares which, it may be hypothesised, were subject to similar pressures of supply and demand. It would seem reasonable to suggest that fine wares for the table operated within a different 'sphere of exchange' to coarse wares for use in kitchen and pantry, and thus that the two were not in direct competition with each other, except perhaps where the most impoverished households were concerned. The proportion of 'fine' to 'coarse' wares can vary considerably between assemblages of the same or different periods, and may be important as a measure of wealth and contact. However, if the comparative success on the market of, say, Oxfordshire and Nene Valley colour-coated wares is to be measured, it is useful to treat these and the remainder of the fine wares in isolation from coarse wares. Mortaria are specialised vessels which often exhibit distribution patterns that are noticeably different with those of other vessels from the same source (e.g. Brockley Hill: see Appendix 3; Oxfordshire wares – Young 1977a); for this reason they have been isolated from the remainder of assemblages. Amphorae have been similarly treated because they, too, are specialised vessels at least in their original function of long-distance bulk carriers.

The maxim established by Orton (1978, 401–2) should be borne in mind when interpreting quantified data: 'one cannot usefully say *by itself* "75% of the pottery at site X is Oxfordshire ware" . . . But we can say that if 75% of the pottery recorded at X is Oxfordshire ware, and only 50% at Y is, then there is relatively more Oxfordshire ware at X than Y. . . . the figures themselves may not be useful individually'. The emphasis in this study is thus placed on inter-assemblage rather than intra-assemblage analysis and interpretation.

2. *Inter-assemblage comparison*

The quantified data provide limited opportunities for making statements of the kind quoted in the previous paragraph. Points of similarity and dissimilarity have been isolated from these data, and from these a series of impressions of the degrees of similarity between sites has been gained. Ideally, objective statistical techniques should be applied to the raw data to provide a check on the subjective impressions. However, it was felt that the size of the quantified data base was not large enough to justify the application of multivariate analysis. Even with the increasing concern shown by pottery reporters for quantification, it is unlikely that a full coverage of the variables of spatial and temporal location and of function will be provided by quantified sites in the foreseeable future, and that presence/absence data will still be required to provide such coverage. A number of statistical measures of similarity between sites/assemblages have been discussed by Doran and Hodson (1975, 135–43), and of these Gower's Flexible Coefficient is deemed particularly useful, as it is able to cope satisfactorily with both presence/absence and quantified data. The correlation coefficients computed by this technique might then be treated to multivariate analysis, such as Principal Components Analysis (Doran and Hodson 1975, 190–7), in the search for major trends of correlation between assemblage components and in order to provide a summary of the relationships between assemblages as units or between sites. The elucidation of production and marketing systems would thus proceed on a more rigorous, objective data base.

The limitation of information on most sites to presence/absence data renders expressions of similarity on a numerical scale both difficult and potentially misleading. However, it was felt desirable to have some such index, and to this end Jaccard's Coefficient was adopted on a limited basis. The formula is cited by Doran and Hodson (1975, 141–2), and is simple to compute, if time-consuming. The coefficient $S_j = a/(a+b+c)$, where a = the number of pottery types that a pair of sites have in common, b= the number of types present at site X but absent at Site Y, and c= the number present at Y but not at X. The shortcomings of presence/absence data render the resulting correlation coefficients crude representations of similarity in comparison with Gower's coefficient, but they do at least provide some check to subjective impressions.

One inherent weakness of Jaccard's coefficient is that it fails to take account of situations wherein the assemblages at site X are effectively subsets of those at site Y. In practice this is often the case, as between a minor, rural site and a neighbouring town (e.g. Charlton and London/Southwark). The correlation coefficient computed in the case of a subset to set pair of sites may be of the same order of magnitude as one computed for two sites with very different 'kitchen ware' assemblages but fundamentally identical 'table ware' assemblages. The latter situation is widespread in the second century in Kent with the existence of several 'kitchen ware' marketing zones but an overall occurrence of exotic 'table wares' such as samian, Nene Valley/Rhineland, and fine grey ware. Constant recourse to the assemblage/pottery type matrices constructed as a preliminary to computation is necessary for the interpretation of the coefficients to be verified.

A second problem results from the treatment of very different quantities of material of any given pottery type as a single score on the matrices. Types of minor significance in terms of numbers of sherds are elevated to the same importance as major types. This raises problems of interpretation particularly where high-status sites such as towns, military bases, or well-appointed villas are concerned, for these tend to have a wide range of exotic 'kitchen wares' occurring in very small quantities that are far more common on sites in different locations. Thus, Canterbury has revealed one or two sherds of first-century West Kent shelly wares (abundant west of the Medway), and Richborough's pottery includes a single Dales Ware jar (Bushe-Fox 1928, no. 147), the only site south of Caistor St. Edmund to do so (Loughlin 1977, 109, fig. 6). A high-status site in one distribution zone may be computed to have a much higher degree of similarity with a site in a second zone than visual inspection of assemblages would suggest.

VI. THE DEMONSTRATION OF SPATIAL TRENDS

The distribution map has long been a primary technique for presenting archaeological data and facilitating the interpretation of those data. The methodology of interpretation was one of the main aspects of the development of archaeological theory and method in the 1970s (e.g. Hodder and Orton 1976; Clarke 1977, with references) invoking and adapting a wide range of techniques developed by other disciplines, in particular geography and plant ecology. One of the main stimulants to this development was the recognition of the fallibility of subjective assessments of distributions: underlying structure may not always be easily discernible to the human eye, and the recognition of only those patterns and structures which the researcher wishes to see is a distinct possibility. These problems have been discussed by Hodder and Orton (1976, 1–10) with particular reference to the archaeology of prehistory.

Two aspects of this discussion may be focused upon: the plotting of both positive and negative data, and the distinction of random from non-random distributions.

Fox's classic study of *The Personality of Britain* (revised edition 1943) is criticised by Hodder and Orton (1976, 3) for failing to take account of the effect of differential patterns of site destruction and fieldwork intensity upon the recovery of archaeological material. The problem of interpreting blank areas on the map may be to some extent alleviated by plotting negative occurrences of relevant material on contemporaneous sites. This approach was applied to studies of Romano-British pottery by Hodder (e.g. 1974b), and has been adopted by the present author on the distribution maps of pottery types. However, the establishment of contemporaneity of sites and assemblages in itself can cause problems. In his studies of, for example, Savernake ware (Hodder 1974c) and Rowlands Castle wares (Hodder 1974a), Hodder assumed that all sites utilised the respective wares simultaneously; he thus plotted and discussed the gross distribution patterns of positive and negative finds. It is often the case that pottery of a particular type was not current in the same areas throughout its overall period of usage – the example of BB2 jars, mentioned in the preceding section and plotted on Figs. 30, 45, and 47 may be cited – and it should not be assumed that a type was in simultaneous use throughout its area of distribution at a certain time in its history. The example of Oxfordshire colour-coated wares indicates that this was not always the case; briefly, in the late fourth century these wares were eclipsed in East Sussex by 'Pevensey' ware (Green 1977, 177–8) but expanded their distribution in East Anglia (Drury 1977, 40). A cumulative distribution pattern may suggest modes of dispersal quite different from those current at any one point in time. The full extent of a pottery type's distribution irrespective of differential periods of use in certain areas is nevertheless of considerable interest; the maps here presented should be studied with reference to the main text in order to ascertain whether such differentiation occurred.

The present author's maps seek to relate the distribution of pottery types to natural and man-made features of the Romano-British landscape (see also Pollard 1983a, 415–73). The non-random behaviour that such features may induce need not always be apparent in the spatial patterning of artefacts or sites, however (Hodder and Orton 1976, 9). Cumulatively, the range of factors that could have influenced the dispersal of pottery may produce a random pattern. A subjective approach to interpretation might result in the false identification of structure in random patterns (*ibid.*, 4–8). The objective search for non-random patterning of artefact and site distributions has been one of the major developmentss in spatial analysis in recent years, but it should not be overlooked that the identification of such patterning is not an end in itself. The processes that resulted in random or non-random patterns remain to be identified; 'one spatial pattern may be produced by a variety of different spatial processes. . . .often one must look to non-spatial evidence to corroborate or disprove theories about spatial processes' (*ibid.*, 8).

The distribution maps published here have not been subjected to tests for randomness. There are two reasons for this omission. Firstly, it was considered (subjectively) that the patterns could be interpreted with reference to kiln/production area location in many instances (e.g. Fig. 22, 48) or to the operation of other factors (Pollard 1983a, 415–73) which have been investigated by previous research (e.g. Hodder 1974b; Loughlin 1977). Secondly, the nature of the area under study, with the coastline a dominant feature of the geography of Kent, places severe limitations on the value of nearest-neighbour analysis in searching for randomness (Hodder and Orton 1976, 41–3). The approach adopted by Hodder and Orton (1976, 44–5) to overcome this problem would be inappropriate to the present study, as it involves the choice of area for analysis such that the nearest-neighbour distance from any site is less than or equal to the distance from that site to the coast. This would seem to rule out many of the most important sites studied by the present author, such as the military bases at Richborough, Dover, Port Lympne and Pevensey, and the civil settlements at Little Shelford (Essex) and Birchington.

It was initially hoped that the comparative efficiency of the major production units in Kent and the surrounding area in supplying their potential hinterland zones might be studied through quantified statistics. Work by Hodder (1974d) suggested that regression analysis would be an appropriate technique: at a generalised level the fall-off gradients thus generated may reflect the comparative 'value' of pottery types, the shallower gradients being equated with types which were marketed in larger quantities at greater distances from their production centres. However, this analysis was curtailed by the weakness of the quantified data base. An alternative approach to regression analysis, involving the measurement of the density of sites with the pottery type under review in bands around the type's source, would seem to be inappropriate in the case of Kent owing to its maritime location; the density of sites greater than 10 km. from either Canterbury or the Cliffe Peninsula area kilns (producing BB2 and grey wares) would inevitably show a marked fall-off due to the inclusion of the Thames Estuary and English Channel in the bands. In the event, sufficient quantified data, expressed in the form of the proportion of one pottery type in assemblages, was collected for one small study to be undertaken (Fig. 48). The number of points was considered to be too small to warrant detailed analysis, but a marked fall-off in quantities outside 10 km. radii from the BB2 kilns around the Cliffe Peninsula is suggested. It would be interesting to examine whether this pattern is confirmed by the excavation and analysis of suitable groups of pottery from other sites of the same period and from sites with somewhat earlier assemblages. The occurrence of large quantities of poor quality imitation BB2 from Greenhithe (Detsicas 1966; nos. 107–109 here; 4.III.2) in a Hadrianic-early Antonine context suggests that the pattern might be somewhat different in this period. The inclusion of Essex material would also be of interest.

The relationship of distance to dispersal of kiln-products has also been investigated by plotting the number of forms of a certain fabric occurring on sites in the study area (Figs. 10 and 11). Empirically, it would appear that the 'value' of a pot varied according to its form/function (Pollard 1983a, 415–73) with the result that higher-value types were distributed over a greater distance than lower-value types. Variation in the number of types present on sites could thus be interpreted as reflecting variation in the economic distance from the source. This may reflect the prosperity, topographical situation, or distance in miles from that source. In the case of Brockley Hill ware, a marked fall-off east and south-east of Southwark is apparent, corresponding to an increase in mileage from the source (north-west of Southwark). In Kent, it is possible to distinguish concentric zones wherein certain numbers of types are to be found irrespective of site-type: 4–6 types west of the Cray, 2–3 types between the Cray and the Medway, and 1 type only (usually mortaria) east of the Medway. This zoning corresponds to increasing distance in miles from the source, and also to the presence of local production centres in Kent. The occurrence of 2–3 types in East Sussex sites perhaps reflects the weakness of the local competitors, particularly in the production of flagons and mortaria (Green 1980). The distribution of late Alice Holt types presents a more complex pattern, in which no one trend appears to predominate. The greatest numbers of types occur in the Darent-Medway area and on Saxon Shore forts (Richborough and Pevensey). Sites nearer to the source (on the Surrey-Hampshire border) contain smaller numbers of types. The pattern is complicated by the presence of local kilns apparently producing similar wares that may not always be differentiated from Alice Holt products, in east Kent and East Sussex (6. VIII). This analysis bears interesting comparison with that published by Lyne and Jefferies (1979, fig. 47) using the number of rims of Alice Holt ware as a proportion of the total number of rims on sites throughout southern England. The latter shows Kent sites to have a small proportion of the ware in comparison with sites in Sussex, Surrey and the middle Thames valley, but too few sites within the area of Kent are included to enable internal variation to be determined with any assurance.

Two further methods of spatial analysis discussed by Hodder and Orton (1976) may be mentioned briefly. Trend surface analysis, the particular value of which is considered to be that 'it allows regional trends to be distinguished from more local ones' (*ibid.*, 174), would seem to be rendered invalid by the shortage of quantified data and the restriction of the majority of sites to a narrow strip along the North Downs and Thames. Moreover, its usefulness as a method of predicting unknown production centres (assuming a single centre to be involved) is in question (*ibid.*, 166). The second method, involving the use of gravity models to examine, for example, marketing hypotheses, has been widely employed by Hodder (1974a; 1974e; Hodder and Orton 1976, 189–95). The underlying concept is one of interaction between centres (e.g. potteries, towns); hypothetical marketing areas are constructed using Reilly's breaking-point formula (Hodder and Orton 1976, 188), the acreage enclosed by town walls or the overall area of pottery kilns of a particular group commonly providing the basic statistics. These marketing areas may then be compared with pottery distributions in order to observe whether there is any correlation

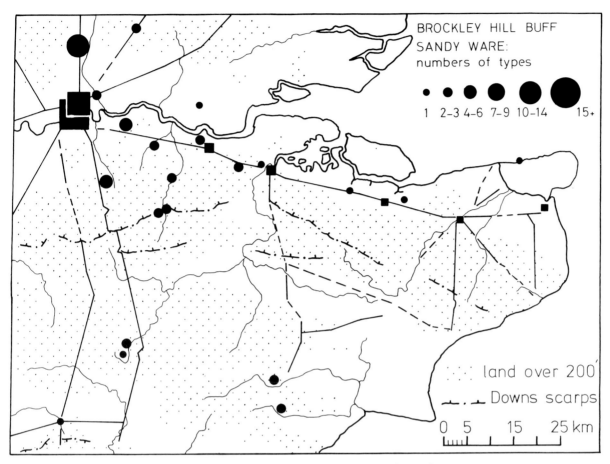

Fig. 10.   Brockley Hill buff sandy ware: numbers of types.

suggestive of a connection between distribution and the scale of production (as assumed to be reflected in the area covered by kilns) or the size of the 'home' market town. There are obvious flaws in this approach, notably the assumptions concerning the area of town or production: defended acreage does not necessarily equate with the overall area of a town, nor need intra-mural population densities be of the same order in all towns, while production units of a given size in terms of scale of production may be dispersed over areas of greatly different acreage for reasons such as availability of raw materials or density of local population and thus local demand. In the opinion of the present author, these weaknesses undermine the principle to an unacceptable degree, and it was felt that the application of this approach would not be useful. Moreover, the dispersed nature of production of north-west Kent/southern Essex BB2 and grey sandy wares would make it difficult to justify the nomination of any one settlement as the 'marketing centre' (Rochester, Springhead and the possible 'small town' at Chadwell St. Mary may all have performed this function). The role of these wares is fundamental to any analysis of marketing patterns in Kent during most of the Roman period. It is possible that most

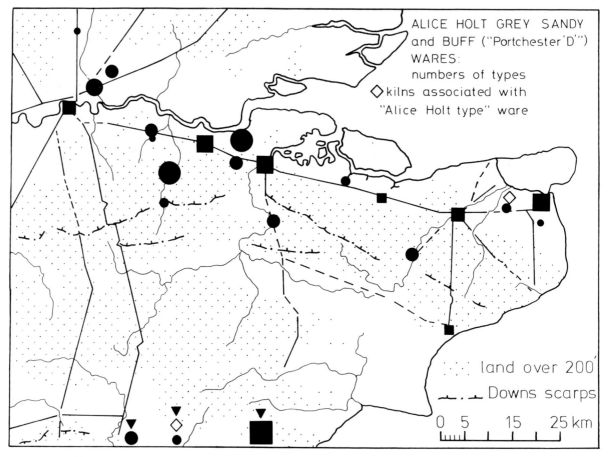

Fig. 11.   Alice Holt grey sandy and buff ('Portchester "D"') wares: numbers of types.

other wares originating in Kent were also produced in a dispersed manner, without the influence of a single market centre, the Canterbury industry being the only certain exception (see Chapter 6).

The interpretations of the distribution maps compiled by the present author, and presented herewith, are thus based upon a subjective, but cautious, visual analysis, checked where possible against quantified data providing a greater clarity to the situations plotted. This approach at least has the merit of not over-stretching the data which, as has been stated above, have been collected from sites diverse in their nature.

CHAPTER 3

THE LATE IRON AGE

I. INTRODUCTION

The study of pottery of the Roman period in Kent, as elsewhere in Britain, would be incomplete without some reference to that of the period immediately preceding the Conquest. Much has been made of the late Iron Age pottery of the south-east of Britain and the light it can shed upon the political history recorded in fragmentary form by Julius Caesar and taken up by occasional literary references emanating from the Roman Empire down to the Claudian conquest of A.D. 43. The invasions of tribal groups from the Belgic areas of Gaul attested by Caesar as having occurred at some time prior to his own raids in strength of 55 and 54 B.C. have prompted several generations of archaeologists to envisage any change apparent in the material record of the late Iron Age as being due to 'intrusive elements', to use the phrase adopted by Ward-Perkins in defining his 'South-eastern B' cultural group (1938, 156). The development of invasion or 'immigration' models of Iron Age Britain has recently been summarised by Cunliffe (1978, 1–10), and need not be reiterated here. It will suffice to observe that the current tenor of studies of this period is to recognise 'a broad cultural continuum' (*ibid.*, 10) from as early as the second millenium throughout the Iron Age. The changes that undeniably occurred are considered in the first instance to be due to the inherent dynamics of economy and society within Britain. 'Intrusive elements' in a ceramic or metal artefact assemblage are more likely, in this climate of speculation, to be attributed to trade and exchange of ideas and objects than to the impositions of invaders upon indigenous culture.

The transformation of thinking that has seen the rejection of many intricate cultural models formulated by scholars of previous generations has not been without its consequences for the archaeology of Kent and its neighbourhood. The two models propounded by Ward-Perkins – the 'south-eastern B' and 'Wealden' cultures (Ward-Perkins 1938, 152–6; 1944, 143–6) – have been generally rejected during the last decade, to be superseded by two schemes of a more cautious nature, invoking sequences of ceramic 'styles' whose significance in terms of society is in their reflection of contact and exchange rather than the homogeneity of ethnic groups. Nevertheless, the ethnic identity of the Belgae, the invaders referred to by Caesar, is not easily rejected. As recently as 1976, a major paper sought to trace the stages of the Belgic expansion in Britain on the basis of ceramic and numismatic evidence (Rodwell 1976a). The precision that this study sought to achieve may be illusory; one of the main inhibitors of progress in unravelling the archaeology of the first century B.C. is the lamentable shortage of sites with a long sequence of occupation, particularly in Kent, an area at the heart of the 'Belgic controversy'.

II.   THE POTTERY OF THE 'AYLESFORD-SWARLING CULTURE'

The passage in Caesar's *Gallic Wars* (v, 12) recording the settlement of maritime areas of Britain by immigrants from the Belgic areas of Gaul in the century of his own subjugation of Gaul has been possibly the foundation for more speculation on the late Iron Age in Britain than any other ancient reference. The excavation of two cemeteries in Kent, at Aylesford (Evans 1890) and Swarling (Bushe-Fox 1925) provided type-sites for the study of 'Belgic' Britain, and the 'Aylesford-Swarling Culture' is entrenched in the literature (see Champion 1976, 10–17, for an historiography, and Cunliffe 1978, 83–93 for a summary of its elements).

The pottery of the Aylesford-Swarling Culture has been the subject of intensive studies by a number of scholars, including doctoral theses in recent years by Thompson (1982) and Tyers (1981). The characteristics of the pottery are much less elusive than its chronology. Vessels are generally wheel-thrown, and evince a penchant for cordons, 'corrugation', and zones of combed or 'furrowed' decoration. Shapes may be angular or rounded, often with pedestal or foot-ring bases, and in some cases clearly derived from the fine platters, beakers, cups and flagons of Julio-Claudian northern Gaul (Figs. 14 and 15). The use of grog temper was extensive, though not universal, particularly in south-east Britain (Thompson 1982). Typological affinities with northern French material are strong, particularly between the assemblages of Kent and the Boulonnais, northern Artois and western Flanders (Tyers 1980, 1981). Chronological studies have tended to look to associated, independently dateable objects, such as metalwork or imported fine pottery and amphorae, for the elucidation of a developmental sequence in the 'Belgic' pottery, either in burials or on stratified sites (e.g. Rodwell 1976a; Stead 1976; Birchall 1965). Opinions voiced in the early 1980s have held that such studies are premature (Tyers 1980; Thompson 1982, 3), though the desire to make sense of the tantalising evidence for dating the late pre-Roman Iron Age in south-east Britain is understandable. The data bases for both funerary (e.g. Stead 1969; Thompson 1978) and domestic (e.g. Partridge 1981; Thompson 1982; Blockley and Day forthcoming) assemblages are expanding gradually, but it is still easier to criticise earlier attempts at chronology than it is to establish a new, more acceptable version (Pollard 1983a, 52–5).

'Aylesford-Swarling', or more appropriately 'Belgic' pottery (in the sense of a distinctive class of pottery, without political, economic or historical implications: Thompson 1982, 5), is, so far as the regions south of the Thames are concerned, primarily a feature of eastern Kentish sites. In Kent west of the Medway valley (except perhaps on the Thames flood plain), and in East Sussex, it is rare, and may be regarded as either intrusive or a product of a cross-fertilisation of ideas (Thompson 1982, 11–14; Green 1980; Pollard 1983a, 55–63).

III.   POTTERY STYLE-ZONES IN LATE IRON AGE KENT

The dearth of 'Aylesford-Swarling' cemeteries west of the Medway valley – Stone-near-Greenhithe (Cotton and Richardson 1941) is the sole known occurrence – may be an accident of discovery. However, the absence of oblique 'furrowed' decoration on west Kent pottery (Fig. 20) provides convincing evidence of regionalisation in pottery styles in late Iron Age Kent. This style (nos. 25, 27–29) was executed on various jar forms in the east, whereas in the west jars were either plain of surface or given horizontal 'furrowed' (rilled) decoration (nos. 1, 2), usually in a wide band. Pre-Conquest copies of Gallo-Belgic and Central Gaulish *Terra Nigra* and *Terra Rubra* platters appear also to be confined almost exclusively to the eastern half of the county. Camulodunum 21/22 (Hawkes and Hull 1947, no. 32) is not uncommon at Canterbury in probable pre-Conquest deposits (e.g. Frere 1954, nos. 40–3, 50; Pollard forthcoming, d, nos. 19, 20, 28), and occurs also at Wye, and at Birchington Minnis Bay (Well 30). It is absent from west Kent, although its imported progenitor, Camulodunum 1, occurs at Bexley (Caiger 1958, no. 4). A generally pre-Claudian date for Camulodunum 21/22 is ascribed by Thompson (1982, forms G1–1/2, 440–447). Flagons tempered with grog and/or organic matter (nos. 35–38 here) are also confined to eastern Kent, but may have post-Conquest origins (4.I below).

The distribution of certain fabrics supports that of forms and motifs in the discernment of what are in effect 'style-zones' (cf. Cunliffe 1978). Independent studies by Thompson (1982, 7–15) and the present author (1983a, 57–62) have revealed some patterning in fabric distributions in Kent. Flint-tempering is found in the Medway valley and eastern Kent in 'Belgic' and 'Gallo-Belgic' forms (e.g. Pollard forthcoming, d, nos. 2, 5, 26, 72, 135, 145) and may be a phenomenon primarily of the earlier 'Aylesford-Swarling' period at Canterbury and elsewhere in east Kent, following a long tradition of potting with flint grit (cf. Macpherson-Grant 1980). The Medway valley itself is the focus for a group of sites with glauconite-rich fabrics employed for 'Belgic' forms. Such fabrics are a feature of 'foot-ring' bowls antedating the 'Belgic' period for the most part (Drury 1978, Form 13; Drury and Rodwell 1973, 53), and have been subjected to a thin-sectioning programme whose results reveal several potential sources in Kent (Peacock and Williams, in Drury 1978, 58). Find-spots of 'Belgic' glauconite-rich fabrics include Quarry Wood, Loose (Kelly 1971: nos. 4–7, 9–11, 18, 19, 23–25, 31, are in these fabrics), Teston (Ocock 1974, nos. 1, 2), and Rochester (see below). Several other sites are listed by Thompson (1982, 11–12). Shelly wares appear to be particularly characteristic of later first century B.C. to late first century A.D. contexts in west Kent, and also in southern Essex (e.g. Philp 1973, 61 – Keston Lower Warbank, and 71 – West Wickham North Pole Lane; Drury and Rodwell 1973, phases 3–5a; 4.I below; Thompson 1982, 7). Diagnostic 'Belgic' vessels are uncommon in shelly wares in these areas, unless one includes simple, utilitarian bead-rim jars and necked storage jars; the cordoned bowl from Greenhithe (Detsicas 1966, no. 48) is exceptional. A ceramic zone where sand-tempering is common has been postulated in south-east Kent, around Deal and Folkestone (Thompson 1982, 14–15), and fine sandy fabrics in 'Belgic' forms are known from Canterbury and Birchington Minnis Bay (Pollard forthcoming, d; no. 89). Vessels with mixed temper are found on occasion throughout Kent (e.g. Pollard forthcoming, d, no. 145; *id.*, 1987, Fabrics 67–70; Ocock 1974, nos. 3 and 4, in a 'grog-and-sand' fabric). Grog was the temper in most widespread use for 'Belgic' forms both in Kent, and more generally throughout south-east Britain. Its distribution spreads beyond the area studied by Thompson (1982, 6), to include Leicester (Pollard forthcoming, f), and the 'Belgic' derivatives found on the fringes of East Sussex in the local grogged 'East Sussex Ware' (Green 1980; Pollard forthcoming, c). Grog-tempered wares in west Kent include vessels whose uncompli-cated forms may not be thought of as distinctively 'Belgic' in style (e.g. Lullingstone Fabric 74: Pollard 1987). Maps plotting the distribution of 'Belgic' vessels in fabrics other than grog-tempered (Thompson 1982, Map 2; Fig. 20 here) demonstrate the position of the Medway valley at the intersection of fabric 'style-zones'. Quarry Wood, Loose, and Teston both have mixed assemblages (Pollard 1983a, 58–9), as has the Aylesford cemetery (Thompson 1982, 12). It is a fourth site, however, which provides the most intriguing example of a mixed assemblage in the Medway valley.

Rochester is located at the lowest crossing point of the Medway at the present day, and a bridge carried the Roman Watling Street across the river. Excavations in 1961 produced a flan mould (for coins?) of 'Belgic' type (Chaplin 1962) which unfortunately has not been published, as well as a number of apparently pre-Conquest features including a slight bank-and-ditch alignment (G. Horner pers. comm.). The settlement has been proposed as a 'tribal focus' or 'oppidum' by Rodwell (1976a, 213, 282), a status cautiously supported by Cunliffe (1978, 92). However, the site possesses all of the qualities listed by Hodder (1979) as befitting a neutral 'port of trade' of the first half of the first century A.D.; the possibility that it lay astride a boundary of social and political importance in this period will be examined below.

Two quite large groups of pottery from the site that produced the coin-mould have been examined by the present author (by kind permission of Mr G. Horner). One group includes a Dressel 1B amphora rim, dateable to the mid-late first century B.C. (Peacock 1971, 165), associated with a variety of coarse wares including grog-tempered ware (50 per cent by vessel rim equivalents), flint-tempered ware (15 per cent), grog-and-sand-tempered ware (11 per cent), shelly ware (10 per cent), and 'glauconite-rich' ware (1.5 per cent). The latter fabric comprises two recognisable forms: a furrowed bead-rim jar and a bead-rim jar or bowl. Definitive 'Aylesford-Swarling' forms comprise only 5 per cent of this assemblage, including a corrugated jar in grogged ware and a biconical bowl in flint-and-grog tempered ware in addition to the furrowed vessel, despite the fact that the Aylesford cemetery itself, considered by Stead (1976) to include later first century B.C. material, lay less than 10 km. upstream. The dominant forms are wide-mouth bead-rim vessels and recurved-rim vessels. The complete absence of wheel-thrown sandy wares and Roman-period fine wares suggests that this assemblage can be considered as entirely pre-Conquest in origin. The second group, a mixed first-century A.D. to early second-century A.D. assemblage, included 32 per cent fine grey ware, 24 per cent wheel-thrown sandy wares, 16 per cent shelly wares and 10 per cent 'flint-and sand' tempered ware. The absence of grog- and solely flint-tempered ware, as well as of the 'glauconite-rich' fabric, is worthy of note in suggesting a decline of these fabrics' usage during the earlier first century A.D. This phenomenon parallels that postulated with regard to flint-tempered ware in east Kent, but is in clear contrast with the predominant use of grogged ware in the latter region (where they comprise 69 per cent of pottery from pre-Flavian/pre-Conquest deposits at 16 Watling St., Canterbury, and 39 per cent of pottery from a mid-first to mid-second century A.D. deposit at Rosemary Lane, Canterbury: see Appendix 5 here).

IV. IMPORTED POTTERY IN LATE IRON AGE KENT, AND THE ISOLATION OF THE LATEST INDIGENOUS WARES

The Claudian conquest of southern and eastern Britain in A.D. 43–47 provides a fixed point in the historical narrative, but is difficult to recognise in the ceramic record. In its wake, it is true, increasingly large volumes of pottery were exported to the burgeoning markets of the new province, and new industries were established in Kent (4.I below). The samian pottery of Gaul found in Kent may all be of post-Conquest date, the Tong crater being one possible exception (Whiting 1927a, 41–3). A large proportion of the Gallo-Belgic fine wares – *Terra Nigra*, *Terra Rubra*, and white wares – belong to the Claudio-Neronian period, although certain earlier forms can be isolated (Rigby 1981; 1982). The quantities of imported pottery dateable with a reasonable degree of certainty to the late Iron Age are low when compared to areas such as Hertfordshire and the Colchester area, even at Canterbury, destined to become the tribal capital of Roman Kent.

The Italian wine amphorae of Dressel 1 form have been recognised more or less confidently at five sites (Appendix 3). Arretine ware is recorded at Canterbury alone, as are ?Central Gaulish flagons (Pollard forthcoming, d) and jars (including nos. 163–164). Micaceous *Terra Nigra* platters, also possibly from Central Gaul, are known from Bexley (Caiger 1958, no. 4) and Canterbury (Rigby 1982). A detailed study of the Gallo-Belgic wares might reveal certain items of pre-Conquest date, but this has yet to be undertaken for Kent, except at Canterbury (see Fig. 18).

The dearth of imports renders identification of the wares in use immediately prior to the Conquest exceptionally hazardous. Attemps can be made at Rochester and Canterbury, and by reference to the range occurring at the Claudian base of Richborough perhaps for north-east Kent in general. Grog-tempered and shelly wares were certainly current, along with some, if not all, variants of flint-based fabrics. A grog-tempered variant found mainly in west Kent and Surrey, 'Patch Grove' ware, was developed during the Tiberio-Neronian period, but on balance seems to be of post-Conquest inception (see nos. 17–21, and 4.I.2 below). Various sandy fabrics may span the Conquest, including a ware found in the Medway valley (nos. 1–9; 4.I.2). The 'glauconite-rich' fabrics appear to have been abandoned in the early part of the first century A.D. at the latest, however. On the southern fringes of the county, the grog-and-siltstone based 'East Sussex Ware' originated in the late Iron Age, and was little influenced by external developments in potting fashions until the mid-second century A.D. (Hamilton 1977, fabric 5; Green 1980; Pollard forthcoming, c).

CHAPTER 4

POTTERY OF THE ROMAN PERIOD IN KENT

INTRODUCTION

The aim of this chapter is to describe the main trends in forms and fabrics that have been perceived in assemblages from modern Kent. The Roman period has been divided for convenience into five chronological blocks: the pre- to early-Flavian, late Flavian to Trajanic, and Hadrianic to Severan periods, the third century, and the fourth and early fifth centuries. Each of these 'sub-periods' witnessed changes in the composition of assemblages, the nature of which varied from period to period, and from region to region across Kent. These changes can seldom be given a narrow date-range of occurrence, owing to the generally poor quality of the stratigraphy of sites and the low incidence of independently-dateable objects such as coins. It is perhaps unlikely that transformations of fashion would have been rapid in a craft as traditionally conservative as potting except when economically expedient. High quality decorative fine wares may provide exceptions to this rule; for example, Greene (1979a, 17) has proposed that 'a sudden expansion must have occurred around AD 40, both in manufacture, distribution, and the range of forms produced' in Lyon colour-coated ware. Further, the hemispherical cup form produced by a wide range of mid-first century A.D. Continental (and British) fine ware industries virtually disappeared around A.D. 70 as a result of 'a combination of changing fashions and economic disruption' (ibid., 139). The Lyon industry provides a rare instance of a rapid decline that is detectable in the archaeological record, owing in all probability to a series of turbulent events in the 60s A.D. that disrupted both its production and distribution centre and its principal markets (ibid., 141). Gallo-Belgic wares and forms provide a second example of a rapid demise, the 'traditional' cup and plate forms (e.g. Hawkes and Hull 1947; Rigby 1973) disappearing rapidly in the Flavian period (Greene 1979a, 118, citing evidence from the Neronian legionary fortress at Usk).

The fine pottery of each period is described for the modern county as a whole. The major wares exhibit little or no differentiation in distribution either spatially or temporally across Kent that can be detected from the present evidence. However, wares from the London area and Hertfordshire-Essex tend to be distributed primarily in west Kent (e.g. Staines ware – Fig. 21, and Hadham oxidised ware – Figs. 34 and 51), while wares from the English Channel regions such as New Forest and Pevensey late colour-coated wares are found mainly in east and south-east Kent. These distributions are nevertheless best discussed on a county-wide level. The coarse wares, in contrast, exhibit marked differentiation between west and east Kent over most of the Roman period, and are described under the regional headings 'the Medway valley and west Kent', 'Kent east and south of the Forest of Blean' (including the valley of the Great Stour) and 'the Swale plain'. The latter region represents the area of overlap of western and eastern styles and marketing zones for most of the Roman period. The area of historic Kent now incorporated into Greater London is included in the 'West Kent' region for convenience, although there are certain distinctions between ceramic assemblages of this area and of the area between the Cray and Medway valleys owing to the proximity of London.

I. THE PRE-FLAVIAN TO EARLY FLAVIAN PERIOD, *c.* A.D. 43–75

1. *The Fine Wares*

The Roman conquest of south-eastern Britain in A.D. 43 does not appear to have had an immediate impact upon the trade in pottery between the indigenous inhabitants of Kent and the Continental fine ware industries. The most widespread 'fine' (as opposed to grog-tempered) high-quality pottery of the pre-Flavian period is of Gallo-Belgic derivation, imported from Gallia Belgica (Rigby 1973) and possibly also from Colchester (Rigby 1981, 160) and other British concerns (e.g. Eccles: Detsicas 1977a). These wares, excepting the Eccles products, may have been circulating in Kent prior to the Conquest: this is certainly the case at Canterbury, and probably also at high-status sites such as Rochester (although there is no positive evidence), Loose Quarry Wood (Kelly 1971), and Worth (Klein 1928 – unpublished material relates to late pre-Conquest – early post-Conquest activity). Two pottery types are predominant amongst 'Gallo-Belgic' wares in Kent: platters in *Terra Nigra* (a grey slip ware) and butt beakers in fine sandy white wares. The former was produced at Eccles by a Claudio-Neronian industry (6.VI.2) alongside colour-coated rough-cast and *appliqué* beakers, and cream fabric flagons and mortaria, but no exportation from the site has been detected. Nevertheless some British '*Terra Nigra*' products may be anticipated in the south-east.

The other wares characteristic of the Gallo-Belgic industries – *Terra Rubra*, white ware flagons, and colour-coated ware beakers – have been recorded much less frequently (see Fig. 18). The popularity of *Terra Rubra* generally appears to have been on the wane in the Conquest period (Rigby 1973), although a similar range of forms (primarily platters and conical cups) continued to be in demand in *Terra Nigra* into the early Flavian period (Rigby 1973; Greene 1979a). Butt-shaped forms apart, Gallo-Belgic beaker forms appear to have been little used in Kent. 'Girth beakers' – delicately-moulded vessels with a constricted waist (Camulodunum, Forms 82–85 – Hawkes and Hull 1947) are known from Canterbury and Hartlip, and various forms from Richborough (e.g. Bushe-Fox 1926, no. 89; 1932, no. 288; 1949, nos. 394 and 400) in *Terra Nigra* including the very thin-walled vessels known as 'Eggshell' ware. (Greene 1979a).

The colour-coated, glazed, and samian products of Central and South Gaulish factories achieved a very limited distribution in Kent. Samian is by far the most frequent imported fine ware of the pre-Flavian period encountered at Canterbury, Richborough, Springhead and elsewhere. Found mainly on sites of urban or villa status (in the latter case probably most often as 'residual' material imported by the occupants during Flavian construction phases), it nevertheless occurs in widely-scattered locations, such as the High Rocks hillfort site in the Weald (Money 1968) and the rural industrial area near Cooling (Dickinson, in Pollard forthcoming, b). The Neronian-Vespasianic period, c. A.D. 55–80, witnessed massive importation of South Gaulish samian ware to southern Britain, as studies of stamped and decorated vessels indicate (Bird and Marsh 1978; Bird 1982b, and forthcoming). The forms are predominantly shallow dishes, bowls and cups. First-century samian of Lezoux origin also occurs in the south-east but very rarely (e.g. Bird and Marsh 1978). These were complemented by beakers in colour-coated wares primarily with 'rough-cast' decoration: particles of sand or fine clay scattered on the surfaces prior to slipping. Paradoxically, the major supplier of these beakers to Britain was not the South Gaulish industry that was responsible for the vast majority of pre-Flavian samian, but the Lyon factories on the upper Rhône (Greene 1979a). However, the beakers, and the cups with which they are associated, are exceedingly rare in comparison with samian products, despite being produced throughout the Claudio-Neronian period. Vessels in Lyon ware regularly occur in pre-and early-Flavian contexts on the major urban sites of London, Southwark and Canterbury, and appear also to have been commonplace at Richborough. Elsewhere Lyon ware has been recorded by the present author on only four sites: Rochester, Wingham, Springhead and Buckland Hill (Fig. 19) to which may be added sherds from Eccles and Faversham (Greene 1979a, 42). Three of these sites are villas of Neronian or Flavian foundation, whilst Rochester was an urban site and Springhead a 'small town', with a religious centre founded probably in the later Flavian or Trajanic period (Penn 1959). The status of Buckland Hill is uncertain. The unusual lead-glazed Central Gaulish ware, also known to British archaeologists as St. Rémy ware, is the only other pre-Flavian import to have achieved an extensive distribution (Fig. 19). It was apparently considerably less common than Lyon ware, however, for example at Canterbury and Southwark (Bird et al. 1978b), although the number of occurrences of flagons in funerary contexts suggests that these forms may have found especial favour as votive objects. Other forms in this ware include cups, beakers and bowls (Greene 1978a, b; 1979a). The colour-coated products of pre-Flavian industries in South Gaul, Central Gaul, Spain and the Lower Rhineland are extremely rare finds in Britain. Richborough is paramount in importance as a location for such discoveries, a reflection no doubt of its function as a military supply base and official port of entry to the Province in the first century A.D. (Cunliffe 1968; Greene 1979a). That these exceptional finds were personal possessions of base personnel rather than traded objects is suggested by the virtual absence of these wares from the nearby town of Canterbury, which carried out a trade in coarse pottery with Richborough (see below). Central Gaulish rough-cast ware alone of the minor colour-coated wares of Richborough has been recognised in the town, and even that could be Flavian rather than pre-Flavian in date, as the cup forms diagnostic of the latter period have not been recorded; all recognisable finds are of beakers, forms produced in both periods. 'Pompeian Red' platters with internal slip were also probably imported from Central Gaul in the pre-Flavian and later periods (Peacock 1977c, Fabric 3), occurring in Claudio-Neronian contexts at Canterbury and Richborough; Mediterranean suppliers of this ware are also suspected to have been operating in the period up to c. A.D. 75 (ibid., 159).

The dominant fine wares on most sites in Kent, certainly in the eastern region, are indigenous grog-, sand- and flint-tempered products of 'Aylesford-Swarling' and 'Gallo-Belgic' derivation. These include globular, biconical and butt-shaped beakers with corrugated, grooved, cordoned and fine combed decoration (e.g. nos. 32 and 33), and flagons (nos. 35–38). The latter two classes, and the conical cups, are clearly derived from Gallo-Belgic prototypes; the platters were certainly widely-used prior to the Claudian conquest, and occur in several fabrics (Fig. 17). The grog-tempered wares are characteristic of east Kent, and are similar to Camulodunum forms (Hawkes and Hull 1947). Camulodunum 21/22 (Thompson 1982, Form G1–1) appears to have been produced in the pre-Conquest period, and occurs mainly at Canterbury (e.g. Frere 1954, nos. 40–43), but also at Wye (unpublished). The apparent absence of this form from Richborough and its rarity in Neronian as opposed to pre-Conquest and Claudian deposits at Canterbury (Frere 1954; Macpherson-Grant 1982; Pollard forthcoming, d) are suggestive of a predominantly pre-Conquest period of usage. Camulodunum 24/27 (Thompson 1982, Form G1–6) is the most common post-Conquest platter, being found in grog-tempered ware in east Kent, flint-tempered ware at Radfield and Rochester, and sandy wares throughout Kent but primarily in central and western districts. The form is almost certainly confined to the Claudian-early Flavian period, as at Camulodunum itself. Other platter forms copied in local wares include Camulodunum 13, 14 and 16, but not, it should be noted, the more intricate forms 4–9. The flagons occur in grog-tempered ware throughout east Kent (Fig. 17); the high degree of similarity between vessels on the various sites is suggestive of a common source, perhaps Canterbury itself. The 'collar-rim' 'Hofheim' forms, (e.g. Camulodunum 144, 161: here nos. 35, 37–39), particularly the two-handled type, are far more common than the disc-rim (no. 36) which has only been noted by the present author at Richborough itself. There does not seem to have been an equivalent range of indigenous products in west Kent, all early flagons in that area being in fine untempered or sandy wares of a higher quality, usually in white-slip wares. The grog-tempered forms of east Kent are found predominantly in Claudio-Neronian layers at Canterbury, Richborough and Wingham; an origin in the late pre-Conquest period cannot be ruled out, however, as the prototype forms of 'collar-rim' flagons were undoubtedly circulating at that time (particularly the white ware Camulodunum 161, on which no. 35 here was based).

Fine ware flagons from several sources are also found on many sites in Kent. Local production is known at Canterbury (Jenkins 1956a, fig. 8, no. 1: no. 56 here) and Eccles (Detsicas 1977a) whilst a large group of white-slipped vessels found on the Medway estuary at Hoo (Blumstein 1956) may indicate a third source. The fabric is recorded at Southwark (Tyers and Marsh 1978, form IA 1) alongside vessels in granular sandy buff ware probably from Brockley Hill (*ibid.*, IA 2 – collar-rim, IB 1 – ring-neck cf. no. 60 here, and ID 1 – disc-rim, cf. no. 36 here; see also Castle 1973a, fig. 2, and 1973b, fig. 2), and fine buff ware (Tyers and Marsh 1978, form IA 3). The Brockley Hill wares of the pre-Flavian period do not seem to have penetrated Kent itself, however.

The end of the Neronian period saw several changes in the supply of fine pottery to Kent. Production and importation of *Terra Nigra* declined markedly, *Terra Rubra* having already fallen from favour in the 50s (Rigby 1973, 20). The Lyon industry suffered a catastrophic series of setbacks in the late 60s from which it was unable to recover, and exports of this ware to Britain undoubtedly ceased at this time (Green 1978a; 1979a). Central Gaulish glazed ware also ceased to be produced during, if not slightly earlier than, the early Vespasianic period (c. A.D. 70–75; Greene 1978b, 31). The samian industry of South Gaul continued its expansion, however, with some simplification of forms presumably designed with acceleration of production in mind. Lyon beakers were replaced by slightly different forms of rough-cast ware from the Lower Rhineland and North Gaul (Greene 1978a; Anderson 1980) and perhaps British sources also, though this has yet to be positively demonstrated. However, these wares do not seem to have had much impact outside of the towns until perhaps as late as the early second century. The Mediterranean(?) 'Pompeian Red' ware (Peacock 1977c, Fabrics 1 and 2) also ceased to be imported in the early Flavian period (*ibid.*, 159). The Canterbury and Brockley Hill industries both expanded in the early Flavian period, supplying between them most of Kent with flagons as well as mortarium, bowl and jar forms (see below, and Fig. 22 particularly). The Eccles production, which as has been said may never have supplied more than the immediate vicinity and perhaps merely the nascent villa-estate itself, evidently ceased during the Neronian period (Detsicas 1977a, 28–9). It is possible that, during much of Vespasian's reign (A.D. 69–79) samian pottery held a virtual monopoly of fine wares in Britain, flagons apart, until the emergence of various grey, red and white wares in the mid-Flavian period (see below).

2. *The Coarse Wares of West Kent*

The problem of distinguishing pre- from early post-Conquest coarse pottery in Kent has been highlighted (in Chapter 3.IV). Champion (1976, 71) has proposed that 'Patch Grove' ware (Pollard 1987, Fabric 73; nos. 17–21 here) originated in the post-Conquest period on the grounds of associations with certain brooch types. Certainly, positive evidence for a pre-Conquest origin is not forthcoming. However, the fabric does occur in pit deposits at West Wickham North Pole Lane that are entirely devoid of characteristic 'Romano-British' sandy wares and of samian ware (Philp 1973, 71), a situation that is indicative of an emergence early on in the sequence of ceramic development in the first century in west Kent. The early forms include bead-rim and everted rim jars, the latter often with finger-tip or slashed decoration (nos. 20 and 21 here). The carinated-shoulder jar (no. 19) appears to be a late first-century development, however. The ware is uncommon along the Thames estuary east of the Darent, for example at Springhead and Rochester (Appendix 5), but is one of the more abundant in western districts (Philp 1973) and also in the interior of central-western Kent (Philp 1963a) in the mid-late first century. The distribution extends into Surrey (Fig. 31), but finds in London, Southwark and Charlton appear to be confined to storage jars, from which it may be inferred that these sites lay outside the main area of usage.

 'Patch Grove' ware is one of a variety of fabrics indigenous to west Kent in the Conquest period. These include shell-, sand-and-shell- and sand-tempered fabrics, all of which exhibit similar formal and technological traits. Hand-forming is predominant, with some trueing-up of the rims on a turntable. The dominant forms are the wide-mouth bead-rim jar or bowl and the everted rim 'S' jar, the former often provided with a groove on the rim thought to have been designed to take a lid. Localised production is probable: the large group of pottery from the Gas Board's pipe trench at Cooling (Pollard forthcoming, b) in sand-tempered ware with sparse shell inclusions is one unit that can be isolated (nos. 1–9 here), with a distribution confined in the main to the Medway valley and Medway/Swale estuaries (Fig. 20). This fabric may span the Conquest, as may other localised wares in eastern Kent and the Medway estuary (see below). Philp's 'Native (local) burnished Wares' (1973, 71) may represent another minor west Kent production unit; although a pre-Conquest date is favoured by the excavator, some sherds are associated with late first/early second century samian (*ibid.*). The published forms include bead-rim necked jars and bowls, sometimes cordoned, and a bag-shape beaker (*ibid.*, fig. 34, no. 306).

 The most common wares are, however, shell- and shell-sand- tempered (nos. 11–16 here). It is possible that the latter represents a technological development of the former, in which case the Cooling fabric should perhaps be given a post-Conquest origin. The 'Granary Ditch' at Lullingstone contained a large pottery assemblage, including a samian dish dated A.D. 55–75 in the primary silt. The pottery 'consists mainly of vessels in coarse, shell-gritted fabric' (Pollard 1987, Group I). Examination of part of the assemblage by the present author suggests that shelly ware predominates, with shell-sand, grogged, 'Patch Grove' and sandy wares also present. A mid-first to early second century group from Rochester (unpublished: see Appendix 5) included 16 per cent shelly wares (nearly 30 per cent if the coarse pottery is taken in isolation from fine wares), nearly 25 per cent (42 per cent) sand-tempered wheel-thrown ware, and 9 per cent (16 per cent) flint-sand tempered hand-made ware probably of Medway estuary derivation (see below). A Flavian-Trajanic group from Springhead (also unpublished: Appendix 5) included 21 per cent (36 per cent) shell-sand ware, 3 per cent (5 per cent) shelly ware, 6 per cent (11 per cent) grogged ware, and 23 per cent (39 per cent) sand tempered wheel-thrown wares. The bead-rim jar is predominant in both shelly and shell-sand wares, although straight sided dishes and everted-rim jars do also occur (see e.g. Philp 1973 and Pollard 1987, Fabric 70). One other form is of particular interest, a large storage-jar with short everted rim and decorated shoulder (no. 16 here; see Harrison 1972, 134, no. 22 also). This form is distributed throughout Kent, southern Essex, and London, but is found primarily west of the Medway and in Essex (Fig. 31). Its period of usage extends from the mid-first to the late second century, long after other shelly wares had disappeared from circulation in Kent and south-east Essex. 'Patch Grove' storage jars also outlived other forms in the ware, surviving into the early third century, and similar phenomena may be observed among the non-sandy wares of Essex and east Kent (see below).

The conflation of 'Patch Grove' ware with 'rather similar pottery. . . .with a poorer surface and orange-red specks in the paste' by Philp (1973, 60) renders assessment of the importance of grog-tempered ware (which in the present author's experience probably includes Philp's 'orange-red specked' ware) somewhat problematical. The 'Granary Ditch' at Lullingstone contained narrow-neck everted rim jars in grey-and-brown fired grog wares (Pollard 1987, Fabrics 67, 74). Other grogged pottery from the villa site includes S-jars, a biconical bowl, and bead-rim jars, the latter in a mixed grog-shell fabric (*ibid.*, Fabric 68). These vessels may all be Flavian or later in date, however. Grog-tempered wares at Southwark are generally Flavian (Tyers and Marsh 1978, forms IIA 1–4, IVF 1, 2, 5), but as the bowls in particular are of forms paralleled by products of the Highgate Wood kilns north of Roman London (Brown and Sheldon 1974) rather than sites to the south of the city this dating need not reflect the west Kent situation. The evidence from Charlton, Springhead and Rochester suggests that grog-tempered wares were little used in the later first century, shell and shell-sand wares being predominant on these sites. However, a pre-Flavian/Flavian deposit at Cobham Park (Tester 1961, Room 4, Layer D) contained somewhat more grog-tempered than shell and sand-shell ware.

The final 'indigenous' fabric to be considered is sand-tempered ware. The origins of this ware, as with 'Patch Grove' and shelly wares, are uncertain. Sandy clays are widespread in Kent, particularly on the coastal plain and under what is now south London, comprising the Eocene Thanet and Woolwich and Reading Beds and the London Clay. To these strata may be added the Pleistocene and Recent Clay-with-flints drift which occur extensively on the higher parts of the Chalk dipslope of the North Downs (Gallois 1965, 59), constituting of flints and clay, with a mixture including sand present in many localities; and the loam or silt Brickearths, mostly head deposits (*ibid.*, 62), superimposed on the Eocene strata of north Kent, particularly in the Great Stour valley and flood-plain, along the Swale catchment area, and in the Upper Medway (in the Weald). Mainman (forthcoming) has demonstrated that the Head Brickearths and London Clay in the vicinity of Canterbury were both suitable materials for potting, producing sandy wares with, in the former case, chalky inclusions. The Brickearths of Kent have been exploited exhaustively for the manufacture of bricks, a further indication of their merit.

Sandy wares were of little or no importance in the century before the Claudian conquest. They comprise less than 2 per cent (by vessel rim equivalents) of the pottery from a late first century B.C./early first century A.D. deposit at Rochester, to which a further 13 per cent of grog-sand and flint-grog-sand wares may be added. The earliest levels at Canterbury, possibly of the mid-late first century B.C., contain virtually no purely sandy wares, but flint-sand and flint-grog-sand fabrics are present. Grog-tempered ware undoubtedly prevailed in the first half of the first century A.D. however, comprising 44 out of 54 sherds of one early layer on the Marlowe Car Park site III (Pollard forthcoming, d), and an even higher proportion of the groups from the lower fills of three out of four of the known late Iron Age ditches in south-east Canterbury (Frere 1954, Cellar L; Pollard forthcoming, d, layers MI 1260/1280 and MIV 732B). The evidence from Faversham (Philp 1968, 76–81) and West Wickham North Pole Lane (Philp 1973, 70–2) supports the hypothesis that sandy wares without a large grog or flint admixture were not produced in the earlier first century A.D.

The east Kent evidence for pre-Conquest sand-tempered wares has been reviewed here in order to provide a general background to discusssion of the problem of their emergence in the west. It may be inferred from occurrences of 'Gallo-Belgic-derived' platters and cups in sandy wheel-finished (if not wheel-thrown) wares throughout west Kent (see Fig. 17) that these wares were being produced by the early A.D. 70s at the latest, as the popularity of Gallo-Belgic forms waned in that decade. Pre-Flavian to Flavian examples occur in pre-Flavian/Flavian contexts at Cobham Park (Tester 1961, no. 12), Rochester (unpublished), Fawkham (Philp 1963, no. 15) and Farningham Calfstock Lane (Philp 1973, nos. 304–5), and in a Flavian deposit at Southwark (Sheldon 1974, no. 15). The pottery from pre-Flavian Southwark includes several other forms in reduced sandy wares, including bead-rim jars (Tyers and Marsh 1978, IIA 5–6), carinated and sub-carinated shoulder necked jars with bead or short-everted rim (*ibid.*, IIC 2, IID, IIN-Q; *q.v.* nos. 93–4, 97 here), butt-beakers (Tyers and Marsh 1978 IIIA), and 'Surrey bowls' (IVK: no. 99 here). The dating of these forms at Southwark is vital to the interpretation of material from West Wickham Fox Hill (Philp 1973, nos. 159, 161–3, 175, 177–80), and Charlton (Elliston Erwood 1916, fig. 21 nos. 3 and 16, fig. 22 nos. 66–7). The internal dating evidence for these two sites is poor; close typological links with the Southwark material allow the suggestion to be made that sandy ware necked jars, at least, were circulating in north-west Kent within a quarter-century of the Conquest. The cordoned, necked jar or bowl is a widespread first-century form in Kent (cf. e.g. Fawkham: Philp 1963, nos. 13–14; Rochester: Harrison 1972, nos. 1, 5 and 11), and lasted well into the second century. Unfortunately, examples in the area between the Cray and the Medway estuary cannot be dated firmly to the pre-Flavian period, and it remains a possibility that, apart from 'fine' forms of Gallo-Belgic derivation, sandy wares were not used in this area until mid-Flavian times. This applies to bead-rim jars as much as to the necked forms. The 'Surrey bowl' has not been recorded in Kent apart from a single example in the east, at Canterbury (Frere 1970, fig. 10 no. 1, in a later second-century context).

The evidence for pre-Flavian mortaria in west Kent is extremely limited. Claudian wall-sided forms have been recorded at Lullingstone Park, near the villa site (unpublished), and also in Southwark (Bird *et al.* 1978b, nos. 16 and 637). Flanged vessels of Hartley's Group 1 (1977; no. 61 here), in white sandy fabrics, occur at Otford Charne Building site (unpublished), Lullingstone villa site (Pollard 1987, type VIE.1(1)), Springhead (Hartley 1977, 6, and unpublished) and Southwark; the period of production of this group of mortaria is *c.* A.D. 55–85 (*ibid.*), but none of the Kent examples need be earlier than *c.* A.D. 80. The same can be said of Hartley's Group 2 flanged mortaria (*ibid.*; no. 62 here), dating to *c.* A.D. 65–100+, which occur at Charlton (Elliston Erwood 1916, fig. 18, no. 5) and Springhead (unpublished), sites with pre-Flavian occupation. The Neronian products of the Eccles industry (Detsicas 1977a) have not been recognised away from the site itself.

West Kent is also lacking in well-stratified occurrences of amphorae suggestive of pre-Flavian importation. South Spanish fabrics occur on several sites with pre-Flavian/Flavian occupation, but only at Springhead (unpublished) can finds be confidently dated to the first century; the form of the relevant vessels is uncertain.

3. *The Coarse Wares of East Kent*

Discussion of the pre- to early Flavian coarse pottery in the easternmost third of Kent is greatly facilitated by the evidence from two sites, Canterbury and Richborough. It is appropriate, therefore, to review these sources prior to more broad-based discussion taking in a number of other sites on the Stour-Wantsum floodplain and the Isle of Thanet.

Canterbury. The excavations of the late 1970s in the Roman civitas capital have placed the study of that city's ceramics on a much firmer footing than was previously possible, as full quantification of closely-dateable contexts has been executed. It is clear from this study (Pollard forthcoming, d) that grog-tempered pottery of 'Aylesford-Swarling' and 'Gallo-Belgic-derived' styles comprised the vast bulk of early to mid-first century A.D. ceramics. The most common forms, accounting between them for perhaps 80 per cent of assemblages, are jars of plain rim (no. 24 here), bead-rim (nos. 25 and 42) and everted-rim type, with or without necks. The necked forms are usually accompanied by cordons or 'corrugation' of the lower neck and shoulder (e.g. nos. 26–29); narrow-aperture necked vessels are frequently encountered, particularly in later pre-Conquest and also post-Conquest contexts. Decoration is primarily of combed or 'furrowed' (deep combing) oblique and/or horizontal type, covering the whole of the body (e.g. no. 25) on all jar forms. Tooled lattice and chevron motifs are particularly characteristic of narrow-necked forms (as at Richborough: Bushe-Fox 1926, nos. 4 and 5), but occur also in wide-mouth necked jars (cf. Bushe-Fox 1932, no. 254 from Richborough). Stabbed decoration is less common, occurring on less than one in ten jars of both pre-Conquest and later first-century A.D. date. 'Comb-stabbing' is confined in the main to wide-mouth necked jars (no. 28 here) in Canterbury and on most sites in east Kent, Richborough being a notable exception to this rule (see below). 'Stick-stabbing' and 'finger-nail-stabbing' (e.g. nos. 29 and 42) is present on all jar forms however. Other forms include lids and straight-sided dishes (no. 34). 'Quoit' or low-pedestal bases are encountered in most pre-Flavian and pre-Conquest groups, presumably associated with necked jars and 'bucket-urns' as on burial sites of 'Aylesford-Swarling' ritual (*q.v.* Birchall 1965).

Bead-rim jars also occur in flint-tempered wares, often with 'furrowed' decoration, and in wares of flint-sand or flint-grog admixture. The stratigraphic evidence suggests that these wares continued to be produced in small quantities well into the first century A.D., although their most important period of usage was probably in the first century B.C. and the earliest years A.D. They are entirely absent from the fills of the late Iron Age ditch at Rose Lane (Frere 1954: examination by the present author) and also in one of the ditches on Marlowe Car Park IV (Pollard forthcoming, d). The early Flavian occupation silt and levelling-up layers on the Marlowe Car Park sites contain less than 3 per cent (vesssel rim equivalents) flint-based wares, and they are entirely absent from Flavian floors on Marlowe Car Park II (*ibid.*).

The evidence for sand-tempered wares in the pre-Conquest period at Canterbury has been reviewed above, and found to be weak. However, the infills of the late Iron Age ditch on 16 Watling Street, and of a ditch and pit on Marlowe Car Park IV (Pollard forthcoming, d) consistently contain small quantities of friable sandy wares, usually wheel-thrown and often containing sparse grog inclusions. The forms are lid-seated shouldered bowls and necked bead-rim and angular everted-rim jars, sometimes with horizontally-combed decoration on the body: they are identical to vessels in the same fabric found in, and in the proximity of, a kiln on Stuppington Lane in the southern suburbs of modern Canterbury (Bennett *et al.* 1980; 5.III.2 below). It is not possible to state with certainty that production began subsequent to the Conquest, but this does seem a distinct possibility. The forms are close enough to local 'Aylesford-Swarling' forms (e.g. no. 30 here) to allow an indigenous origin for the ware independent of the infusion of Continental prototypes to be contemplated, although the lid-seated form is closer to west Kent than east Kent coarse wares of the late Iron Age (no. 12). The ware achieved a small degree of success against the predominant grogged wares, comprising as it does between 5 per cent and 13 per cent of pre-Flavian pottery from the Marlowe Car Park sites. It does not appear to have survived far into the Flavian period, as only 6 sherds out of 224 (0 per cent by vessel rim equivalents) were recovered from a floor level of this date.

A second sand-tempered industry also developed in the pre-Flavian period at Canterbury. The fabrics are generally of a higher quality, being more compact and lacking the minor grog admixture. The forms are markedly different from those of Stuppington Lane, including tall-necked bead-rim jars, carinated flange-rim bowls, everted-rim vessels, lids and flagons (nos. 47–57 here). They have been found on two kiln sites, one immediately east of the Roman city of Canterbury in Reed Avenue (Jenkins 1966a; Swan 1984, 392) and one to the north, in St. Stephen's Road (Jenkins 1956a, 50–56). The forms of the tall-necked jar and carinated bowl are quite closely paralleled by 'Arras' grey wares of northern France (de Laet *et al.* 1970, 19–20, fig. 16–17; Tuffreau-Libre 1980b, especially fig. 10, no. 9 and fig. 14, no. 5; Richardson and Tyers 1984), suggestive of an origin for the industry lying with immigrant North Gaulish potters (5.III.2). Finds of these forms on occupation sites in Canterbury suggest that it was first produced in the Neronian period (A.D. 54–69), as it is present only in a disturbed pre-Flavian context on 16 Watling Street, and is absent from most contexts of this date on Marlowe Car Park IV. This hypothesis is supported by the Richborough evidence; several vessels were found in a pit containing 13 coins of Claudius I (Bushe-Fox 1926, Pit 14: nos. 20 and 21, plus unpublished lids and a jar with horizontal burnished lines on the neck), and a number of other examples were recovered from Pit 33, dated to A.D. 50–75 (Bushe-Fox 1932, nos. 194, 195, 213, 256, and 260) along with forms which should be slightly later in their inception than those from the Reed Avenue kiln, on the evidence from Canterbury (see below). Deposits of *c.* A.D. 60–75 date at Canterbury contain under 4 per cent of the ware, compared with nearly 17 per cent on an early-mid Flavian floor (Pollard forthcoming, d.). The industry did not influence the producers of grog-tempered ware, either in the range of forms that they turned out or in the portion of the market that the latter supplied: grog-tempered ware consistently comprises between 68 per cent and 75 per cent of pre-Flavian and early Flavian pottery assemblages. It seems likely however that the 'Stuppington Lane' industry was eclipsed by the Reed Avenue/St. Stephen's Road ventures.

Mention should be made of a series of small jars or beakers in grey sand- or grog-sand-tempered wares found throughout east Kent in the later first century A.D. These are of ovoid form with small bead-rims, sometimes necked, and slash-incised decoration (cf. no. 42 here). They appear to have originated in the pre-Flavian period at Canterbury (cf. Jenkins 1950, Pit RI, nos. 26–27, in grog-sand ware), although no certain examples in these fabrics have been found in pre-Flavian levels on Canterbury Marlowe Car Park sites I and IV (Pollard forthcoming, d). At Richborough they occur in pits of Claudio-Neronian (e.g. Pit 14: Bushe-Fox 1926, no. 17), mid to late first century (Pit 179, Bushe-Fox 1949; vessel unpublished) and late first to mid-second century date (Pit 121, *ibid.*; vessel unpublished). The forms were also produced in grog-tempered wares in the pre-early Flavian period (no. 42 here). The source of this pottery is unknown, but may well represent a third sandy ware producer in the Canterbury area at this time. The mortaria and amphorae from Canterbury and Richborough are dealt with in the general discussion of coarse wares in east Kent, below.

Richborough. Unlike Canterbury, which was occupied continuously from at least the early first century A.D., Richborough was effectively a virgin site when the Roman bridgehead was established in A.D. 43 (Cunliffe 1968). The pottery from the two pre-Flavian (possibly Claudian) pits examined by the present author (Pit 14 – Bushe-Fox 1926, and Pit 35 – Bushe-Fox 1932) is thus certain to be uncontaminated by residual material. It comprises grog-tempered (including Bushe-Fox 1926, nos. 1, 3, 5, 6, 8, 18, 19), 'Reed Avenue/St. Stephen's Road' sand-tempered (references above, plus Bushe-Fox 1932, nos. 218 and 315), and miscellaneous sand-tempered wares including bead-rim (Bushe-Fox 1925, no. 17) and lid-seated jars, the latter with a shell/chalk admixture, and a reeded-rim dish (unpublished: cf. Marsh 1978, Type 26). A reeded-rim bag-shape jar (Bushe-Fox 1926, no. 11; cf. no. 68 here) may be intrusive. This assemblage is similar to the Canterbury material described above, but it should be observed that the 'Stuppington Lane' and flint-based wares are missing. The sand-shell/chalk jar may be an import from Essex or west Kent.

Late Claudian-Vespasianic pit groups include a similar range to those of Claudian date, but with two noteworthy additions. The bulbous-carinated bowl (no. 59 here) is in a 'Reed Avenue/St. Stephen's Road' fabric, but does not feature in any known Canterbury kiln group. The Canterbury and Richborough evidence together suggests that it was produced in east Kent, probably slightly later in origin than the 'Reed Avenue' forms and outliving them by a decade or two (see below, 4.II.3). The second 'new' type is the 'comb-stabbed' beaker with a bead-rim and sometimes a neck (nos. 39, 40 here). This form is paralleled by Camulodunum 108 (Hawkes and Hull 1947), and is present in both sand- and sand-grog-tempered wheel-thrown wares in several pits ranging in date from *c.* A.D. 50–80 to *c.* A.D. 80–110. It is extremely rare elsewhere in Kent, examples having been recorded only at Eastry (Pollard 1982, no. 19) and Rochester (unpublished), plus two vessels from Southwark (Bird *et al.* 1978b, nos. 557 and 798). This phenomenon, plus the abundance of the form at Colchester (Hull 1958) in later first-century levels, leads to the hypothesis that the Richborough vessels were produced by potters working in an 'Essex tradition' in the immediate vicinity of the military base, or were imported from

Colchester itself. A series of grog-tempered jars with 'rope impressed' decoration of the shoulder (no. 45 here), and/or lugs (nos. 44 and 46) occurring at Richborough in unstratified and late first/early second-century contexts but only at Eastry and Birchington (both unpublished) elsewhere in Kent may also represent production at Richborough or importation with very limited redistribution. They are paralleled by vessels from Vindonissa (Ettlinger 1977, fig. 5.2, nos. 8 and 13) and by late Iron Age material from Lincolnshire (Elsdon 1975), but not by finds in south-east Britain. The possibility that they were brought into Richborough by military units as personal possessions or quartermasters' stores should not be overlooked (these jars are further discusssed in 6.III.2).

Other Sites in East Kent. Grog-tempered wares of Canterbury/Richborough forms comprise the overwhelming majority of coarse ware vessels ascribable to the period under discussion. These include 'comb-stabbed' necked storage jars at Wye, Eastry and Highstead as well as the more commonplace furrowed and tooled schemes. Flint-tempered wares are also present, in very small quantities, on sites throughout north-east Kent and in the Great Stour valley. As at Canterbury these may be predominantly pre-Conquest in date, as the absence of such wares at Richborough suggests.

The most striking feature of the rural assemblages is the virtual absence of sand-tempered wares other than the later Flavian Canterbury forms (see below). Highstead is the only site known to have received 'Reed Avenue'/St. Stephen's Road' wares, the evidence there being confined to a single tall-necked jar rim (unpublished). This is all the more remarkable as both Birchington and Wingham had access to the generally rare pre-Flavian imports from Central Gaul (glazed ware at Birchington, Lyon ware at Wingham), and Wingham also contains a variety of Gallo-Belgic fine wares rivalled only by the Hartlip villa (see below) amongst other rural sites in Kent. Moreover, it should be remembered that Wingham lay very close to Watling Street, the road linking Canterbury and Richborough. The absence of 'Stuppington Lane' ware is less surprising, as this was not a particularly high quality product, and it is not found at Richborough either. Hand-formed sandy wares are occasionally encountered, for example at Worth where they comprise Gallo-Belgic forms and a plain-rim jar, and at Birchington where bead-rim necked and neckless vessels occur. Birchington also exhibits an informative example of localised pottery production and distribution of 'Aylesford-Swarling' types. The fabric is fine, hand-made, with sparse fine sand inclusions, buff in colour, and comprises bead-rim and lid-seat neckless jars (including one with an *appliqué* cup or lug on the shoulder), S-shape jars and bowls, necked bead-rim jars, and a lid. Two body sherds in a similar ware have been found at Canterbury, one in a Neronian/early Flavian context, but otherwise the ware is confined to Birchington Minnis Bay.

Exotic coarse wares are also extremely rare outside of Canterbury and Richborough. The Camulodunum 108 and 'rope-impressed' vessels have been referred to above, whilst the west Kent/south Essex shelly storage jars occur only in Highstead amongst rural sites. None of the east Kent occurrences of this type need be earlier than late Flavian however. Claudian 'wall-sided' mortaria have not been found away from Canterbury and Richborough, although a flanged mortarium of Hartley's Group 1 (1977) occurred at Eastry, and examples of her group 2 (*ibid.*) at Eastry, Birchington and Wye. It is possible, therefore, that mortaria were adopted on rural sites before mid-Flavian times, but by no means certain. A Greco-Roman amphora of Camulodunum 184 at Folkestone may be a pre-Flavian import, but Peacock (1971, 167) notes that this form may have been produced in the Flavian period also. Other occurrences of amphorae on rural sites, which are widespread, cannot be dated with confidence either by typology or stratigraphic associations to the pre-Flavian period, except for first-century B.C. Dressel 1B finds at Highstead (Arthur forthcoming) and Worth. Canterbury and Richborough both exhibit a wide variety of pre-Flavian amphorae (Arthur 1986), further emphasising the differentiation between these sites and the countryside around them in this period.

4. *The Coarse Wares of Central Northern Kent*

There is considerable differentiation between sites around Faversham Creek on the one hand and those to the west up to the Medway at Rochester. Mid-first century groups at Faversham (Philp 1968, nos. 174–233) and pre-Flavian/Flavian ditch fills at Brenley Corner (Jenkins 1973; 1974; interim reports) are similar in many respects to those of rural sites in north-east Kent. Grog-tempered wares of Canterbury forms predominate (88 per cent of coarse wares at Brenley Corner, excluding a complete amphora rim), alongside 'calcite-gritted' S-shape bowls and bead-rim jars at Faversham, and sand-tempered necked jars at both sites. It is possible that the Faversham examples (Philp 1968, nos. 193, 194) are of 'Stuppington Lane' ware, but this hypothesis is based on the published descriptions alone.

There is kiln and waster evidence for the production of flint-tempered wares in bead-rim and S-jar forms on the Upchurch Marshes in the pre-Flavian period (Noël Hume 1954; Jackson 1962, 1972/3). This ware clearly achieved only a very localised distribution, being found no further east than Radfield (Baxter and Mills 1978; unpublished material), or further west than Rochester, both less than 15 km. away. These two sites also received finely flint-gritted 'Gallo-Belgic' platters (cf. Camulodunum 27), probably manufactured in the same area in the mid first century A.D. Flint-sand tempered ware comprised 11 per cent of a mid-first to early second-century A.Ð. group at Rochester (unpublished: see Appendix 5); alongside 16 per cent shelly ware and 24 per cent sand-tempered wheel-thrown wares (4.I.2). Grogged ware would appear to have been predominant at Radfield, however, with shelly wares extremely rare both here and at Brenley Corner (two sherds at the former – one a shell-sand bead-rim jar – and one at the latter site). The collection from Hartlip villa, which comprises mostly fine pottery, also includes a shell-sand tempered bead-rim jar, and a Canterbury-type grog-tempered platter. Hand-made sandy wares, not necessarily of mid-first century A.D. date, at Radfield include bead-rim jars with furrowed decoration, and a bead-rim cordoned S-jar.

Furrowed wares are an important feature of the pottery of the Medway-Swale region, as they form a typological link with the east, rather than the west, of Kent. 'West Kent' mid-first century coarse wares are present only in very small numbers east of Rochester, the 'Cooling' sand-with-shell fabric being found only at Ospringe, (one sherd, unstratified), and 'Patch Grove' ware also only at Ospringe, but in a late second/third-century burial group (see Figs. 20 and 31). 'Reed Avenue/St. Stephen's Road' Canterbury wares are entirely absent from the region. Jaccard's correlation coefficients, taking in all wares possibly attributable to the pre-Flavian period, imply that Rochester has a greater similarity to Radfield (53 per cent) than to Brenley Corner (33 per cent), but Canterbury also exhibits these characteristics (60 per cent and 43 per cent, respectively). By the same measurement Canterbury and Rochester show a 53 per cent similarity, but Radfield and Brenley Corner a lower rating (33 per cent). These figures are difficult to interpret in terms of trade inclination; it may be that Radfield was in a position to absorb trade and influences from both west and east; its pottery exhibits a wider range of both fine and coarse ware of this period than does that of Brenley Corner. The latter site's assemblage is a minor subset of that of Canterbury, which explains the low correlation (2.V.2).

It is possible that both amphorae and mortaria were being received on the rural sites of this area prior to the mid-Flavian period. Radfield's pottery includes mortaria of both Groups 1 and 2 (Hartley 1977), whilst sherds of a South Spanish Dressel 20 amphora were recovered from one of the ditches at Brenley Corner, a mid-late first century context. Claudian 'wall-sided' mortaria, and amphora forms especially typical of the early-mid-first century A.D. (Dressel 2–4: Peacock 1971, 165–6) have not been recognised, however.

5. *The Significance of the Claudian Conquest for Pottery Studies in Kent*

A brief study of the ranges of pottery in pre-Claudian and Claudian-Vespasianic Kent might give the impression that the imposition of Roman authority brought about significant changes in the trade and production of pottery in Kent. Pre-Conquest imported fine wares were virtually confined to Gallo-Belgic wares, Arretine being found only at Canterbury and pre-Conquest(?) South Gaulish samian at Tong near Sittingbourne (a Drag. 11 with medallion and St. Andrew's Cross motifs: Whiting 1927a, 41–3). The Conquest brought in its wake a large variety of wares from central and southern Gaul, including large quantities of South Gaulish samian that must have made a considerable impression on Canterbury's volume of trade. Wheel-thrown sand-tempered wares were produced at Canterbury probably by potters of northern Gaulish origin, and other wares in generally similar fabrics, if not forms, were used at Southwark and possibly also in north-west Kent. A wide range of exotic forms was produced within twenty years of the Conquest at Eccles, whilst an industry producing mortaria may well have established itself in east Kent in the Neronian period (Hartley 1977, 11–12). Flagons of mainly pre-Flavian forms (the 'Hofheim' collar-rim, no. 56 here) are widely distributed, both in fine wares and local grog-tempered wares. At least two coarse wares appear to have originated in the Conquest period, 'Stuppington Lane' sandy ware at Canterbury and 'Patch Grove' ware in south-west Kent and east Surrey.

The preceding sections have made it clear, however, that most of these changes affected only a handful of sites, primarily on Watling Street and in the vicinity of the military supply base at Richborough. Pre-Flavian samian, it is true, has been recorded on several rural sites away from these areas of major Roman influence, but not in contexts necessarily of this period: the pottery could have been brought into these sites at any time in the Flavian period (cf. Orton and Orton 1975 for a study of the longevity of samian ware). Even Gallo-Belgic fine wares, white ware butt-beakers aside, are rarely encountered except on roadside and urban sites. Claudian-early Neronian 'wall-sided' mortaria have only been recorded on one non-urban site (the implication being that Roman methods of food-preparation were not generally adopted at this time), whilst there can be no certainty that the ?east Kent mortarium industry supplied rural sites any earlier than the 70s. Certainly there seems little doubt that the Eccles industry was not a speculative enterprise aimed at a wide civilian market, but an estate concern (6.VI.2). The 'northern Gaulish' sand-tempered ware industry at Canterbury was also evidently aimed at a very limited market, in this case the military base at Richborough and the city itself. The other pre-Flavian sandy ware industry at Canterbury appears only to have concerned itself with the urban trade.

The broad pattern of British pottery 'style-zones' that can be traced back to at least the first century B.C. (see Chapter Three) was not broken down in the aftermath of the Conquest. It is

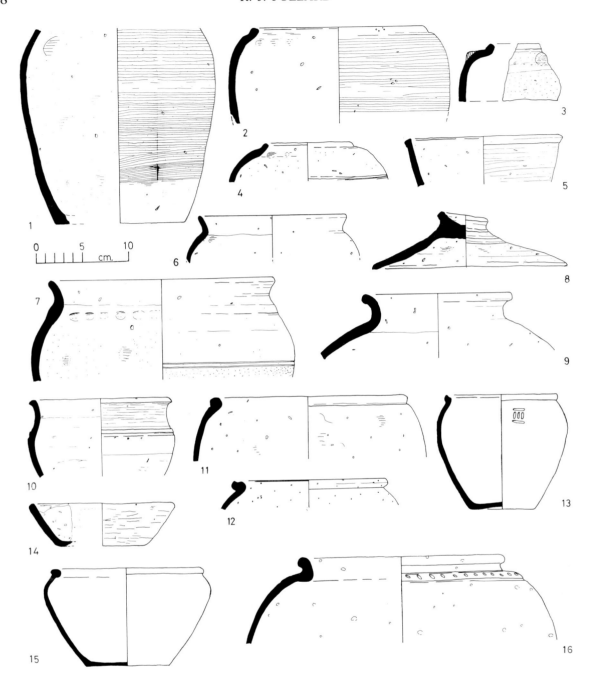

Fig. 12.   Pottery forms nos. 1–16 (Scale: ¼).

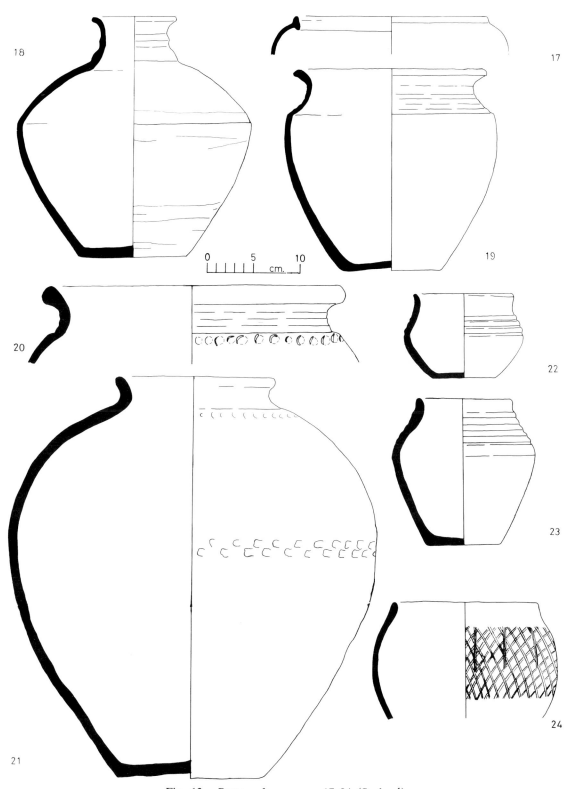

Fig. 13. Pottery forms nos. 17–24 (Scale: ¼).

Fig. 12. **1–9**:   'Cooling' sand-and-shell tempered ware.

1. Combed jar, Pollard forthcoming, b, no. 1. **2**. Combed bead-rim jar, *ibid.*, no. 2. **3**. Bead-rim jar with applied boss, *ibid.*, no. 4. **4**. As no. 2 above, *ibid.*, no. 6. **5**. Bead-rim dish or salt-cake mould, *ibid.*, no. 17. **6**. Everted-rim jar, *ibid.*, no. 7. **7**. As no. 6 above, *ibid.*, no. 11. **8**. Lid, *ibid.*, no. 19. **9**. Rolled-rim necked jar, *ibid.*, no. 14.

10:   Sand-and-grog tempered ware with sparse shell; cordoned S-bowl, *ibid.*, no. 25.

11–13:   Sand-and-shell tempered ware.

11.   Bead-rim jar, *ibid.*, no. 26. **12**. Lid-seated bead-rim jar, *ibid.*, no. 30. **13**. As no. 12 above, with graffito (cf. Jones 1972), Bushe-Fox 1932, no. 245.

14–16:   Shell-tempered ware of late Iron Age to early Romano-British period.

14. Plain-rim dish, Pollard forthcoming, b, no. 36. **15**. Bead-rim of so-called 'Charlton' form (Ward-Perkins 1944, 150) on shouldered bowl, Philp 1973, no. 286. **16**. Storage jar of 'Thames Estuary' type, Richborough, unpublished.

Dating: 1–10: (Late first century B.C. to) first century A.D. 11–13: (Early to) mid- to late first century A.D. (to early second). 14–15: As nos. 1–10 (to early second). 16: Mid- first to late second/early third century A.D.

Fig. 13. **17–21**:   'Patch Grove' ware.

17. 'Charlton' bead-rim jar, Philp 1973, no. 275. **18**. Narrow-mouth storage jar, *ibid.*, no. 258. **19**. Everted-rim jar with corrugated, carinated shoulder, Tester and Caiger 1954, no. 6. **20**. Corrugated-neck bead-rim wide-mouth storage jar with finger-tip decoration, *ibid.*, no. 2. **21**. Everted-rim narrow-mouth storage jar with finger-tip decoration, Whiting *et al.* 1931, no. 461.

22–24:   'Aylesford-Swarling' grog-tempered ware.

22. Cordoned biconical bowl, Birchall 1965, no. 90, from Deal.

23. Corrugated biconical jar or beaker, *ibid.*, no. 33, from Swarling.

24. Plain-rim jar, Bushe-Fox 1932, no. 247.

Dating: 17: Mid- first to early second century. 18: Mid- first to early third century A.D. 19: As no. 17. 20–21: As no. 18. 22–24: Mid- first century B.C. to mid- first century A.D.

Fig. 14. **25–31**:   Fabric as nos. 22–24 above.

25. Furrowed bead-rim jar, Bushe-Fox 1928, no. 136. **26**. Bead-rim S-jar, Birchall 1965, no. 19, from Swarling. **27**. Corrugated furrowed bead-everted-rim jar, Frere 1970, fig. 9, no. 10. **28**. Corrugated bead-rim necked jar, furrowed and comb-stabbed, Richborough, unpublished. **29**. Form as no. 28 above, with stabbed and furrowed decoration, Frere 1954, fig. 4, no. 10. **30**. Bead-rim necked beaker, Bushe-Fox 1926, no. 6. **31**. Butt-beaker, Tester and Bing 1949, no. 42.

Dating: 25–26: Late first century B.C. to first century A.D. 27: As nos. 25–26 (to early second century). 28: First century A.D. (to early second). 29: As no. 27. 30–31: As nos. 25–26.

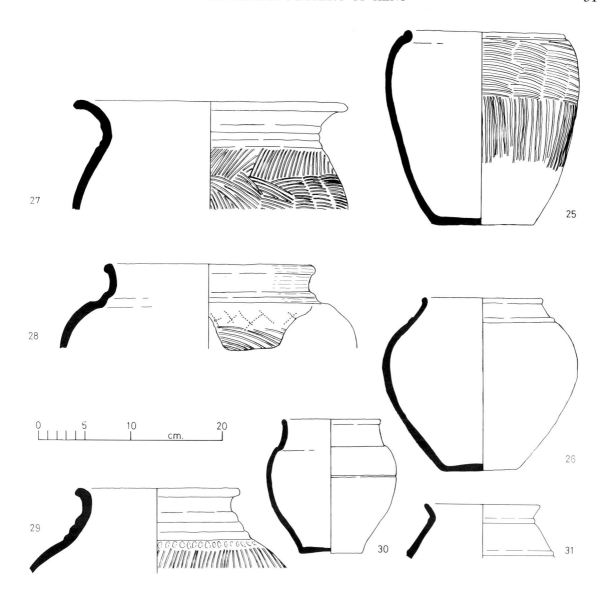

Fig. 14. Pottery forms nos. 25–31 (Scale: $\frac{1}{4}$).

Fig. 15.   **32–39:**   Fabric as nos. 22–24 above.

32. Platter of Camulodunum Forms 21/22 (Hawkes and Hull 1947), Frere 1954, fig. 5, no. 40. **33.** Platter of Camulodunum Forms 24/27, Bushe-Fox 1926, no. 10. **34.** Dish with outcurved rim, Bushe-Fox 1932, no. 238. **35.** Flagon derived from Camulodunum Form 161, *ibid.*, no. 188. **36.** Disc-rim flagon, cf. Camulodunum Forms 148–150, *ibid.*, no. 190. **37.** 'Hofheim' collared-rim flagon derived from Camulodunum Form 140, *ibid.*, no. 187. **38.** Form as no. 37 above, *ibid.*, no. 186. **39.** Comb-stabbed bead-rim necked beaker, *ibid.*, no. 250.

40–41:   Fabric uncertain; both grog-tempered and sandy fabrics are associated with no. 40 type in east Kent.

40. Comb-stabbed short-everted-rim jar, Bushe-Fox 1926, no. 47. **41.** As no. 40 above, but a flask, Bushe-Fox 1949, no. 387.

42:   Fabric as nos. 22–24 above; incised-shoulder bead-rim jar, Bushe-Fox 1926, no. 19. Fine sandy grey ware versions are also found in east Kent.

43:   Fine grey ware; cup derived from Camulodunum Forms 56/57, Bushe-Fox 1932, no. 211. This form also occurs in fine grog-tempered ware in east Kent (e.g. Macpherson-Grant 1982, no. 225).

44:   Fabric uncertain, possibly grog-tempered ware; bead-rim jar with applied lugs, Cunliffe 1968, no. 582.

45:   Sand, charcoal and grog-tempered ware; everted-rim necked jar with applied lugs and impressed 'maggot' or rope-impressed decoration; Richborough, unpublished.

46:   Grog-tempered ware, short-everted-rim necked corrugated jar, with lugs and comb-stabbed decoration; Richborough, unpublished.

Dating: 32: Very late first century B.C. to mid- first century A.D. 33: Claudian to Flavian. 34: First century A.D. 35–38: As no. 33. 39–41: Flavian to Trajanic. 42: First century A.D. (to early second); Claudian to Trajanic in sandy ware. 43–46: Very late first century B.C. to first century A.D.

Fig. 16.   **47–54:**   'North Gaulish' Canterbury sandy grey ware.

47. Everted-rim necked jar with applied 'vases'; Canterbury, Reed Avenue kiln, unpublished. **48.** Form and source as no. 47 above. **49.** Bead-rim tall-necked jar with burnished lines on neck, Bushe-Fox 1932, no. 256. **50.** Everted-rim dish; source as no. 47 above. **51.** Flange-rim carinated rilled bowl; source as no. 47 above. **52.** Everted-rim jar; source as no. 47 above. **53.** Bead-everted-rim flagon, two(?)-handled; source as no. 47 above. **54.** Bead-rim tall-necked jar; source as no. 47 above. (Nos. 47–48 and 50–54 drawn by kind permission of Dr F. Jenkins).

55:   'North Gaulish' Canterbury ware: fine micaceous orange-buff; bevelled-rim moulded-neck flagon, Jenkins 1956a, fig. 8, no. 7, St. Stephen's Road Area II kiln.

56:   'North Gaulish' Canterbury ware: fine, sometimes sandy, reduced/oxidised misfired wasters; 'Hofheim' collared-rim flagon, ribbed handle, *ibid.*, fig. 8, no. 1, same site.

57:   Fabric as nos. 47–54 above; plain-rim lid, *ibid.*, fig. 8, no. 18, same site.

58:   'North Gaulish' Canterbury sandy oxidised ware, short-everted-rim; *ibid.*, fig. 5, no. 4; St. Stephen's Road Area I kiln.

59:   Fabric as nos. 47–54 above; flange-rim offset-S bowl, Bushe-Fox 1932, no. 215.

60:   Canterbury sandy orange/buff ware; 'cylindrical'-ring neck flagon, Kirkman 1940, no. 48; Dane John Kiln.

61:   South-east Britain/north-east Gaul sandy white ware, flint and quartz trituration grit; mortarium, Hartley Group 1 typical form, Hartley 1977, no. 1A.

Dating: 47–52: *c.* A.D. 50–80. 53: *c.* A.D. 50 to Trajanic. 54–56: As no. 50. 57: As no. 53. 58: As no. 50. 59: Flavian to Trajanic. 60: Claudian to Flavian. 61: Neronian to Flavian.

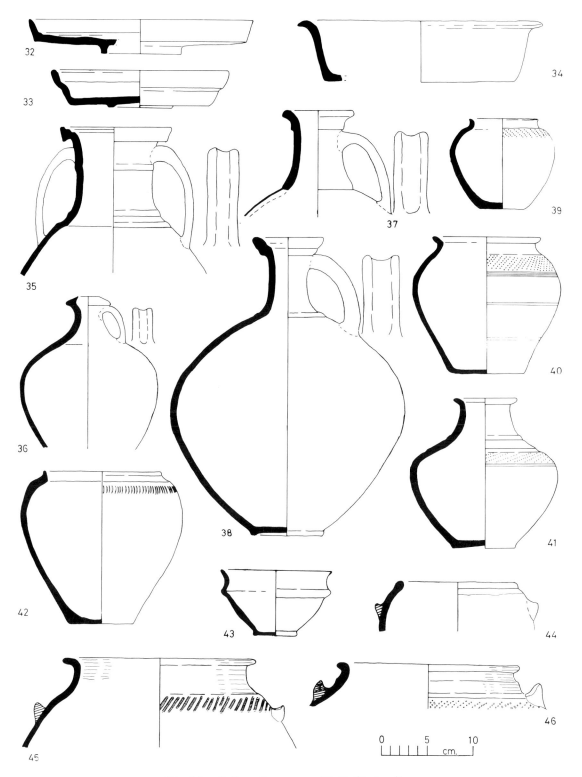

Fig. 15. Pottery forms nos. 32–46 (Scale: ¼).

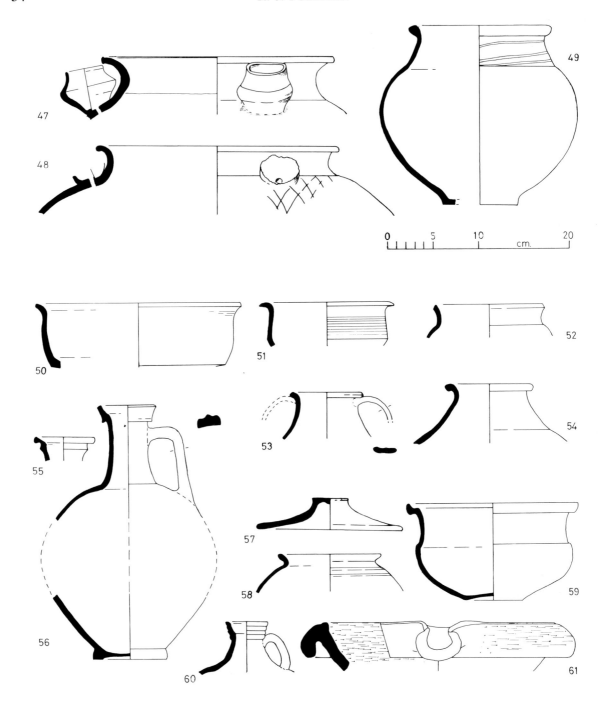

Fig. 16.   Pottery forms nos. 47–61 (Scale: ¼).

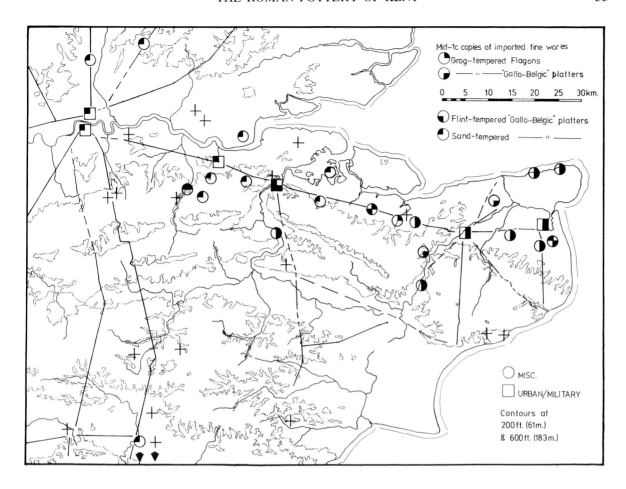

Fig. 17.   Mid- first century A.D. copies of imported fine wares: Distribution. + = absent ('Gallo-Belgic' includes
Camulodunum Forms 21/22).

true that 'west Kent' shelly wares are occasionally found on east Kent sites, but these need not
all be of post-Conquest importation and in any case may well have been acquired through
indigenous mechanisms of trade and exchange rather than through any method consequent
upon the imposition of the Roman systems of taxation and administration (Pollard 1983a,
474–535). 'Patch Grove' ware provides a link between Kent and Surrey that is not clearly visible
in the Iron Age, but little is known of the Surrey area in the century before the Conquest, and it
is possible that this 'link' may have been established prior to the Conquest through other wares.
The forms of 'Patch Grove' ware, and the infrequency with which it is found on urban and 'small
town' sites (see Tyers and Marsh 1978, and Appendix 5 below), do not suggest that it was
particularly influenced by fashions and institutions introduced by Continental immigrants.
Rather, it is best seen as a purely indigenous development coincident with the establishment of
Roman rule. That it achieved a wide distribution in the pre- to early Flavian period within an
essentially rural area supports this view, for it clearly contrasts markedly with the highly
localised distribution of the wares of the two 'Roman' industries of the pre-Flavian period, the
Eccles and 'Reed Avenue/St. Stephen's Road' concerns. Moreover, it is thought that the

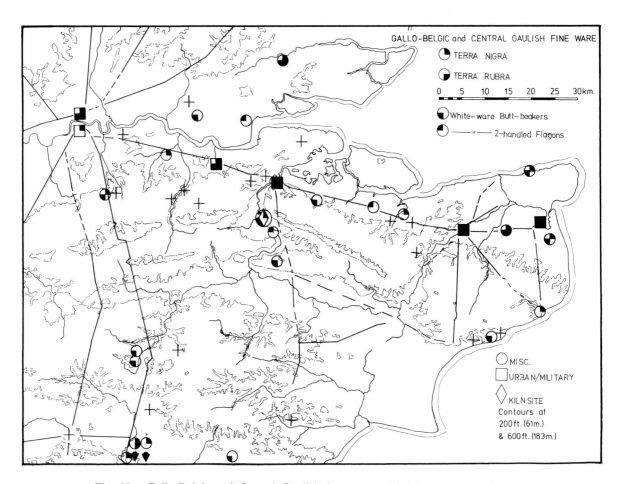

Fig. 18.   Gallo-Belgic and Central Gaulish fine wares: Distribution. + = absent.

Roman system of commercial trade involving market or monetary transactions was inhibited by taxation in kind, imposed by the military authorities in the early post-Conquest years (Hopkins 1980, 103; Pollard 1983a, 474–535). It may be erroneous to suppose that the Conquest provided an immediate stimulus to the production and marketing of coarse pottery, except where there was direct contact with an imperial consumer such as the Richborough base represented, or a burgeoning township. The foundation of the London-Southwark community may explain the development of the sand-tempered wheel-thrown ware pottery found on pre-Flavian sites in north-west Kent and Surrey. The forms are mostly based on indigenous pre-Roman types, as has been observed by Tyers and Marsh (1978, 553). The introduction of sandy wares may have been a response to Gallo-Roman practice, but this need not have been the case. It is clear that a wide variety of fabrics was produced in the late Iron Age; experimentation by native potters may have resulted in the adoption of this kind of fabric. This would seem to be the case at Highgate Wood in north London, where first-century pottery exhibits some fabric differentiation between simple jar forms and 'finer' wares, the latter containing a higher proportion of sand in what are basically grog-tempered wares (Brown and Sheldon 1974, 224).

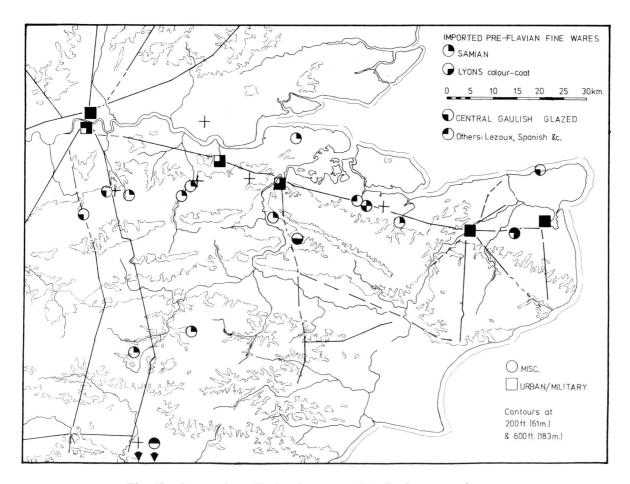

Fig. 19. Imported pre-Flavian fine wares: Distribution. + = absent.

There would seem to be no compelling evidence to support the view that the Claudian conquest brought about any rapid, radical change in the production and distribution of pottery in Kent. Developments that can be traced during the pre- to early Flavian period either affected only a very small portion of the population, or can be attributed to the craft of indigenous potters. There remains one great exception to this rule, and that is the introduction of the flagon as an object of common usage. Pre-Flavian forms in a variety of fabrics are present on sites of all types in every locality, particularly in east Kent and along the Thames flood plain. Although the stratigraphic evidence does not provide firm proof, there is a strong possibility that the widespread adoption of the flagon was a direct result of the Conquest. Dannell (1979, 178) has observed that even in Essex the numbers of later first-century B.C. amphorae do not suggest that wine-drinking became a widespread habit. Finds in Kent of these amphorae (Dressel 1B) are more thinly scattered than north of the Thames (see Appendix 3), although the buckets found in burials at Aylesford and Swarling possibly provide supporting evidence for the consumption of wine at this period (Stead 1971). The lack of known examples of Greco-Roman wine amphorae (except perhaps at Canterbury), the small number of finds of Gallo-Belgic fine

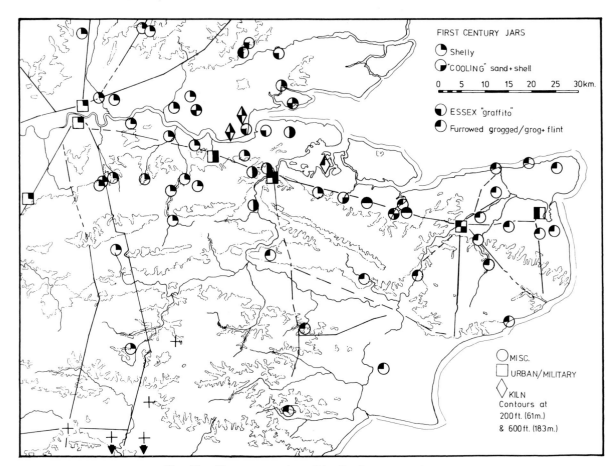

Fig. 20.   First-century jars: Distribution. + = absent.

ware flagons (see Fig. 18 and Appendix 3), and the apparently late introduction of flagons to the range of forms produced in grog-tempered ware in east Kent (Pollard forthcoming, d), provide negative evidence in support of the hypothesis that wine was a little-used commodity in pre-Conquest Kent. The amphorae from Canterbury have been studied by Paul Arthur (1986): it will be of interest to learn whether there was a significant increase in the importation of wine-amphorae in the mid-first century A.D. coincident with the introduction of flagons in large numbers to the city. Further study of amphorae, from rural sites, would be required to follow up such an observation, and might have an enlightening rôle to play in the study of trade between town and country in the Roman period.

II. THE MID-FLAVIAN TO TRAJANIC PERIOD, c. A.D. 75–120

1. *The Fine Wares*

This period witnessed the burgeoning of several fine ware industries in south-eastern Britain, the most important of which in quantitative terms were, for Kent at least, the fine grey ware producers. Other wares encountered with lesser frequency include fine oxidised, painted, mica-dusted, marbled, stamped, lead-glazed and fine white wares. Continental importation was dominated for most of the period by South Gaulish samian ware, but the quality of this region's output declined during the late first century, resulting in a virtual cessation of supply to most of the Empire (Johns 1971, 23). Central Gaulish potteries at Les Martres-de-Veyre inherited the trade in samian to Britain, but sites throughout the south-east show a marked fall-off in stamped samian in the last decade of the first century, a trend which the Central Gaulish potteries were able at first to reverse with only limited effectiveness (cf. Bird and Marsh 1978, 527–30; Bird 1982b and forthcoming). The coincidence of this shortfall in the supply of samian with the production of a variety of fine wares in Britain has been remarked upon by Marsh (1978, 207–8), and will be further discussed below.

The range of pottery types imported to Britain in the mid-Flavian to Trajanic period, samian apart, appears to have been restricted in the main to beakers. Exports of Gallo-Belgic pottery to Britain ceased to flow in appreciable quantities in the early Flavian period; although *Terra Nigra* bowls of Flavian date do occur (Greene 1979a, 111–14), these are not necessarily of Gaulish origin. The Rhineland exported small quantities of mica-dusted wares to Britain in the late Neronian and Flavian period, these being predominantly short everted-rim globular beakers sometimes with bossed decoration (Marsh 1978, 120–2, 151–3 and Types 20.1 and 22.1–2). Colour-coated 'bag-shaped' beakers with delicately-moulded 'cornice' rims and rough-cast clay embellishment were also imported from the lower Rhineland (Greene 1978c), their fine white fabric contrasting with broadly similar forms in grey/red ware from North Gaul (Anderson 1980, lower Rhineland Fabric 1, North Gaul Fabric 1). Ovoid beakers, also in colour-coated white ware, were imported from Central Gaul; these vessels have a short-everted rim and usually either rough-cast or *'en barbotine'* decoration, the latter being applied prior to slipping and often in 'hairpin' motifs (Greene 1978a, fig. 2.3, no. 2). None of these non-samian imports appears to have found a wide market in Kent at this time, being confined in the main to Canterbury and Richborough (see Appendix 3). Lower Rhineland colour-coated beakers did expand their distribution in the Hadrianic-mid-Antonine period, however, to include settlements of all types in every locality (4.III.1).

The evidence for production of fine reduced wares on the Upchurch Marshes comprises wasters from various sites (Noël Hume 1954) and a beaker from a kiln at Bedlam's Bottom, Iwade (Ocock 1966). Forms characteristic of this industry first appear at Canterbury and Richborough in deposits with *termini post quos* in the late A.D. 70s–80s (e.g. at Richborough: Pits 34 and 40 – Bushe-Fox 1932, and Pit 194 – Bushe-Fox 1949; at Canterbury the floor of the Flavian building R1 – Pollard forthcoming, d). Sherds are also present at Lullingstone in the 'Granary Ditch', a context thought by the excavator to pre-date the construction of the villa *c*. A.D. 80–90 (Meates 1979). The potteries supplying these sites may thus pre-date the inception of fine reduced 'London Ware' production in London (Marsh and Tyers 1976), which is dated to *c*. A.D. 90 on the basis of occupation site evidence from Southwark and London (Marsh 1978, 199). Fine grey wares appear to have rapidly achieved a strong custom throughout Kent. The Domitianic (?) floor level at Canterbury alluded to above included over 14 per cent of these wares (vessel rim equivalents, excluding samian), although a Vespasianic-Trajanic context in the city contained only some 5 per cent (including samian), a figure echoed in a deposit of similar date at Springhead (see Appendix 5).

The early forms in fine grey ware include biconical, butt-, shouldered, globular and 'poppyhead' beakers (nos. 119, 122, 126–7 and 129 here), biconical and S-shape jars or bowls (nos. 121 and 125), and segmental, campanulate and hemispherical bowls (nos. 130–132, 134, and cf. 136). The shouldered and butt-beakers are generally mid-Flavian in date, the other forms longer-lived. Pit 34 at Richborough includes a large assemblage in this ware dateable to the Domitianic-Trajanic period (Bushe-Fox 1932, nos. 226–7, 233, 271, 273, 280–4, 289–91, 305, 311 and 325, plus unpublished material). There is some evidence to suggest that more than one industry was responsible for supplying fine grey ware, and the oxidised ware produced in similar forms, to Kent in the Flavian-Hadrianic period. There exists in north-east Kent a group of sites from which have been recovered butt-beakers and pedestal jars decorated with fine combed chevron or 'compass-scribed' arc motifs (see Appendix 3, and nos. 122–3; Fig. 27). The forms are dateable to the late first century on typological grounds and on their occurrences at Canterbury and Richborough. The form-motif combination is virtually unknown in more westerly areas, (one from Dartford – Dale 1971, no. 1 – being the sole exception known to the present author), although narrow-neck jars with these motifs were evidently produced in London (Marsh and Tyers 1976, nos. 135–140). Plain and rouletted versions of these forms are known from the Upchurch Marshes (e.g. Wood 1883, 109, no. 2, and unpublished material in Rochester Museum), whilst the motifs occur on bowl and beaker forms from the marshes (e.g. Roach Smith 1847, 136, and unpublished material in Rochester Museum). It is possible that the north-east Kent vessels were produced on the Upchurch Marshes specifically for this non-local demand, but it may also be proposed that they represent an otherwise-undetected fine reduced ware industry operating in east Kent. Flanged-rim bowls also exhibit a bias in distribution towards eastern Kent. They comprise roughly 40 per cent of the fine reduced ware group from the later first-century A.D. ditch fills at Brenley Corner (unpublished; q.v. Appendix 5), and 35 per cent from a similar context at Wye, which contained coins of Vespasian and Titus (unpublished: q.v. Appendix 5). The form would seem to be less common at Canterbury and Richborough, but it is present on most sites in east Kent. Two vessels are included in the Hartlip villa collection, although the form has not been recorded on the Upchurch Marshes by the present author. West of the Medway it is virtually absent from the large assemblages at Lullingstone (Forms VE.4, VE.5: Pollard 1987) and Springhead (one unpublished vessel) despite the presence of contemporary forms in the same fabric. The excavations in north-west and west-central Kent published by Philp (1963a, 1973) have failed to produce any relevant published material. The form was, however, manufactured in London (Marsh and Tyers 1976, nos. 141–148, 151; Marsh 1978, Types 31, 33, 34,) to which source the Lullingstone vessel may be ascribed on typological grounds. On the Continent, it is most common in Upper Germany and Raetia, where a Claudian to Flavian date-range is applicable (Greene 1979a, 115), whilst in Britain it occurs widely as late as the early second century (Marsh 1978, 168). The absence of vessels from the collections and published material examined by the present author that were derived from the Upchurch Marshes does not allow the eastern Kent material to be ascribed to that area with any confidence, although such a source cannot be ruled out, as vessels have been recovered from sites close to the marshes (Bayford-near-Sittingbourne and Hartlip).

The distribution of a quite distinctive group of painted wares (Fig. 26) suggests the extent of the primary sphere of exchange of fine wares from the Upchurch Marshes. The forms include S-jars and carinated and hemispherical bowls broadly similar to the samian forms Drag. 30 and 37 (nos. 138–140 here). They are usually found in oxidised forms with either a cream slip and red-brown paint or a red smoothed surface with cream paint. The majority of find-spots fall within a 25 km. radius of the Upchurch Marshes, including two sites on the marshes themselves. Sherds of two vessels have been recorded from Canterbury (Macpherson-Grant 1982, no. 150, and unpublished), and none, to the knowledge of the present author, from London or Southwark. Several vessels were recovered from Richborough, however (see Appendix 3), in contexts dated to within the Flavian-early Antonine period. The high density of find-spots within 15 km. of the Upchurch Marshes (six out of ten sites), including occurrences in collections of mere handfuls of sherds, suggests the hypothesis that these were either a local product or an exotic ware from an unknown source that was intensively traded or exchanged within the neighbourhood of the most obvious point of importation, Rochester.

Fine oxidised wares of the Flavian-Trajanic period include biconical, globular and shouldered beakers, hemispherical and carinated bowls often with 'compass-scribed' arcs (nos. 136 and 137 here), and segmental bowls with bead- and flange-rims (nos. 163–4, 166), and flagons, including ring-necked (cf. no. 73) and plain-conical rim (no. 160) forms. Flagons in both oxidised and white-slip wares are more common in central-northern Kent, which was on the fringes of the distribution areas of Brockley Hill and Canterbury ware flagons (see below, and Fig. 22), than elsewhere, but are found in all regions. Shouldered and butt-beakers also occur in white-slip ware, but bowls and dishes do not. White-slip and oxidised wares may well have been produced alongside reduced and painted wares on the Upchurch Marshes, though the evidence from antiquarian reports and collections (e.g. Roach Smith 1847, 1868) suggests that the numbers of vessels in these wares that were recovered were very small in comparison to those in reduced wares. The Hoo assemblage (Blumstein 1956) included cordoned S-jars (cf. Camulodunum 220B – Hawkes and Hull 1947), shouldered beakers (cf. Richborough 250 and 285 – Bushe-Fox 1932) and a butt-beaker, an assemblage which, taken in conjunction with the range of flagon types (collar-rim 'Hofheim' types predominantly, plus ring-neck and plain-conical rim forms, cf. nos. 56, 155 and 160 here), should be dated to the A.D. 70s at the latest, that is at the period of transition between the first two periods discussed in this chapter. The proportions of reduced to oxidised to white-slip wares vary; in western and central-northern Kent they are of the order of 2:1:1 to 4:1:1 (see Appendix 5), while at Canterbury white-slip is generally the rarest of the three wares, and both this and the oxidised fabric may be entirely absent from some contexts. Reduced wares are ubiquitous, however.

The London area potteries do not seem to have produced oxidised-surface, white-slip or geometrically painted wares, although painted vessels of 'marbled' decoration do occur (Marsh 1978). A recent survey of the Flavian-Trajanic fine wares of the London area suggests that fine reduced, mica-dusted, 'eggshell' and 'marbled' wares were all produced in or around the City in this period (ibid.). Oxidised 'London' (i.e. fine-combed, 'compass-scribed', and rouletted) wares are considered to be 'seconds' (ibid., 198), that is vessels whose firing rendered them imperfect by virtue of colouration (or in other cases minor warps in the form). The 'eggshell' wares are so named owing to the thinness of their walls, and are extremely rare in Kent, only two occurrences having been noted by Marsh (ibid., 130–1), to which may be added sherds of hemispherical cups from Canterbury (unpublished, cf. Marsh 1978, Type 13.6). 'Marbled' wares in white to orange fabrics with orange-brown brushed/wiped paint (over white-slip when the fabric is oxidised) have been recognised by the present author at Springhead and Richborough (Fig. 21: the sherd from Brenley Corner is probably a mottled-slip Central Gaulish white ware beaker, cf. Greene 1978a, fig. 2.3 no. 2). Fine reduced 'London' ware may be widespread in Kent, but macroscopic differentiation of London and Upchurch fabrics is hazardous, and has not been pursued by the present author. Marsh's selective gazetteer (1978, 125–9) of 'compass-scribed' wares includes sites throughout Kent. His contention that London fine ware products, including the fine reduced wares, are generally unlikely to have been distributed much over 20 miles (32 km.) (*ibid.*, 202) is supported by the evidence of the most frequently encountered product, mica-dusted ware, with six out of nine sites falling within a 30 km. radius of London (Fig. 21). Platter, cup, beaker and flagon forms in this ware have been found on Kent sites (Appendix 3), but not *paterae* or biconical strainers (Marsh 1978, Types 32 and 46, respectively). In general, identifiable London products are rare in Kent; the present author has seen no more than eight sherds from any one site of 'eggshell'/'marbled'/mica-dusted wares, Springhead containing that number of finds.

Three other wares thought to have been manufactured to the north or west of London ought to be mentioned: cream ware 'ring-and-dot' beakers, 'Staines' lead-glazed ware, and 'London-Essex' stamped wares. The first-named are globular vessels with short-everted rims and usually decoration of rings and dots *'en barbotine'*. They have been discussed by Green (1978b), who suggests a date-range of Neronian-Flavian, and a source in the South Hertfordshire/North Middlesex area. They appear to have been common in London and to a lesser extent Verulamium, but rare elsewhere in south-east Britain: five sites are known in Kent, each comprising only a single sherd with the exception of Richborough (four sherds, Appendix 3 and Fig. 21). The lead-glazed wares of Roman Britain have been discussed by Arthur (1978); his 'south-east English' group includes globular beakers, 'imitation Dr. 30 beakers, Dr. 37 bowls' (*ibid.*, 300) and pear-shaped flasks, in a grey to red-brown ware with white barbotine decoration, the whole covered by a translucent glaze usually appearing a medium green and yellow over the barbotine. Wasters from Staines suggest a source thereabouts for at least some of the group. Six find-spots are known in Kent, four of which are west of the Medway (Fig. 21 and Appendix 3). On the grounds of the distribution, a riverine traffic down the Thames was envisaged by Arthur (*ibid.*); the apparent scarcity of the ware at Richborough (one sherd only seen by the present author) suggests that beyond the mouth of the Thames the volume of this trade, as of that in other fine wares from the London area, was small in the extreme. A Flavian-Hadrianic date encompasses all dateable finds of this ware. The stamped wares of Rodwell's Group 2C, the only one of his 'London-Essex' groups (Rodwell 1978) known to have been found in Kent, are entirely confined to the western part of the county (Fig. 33; Rodwell 1978; Philp 1980). The fabric is fine, sandy, and usually oxidised, with bar- and ring-stamps; forms are predominantly carinated sub-cylindrical bowls, plus, possibly, hemispherical bowls (Rodwell 1978). Only seven sherds have been published from Kent and its bordering districts, three of which come from Springhead. The four sites – Springhead, West Wickham, Fawkham and Titsey – all fall within a 30 km. radius of London, but outliers to the south of the Thames are represented by two find-spots in Sussex (see Appendix 3). Rodwell (1978) has argued in favour of a source in the Hadham area of east Hertfordshire, but no wasters or kilns are known. The dating of the ware is also open to speculation, but an origin in the mid-Flavian period seems likely (*ibid.*), with a termination of production within the first half of the second century.

The development of Romano-British fine ware industries in the Flavian period may be considered to have been the result of two processes: the economic progress of the province and the demise of competitors on the Continent. The former is fully discussed elsewhere (Pollard 1983a, 480–92); briefly, the taxation system was reformed during the Flavian period, possibly involving a switch from taxation in kind to taxation in cash, at least in the south-eastern half of

Britain (Fulford 1981). This reform broadly coincides with the foundation of a considerable number of villas in Kent and elsewhere, and with the development of civic building in Canterbury (Wacher 1975; Blockley and Day forthcoming). These processes provided conditions beneficial to the expansion of trade in the province, through which pottery industries such as those producing fine grey and painted wares in north Kent were able to spring up. These developments also coincided with the decline in importation of Gallo-Belgic wares in the early Flavian period (see above), and the demise of the Lyon and Central Gaulish glazed ware concerns. It is possible that the trade in Gallo-Belgic wares slackened as a direct result of the expansion of Romano-British industries, but the dating evidence from Kent suggests that the local fine grey industries emerged some little time after the waning of the Gallo-Belgic trade. This emergence coincided, or was soon followed by, a marked fall in samian importation in the last two decades of the first century. The conventional dating of most of the various industries in and around London to a foundation c. A.D. 80–90 suggests that these were enterprises which from the outset sought to exploit what must have been something of a vacuum in the market for fine pottery. The pre-existing(?) fine ware industries undoubtedly also reaped the benefits of such a situation. It is interesting to note, however, that few of the fine wares produced in the south-east in this period faithfully copied samian ware: the basic South Gaulish forms were widely copied, or, debatably, used as prototypes, particularly forms Drag. 18/31, 27, 30 and 37. Red wares are uncommon relative to reduced wares amongst the fine wares used in Kent, and the London industries do not seem to have produced red wares at all (see above). This phenomenon is in marked contrast with the situation in the later third and fourth centuries, when a wide range of potteries large and small turned out red wares of general similarity to the samian forms of the late second and early third centuries (see below); it is difficult to escape the conclusion that by the end of the Flavian period red fine wares had not made the impact upon the consumer that is later so strongly in evidence.

The flagons of the Flavian-Trajanic period have been partially described above. In addition to fine oxidised and white-slipped fabrics, a variety of buff and white wares occur, the later including fabrics with a greenish tinge suggestive of a clay source in the Gault stratum that lies at the foot of the North Downs escarpment in Kent and Surrey. The Otford pottery was probably in operation in the early/mid Flavian period, producing vessels in 'red clay, changing even in the same vessel to yellow or brown' (Pearce 1930, 161; nos. 102–106 here). Unfortunately, this pottery appears to have been lost subsequent to excavation. The significance of the Otford concern is discussed below (6.VI.1). The Canterbury, Brockley Hill and London industries also produced flagons, the last-named in mica-dusted ware (Marsh 1978, Types 1–4). Between them Canterbury and Brockley Hill distributed their products throughout Kent (Fig. 22), although the small numbers of these wares in the Medway valley area in comparison with the greater quantities found in east and west Kent, respectively, suggests that direct competition between the two was on a small scale; the oxidised and white-slipped wares suspected of being produced on the Upchurch Marshes were probably the major supplier to the Medway valley area. The forms of this period include globular vessels with ring-necks (no. 73 here), 'pulley-rims' (no. 77), and pinched-spout jugs (no. 74). The disc-rim flagon (cf. no. 36) appears to be confined to the first century, but the dating evidence is not entirely clear on this point. The flagon formed an intimate part of pottery production at both Canterbury and Brockley Hill, and was one of the most widely-distributed forms of these industries (see below, and Pollard 1983a, 351–83).

2. *The Coarse Wares of West Kent*

The mid-Flavian to Trajanic period witnessed the demise of grog- and shell-tempered wares in west Kent, and the emergence of wheel-thrown sand-tempered wares throughout the area. The rate of change from the use of fabrics that were well-established in the Conquest period to the adoption of wheel-thrown sandy wares is difficult to gauge, owing to the paucity of well-stratified sequences. Moreover, it would appear that in more western parts, notably the Darent, Cray and Ravensbourne valleys, 'Patch Grove' ware increased in popularity up to the Trajanic period. Exotic coarse wares include Brockley Hill buff sandy ware, London, Highgate Wood and Alice Holt grey sandy wares.

The stratigraphic sequence at Southwark allows some valuable information on the development of pottery in this period to be deduced (Tyers and Marsh 1978). Grogged and shell-tempered wares were apparently out of use by the turn of the century, with the exception of storage jars (*ibid.*, forms IIL and IIM) in both fabric types. Sand-tempered ware from a variety of sources virtually monopolised the market in coarse wares. This phenomenon does not seem to be so emphatic on rural sites to the south-east of Southwark, however. Here, shell-tempered wares were undoubtedly little-used after the Flavian period, if at all. 'Patch Grove' ware enjoyed its apogee in the late Flavian and Trajanic years, supplying rural sites throughout the area of the Darent valley and westernmost Kent with necked wide-mouth storage jars, carinated-shoulder jars and bowls, S-profile narrow-neck jars and wide-mouth bowls, and bead-rim jars and bowls (nos. 17–21 here). Meates (cf. Pollard 1987, Fabric 73) has dated the 'Patch Grove' ware at Lullingstone villa mainly to the Flavian-Trajanic period, considering Antonine occurrences as implicitly residual with the exception of storage jars. These forms are also abundant in the upper Darent valley site of Otford (Charne building site, – unpublished except for an interim note: Meates 1954), and in the Bromley – West Wickham area of what is now south-east London (Philp 1973). Shelly wares are absent at Otford Charne, though present at the Otford 'Progress' villa site, which was founded at a somewhat earlier date in the first century A.D. (Appendix 1); they are also confined to two sherds on a late first/early second century A.D. plus site at Bromley Oakley House (Philp 1973), from which nearly 300 'Patch Grove' ware and 350 'Romanised' sandy and fine wares were recovered. The total assemblage from an early second to mid-fourth century site at Joyden's Wood, in the lower Cray valley, included some 10 per cent 'Patch Grove' ware (by vessel rim equivalents) but only storage jars (as no. 16) in shelly ware. Further east both 'Patch Grove' and shelly wares, storage jars excepted, were little used in this period: a rural site at Greenhithe (Detsicas 1966) included a Trajanic-early Hadrianic pit fill in which just over 2 per cent and 10 per cent, respectively, of these wares were recovered. The evidence of residual material at Springhead and Rochester (Appendix 5) suggests that, as at Greenhithe, shell and shell-sand wares may have continued in production somewhat later than in western districts, being superseded by sandy wares alone.

The locally produced sandy wares of this period comprise for the most part bead-rim jars and cordoned necked jars and bowls (nos. 91–94 here), following the formal traditions of grog-tempered and shell-tempered wares. These occur throughout west Kent; one kiln site, at Chalk (Allen 1954) is known, but this may date to the Hadrianic-Antonine period on the grounds of the BB2 vessels also produced there (see below). The Highgate Wood industry, in north London, produced bead-rim and short-flange-rim jars and bowls in grogged and, less frequently, sandy wares up to the end of the first century (Brown and Sheldon 1974, Phase II).

The Trajanic-Hadrianic (Phase III) potters concentrated on necked jars with decorated shoulders (no. 95 here), which comprised 45 per cent of the pottery (rim count) from Phase III; other forms included 'poppyhead' beakers (no. 144 and cf. nos. 129 and 146) and everted-rim neckless jars (18 per cent), flanged bowls (18 per cent – cf. no. 96 here), pie-dishes (c. 10 per cent – cf. no. 110 here), and bead-rim jars (8 per cent). These were all made in a fine sandy fabric, with a silver-grey or white slip. Highgate Wood itself appears to have been a small-scale pottery, thought to represent an indeterminable number of similar enterprises in the London area (ibid.). Wares of 'Highgate Wood type' are common in Trajanic-Hadrianic levels at Southwark (Tyers and Marsh 1978, 559, 575) the necked jars being the most frequently encountered jar form of the period. Necked jars and 'poppyhead' beakers of 'Highgate Wood types' are widespread in Kent, but occur only rarely in sites east of the Darent valley (Fig. 32). They, in combination with flanged bowls, comprise some 8 per cent (vessel rim equivalents) of the early second to mid-fourth century pottery from Joyden's Wood, although much of this 8 per cent is possibly Hadrianic-Antonine in date (see below). The mainly Trajanic pit fill at Greenhithe contained none of this ware, but a Hadrianic-early Antonine rubbish level (Appendix 5) included necked jar and 'poppyhead' beaker forms to the sum of less than 1 per cent of the assemblage. General second-century levels at Springhead and Rochester were devoid of 'Highgate Wood type' wares, although they have been recovered from mixed deposits (Appendix 3). Presumably, the competition from the Upchurch Marshes fine wares and sandy ware producers of 'Shorne type' served to restrict the distribution of 'Highgate Wood type' to western districts.

A number of other coarse wares of the mid-Flavian-Trajanic period exhibit similar ranges of distribution to 'Highgate Wood type' wares. Grey sandy wares of forms essentially identical to those in the London Copthall Close waster group (Marsh and Tyers 1976), including necked jars sometimes with a carinated shoulder and reed-rim (carinated?) bowls, are found in the Cray valley and to the west, but not in the Darent valley (Fig. 24 for grey ware reed-rim bowls). It is interesting to note that reed-rim bowls of mid-Flavian to Antonine date at Southwark are entirely in the buff and cream-slipped red sandy fabrics typical of the Brockley Hill-Verulamium region (Tyers and Marsh 1978, 573), although grey ware jars of Copthall Close forms do occur (ibid., Type IIC). The buff ware bowls were probably more common in Kent than those in grey wares: at Joyden's Wood three vessels of the former and one of the latter were recovered (unpublished).

The Brockley Hill-Verulamium potteries supplied a wide variety of flagon, mortarium, jar, bowl and amphora forms to the London area in the later first and first half of the second centuries (cf. Tyers and Marsh 1978, and Pollard 1983a, 365–83). The range of forms is in many ways similar to those of the contemporary Canterbury industry (below; ibid., 351–64; Richardson 1948; Tyers and Marsh 1978; cf. nos. 63, 65–8, 70–1, 73–7 here). The widest range of form types occurs on sites west of the Cray valley (Fig. 10). East of the Cray, excluding Joyden's Wood, only single examples of a reed-rim bowl and a handled globular 'honey-jar' (Tyers and Marsh 1978, Type IIK) have been found (Appendix 3). Brockley Hill-Verulamium types comprise 3 per cent of the Joyden's Wood assemblage, but less than 1 per cent of the Trajanic pit-fill at Greenhithe; rim sherds are absent from general second-century levels at Springhead and Rochester. Flagons and mortaria tend to be the only forms found on sites east of the Cray valley (Pollard 1983a, 455–9).

The wares described above were produced in either west Kent or the London–South

Hertfordshire area. However, the mid-Flavian to Trajanic period also witnessed importation of coarse wares from the Alice Holt forest on the Surrey/Hampshire border. Alice Holt wares achieved a limited circulation in Southwark in the pre-Flavian period (see above), possibly extending this market into north-west Kent. Bead-rim jars (no. 98 here) and bead- or short-everted 'figure–7' rim necked jars (nos. 93 and 97) are the forms most frequently encountered, the former being of pre-Flavian to early second-century date at Southwark, the latter of Flavian to early Antonine date (Tyers and Marsh 1978, Types IIA 12–14, IIC, IID). Lyne and Jefferies (1979, 52, and Appendix 3) have suggested that Alice Holt ware at London 'simply vanished' at the end of the Flavian period after a considerable popularity there in the A.D. 70s and 80s. The differentiation between London and Southwark pottery assemblages of the Trajanic period, highlighted by the absence of grey ware reed-rim bowls at the latter site and Alice Holt wares at the former, is an intriguing phenomenon that will be well worth studying when more quantified material has been published from both settlements. It is clear that north-west Kent and London represented the eastern fringe of early Alice Holt ware distribution, find-spots in Kent being confined to Charlton and possibly West Wickham and Hayes (Fig. 37, and Appendix 3).

The ultilisation of mortaria in food preparation appears to have been adopted at all levels of society (as represented by settlement hierarchy) by the end of Trajan's reign. Brockley Hill wares achieved a virtual monopoly of the west Kent market during the Flavian-Trajanic period to the exclusion of wares from the known Canterbury kilns (see below). Vessels of Hartley's Group 2 (see above and no. 62), and in fine white wares, are also present, but in small quantities. The forms most frequently encountered in Brockley Hill (and, in the Trajanic period, Verulamium) wares are hook-flanged (cf. nos. 71, 117 here): these have been found on at least thirteen sites in all parts of west Kent, and in central and eastern regions also (see below).

Amphorae probably also achieved a wide circulation by the end of this period. Rural sites of the Flavian to early Antonine period generally include fragments of amphorae (cf. Philp 1973), including examples of the globular Dressel 20 that carried olive oil from the area of south Spain between Seville and Cordoba (Peacock 1971, 170). This form occurs in a well-stratified late first-early second-century context at Springhead (unpublished) and was, according to Callender (1965, 19), the commonest of Roman amphorae forms. Fine buff, and Brockley Hill, amphorae also occur on sites of this period, the latter only at Charlton (Elliston Erwood 1916, fig. 19, no. 6). South Spanish elongate amphorae (Dressel 7–11) were possibly imported to west Kent in this period, apparently ceasing to be produced during the early second century (Peacock 1971, 171).

3. *The Coarse Wares of East Kent*

The Flavian period witnessed the expansion of the Canterbury pottery industry from an apparently small-scale concern, supplying almost solely Canterbury itself and the military base at Richborough, to one that dominated the market for coarse pottery throughout east Kent. At the same time the production of grog-tempered ware and of traditional 'Aylesford-Swarling' forms, including those produced in grog-sand and sand-tempered wares in the pre-Flavian period, declined almost to the point of complete termination. Exotic coarse wares are almost entirely confined to Canterbury and Richborough, excepting mortaria from Brockley Hill.

The rate of expansion of the Canterbury industry is at present difficult to gauge; it is clear that new forms were introduced in the mid-Flavian period, including reeded and lid-seated bag-shape and necked globular jars (nos. 68 and 64 here), reeded and lid-seated carinated bowls and straight-sided dishes (nos. 70 and 69), short-necked jars often with a shoulder cordon (nos. 63, 65), and hook-flange mortaria (no. 71). Other forms of this period include bulbous-carinated lid-seated flanged bowls (no. 59), lids (e.g. nos. 57, 66–7), ring-necked flagons (no. 73), 'pulley-rim' flagons (no. 77) and pinched-mouth jugs (no. 74). The jar, bowl, dish and jug forms are usually in grey wares, although oxidised vessels do occur on occupation sites, suggesting that these were also acceptable to the consumer. Flagons and mortaria are found in a wide range of colours from brick-orange through buff to off-white, often with a buff to white wash. The Canterbury wares are all sand-tempered, usually coarse but often, with flagons and mortaria, fine in terms of the size and abundance of inclusions (see Appendix 2). Jugs and bulbous carinated bowls may have been produced by the pre-early Flavian 'Reed Avenue/ St. Stephen's Road' industry; although examples have not been found on kiln sites of this industry, they do occur in a pit group at Richborough (Bushe-Fox 1932, Pit 33) dated to c. A.D. 50–75 in which other forms of this industry are present, but from which the mid-Flavian-plus types are absent (*ibid.*, nos. 194–5, 213, 215–6, 219, 221, 256, and 260). Ring-necked flagons, lids and short-necked jars may also belong to the earlier industry, perhaps in a 'transitional' phase later in the short life of that industry: these forms were found at St. Stephen's Road Kiln II alongside typical 'North Gaulish' forms and 'Hofheim' flagons (Jenkins 1956a, fig. 8).

It is likely that by the turn of the century grog-tempered wares had been almost entirely eclipsed, excepting possibly the small-scale production of storage jars and necked jars with wiped surfaces of a 'scarred' appearance and incised or tooled linear decoration (e.g. Williams 1947, fig. 7, no. 1; Bennett *et al.* 1980, fig. 12, and possibly Williams and Frere 1948, no. 38). Flavian-Trajanic groups from Canterbury and Wye suggest that considerable quantities of grog-tempered wares of pre-Flavian types were still in use in the Flavian period, as these comprise over 40 per cent and 32 per cent of these groups, respectively. Sandy wares of Canterbury type, with mid-Flavian-plus forms, predominate at the former site and comprise the totality of the site at Wye, accounting for 31 per cent and 27 per cent of these assemblages. A Domitianic-early Hadrianic pit group at Richborough (Bushe-Fox 1932, Pit 34) includes only one or two possible grog-tempered vessels (*ibid.*, nos. 224, 250; the latter is illustrated as no. 39 here), and fourteen Canterbury sandy ware vessels (Bushe-Fox 1932, nos. 220, 222, 232, 261–3, 269, 316 and unpublished material). Canterbury wares were distributed throughout east Kent, including the upper Stour valley (Eames 1957, fig. 5, no. 11), and central-northern Kent (see below, and Figs. 24 – eastern Kent grey wares – and 30). Mortaria were sometimes stamped: one potter, IVVENALIS, has been recorded in Canterbury (no. 71 here), Richborough (Bushe-Fox 1926, 88, no. 6 – see also Hartley 1968) and Boulogne (*Corpus Inscriptionum Latinarum*, xiii, 10006, 42). The same stamp is also known from an amphora at Richborough (Bushe-Fox 1949, 244, no. 43 (A), implying production of both forms of vessel by the same industry. Hartley (1968) dates the potter Juvenalis' activity to c. A.D. 90–130, and considers east Kent the likely production centre. Other potters who probably worked in the same industry include Valentinus (Hartley, forthcoming; see below) and ones with partially legible or illegible stamps from Richborough (Hartley, 1968, 182, no. 144) and New Ash Green in west Kent (pers. exam.).

Competition with the Canterbury industry (flagons and mortaria apart) would appear to have been confined to a handful of concerns of local significance only and a very small trade in imported coarse wares. There are no kilns of this period known in east Kent outside of Canterbury. An enigmatic group of sandy ware jars from Richborough (nos. 85–88 here) hints at production there: formally a late first-early second date would be appropriate (5.IV.2). Fabric examination under a hand-lens of reed-rim bowls and bead-rim necked jars from Wye suggests that certain vessels, in a finer sandy fabric than that commonly used for Canterbury grey wares, may be from a third, probably local, source.

The importation of coarse pottery to east Kent in this period (amphorae apart) seems to have been almost entirely confined to mortaria from Brockley Hill (vessels at Wye, Canterbury, Richborough and Dover – see Appendix 3) and possibly potteries producing fine white wares, if these were not local products (cf. Hartley 1968). Vessels of Hartley's Group 2 (1977), possibly Kent products, occur on several sites throughout the region, suggesting that, as in west Kent, mortaria were generally adopted by the turn of the century. There are a handful of 'poppyhead' beaker sherds from Canterbury, Richborough and Dover of 'Highgate Wood type' fabric, in unstratified contexts. Alice Holt grey wares are represented by bead-rim jars at Canterbury and Highstead, and a 'Surrey bowl' (as no. 99 here) in an Antonine context but possibly imported in the Flavian-Trajanic period (Frere 1970, fig. 10, no. 1). Sherds of Brockley Hill buff ware occur at Birchington, of uncertain form, and a reed-rim bowl in the same ware was recovered from a pit dated late first-mid second century at Richborough (Pit 182, Bushe-Fox 1949; this vessel unpublished). Comb-stabbed beakers of Camulodunum 108 form (Hawkes and Hull 1947: see discussion above, pre-early Flavian period) occur in several pit groups of late first to early or mid second-century date at Richborough, this period coinciding with their greatest popularity at Colchester (Hull 1958), and other examples have come from Canterbury (unpublished, in a late Flavian-Trajanic context from Marlowe Avenue) and Dover (Willson 1981, no. 827, unstratified).

Amphorae probably occur on most sites of this period although firm stratigraphic evidence to support this proposition is lacking. Body sherds and Dressel 20 rims, of South Spanish fabric, are widely found on sites whose life-span included the Flavian-Trajanic period. Other types include Dressel 30 (South Gaulish) and Dressel 7–11 (South Spanish) at Highstead (Arthur forthcoming) and a possible Dressel 30 from Wye. Canterbury and Richborough exhibit a wide variety of amphorae (cf. Arthur 1986; Callender 1968), including possible east Kent products (see above for Juvenalis stamp; also Jenkins 1950, no. 48, in an oxidised Canterbury fabric) of the late first and second centuries. Canterbury amphorae are further discussed below 4.III.3).

4. *The Coarse Wares of Central Northern Kent*

There is a lack of closed mid-Flavian to Trajanic groups from this area on which to base discussion of the pottery of this period and its implications for studies of continuity, trade and exchange. It is clear from studies of groups of mid-to-late Flavian date at Brenley Corner and mid-first to mid-second century date at Radfield (Baxter and Mills 1978, the Pit; and unpublished material) that grey sandy wares of Canterbury origin achieved only very limited penetration of the area between the Forest of Blean and the Medway. One lid-seated jar and one flange-rim bowl have been recovered from Radfield, in unstratified levels, whilst Brenley Corner's pottery includes one reed-rim bowl and one lid-seated jar from late second to mid-third-century pits, and two lid-seated jars and a reeded-flange-rim vessel from unstratified

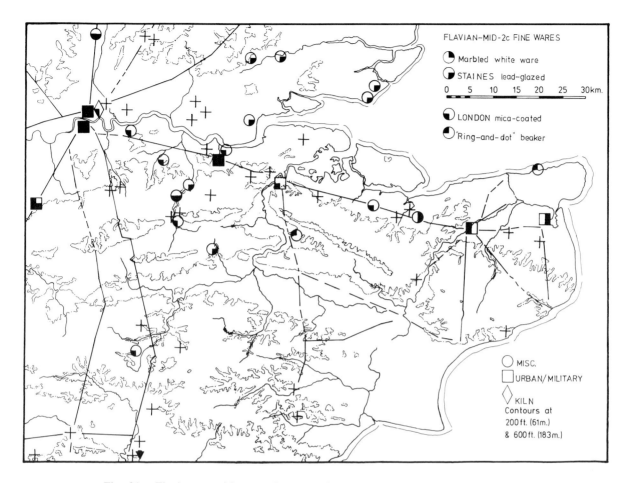

Fig. 21.   Flavian to mid- second-century fine wares: Distribution. + = absent.

contexts. Other grey sandy wares may be of Canterbury origin, but it seems possible that necked jars and jar/bowls in this type of fabric were being produced locally in this period; a kiln at Bedlam's Bottom on the Upchurch Marshes (Ocock 1966) contained a biconical bowl in this fabric (cf. Harrison 1972, no. 4), associated with a globular 'poppyhead' beaker in fine grey ware. Other sherds in the immediate vicinity included 'poppyhead' and biconical beakers and body sherds with 'compass-scribed' arc decoration in fine grey ware, suggestive of a late first- to early second-century date (the pottery is unpublished). An unstratified, blistered necked jar or bowl with lattice decoration on the shoulder in grey sandy ware from the Slayhills Marsh north of Upchurch may also be of this date (Noël Hume 1954, fig. 1, no. 7).

Pottery of west Kent and London-area origin is also rare in this region. 'Highgate Wood type' vessels have been found at Bayford near Sittingbourne in a later first- to second-century funerary assemblage (Payne 1877, 47), and at Brenley Corner in a late second to mid-third century pit. Brockley Hill flagons and mortaria have also been recovered from the area, plus a

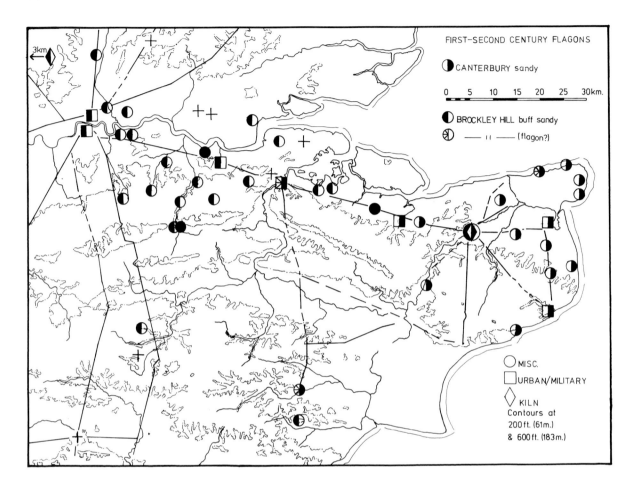

Fig. 22.   First- to second-century flagons: Distribution. + = absent.

'honey-jar' (Tyers and Marsh 1978, Type IIK) at Hartlip. Alice Holt wares, and London Copthall Close type wares (excluding the ubiquitous ovoid necked jar) are entirely absent. Wheel-thrown sand-tempered bead-rim jars are amongst the most typical mid-Flavian to Trajanic types.

The Jaccard correlation coefficients for the Flavian and the Trajanic-Hadrianic periods suggest that, whilst Brenley Corner is more similar to Canterbury (71 per cent and 63 per cent of the respective periods, taking all types studied into account) than is Radfield (57 per cent, 48 per cent), these roadside sites exhibit mutual similarity to Rochester (around 50 per cent for both sites in both periods) and to each other (53 per cent, 43 per cent). The similarity between Rochester and Canterbury in the two periods is expressed as, successively, 42 per cent and 56 per cent. Although significance tests for Jaccard's coefficients have not been formulated, intuition suggests that these figures, with the possible exception of those of Canterbury-Brenley Corner, emphasise neither marked positive nor negative correlation. Certain wares, such as

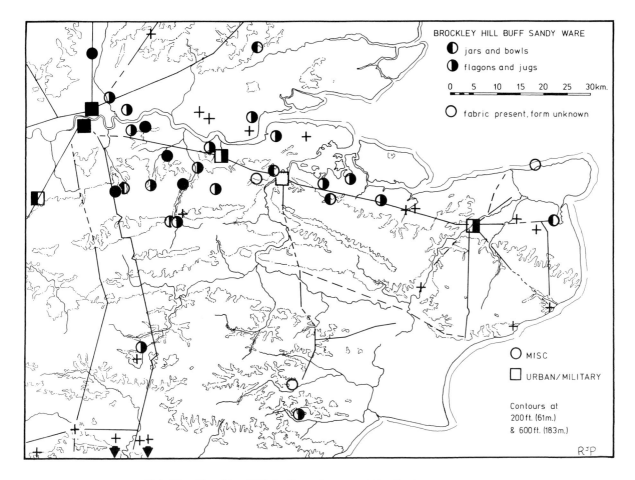

Fig. 23. Brockley Hill buff sandy ware: Distribution. + = absent.

samian and white-slip fine wares, are common to all, or to three out of the four, sites. Others occur only on western or eastern members of this group of sites. Assemblages that include material of this period suggest that the region of central-northern Kent was on the fringes of both west Kent and east Kent 'style zones', incorporating elements of the pottery of both regions without being dominated by either. This situation is underlined by the distribution of flagons current in the Flavian-Trajanic period (Fig. 22), and of mortaria; both Brockley Hill and Hartley Group 2 vessels have been found at Radfield, and mortaria in the former ware also occur at Hartlip and Brenley Corner. White ware mortaria appropriate to this period occur at Brenley Corner. As elsewhere, the mortaria, and also the amphorae, appear to have been utilised on both villas and roadside settlements. It should be recognised, however, that amphorae were not necessarily imported to the site at which they were deposited for the contents that they carried when shipped out from their source. It is possible that certain classes of site received only empty amphorae for general use, or amphorae refilled with a second commodity at some dispersal point.

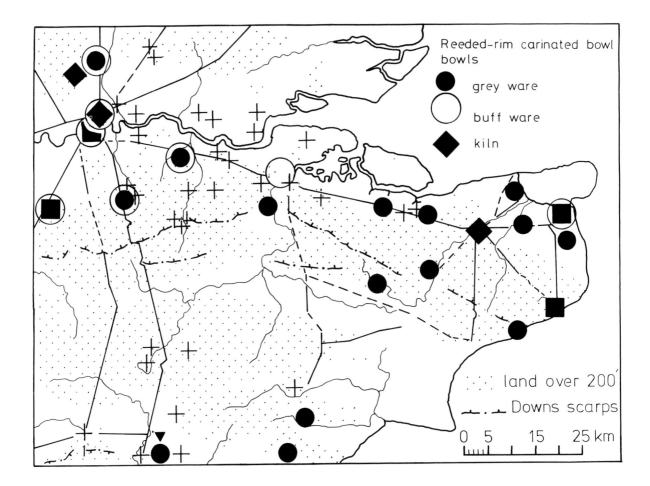

Fig. 24.   Reeded-rim carinated bowls: Distribution. + = absent.

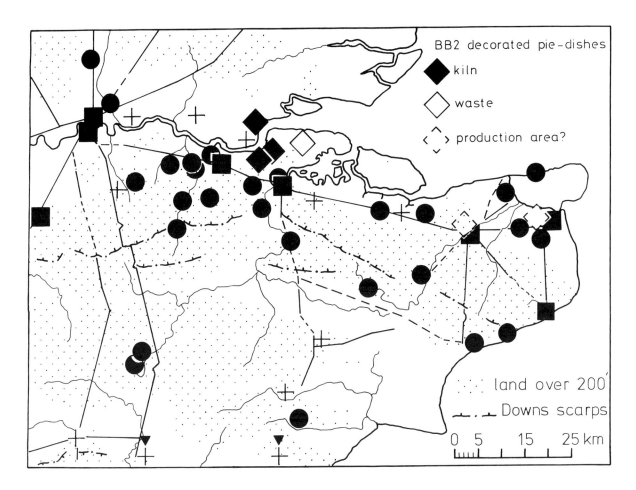

Fig. 25. BB2 decorated pie-dishes: Distribution. + = absent.

R. J. POLLARD

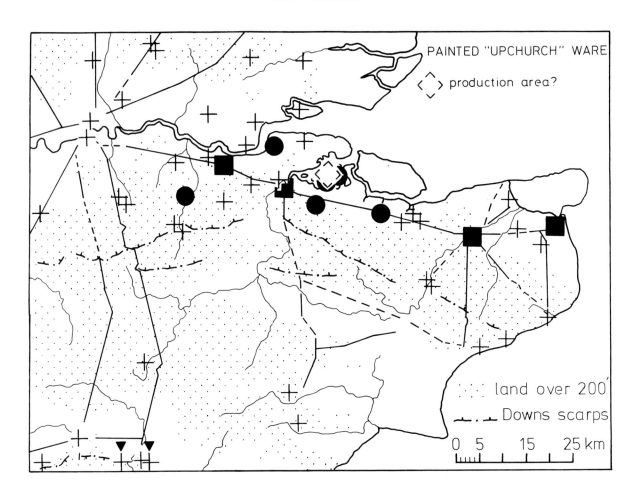

Fig. 26.   Painted 'Upchurch' ware: Distribution. + = absent.

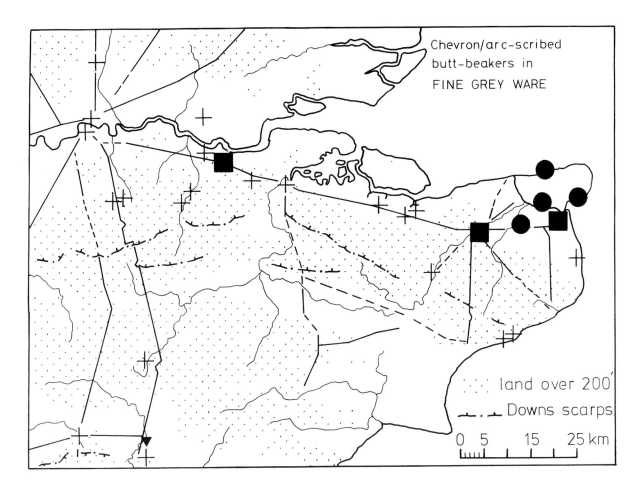

Fig. 27. Chevron/arc-scribed butt-beakers in fine grey ware: Distribution. + = absent (cf. Fig. 41, nos. 122–123 for types).

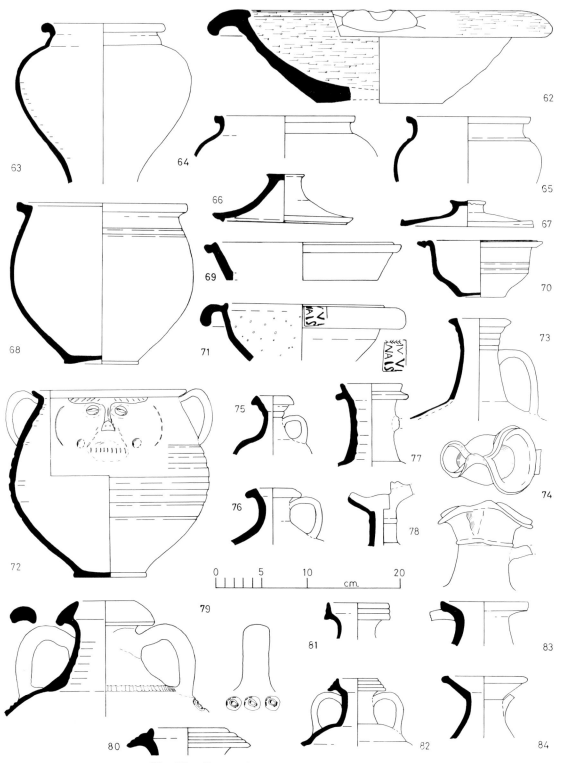

Fig. 28.   Pottery forms nos. 62–84 (Scale: ¼).

Fig. 28. **62**: South-east Britain/north-east Gaul sandy white ware, flint and quartz trituration grit; mortarium, Hartley Group 2 typical form, Hartley 1977, no. 3A.

63–70: Canterbury sandy grey ware.
63. Rolled-rim necked pear-shaped jar, Bennett *et al.* 1978, no. 13, North Lane kiln. **64**. Lid-seated angular-rim necked jar, *ibid.*, no. 2. **65**. Angular-rim necked jar, Jenkins 1960, no. 15, Whitehall Gardens kiln I. **66**. Bead-rim lid, Bennett *et al.* 1978, no. 12, North Lane kiln. **67**. Triangular-rim lid, Jenkins 1960, no. 8, Whitehall Gardens kiln I. **68**. Lid-seated bag-shaped jar, Bushe-Fox 1949, no. 405. **69**. Lid-seated flange-rim dish, Frere 1954, fig. 8, no. 78. **70**. Reeded-rim carinated bowl, Bushe-Fox 1926, no. 80.

71: Canterbury sandy oxidised ware, flint trituration grit; bead-and-hooked-flange mortarium, with a double-row stamp of Juvenalis: IVVENALIS; Williams 1947, fig. 7, no. 7.

72–73: Canterbury sandy orange/buff ware.
72. 'Face-urn' with applied features, probably three-handled; East Studdale, unpublished. **73**. Thickened-lip conical ring-neck flagon, Jenkins 1960, no. 2. Whitehall Gardens kiln I.

74: Fabric as nos. 63–70 above; pinched-mouth 'figure-8' jug, *ibid.*, no. 6.

75. Canterbury fine buff ware, triangular-lip ring-neck flagon, Kirkman 1940, no. 51, Dane John kiln.

76. Fabric as nos. 63–70 above, triangular-rim flagon, *ibid.*, no. 49.

77–84: Canterbury orange/buff wares, sandy, except for no. 81, which is fine.
77. 'Pulley-rim' flagon, Jenkins 1960, no. 4, Whitehall Gardens kiln I. **78**. Tubular-spout flagon imitating bronze vessel prototype (Marsh 1978, Type 2), Kirkman 1940, no. 56, Dane John kiln. **79**. 'Hammerhead'-rim flagon or storage jar with stamped decoration, *ibid.*, no. 40. **80**. Ringed-flange-rim flagon, possibly two-handled, *ibid.*, no. 41. **81**. Cupped-ring-neck flagon, *ibid.*, no. 58. **82**. Form and source as no. 80 above, *ibid.*, no. 46. **83**. Angular-everted-rim flagon, *ibid.*, no. 54. **84**. Bead-rim cupped-mouth flagon, *ibid.*, no. 53.

Dating: 62: *c.* A.D. 65–100. 63: Late first to fourth century. 64: Late first to early second century. 65–66: Late first to third quarter second century. 67: As no. 63. 68–70: As nos. 65–66. 71: *c.* A.D. 90–130. 72: As nos. 65–66. 73: Flavian to first half second century. 74: As nos. 65–66. 75: Mid- to late second century. 76–78: As no. 73. 79–84: Mid- second to early third century.

Fig. 29.   **85–88**:   'Richborough' sandy reduced ware.
                        85. Rolled-rim necked jar, Richborough, unpublished. **86**. As no. 85. **87**. As no. 85.
                        88. Base, probably of jar, Richborough, unpublished.
            89:   Sandy reduced hand-formed ware; lid-seated jar, Pollard forthcoming, b, no. 42.
            90–94:   West Kent sandy reduced wheel-thrown wares.
                        90. Bead-rim jar, Whiting *et al.* 1931, no. 407. **91**. Bead-rim jar, burnished rim and shoulder,
                        Detsicas 1966, no. 117. **92**. Everted-rim S-bowl, *ibid.*, no. 157. **93**. Carinated-shoulder
                        bead-rim necked jar, Philp 1973, no. 162. **94**. Sub-carinated-shoulder bead-rim necked jar,
                        Tyers and Marsh 1978, Type IIN type-sherd.
            95–96:   'Highgate Wood' fine sandy grey ware.
                        95. Bead-rim necked jar with tooled decoration, Tyers and Marsh 1978, Type IIE
                        type-sherd. **96**. Hooked-flange-rim bowl, *ibid.*, Type IVF type-sherd.
            97–99:   Alice Holt sandy grey ware.
                        97. 'Figure-7' angular-everted-rim necked jar with tooled or incised decoration, Tyers and
                        Marsh 1978, Type IID.1 type-sherd. **98**. Bead-rim jar, Holmes 1949, fig. 1, no. 5. **99**. 'Surrey
                        bowl' lid-seated dish, *ibid.*, fig. 1, no. 2.
            100–101: BB1, Dorset source probable.
                        100. Flange-rim 'pie-dish', Gillam 1970/Types 220/221; Tyers and Marsh 1978, Type IVG 2
                        type-sherd. **101**. Bead-everted-rim jar, Gillam 1970, Type 125 type-sherd.
            Dating: 85–88: Late first to early second century (?) 89–94: Late first to early second century.
                        95: Late Flavian to late Hadrianic (rarely Antonine) (Southwark). 96: A.D. 85–140
                        (Southwark). 97: Pre-Flavian to early Antonine (Southwark). 98: Pre-Flavian to early
                        second century (Southwark). 99: *c.* A.D. 75–200 (Millett 1979; Southwark). 100: *c.* A.D.
                        125–150+ (Southwark); second century (Gillam 1970). 101: Hadrianic/early Antonine
                        (Southwark); second century (Gillam 1970).

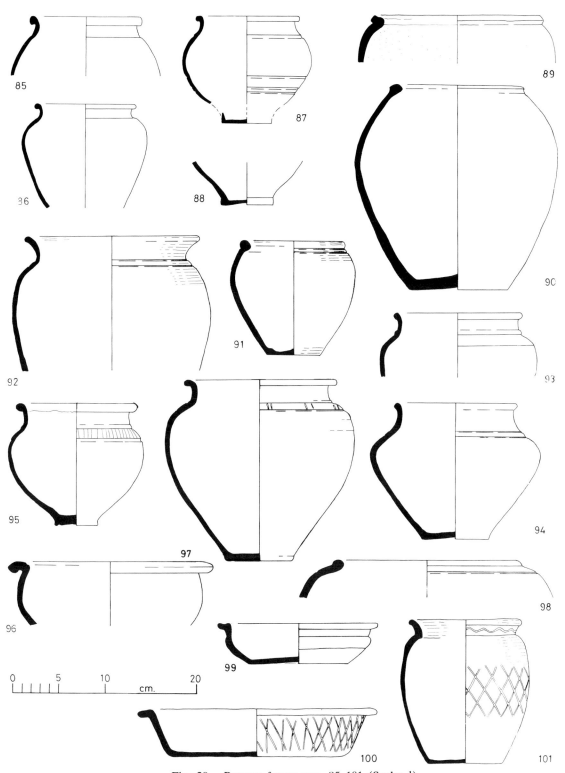

Fig. 29. Pottery forms nos. 85–101 (Scale: ¼).

III. THE HADRIANIC TO SEVERAN PERIOD, *c.* A.D. 120–220

1. *The Fine Wares*

Fine ware assemblages of the century following the death of Trajan are dominated by two fabrics: Central Gaulish samian and Upchurch(?) fine grey ware, the former primarily supplying cups and open bowls, the latter beakers. Imports of colour-coated wares from the Continent reached a wider market than in previous years: the white-fabric dark slip lower Rhineland wares are particularly frequent in occurrence on all classes of site throughout Kent, as are the black-slip Central Gaulish beakers and cups imported alongside red-slip samian during the second half of the second century. The varied wares originating in the London area are generally thought not to have been produced after *c.* A.D. 130 (see 4.II.1, and Marsh 1978, 199), and the oxidised, white-slipped, and painted wares possibly emanating from the Upchurch Marshes industry would also seem to have been discontinued around that time, apart from production of flagons in oxidised and white-slipped wares and beakers in oxidised ware. Further afield, however, two Romano-British fine ware industries burgeoned in the Hadrianic-early Antonine period (*c.* A.D. 120–160), in the lower Nene Valley around Durobrivae (modern Water Newton: Howe *et al.*, 1980), and around Colchester (Hull 1963). The role that these two industries played in the supply of fine pottery is uncertain, owing to similarities of fabrics and forms to Continental imports and to each other (Orton 1977b, 41; Anderson *et al.* 1982). Towards the end of the period under review supplies of samian ware from Central Gaul declined in quantity, particularly in the last decade of the second century, and were effectively terminated at the end of the century (Johns 1971, 25), leaving a small-scale trade in East Gaulish samian, which was accompanied by black-slip beakers known as Trier 'Rhenish ware' or *Moselkeramik*, that continued during the first half of the third century. East Gaulish samian was imported from the Hadrianic period onwards, but was always very much in the shadow of the giant Central Gaulish industries, particularly those at Lezoux and Les Martres-de-Veyre, until their sudden demise.

The publication of samian pottery has tended to be isolated from that of the remainder of Roman pottery in Britain, owing to its especial qualities as a dating medium that are a result of the industrial practices of stamping vessels with potters' marks and utilising distinct figure-types in relief-moulding. The analysis of these techniques enables inter-site links to be established, and hence provides the facility to date one site by analogy with the samian from another site for which independent dating evidence such as building inscriptions or literary evidence for military campaigns can be adduced. It is an unfortunate consequence of this isolation that quantities of samian, and the frequency of different classes of vessel, have rarely been related to those of other wares in the publication of excavation reports and pottery syntheses (cf. e.g. Green 1976, 282, and Orton 1977b, 43). This shortcoming has been, for the present study, exacerbated by the necessity, recognised quite correctly by excavators, of submitting samian to specialists for analysis; consequently, the samian has all too frequently been unavailable for study by the present author with a view to quantification in line with that undertaken with other types of pottery. Published quantified statistics on samian tend to be based either on a 'minimum numbers of vessels' approach (e.g. Bird 1982b and forthcoming) or on 'numbers of stamps/decorated sherds per ten/five year period' (e.g. Bird and Marsh, 1978). Clearly the latter takes account of only a small portion of the samian assemblage, and in published form differentiation by source area has not been attempted. The former method is not comparable with the vessel rim equivalents method adopted by the present author.

Graphs of the 'numbers of stamps/decorated sherds per ten/five year period' tend to show a rise from around A.D. 120, when the Central Gaulish factories were expanding, peaking in the mid-Antonine period (c. A.D. 150–170), and falling off thereafter to the end of the second century, beyond which only a trickle of imports primarily from East Gaul, but also including vessels from Raetia (the Westendorf industry; e.g. Simpson 1970, 111, no. 15, from Canterbury), continued to flow until the mid-third century. The quantified data accumulated by the present author (Appendix 5) suggests that samian (taking all sources together) generally comprises between 5 per cent and 10 per cent of Hadrianic-Severan pottery assemblages; further study should reveal whether the figure of 23 per cent from the well at Canterbury Rosemary Lane (Bennett et al., 1982; quantification by the present author, published in Appendix 5 of the present volume) is abnormally high or not. The sites for which quantified Hadrianic-Severan groups are available are mostly from urban or 'small town' settlements, but the figures from two late-second to mid-third century groups from Brenley Corner, a roadside industrial/agricultural settlement with a shrine or small temple, accord with those from Rochester and Springhead of similar date; further data are required from both rural and urban sites before any patterning in the distribution of samian can be usefully determined. The intensity of usage of East Gaulish third-century wares on different classes and locations of site is a field of especial interest, as the study of East Gaulish Trier 'Rhenish' ware by the present author (Fig. 39) suggests that these black-slip beakers achieved an uneven distribution restricted in the main to urban sites and some villas.

The most frequently-occurring samian forms of this period (Hartley 1969) are bowls, particularly Drag. 18/31, 37, and the Antonine introductions Drag. 31 and Drag. 38; cups, primarily Drag. 33 (Drag. 27 being made only until the mid-second century); and mortaria. The latter class of vessel was first introduced in the samian ware range in the second half of the second century, and became one of the more common mortarium fabrics on Kent sites in the late Antonine period, ushering in a fashion for 'fine ware' mortaria that continued in Britain and elsewhere into the fifth century (see below, and cf. Young 1977a).

The colour-coated wares of the period from c. A.D. 130–150 are mainly bag-shaped rough-cast beakers, sometimes folded, the production of Central Gaulish colour-coated ovoid beakers having terminated some time during the reign of Hadrian (A.D. 117–138) (Greene 1978a, 17). Everted-rim globular rough-cast beakers were also produced in the lower Rhineland (Anderson 1980, fig. 8, no. 2,), and Colchester (Hull 1963, Form 396). The bag-beakers occur in a variety of fabrics, but are always cast with clay particles rather than sand. The primary supplier to Kent appears to have been the lower Rhineland, the most common fabric from which is a white ware with dark brown, grey or black slip (Anderson 1980, 14–20, Fabric 1). Grey and buff-orange wares from North Gaul (ibid., 28–34) are also known, at least at Canterbury (M. Green, pers. comm.). A number of other sources may be represented, in grey, brown, red and buff fabrics; amongst these may be Colchester, which was producing colour-coated beakers from the mid-second century onwards, if not earlier (Hull 1963, Forms 391, 392, 396; Anderson 1980, 35–8). Colchester fabrics range in colour from buff through orange to brown or grey, and are often impossible to distinguish with a hand-lens from Nene Valley products. However, the latter source does not appear to have produced rough-cast wares and may not have begun production of colour-coated wares on an appreciable scale until the latter half of the second century (Howe *et al.* 1980, 7). Although widespread in occurrence (Appendix 3), rough-cast wares appear to have been a rare commodity; of the sixteen assemblages examined at first hand or through publications that include material of *c.* A.D. 120–180 date (the latter being the *terminus ante quem* for rough-casting proposed by Anderson 1980) rough-cast wares feature in only seven, in which they comprise up to 4.4 per cent of the total assemblage (excluding samian: Appendix 5).

The second half of the second century witnessed the eclipse of rough-casting by decoration *'en barbotine'* and of rouletting. These techniques were both utilised by Nene Valley, Rhineland, Colchester and Central Gaulish (black slip 'Rhenish') colour-coated ware industries. Trier 'Rhenish' ware was decorated mainly with paint and rouletting, however. The zoomorphic 'hunt cup' and anthropomorphic motifs rendered *'en barbotine'* on bag-shaped beakers are particularly well-known; in the Nene Valley ware, at least, they are virtually confined to the period *c.* A.D. 150–225 (Howe *et al.* 1980, 8). Bag-beakers were still apparently the most common forms produced in the Antonine-Severan period (Hull 1963, Forms 391–2; Greene 1978a, fig. 2.3, nos. 4, 9; Howe *et al.* 1980, nos. 26–34, 37, 44–7; Anderson 1980, 6–7, Form 2), but necked or everted-rim vessels with globular, elliptical and ovoid bodies, sometimed folded, are also known (Hull 1963, Forms 396, 406; Greene 1978a, fig. 2.3, nos. 5–6; Howe *et al.* 1980, nos. 35–6, 40–1; Anderson 1980, 7, Forms 3 and 4). Globular and ovoid jars or large incised beakers with *'en barbotine'*, *appliqué* and moulded decoration occur in second-century samian ware (Déchelette·68, 72–4: Hartley 1969; Johns 1971), but are rare in comparison with bowls, cups and mortaria in both the Central and East Gaulish industries' output (e.g. Bird forthcoming). Until recently it was believed that the majority of white fabric colour-coated barbotine bag-beakers found in southern Britain were products of the Nene Valley industry (Greene 1978c); however, petrological analysis of fabrics from Silchester, Canterbury and elsewhere (Anderson *et al.* 1982) has revealed the probability that the lower Rhineland industry took a dominant role in the trade in this type of pottery. Nene Valley/Lower Rhineland, Colchester, and Central Gaulish 'Rhenish' colour-coated wares all reached a diverse, widespread range of sites in Kent, all three wares often being represented even on rural sites although rarely on settlements below villa status (Fig. 39). The three wares together account for less than 4 per cent of quantified assemblages of second and mid-second to mid-third century dates (Appendix 5), suggesting that the introduction of new pottery styles, and the emergence of the Nene Valley and Central Gaulish 'Rhenish' wares did not occasion an expansion of the market for colour-coated wares. The introduction of barbotine-decorated bag-beakers in southern Britain is dated to the middle of the second century; *c.* A.D. 140 at Verulamium (Wilson 1972), and *c.* A.D. 150 at London Angel Court Walbrook (Orton 1977b). This date would also suit Central Gaulish 'Rhenish' ware (Greene 1978a, 19), but Trier 'Rhenish' ware may not have been introduced until the final years of that century lasting into the mid-third century (*ibid.*).

Colour-coated wares of the Hadrianic-Severan period in southern Britain are almost wholly confined to beakers. However, 'Castor boxes' – angular narrow-based vessels with a ceramic lid (Howe *et al.* 1980, no. 89) – may have been produced from the end of the second century, and hemispherical and carinated cups or bowls occur in Central Gaulish 'Rhenish' ware (Greene 1978a, fig. 2.3, nos. 7–8). Platters in 'Pompeian Red' ware from the Continent, possibly west Flanders (Peacock 1977c, Fabric 7, form as *ibid.*, fig. 3, no. 15) have been found in levels dated to within the late second to mid-third century at Lullingstone villa (Meates 1953, no. 128) and Dover (unpublished): the Continental evidence suggests production between the Flavian period and the early third century (Peacock 1977c, 159), but there is no evidence of importation to Kent prior to the late second century. Colour-coated flagons were produced at Colchester in the period under review; these are described below.

Limited production of mica-dusted wares occurred at Colchester and Canterbury, probably in both cases in the later second century. The forms produced at the former city include bag-beakers (Hull 1963, Form 391) and flagons with knobbed handles, some of which have tube-spouts (Hull 1963, Forms 361 and 362; cf. no. 78 here). These have occasionally been found in Kent (Appendix 3). A kiln associated with mica-dusted 'face-mask' jars (cf. no. 72 here, in orange-buff 'Canterbury' ware) has been recorded on the south side of Canterbury (Jenkins 1956b), but no details are available (cf. Swan 1984, 391, Whitehall Road).

The range of forms produced in fine grey wares underwent some significant changes in the second quarter of the second century. Biconical beakers and jars, segmental and hemispherical bowls, and campanulate cups were all discontinued; with the abandonment of the biconical forms the last vestiges of what could loosely be described as a 'Gallo-Belgic' influence disappeared, production of butt-beakers and pedestal jars having been terminated by the Trajanic period. It is interesting to note that both biconical and butt-beaker forms are thought to have continued as part of the Oxfordshire grey ware range throughout the second century (Young 1977a, Types R25–6 and 29), as were carinated, hemispherical and campanulate derivatives of samian forms Drag. 29/30, 37 and 27 in reduced oxidised wares (*ibid.*, Types R64 and O.42, R68 and O.45, and R62, respectively). Flanged hemispherical and bead-rim 'Drag. 18' straight-sided bowls in both reduced and oxidised Oxfordshire wares are, however, generally confined to the late first-early second century (*ibid.*, Types O.39 and R70, and R60, respectively). Further work needs to be done on the Oxfordshire wares in order to refine their dating, if this is possible. The contrast between the rural setting of the Oxfordshire industry and the location of the Upchurch industry close to a major inter-provincial trade route (the Thames estuary) with trade links with the civitas capital and the *Classis Britannica*, is striking; the possibility that these differences of location influenced the dissemination of fashion developments is raised by this apparent conservatism on the part of the potters of the former industry.

Beakers were by far the most important class of vessel, quantitatively, produced by the fine grey ware suppliers to Kent in the Hadrianic-Severan period. The dominant form is the 'poppyhead' beaker; strictly speaking this term should be confined to vessels with an everted rim, paralleling the poppy seed-head in form (nos. 145 and 150 here; cf. Tyers 1978, 61). However, the common association of vessels of this form with a decoration of panels of barbotine 'comb-applied' dots has often led to other beakers with this motif being given the name of 'poppyhead' including cornice rim and bead-rim types (e.g. no. 144). The dot-panel motif appears to be mainly of second-century date, vessels of the third century being either plain or rouletted (no. 150), the latter variations being introduced in the late second century. The typological development of these beakers has been investigated in depth by Tyers (1978); later vessels tend to be of narrower, more elliptical, shape, often with taller rims than their more globular predecessors of the early- to mid-second century. The form apparently continued well into the third century (see below) in Kent at least. Bag-shaped vessels occur throughout the period. Several plain vessels from the Ospringe cemetery (Whiting *et al.* 1931, e.g. no. 125) are smaller than is usual for the form, suggesting that they were especially produced as votive pieces; their size, and plainness, could have reduced production costs in terms of raw materials and labour time, rendering them cheaper to acquire than larger, decorated vessels designed for domestic functions. 'Poppyhead' beakers account for between 30 per cent and 60 per cent of fine grey ware assemblages of Hadrianic to mid-third century date quantified by the present author; other forms that regularly figure in groups of this period include rouletted bag-beakers (cf. no. 147 here), everted-rim beakers and jars with tooled decoration of BB2 type (cf. no. 191), and necked bead-rim globular bowls. The first two types are particularly characteristic of the later second and third centuries, paralleling the development of colour-coated and BB2 wares respectively (cf. Greene 1978a, and Howe *et al.* 1980, for colour-coated ware, and the following section for BB2).

The late second century witnessed an expansion in the range of fine grey ware products. Tall-necked globular-bodied 'bulbous beakers', sometimes folded, were produced from this time until the demise of the industry at the turn of the fourth century (nos. 152–4 here; cf. Noël Hume 1954). These forms were presumably derived from black-slip 'Rhenish' ware imports, folded vessels having been previously confined to cornice-rim and short-everted rim types. A number of unusual forms is represented in the mid-second to early fourth century cemetery at Ospringe (Whiting *et al.* 1931), including multi-cordoned 'sugar loaf' beakers (no. 151 here) and sub-globular carinated 'poppyhead' beakers (no. 146 here); these forms have yet to be recognised on occupation sites, however. The Ospringe material also includes a variety of flasks including flange-neck and bead-everted rim types, in reduced and oxidised wares (nos. 169–173 here). The flange-neck is also encountered on flagons, and would seem to be a development of the very late second or early third century; it was also produced in Oxfordshire, in a variety of wares, from *c.* A.D. 240 onwards (Young 1977a, Types W21, C8 and O.4). Flasks in fine reduced and oxidised wares are more typical of eastern Kent than the Medway valley and western districts, where fine sandy ware products predominate (see below).

The fine reduced wares of the Hadrianic-Severan period in Kent may all have emanated from the Upchurch industry, there being no obvious regional sub-groups of forms as were recognised in the Flavian-Trajanic period. The operation of potteries producing 'Highgate Wood types' in the London area precluded intensive marketing in the extreme north-west of Kent and in London and Southwark; even as far east of London as Joyden's Wood, 'Highgate Wood types' outnumber fine reduced wares by a ratio of 5:2, taking the total assemblage recovered from that site into account. The quantified evidence from other sites in Kent (Appendix 5) leads to the suggestion that fine reduced wares declined in importance in west Kent and the Medway valley, in relation to other wares, during the later second and third centuries, although this decline is less marked, if the fine wares are studied in isolation from the remainder of the pottery. The development of beaker and flask production by the 'Cliffe Peninsula' sandy ware industry (4.IV.2) may have been the prime cause of this phenomenon. This would explain why the decline is not apparent at Canterbury, for 'Cliffe Peninsula' 'fine' forms are rare in the city, and infrequently found in east Kent generally (Fig. 46). Fine reduced wares, of possible Upchurch origin, also occur in southern and eastern Essex, for example at Mucking (Romano-British cemetery III, burials 1014, 1028 and 1031; and cemetery II, burial 903, with mid- to late second-century samian), Billericay (unpublished), Little Shelford (e.g. James and James 1978, no. 9, and unpublished material) and Little Oakley, to the north of Colchester (unpublished). It would seem that the dot-panel 'poppyhead' beaker was not manufactured at Colchester (Hull 1963), and appears to have been more common along the Thames estuary than in eastern and northern Essex (C. Going, pers. comm.). The fabrics of Mucking vessels suggest local production as well as possible importation from the Medway marshes and the London area;

certainly beakers were amongst the third-century repertoire of the Mucking potters (Jones and Rodwell 1973, Type Q, nos. 99–100, and Type R, nos. 101–107).

Fine oxidised wares and white-slipped wares of the Hadrianic-Antonine period appear to have been almost entirely confined to flagons, the forms including cupped-rims (no. 159 here), cupped-ring necks (nos. 156 and 161), large bead-and-ring necks (no. 155), 'hammer-head' and triangular-ringed rims (no. 157) and tall-necked vessels with conical ringed upper necks (no. 158). Bag-shaped bodies are common (cf. Whiting *et al.* 1931), but globular and elliptical shapes are also found. The very late second century (the early Severan period, roughly speaking), witnessed the introduction of flange-neck types, as mentioned above; these occur in both oxidised and white-slipped wares, and as flagons and flasks (nos. 167–9). Beakers also occur in oxidised ware (e.g. no. 147) but are much less common in this fabric than in reduced ware. Bead-and-hooked flange segmental bowls or dishes have been recorded (e.g. at Rochester, unpublished) in second- to mid third-century contexts; it is conceivable that these were designed as small mortaria, as white-surface bowls are otherwise virtually unknown in Kent.

The range of fine oxidised wares increased in the late second or early third century with the apparent reintroduction of segmental and hemispherical bowls, presumably stimulated by the sharp drop in the volume of samian imports. The forms include loosely-derived variations of samian forms Drag. 31, 32, 36, 38, and Ludowici Tg/Drag. 36/Curle 15 (nos. 166, 165, 164, 161 and 162, respectively, here). Copies of the conical cup Drag. 33 are also known, but would seem to be rare (cf. Whiting *et al.* 1931). It is possible that the production of bowls in the Severan period represented a direct continuation of the Trajanic production, but this hypothesis is not supported by the stratigraphic associations of these forms at Rochester, Springhead or Canterbury, and would in any case seem unlikely given the massive scale of importation of Antonine samian. However, the Oxfordshire industry may have continued production of oxidised samian copies throughout the second century (Young 1977a, Types O.41, 42 and O.45), with a new range of oxidised and colour-coated products being introduced in the mid-third century (*ibid.*, Types O.44, O.47, C49, C51, C55, C58, C97 and possibly C88). The Oxfordshire oxidised wares, as discussed above, require further research on their dating, should this prove possible, with freshly excavated material. It may be significant, however, that there was a hiatus in the production of segmental flange-rim forms (*ibid.*, O.39 and O.44) in the later second and early third centuries, and that the Drag. 38 derivatives were not introduced until the mid-third (O.47, C51) after the demise of samian importation and the recession in the Oxfordshire industry between *c.* 180 and 240 (*ibid.*, 235–6). The industry might be expected to have produced Drag. 38s in the Antonine period had it been directly competing with samian at that time.

Potteries producing 'Highgate Wood type' ware continued to supply Southwark, and possibly the extreme north-west of Kent also, with 'poppyhead' beakers up to the late Antonine period, although the Highgate Wood site itself ceased production around A.D. 160 (Brown and Sheldon 1974, 230). The final phase of the Highgate Wood industry included 'BB2' medium-everted-rim jars, and triangular-rim pie-dishes, with lattice tooled decoration, and dog-dishes with wavyline tooled decoration (*ibid.*, nos. 82, 79, and 91) in the range of products; one possible vessel of the 'BB2' jar form was recovered at Joyden's Wood, and parallels with Highgate Wood are cited for a 'miniature jar' form at Southwark, resembling BB2 and reduced fine ware everted-rim beakers (Tyers and Marsh 1978, form IIF 11). The evidence for 'Highgate

Wood type' wares at Southwark in the period *c.* A.D. 130–160 is less than for the Trajanic-mid Hadrianic period (*ibid.*) from which it may be concluded that the majority of Kent material is also likely to be pre-Antonine.

Fine grey wares, with sparse to abundant quartz inclusions, were also imported from North Gaul in the latter half of the second and the early third centuries. The vessels are of 'Arras ware', produced in the Nord and Pas-de-Calais departments of France (Tuffreau-Libre 1980a, 1980b) and included tall-neck beakers (*ibid.*, 1980a, fig. 31, nos. 6 and 7; fig. 32, no. 4: no. 177 here), carinated bead-rim bowls with sub-vertical upper walls (*ibid.*, fig. 11, nos. 4 and 6), and carinated flaring-wall bowls (*ibid.*, fig. 7, no. 7). Several examples have been recognised by the present author from the *Classis Britannica* fort at Dover (Philp 1981, e.g. nos. 512, 515, 568, 669, 694 and 853), and other vessels may also be represented on this site (*ibid.*, e.g. nos. 646 and 661). Beakers are also known from Higham, Birchington, Richborough and Folkestone, and a sub-vertical-sided carinated bowl from Canterbury (all unpublished; the Canterbury vessel is Pollard forthcoming, d, no. 200). These fine wares are accompanied by coarse sandy grey ware jars, probably also of North Gaulish origin, at Dover (no. 176 here; see below). The 'Arras' industry in North Gaul produced these forms of beakers and sub-vertical carinated bowls from the first into the third or fourth century A.D. (Tuffreau-Libre 1980a, 223–5), but the Dover evidence suggests that the mid-Antonine to Severan period was the only time at which imports entered Britain on an appreciable scale (cf. Richardson and Tyers 1984, for evidence from London).

The flagons of the Hadrianic-Severan period have been discussed in part in the preceding paragraphs. The typological development of the various industries involved in flagon production is closely similar during the second century; the cupped ring-neck flagon would seem to have been a particularly common product of the Brockley Hill-Verulamium region from *c.* A.D. 120/125 to the end of the second century (Tyers and Marsh 1978, forms IB 7–10) and was accompanied by pinch-mouth jugs. Oxidised sandy and fine fabrics with cream slips were introduced in the Hadrianic and early Antonine periods to supplement the buff sandy fabric that had been used since the inception of the industry. There may have been a marked decrease in the scale of production of the industry around A.D. 160 (*ibid.*), but flagons and mortaria apparently continued to be turned out into the early third century. White-slipped and buff fine and sandy wares are the most frequently encountered flagon fabrics in the Hadrianic-Severan period in west Kent, but the role played by the Brockley Hill-Verulamium industry in supplying vessels to this region is unclear. Flange-neck forms do not seem to have been produced by this industry, perhaps because of its waning in the last years of the second century.

The range of flagon forms produced by the Canterbury industry in the Hadrianic-Antonine period is well illustrated by the pottery from the Dane John kiln site (Kirkman, 1940, nos. 40–58; nos. 75–6, 78–84 here) and Whitehall Road kiln III (Jenkins 1960, fig. 5, nos. 18–20, 22). These include cupped ring-neck, 'hammerhead' plain and ringed, triangular bead-and-ring neck and cupped bead-rim forms, as well as pinched mouth jugs (no. 74 here) in grey sandy ware. The fabrics cover a wide degree of coarseness, and are usually buff to orange in colour (*q.v.* 4.III). They were distributed throughout east Kent (Fig. 22), particularly east of the Forest of Blean where the white-slipped and oxidised fine wares of Ospringe cemetery forms (see above) were apparently uncommon by comparison. The Canterbury industry of the late Antonine-Severan period appears to have found itself in difficulties (5.III.4) from which it failed to recover; the flanged-neck form does not occur on kilns sites of the Canterbury industry and, as with the Brockley Hill-Verulamium industry, may never have been introduced. Third-century flagons are rarely encountered, being supplanted throughout Kent by handle-less flasks mostly in grey wares.

2. The Coarse Wares of West Kent

The whole of the Hadrianic-Severan period throughout west Kent is dominated by the sand-tempered, wheel-thrown products of kilns along the lower Thames valley. These kilns, as they are known at present, are concentrated around the Cliffe peninsula in Kent, and the gravel terrace opposite the peninsula in Essex (Figs. 5 and 69). There are in addition several kiln sites dotted around west Kent, at New Ash Green (Cockett 1976) and Springhead (Jessup 1928), and also in Essex (see Tyers and Marsh 1978, 539–40, Goodburn 1978, 449–50 and Swan 1984). The pottery produced in these kilns may be conveniently divided into three fabrics: coarse sandy ware, fine burnished sandy ware, and slipped sandy ware. These are usually black or grey in colour, although brown vessels are not uncommon particularly in third-century assemblages. The pottery represented by kiln waste from Grays Thurrock Palmers School in Essex (Drury 1973, 118) was, on present knowledge, unique in having produced fine red, white-slipped flagons, and cream ware flagons and mortaria, alongside reduced wares.

The development of the scattered pottery industries of west Kent and south Essex in the Hadrianic-Antonine period resulted in the almost total exclusion of other coarse wares from the market. Dorset-produced black sandy ware (BB1) and Brockley Hill-Verulamium sandy wares occur at Southwark, and shell-tempered, grog-tempered and 'Patch Grove' storage jars are widespread. Mortaria and possibly black-burnished wares were imported from Colchester, and mortaria from a number of other sources are also known. Amphorae from southern Spain and southern Gaul continued to be imported into the province, possibly in larger quantities than in the Claudian-Trajanic period (see below).

The existence of local kiln sites, producing reduced and brown sand-tempered, wheel-thrown or wheel-finished wares, in west Kent may be hypothesised in the late Flavian-Trajanic period, if no earlier, on the grounds that certain forms in such wares are widespread in the area and were not produced by known industries in the London area, the Surrey-Hampshire border, or in east Kent (see above). One such kiln has been excavated on the Upchurch Marshes, probably of Trajanic date (Ocock 1966). The manufacture of coarse sand-tempered wheel-thrown bead-rim jars and necked bowls at Chalk (Allen 1954), possibly in the Hadrianic to mid-Antonine period, followed the tradition established in the preceding period. However, the necked bowls were slipped and burnished whereas vessels of pre-Hadrianic date tend to be burnished only. A more important distinction between production in pre-Hadrianic and Hadrianic-Antonine times in north Kent lies in the range of forms; to the long-established bead-rim jar (no. 90) and necked jar or bowl (no. 92) were added everted-rim jars (cf. no. 115), short-flange-rim decorated 'pie-dishes' (cf. nos. 110–111) and plain-rim decorated or undecorated 'dog-dishes' (cf. nos. 113 and 184, and Gillam and Mann 1970, fig. 2, no. 19). These three forms – the everted-rim jar, the pie-dish, and the dog-dish – together comprised the vast bulk of what is generally referred to as 'Black-burnished ware category 2' ware (usually abbreviated to BB2).

BB2 was first defined by Gillam (1960) in his report on the pottery from the Mumrills fort on the Antonine wall. The suffix '2' is applied to distinguish this ware from a broadly similar ware produced originally in Dorset and later elsewhere in Britain, which is known as BB1 (*ibid.*; see below, this section also). In essence, BB2 is a wheel-thrown, sand-tempered, reduced fabric, covered overall (dishes) or in part (jars) with a slip that is normally also reduced, but very occasionally white; slipped zones are burnished to a varying degree, and the lower, unslipped, portion of the jar wall is also burnished. Decoration is restricted to tooled oblique, vertical, and latticed lines on the exterior of jars below the shoulder, and to these motifs plus wavy lines on the exterior of dishes (see Farrar 1973, 84). BB2 of the period up to *c.* A.D. 180 is different in several respects from that of the late-second to mid-third century; it is convenient, therefore, to describe the coarse pottery of west Kent in the former period separately from that of the latter.

The production of BB2 seems to have begun during the reign of Hadrian. It was believed until recently (e.g. Farrar 1973) that the main centre was Colchester, as Hull's research revealed that the major forms were associated with kilns there (1963): the decorated pie-dish (*ibid.*, Form 37), the plain pie-dish (Form 38), the dog-dish (Forms 40A and 40B), and the everted-rim jar (Form 278). Williams (1977, 195–6) pointed out that Forms 37 and 278 also incorporated non-BB2 grey wares; the supposed BB2 vessels from kiln sites could not be found, and a sample of local Colchester sand was used as the basis for discussing the allocation of petrologically-analysed vessels from various parts of Britain to a Colchester source. Williams concluded that Colchester was the main, if not the sole, supplier of BB2 to Scotland in the early Antonine period, and that it was also the 'single largest supplier of BB2 in the south-east' (*ibid.*, 207–13). He recognised that BB2 emanated from kilns along the Thames estuary, and in addition, postulated sources in east Kent and at other, undesignated, locations. An origin earlier than the Hadrianic period also seems less likely than was believed by Williams (*ibid.*, 207).

The one piece of evidence submitted by Williams to support Flavian exportation of BB2 from Colchester, a pie-dish from Canterbury in a Claudio-Vespasianic context (Jenkins 1950, fig. 11, no. 28), came from a pit cut by later Roman features, and thus quite possibly contaminated by intrusive material (see also 4.III.3).

The kiln site at Chalk is, on the grounds of vessel typology, the earliest of the Thames Estuary BB2 potteries at least in Kent. The bead-rim jars (Allen 1954, nos. 5–10; cf. no. 90 here) date mainly to the early to mid-second century and have not been found on other kiln sites except in very small numbers suggestive of residual or imported material rather than contemporary on-site production. The other forms apparently produced at Chalk include everted-rim BB2 jars with a curved 'cavetto' rim (cf. Gillam 1970, Type 222–decorated, and Types 225 and 313–plain; Gillam and Mann 1970, fig. 2, no. 22–decorated), decorated BB2 dog-dishes (Gillam 1970, Type 328; Gillam and Mann 1970, fig. 2, no. 23, and possibly no. 19) and slipped necked bead-rim jars with tooled chevrons on the shoulder. The last-named form satisfies all the criteria proposed above (*q.v.* Farrar 1973, 84) for BB2; however, it was apparently not used in the northern military zone (cf. Gillam 1970), and has consequently been overlooked in discussion of BB2 in the south-east of Britain (cf. Farrar 1973; Williams 1977). It is proposed here that vessels of this form should be designated BB2 when slipped: unslipped wares fall into the 'burnished ware' category mentioned at the beginning of this section. The slipped necked jar or bowl was produced throughout the timespan of BB2 from the Hadrianic period into the fourth century alongside unslipped, burnished vessels of the same form; other slipped forms were introduced late in the second or early in the third century (see below).

The evidence for BB2 production beginning in the Hadrianic period comes from Southwark and Greenhithe. The earliest BB2 at Southwark comprises shallow decorated pie- and dog-dishes (Tyers and Marsh 1978, types IVH 1 and IVJ 2) and lattice-decorated everted-rim (*ibid.*, IIF 10) and bead-rim (IIA 17) jars, in contexts dated to around A.D. 120/130. The jars include 'grey-ware imitations'; the latticed bead-rim jar (no. 114 here) was recognised by Gillam and Mann (1970, fig. 2, no. 14) to be a form produced in BB2, but so far no kiln sites are known to have produced it, and it is extremely rare on sites in Kent (only eight vessels, from four sites, are known to the present author, plus examples from London, Southwark and Enfield – see Appendix 3). The Greenhithe evidence is less reliable, since only single features of each relevant period can be studied, but the site is valuable in this context both for the contrast which its status – a rural farmstead apparently – provides with suburban Southwark, and for the insight which its pottery gives on the development of BB2 in north Kent. A mainly Trajanic pit group is devoid of BB2 (Detsicas 1966, Pit 1; see Appendix 5 here), being dominated by wheel-thrown (44 per cent by vessel rim equivalence) and hand-made (18 per cent) unslipped sandy wares. A large assemblage from a well-stratified rubbish layer of Hadrianic-early Antonine date (*ibid.*, layer 17) contained similar proportions of these fabrics, but also nearly 6 per cent BB2 (Appendix 5). A mid-second century group from an oven (*ibid.*, Oven 1) comprised almost solely sandy wheel-thrown ware (23 per cent) and BB2 (73 per cent). Tyers and Marsh (1978, 580–2) have demonstrated that 'within a short time of their introduction black-burnished wares (primarily BB2) and their imitations came to dominate the coarse ware assemblage': this is particularly true of BB2 types in the Antonine period. Unfortunately, the Southwark evidence is presented in the form of an unspecified type of 'numbers of vessels represented' analysis, and cannot be compared directly therefore with the statistical evidence compiled by the present author.

The development of the sand-tempered wheel-thrown ware industry in north Kent led to the apparently rapid demise of other wares in use in the area, both local and imported. 'Patch Grove' ware at the Lullingstone villa is dated by the excavator (Meates, pers. comm.) mainly to the Flavian-Trajanic period, with examples occurring in Antonine contexts. Other sites in the Darent valley and more westerly areas, such as Joyden's Wood (Tester and Caiger 1954) and the Otford 'Charne' site (Meates 1954) do not provide sufficient stratified sequences to enable the decline of 'Patch Grove' ware to be dated; it is clear that large 'storage' jars continued to be used throughout west Kent, and even east of the Medway, to the end of the second century and into the third, as were shell-tempered storage jars. It can be assumed with confidence that few, if any, 'Highgate Wood type' or 'Brockley Hill-Verulamium' jars or bowls were imported into west Kent after the Hadrianic period, since these virtually disappeared from Southwark within the first half of the second century, in the case of 'Highgate Wood' types as early as *c*. A.D. 130 (Tyers and Marsh 1978, 581).

The introduction of BB2 in the south-east of Britain also stifled the small-scale trade (up the Thames Estuary) in BB1, presumably from Dorset (cf. Williams 1977), that took place during the Hadrianic period. At this time the hand-made, sand-tempered, 'Black-burnished ware 1' from Dorset was becoming established in the northern military zone (Gillam 1973), and also in the Severn estuary region (Williams 1977, 200). The occurrence of flange-rim dishes and bead-lip everted rim jars (nos. 100–101 here) at Southwark, London and Enfield in Hadrianic-early Antonine contexts implies the extension of this coastal trade to the Thames Estuary also; however, second century BB1 forms are extremely uncommon elsewhere in the south-east (Fig. 35 and Appendix 3) and occur in contexts avowedly earlier than the very late second century only at Richborough. This suggests that the Thames cargoes were transported to London alone, from which a very limited redistribution was achieved. The Richborough vessels could represent the occasional landing of a small part of the cargo at the Wantsum Channel port, or the dumping of vessels found to have been broken in transit. Fulford (1981, 202–3) has suggested that Dorset BB1 was transported up the west coast of Britain as a makeweight in cargoes of official supplies of essential commodities such as grain, rather than as a cargo by itself. The very small quantities of BB1 reaching the London area over a period of perhaps twenty years would also seem to fit this hypothesis of a subsidiary cargo; it is plausible that the burgeoning provincial capital required commodities that could be supplied from the south-west, perhaps food-stuffs or raw materials. The development of the BB2 industry in the Thames estuary and Colchester presumably rendered even this minor level of long-distance trade in coarse pottery unviable.

The introduction of BB2 to the range of coarse pottery current in west Kent in the second quarter of the second century is a manifestation of a highly popular fashion for lattice-decorated everted rim jars and triangular-rim pie-dishes. Not only are these forms ubiquitous in west Kent in slipped, wheel-thrown wares (Figs. 25 and 30), but there is also a variety of unslipped, sand-tempered, often hand-made vessels extant from sites of the Hadrianic-early Antonine period which imitate 'genuine' BB2 in varying degrees of accuracy. Such vessels comprise nearly one quarter of the pottery from the rubbish deposit of this period at Greenhithe (e.g. nos. 107–109 here; see Appendix 5), in contrast with their total of only 7 per cent in the mainly Trajanic pit from that site. Early 'BB2 imitations' have also been recorded by the present author from Charlton, the Otford 'Charne' site and Springhead (all unpublished); Williams (1977, 198) considered that two vessels from Rochester (Harrison and Flight 1968, fig. 13, nos. 18 and 19) were in the same fabric as the Greenhithe vessels. It is conceivable also that the triangular-rimmed pie-dishes from Southwark published as BB1, but without parallels in the north of the province, are in fact 'BB2 imitations' of local production (Tyers and Marsh 1978, type IVG 3, dated to c. A.D. 120–150+), although they occur somewhat earlier at this site than 'genuine' BB2 pie-dishes (ibid; type IVH). The development of the BB2 industry of the lower Thames is discussed further below (5.II; 6.V). It should be noted here that the present author contends Williams' allocation of the Greenhithe material described above as BB2, on the grounds that it is neither slipped nor, in some cases, wheel-thrown (Pollard 1981a).

The 'imitation' BB2 of Greenhithe and elsewhere did not remain in production later than the early Antonine period. However, bead-rim jars and necked jar-bowls in grey sandy wheel-thrown wares continued to be made alongside BB2 throughout the timespan of the latter. Bead-rim jars probably declined in usage during the third quarter of the second century: kilns producing BB2 wares of c. A.D. 180-plus forms did not include bead-rim jars amongst the associated unslipped grey wares (see below), and the ratio of bead-rim to BB2 everted-rim jars in a deposit of c. A.D. 150–220/250 at Rochester is markedly lower than that in a deposit of c. A.D. 90–180 from the same site (2:7 and 7:5, respectively; Pollard 1981a). The Greenhithe sequence (Detsicas 1966: quantification by the present author) also exhibits a fall-off in the discard of bead-rim jars against BB2 everted-rim jars. The necked jar-bowl appears to have been used in smaller numbers than either of these forms during the Hadrianic to mid-Antonine period. In contrast with the production of jars and necked forms in BB2, burnished wares and plain wares, dishes appear to have been regularly produced only in BB2 during this time. The lattice-decorated pie-dish, found on kiln sites at Higham (Kiln C: Catherall 1983) and Chalk (Allen 1954) in Kent, was by far the most common form, with plain and decorated dog-dishes, and pie-dishes with oblique or wavy linear motifs (nos. 182 and 112 here) comprising the remainder. Other forms present in grey sandy ware include lids and everted-rim storage jars of identical style to those in shelly ware. These storage jars are, however, much less common than their shelly counterparts, having been found on only four sites in the Thames estuary to the knowledge of the present author to a total of five vessels (Appendix 3, and Fig. 31).

The range of vessels manufactured in BB2, burnished and plain reduced sandy wares in west Kent underwent considerable revision in the late second century. Evidence from both the northern military zone and from Southwark places the introduction of the quarter-round 'cavetto' everted rim form on BB2 jars (Gillam 1970, Types 143–4; Tyers and Marsh 1978, types IVH 5–7; nos. 181 and 183 here) in this period. A synchronous decline in the manufacture of decorated pie- and dog-dishes may be envisaged, excepting perhaps pie-dishes with oblique linear decoration (Gillam 1970, Type 310); certainly the evidence from occupation deposits of the first half of the third century favours the proposition that the former decorated forms were not produced after the first decade of that century (Gillam 1970). The bead-rim BB2 jar was also discarded around this time. The ubiquity of the plain pie-dish in late second to mid-third century contexts renders the presence or absence of the form from broadly second-century contexts a valuable indicator of date: assemblages from which the form is absent are almost certain to be pre-c. A.D. 180 in accumulation (cf. Gillam 1973, 60). It is primarily this phenomenon that enables the introduction of fine burnished ware tall-necked bulbous beakers (cf. no. 152 here), pear-shaped cavetto-rim folded jars (no. 192), flasks (no. 195), narrow-neck slim jars (e.g. no. 196) and necked jar-bowls with a wavy line on the lower neck (no. 194) to be placed with confidence in the late second or early third century rather than any earlier. The plain coarse ware everted-rim lid-seated jar (no. 201) was probably also a product of this period; the pear-shaped necked triangular-roll-rim jar (nos. 197–9) may have featured in the 'pre-plain pie-dish' range of forms, but it was undoubtedly turned out in much larger numbers relative to other forms from the late second/early third century onwards (cf. Colchester: Hull 1963, Form 268; and Alice Holt: Lyne and Jefferies 1979, Class 3C). Heavy bead-rim storage jars (no. 202) were produced from the late second century onwards at Mucking (Jones and Rodwell 1973, Type S) but possibly not in Kent. An element of standardisation is apparent in the new fine-burnished range, for wavy lines and burnished zones were employed by the potters of the Cliffe peninsula on this ware almost to the complete exclusion of other motifs (at Higham, Pollard 1983b; and amongst the kiln waste from Cooling – unpublished). This style was also popular at Mucking, on necked jar-bowls (Jones and Rodwell 1973, Type K), narrow-neck slim jars (ibid., Type N), flasks (ibid., Type O) bag beakers (ibid., Type R, no. 107) and even heavy roll-rim recurved-shoulder jars (ibid., Type S, no. 110, cf. no. 202 here) during the late second and third/early fourth centuries. Plain bag- and necked bulbous-beakers in fine grey ware may also have been produced at Cooling (unpublished), but are absent from Higham. Local variation in the production of these wares is detectable from the study of kiln site and occupation site material. Thus the combed-shoulder motif found at Joyden's Wood (no. 193 here) has not been recorded by the present author on any other site in Kent or Essex. This form may, admittedly, be pre-Severan in date, but is almost certainly not earlier than mid-Antonine according to its on-site asssociations. The wavy line does not seem to have been present on this site, although the heavy abrasion of the material may have resulted in the loss of decoration. The use of diamond-rouletting (Jones and Rodwell 1973, e.g. no. 82) and roller-stamping (ibid., nos. 83 and 99) appears to have been confined to the Mucking area kilns so far as the lower Thames potteries are concerned, though roller-stamping is recorded on bag- and globular recurved-rim colour coated beakers (Hull 1963, Forms 391 and 396, fig. 58, nos. 16 and 18) and on buff pedestal-vases from the vicinity of kilns at Colchester (Hull 1963, Form 207, fig. 71, nos. 6–7; Mucking produced grey ware versions of this form: Jones and Rodwell 1973, Type N). Diamond-rouletting has not been seen in Kent, and only two examples of roller-stamping have been recorded, at Lullingstone (Pollard 1987, fig. 86, no. 408) and Springhead (unpublished). These motifs are absent from the Billericay kiln material. The hypothesis of quite discrete distribution areas for the products of different groups of kilns in north Kent and southern Essex may be proposed on the evidence of these motifs. That of the Cliffe peninsula appears to have taken in the Medway and Darent valleys and the land between them, with smaller quantities and fewer types being marketed beyond this core area (cf. Figs. 45–48 here) in both west and east Kent. The predominant forms in west and central northern Kent and in southern Essex are the cavetto-rim jar and plain pie-dish in BB2, and the pear-shaped necked roll-rim jar in plain sandy ware.

Coarse ware mortaria in west Kent of Hadrianic to Severan date are predominantly in fine and sandy white wares, particularly the hook-flanged form with a bead level with the flange top (nos. 116, 118 here), and a form with a near-vertical flange. These were both produced at Colchester (Hull 1963, Forms 497 and 501, respectively), the former in the late Hadrianic-Antonine period, the latter from the later second into the third century. K.F. Hartley's research on mortaria stamps has indicated that products of the Colchester potters of c. A.D. 140–200 were distributed throughout Kent (including New Ash Green, Springhead and Rochester: Hartley 1963; 1972), East Anglia and the Home Counties, as well as in the northern military zone (Hartley 1973a, fig. 7). The hook-flange rim form was also produced at Canterbury, in both white and oxidised wares (Jenkins 1960, no. 21; Kirkman 1940, nos. 5–10), and possibly at or near Rochester also in white ware (Hartley 1972; nos. 116–118 here). The scarcity of oxidised vessels in west Kent, in comparison with their abundance in east Kent, suggests that the former area drew its supplies mainly from Essex and perhaps local potteries. Cream ware mortaria production is also attested at Grays, Thurrock (Drury 1973) during the period c. A.D. 150–250, but the range of forms has not been published.

The supply of mortaria from the Brockley Hill-Verulamium industry to Kent appears to have ceased during the Hadrianic period, except to sites in the immediate vicinity of Southwark (e.g. Charlton and Greenwich), which contain forms of the mid- to late second century (Charlton: Elliston Erwood 1916, fig. 18, nos. 2 and 3). The loss of the bulk of the Kent market coincided with the eclipse of this industry's trade to the northern military zone by the expanding Mancetter-Hartshill concern (Hartley 1973a, 42). Vertical-flanged 'hammer-head' white sandy mortaria with quartz trituration grit (Gillam 1970, Type 272), possibly from a source in west Surrey (where they are most common: e.g. Hanworth 1968; C. Smith 1977; cf. Hartley 1973a), occur on several sites in contexts of the late second and third centuries (Appendix 3). Other 'hammer-head' (no. 180 here) and triangular-flange vessels, in fine or sandy oxidised ware sometimes with a white wash and flint trituration grit, may have been imported from east Kent in the late second and third centuries. Occasional vessels from the Rhineland industry at Soller, including examples with the stamp of Verecundus, were imported probably during the latter half of the second century (Hartley 1973a); these are in an orange to buff and white sandy fabric with quartz trituration grit, and include thick-horizontal flange (e.g. Bird et al. 1978b, fig. 218, nos. 1820–1 from Southwark) and hook-flange forms.

These are virtually the only coarse wares, apart from amphorae, to have reached west Kent from the Continent in the Hadrianic-Severan period. An exception that is unique, to the present author's knowledge, is a lid-seated jar of Urmitzer ware type (cf. Fulford and Bird 1975, form 4, but with a groove in the rim externally) from a late second to mid-third century context at the Lullingstone villa (Meates *et al.* 1952, no. 47), examined by the present author. Urmitzer ware was produced in the Rhineland in the second and third centuries (M. Redknap, pers. comm.). The fabric (Pollard 1987, Fabric 77) is broadly similar to Fulford and Bird's fabric 2 (1975), but somewhat coarser in grain size than the sherds described therein; a Rhine valley source was postulated for the latter (*ibid.*, 173). The vessels in this ware published by Fulford and Bird include examples from the Portchester Saxon Shore fort, which was founded in *c.* A.D. 270/80, and one from a burial at Lankhills, Winchester, dated to *c.* A.D. 300–350 (*ibid.*, 178). The Lullingstone vessel, and the Soller mortaria, may have entered the province as a bi-product of the trade between Britain and the Rhineland in lava millstones which took place during the first and second centuries, or possibly alongside Rheinzabern samian ware (for wider discussion of this trade route, see du Plat Taylor and Cleere 1978).

The trade in olive oil with Baetica (southern Spain), transported in the globular Dressel 20 amphorae, continued throughout the second century, probably in greater bulk than before: the majority of dateable occurrences of south Spanish fabrics in west Kent fall in this century (cf. Peacock 1971, 171). The elongated Baetican Dressel 7–11 amphorae, carrying marine products, may not have been produced after the early part of the second century, however (*ibid.*). Another amphora form particularly common on a province-wide level was Dressel 30 (Pélichet 47), a cone-shaped vessel used to transport wine from southern Gaul; Peacock (1978, 49) has suggested that this trade reached its peak in the late second century and may have continued into the third.

3. *The Coarse Wares of East Kent*

The Canterbury industry continued to dominate the market for coarse wares, including mortaria, and flagons throughout the Hadrianic to mid-Antonine period. The introduction of BB2 in south-east Britain appears to have stimulated local production of decorated pie-dishes and everted-rim jars, but the latter remained a very minor component of assemblages throughout the second century. However, coastal sites, particularly Richborough and Dover, exhibit a higher incidence of fine-quality BB2 jars and dishes than do other sites such as Canterbury and Wye. It is proposed that the BB2-producing potteries of the lower Thames and Colchester established a trade route around the east coast of Kent which, at Dover, if nowhere else, eclipsed the Canterbury industry during the A.D. 130s. At Canterbury itself this trade appears to have remained at a low level until the latter half of the second century; the incidence of characteristic Canterbury jar and bowl forms falls off in contexts of this period, suggesting that the industry found itself in difficulties in the final quarter of the century, if not before. The early years of the Severan dynasty witnessed the re-emergence of grog-tempered wares, mostly thick-everted rim jars, as a commonplace fabric throughout east Kent. Reduced sandy ware jars also continue to occur in large numbers, but are different in detail from those of the Flavian-Antonine Canterbury industry.

The importation of coarse pottery to east Kent in the Hadrianic-Severan period appears to have been confined in the main to BB2, and to mortaria and amphorae. Comb-stabbed 'Camulodunum 108' beakers (Hawkes and Hull 1947; Hull 1958) were not used at Richborough later than the early second century, and Dorset BB1 had only a very limited currency possibly confined to Richborough and of Hadrianic date. There is circumstantial evidence for the shipment of North Gaulish coarse wares, primarily jars, to Dover in the late second and early third centuries, but these do not seem to have been redistributed to other settlements from the port. Mortaria and amphorae were drawn from the same exotic sources as supplied west Kent during the Hadrianic-Severan period, excepting the Brockley Hill-Verulamium industry whose products are confined to the extreme north-west of Kent (south-east London).

The range of forms and fabrics known to have been produced by the Canterbury industry changed but little from the time of Trajan down to the final years of the second century. The bulbous-carinated flange-rim bowl (no. 59 here) was probably discarded around the end of the first century, and the 'pulley-rim' flagon (no. 77) soon followed. Thenceforth, the range of jars, bowls, dishes and lids was not augmented, except for the production of 'face-mask' jars (no. 72) in mica-dusted and plain wares probably during the latter half of the second century, if not before. New forms of flagon, amphorae (or large flagons) and mortaria were introduced, however, as is evinced by the kiln debris on the Dane John (Kirkman 1940) and Whitehall Road Kiln III (Jenkins 1960, nos. 18–23). The flagons include cupped ring-neck (cf. no. 161 here), ringed flange-rim (nos. 80–82), triangular-bead-and-ring-neck (no. 75), plain flange-rim (no. 76), cupped bead-rim (no. 84) and angular-everted rim (no. 83) types in fine and sandy buff and oxidised wares, sometimes with a pale wash. Pinch-mouth jugs in grey sandy ware (no. 74) also continued to be made. The 'amphorae' comprise large two-handled necked vessels in oxidised sandy ware, with plain (no. 79) and ringed (Jenkins 1960, no. 22) flange rims. Simple ring-stamps (no. 79) or pads of applied clay (Pollard forthcoming a, no. 50) were sometimes, if not always, used to mask and perhaps strengthen the junction of handle to shoulder. The mortaria of the second century tended to exhibit heavy flanges with hooked lips (cf. Colchester 497: Hull 1963; and nos. 116 and 118 here); sometimes the flanges are almost vertical, producing a 'wall-sided' (i.e. thickened upper wall) profile (cf. Colchester 498: Hull 1963). A second form that is frequently encountered has a more or less triangular pendant flange with a high rounded bead (Kirkman 1940, no. 17; a variant of Colchester 197, e.g. Hull 1963, fig. 65, no. 7). These forms are often embellished with 'herringbone' style potters' stamps on the flanges; four different stamps were associated with the mortaria from the Dane John site (Kirkman 1940, no. 8a on vessel no. 8; a slightly different stamp on nos. 9 and 10, not illustrated, of the same size as 8a but with 6 'ribs' on either side of the 'spine' of different spacing to those on 8a; a smaller stamp on no. 20, and a second 'small' stamp with 3 'ribs' on either side, vessel form as no. 15, unpublished). Unlike the Canterbury/Kent name-stamps of the Trajanic-early Antonine period (4.II.3) which are found on oxidised wares, (Hartley 1968, fabric C, nos. 29 and 114; Williams 1947, fig. 7, no. 7; Hartley 1981, fabric 3, no. 367), 'herringbone' stamps are usually associated with fine buff wares (Hartley 1968, fabric A: nos. 107, 108, 110; id., 1972, no. 29; 1981, fabric 1, no. 364) indistinguishable from Colchester products (Hartley and Richards 1965, 35). Oxidised fine and sandy wares did continue in use, however, and became the sole fabric employed for 'East Kent' mortaria from the end of the second century and throughout the third. 'Herringbone' stamps appear to belong mainly to Antonine production at Colchester (Hartley 1963), and a similar date-range for Kent material may be assumed. The Kent stamps are incorporated in a definitive volume on Roman mortarium stamps in Britain currently in preparation by K.F. Hartley (pers. comm.).

The Canterbury industry, and possibly also rural potteries producing Canterbury-type wares (see the preceding period above), continued to supply the bulk of coarse pottery used by the inhabitants of east Kent up until the final years of the second century, with the consequence that there is very little differentiation, if any, in the range of wares and types found in the civitas capital and on rural sites. There is little evidence for a wider market for Canterbury wares, however; it will be observed in the following section that these wares achieved little success in trade west of the Forest of Blean, except in mortaria and to a lesser extent in flagons. K.F. Hartley has written of a 'herringbone' stamp die from Dover that 'all the known stamps from the same die have been found in Kent and manufacture there, perhaps in the Canterbury area, is certain' (1981, 203, no. 394); and of the single die used by Valentinus, a potter probably of *c*. A.D. 110–160, that 'his fabric [the oxidised sandy ware] and the distribution of his work clearly indicate manufacture in Kent' (*ibid.*, no. 367). However, stamps probably of this potter are widely distributed in Britain, including examples at Caerleon, Corbridge, London, the Upchurch Marshes and Wroxeter as well as east Kent finds at Dover, Canterbury and Highstead (Hartley forthcoming). This evident success in a highly competitive long-distance commerce contrasts strongly with the localised marketing of grey wares, flagons and the 'herringbone' die mortaria described above.

There is a small body of evidence pointing to a contraction in the spatial extent of the Canterbury industry's marketing area during the early or mid-second century, excepting the widespread Valentinus mortaria. The virtual absence of Canterbury grey wares from primary deposits of Period II of the *Classis Britannica* fort at Dover (Philp 1981: examination by the present author, report incorporated in the site archive), dated to *c*. A.D. 155/160–180 is significant evidence for this contraction. Canterbury wares do occur in secondary (e.g. the Period II demolition of structure B.25–Willson 1981, 234–5, nos. 709–11, 719) and unstratified (e.g. associated with structure B.32–*ibid.*, 244–5, nos. 824, 826, 828, 831, 833) deposits. The extreme rarity of primary Period I (*c*. A.D. 125–150/155) deposits renders elucidation of the pottery of this period difficult; the Canterbury grey wares in secondary and unstratified deposits could have derived from this period, but unfortunately the samian ware from these specific layers containing 'Canterbury wares' is not published separately from other layers (cf. Bird and Marsh 1981, 200, 'Unstratified deposits' with Willson 1981, 245, 'structure B.32 Unstratified Deposits'), and it cannot, therefore, be ascertained whether Hadrianic-early Antonine or entirely pre-Hadrianic samian was associated with the Canterbury grey wares. The latter case would suggest that the Canterbury grey wares were mostly from pre-Period I 'Unfinished *Classis Britannica* Fort', tentatively dated to A.D. 117 (Philp 1981, 1), as Hadrianic-early Antonine samian was abundant on the site as a whole (Bird and Marsh 1981, 202). Either way, it is clear that the Canterbury grey ware industry had lost the Dover market by the time of the Period II occupation, at least twenty years before the collapse of the industry itself. A small body of second-century pottery from pre-Saxon Shore fort pits at Richborough (Bushe-Fox 1932, Pit 52; 1949, Pits 77 and 113) includes only one possible 'Canterbury' grey ware, a necked roll-rim jar (unpublished): the absence of characteristic forms such as reed-rim bowls and bag-shape lid-seated jars, present in Flavian-Hadrianic pits (e.g. Bushe-Fox 1932, Pit 34; 1949, Pit 101) is suggestive of a waning Canterbury ware currency. Flagons and mortaria possibly from Canterbury did continue to find a market at both Dover and Richborough, however (mortaria: Hartley 1981, 1968).

An external factor of undoubted significance in the decline of the Canterbury industry was the expansion of the Thames estuary sandy grey/BB2 and Colchester mortaria/BB2(?) industries.

Hartley (1968, 174) has shown that the mortaria of the latter industry encroached upon the Kent products' markets share at Richborough in the second century, and were even able to compete in Canterbury itself with the indigenous pottery (Hartley 1963; 1973a, fig. 7) during the Antonine period. Colchester mortaria of this date have also been recorded at Dover (Hartley 1981) and Highstead (Hartley forthcoming). The most common coarse ware in use at Dover in Periods II and III (c. A.D. 155–180 and 190–210) would appear to have been BB2, and grey sandy ware roll-rim necked jars (e.g. Willson 1981, 222–9 and 235–41). The latter could conceivably be of Canterbury origin, but the lack of other characteristic Canterbury grey wares here makes this improbable. The roll-rim necked jar was a ubiquitous product of the later second and third centuries (e.g. in the lower Thames industries, such as Mucking – Jones and Rodwell 1973, Type J – and Higham – Pollard 1983b, Gross Form XVI; and at Colchester – Hull 1963, Form 268), and the possibilities of importation of these vessels from the Thames estuary or local production at Dover cannot be disregarded. A Colchester source is unlikely, as the Dover pottery does not exhibit the shoulder groove(s) characteristic of that industry.

BB2 pie- and dog-dishes were in widespread use in east Kent prior to the collapse of the Canterbury grey ware industry. Unfortunately, a lack of independent dating evidence and well-stratified groups have frustrated attempts to assess the rate and periods of introduction of the ware to most sites in the east. There is no certain evidence of BB2 at Canterbury antedating the Hadrianic period: the vessel cited by Williams (1977, 207) from one of Jenkins' sites (1950, fig. 11, no. 28) came from a late first-century pit cut by third-century pits, and no well-sealed examples have come to light during the recent campaign of excavations undertaken by the Canterbury Archaeological Trust (Macpherson-Grant 1982; Pollard forthcoming, d). It is probable that BB2 first occurred in east Kent in the Hadrianic period: several pits with fills of Flavian-early Hadrianic date (Bushe-Fox 1932, Pit 34, no. 339) or late first to mid second (Bushe-Fox 1949, Pit 182: unpublished jar of Gillam 1970, Type 139; Cunliffe 1968, Pit 255: unpublished bead-rim jar of Gillam and Mann 1970, fig. 2, no. 14, and dog-dish of Gillam 1970, Type 328) contain BB2, but only a single first-century pit (Bushe-Fox 1949, Pit 76, pre-Flavian) held a BB2 vessel (a pie-dish with stubby triangular rim and lattice, unpublished), possibly to be interpreted as intrusive. The earliest BB2 in east Kent may have come from more than one source: Williams suggested a Colchester origin for a pie-dish from a late first- to early second-century deposit at Canterbury (Williams 1977, 208), but postulated a Kentish source for a group of six vessels from Richborough including lattice decorated pie-dishes and a decorated dog-dish from late first to early second century contexts (ibid., 207: Group XVII). That this source continued to supply Richborough in the late second to mid third century is implied by the inclusion of a plain pie-dish (datable by typology to c. A.D. 180–250) in this group. A third source, perhaps in the vicinity of Canterbury, is represented by a series of coarse-grained, soft, semi-matt BB2 lattice-decorated pie-dishes from Canterbury occurring in early to late second-century contexts (e.g. Pollard forthcoming, e, no. 7); the fabric is easily distinguished from the finer-grained, hard, glossy vessels from the Richborough groups, bearing a closer resemblance to the Greenhithe BB2 copies (see above).

These Canterbury vessels, and the finer BB2 dishes that are found alongside them, formed only a small proportion of the city's pottery in the first half of the second century in comparison with the much greater numbers of vessels recovered from contexts of c. A.D. 150–220. 17 per cent of the pottery from a well filled in this period (Macpherson-Grant 1982, Well 101; quantification by the present author) comprised BB2, all of it of plain dish forms, suggesting a large-scale importation of BB2 after *c.* A.D. 180. Other contexts from Canterbury contain varying quantities of plain and decorated BB2 dishes, but a consistent feature is the low incidence often amounting to a complete absence of BB2 jars, particularly in contexts with *termini ante quos* in the early third century. This is in marked contrast with Dover, where everted-rim, cavetto-rim and bead-rim BB2 jars seem to have been abundant in Period III (e.g. Willson 1981, nos. 737, 739, 742, 745, 747, 750–2, 756, 759, 772, 775: identification by the present author), although present in smaller numbers in Period II (Willson 1981: probably one only – no. 606 – from a dump containing 52 published vessels). BB2 jars also occur in several second/early third-century pits at Richborough (Bushe-Fox 1932, Pit 52, no. 251; 1949, Pit 113, no. 464; Pit 182, unpublished; Pit 184, no. 427; Cunliffe 1968, Pit 255, unpublished). BB2-derived jars have been recovered from sites in east Kent (e.g. Folkestone and Highstead, both unstratified and unpublished), but on the whole the forms appear to have had little impact in comparison with their ubiquity in west Kent, and with BB2 dishes throughout Kent (cf. Figs. 25, 30 and 45). The existence of a direct trade between BB2 potteries on the Thames and perhaps at Colchester and coastal sites such as Dover and Richborough may be postulated; seaborne transportation of this ware to the northern military zone may be considered a certainty (Gillam 1973; Breeze 1977; Williams 1977) from *c.* A.D. 140–250, as may the delivery of Colchester mortaria to Kent. It is plausible that the *Classis Britannica*, in its role as a supply unit, was directly involved in this movement of material at least to military sites, but the existence of 'military contracts' for pottery to the northern zone is a contentious issue (cf. Gillam 1973; Breeze 1977; Williams 1977; Fulford 1981; Pollard 1983a, 492–505). The shape of jars lends itself less readily to compact stowage than does the conical dish, and it may have been the extra cargo space required, and greater vulnerability to breakage, that discouraged intensive trading in BB2 jars to inland sites in east Kent wherein some reloading onto shallow draft vessels and/or overland carriers would have been unavoidable. It is noticeable also that the jar and flask forms of the third-century lower Thames BB2 and burnished ware industries are also much rarer in relation to BB2 dishes of that period than in west Kent and southern Essex (Figs. 45–46 and Appendix 3), throughout east Kent even at Dover and, on evidence of published material, Reculver (Philp 1957; 1959).

The expansion of the importation of BB2 to east Kent in the last quarter of the second century coincided broadly with a marked decline in the production of Canterbury sandy wares. However, it must not be assumed that the pressure exerted by other industries was the sole, or even the primary, cause of this demise of the urban industry's fortunes. Fulford (1977b) has argued convincingly that a general shift of emphasis from urban to rural production was experienced in the late second and early third centuries, coinciding with a widespread recession in the pottery industry (Pollard 1983a, 378–83, 492–519; cf. Hull 1963, and Young 1977a). The degree of temporal finesse that is afforded by the dating evidence for south-eastern Roman Britain – primarily coins and pottery – is not good enough to allow the details of the decline of Canterbury and the rise of the BB2 industries to be recovered; it is possible that the success of the latter was a consequence, not a prime cause, of the failure of the former. The BB2 industries were not the sole heirs to the Canterbury markets, however. Small quantities of BB1, probably from Dorset, have been recovered from late second to early/mid third-century contexts at Dover (e.g. Willson 1981, nos. 468, 696, 773, 871, and 877) and possibly Reculver (Philp 1957, nos. 27 and 30), whilst second- to early third-century forms have occasionally been recognised in Canterbury. This ware was virtually absent from east Kent during the Hadrianic period, when it was exported to London (see above), but is a regular find on third/fourth-century sites throughout Kent (Figs. 35–36), particularly from the mid-third to the mid-fourth century (4.IV, 4.V). The occurrence of a number of grey sandy ware jars at Dover in contexts of the late second to mid-third century that broadly resemble North Gaulish types (no. 176 here; cf. Tuffreau-Libre 1980b, fig. 13, nos. 1 and 2; Willson 1981, nos. 581, 636, 639, 643, 668, and 699) suggests that direct shipment of coarse wares from the Continent (Boulogne perhaps, as this was the site of a *Classis Britannica* base opposite Dover) to Dover took place without any redistribution within Britain; these vessels may have accompanied the fine grey sandy 'Arras' ware that is occasionally found on sites in east and north Kent (see above); however, the decoration is not apparently paralleled by material from the Nord/Pas-de-Calais region of France (Tuffreau-Libre 1980a).

The most significant new fabric to be found in east Kent in Severan contexts, in terms of quantity, is a grog-tempered ware of almost certain indigenous production. This is characterised by high firing, in an atmosphere of reduction or resulting in insufficient oxidation, often to the point of vitrification, giving a silver-grey or occasionally glassy grey-green surface. Grog and quartz are the major inclusions, occurring in varying ratios and size ranges; a grogged fabric with sparse quartz is particularly common, but quartz with sparse grog is also encountered. The name 'Native Coarse Ware' has been applied to the Canterbury material (Pollard forthcoming, d) as a convenience; the wiping of the lower exterior of jars, producing a scarred appearance, and the penchant for simple linear burnished motifs, recall the grog-tempered wares of the first century B.C. to the early second century A.D. (see above), although the coarse-combing of the latter period does not occur. It is possible that these late Iron Age-derived wares continued to be produced in small numbers, particularly as storage jars, during the second century (cf. Gaunt 1974, no. 3). The techniques exhibited by the 'Native Coarse Ware' are at variance with those of the Canterbury sandy ware industry which it succeeded: the high firing is only an occasional feature of the latter, more often encountered in kiln waste than occupation site material. Hand-forming, perhaps involving a turntable as well as coiling, seems probable, with the rim sometimes trued-up on a wheel of some kind. The upper body and rim are usually burnished (no. 179 here). Jars are by far the most common forms, including simple everted rims and angular everted or rolled rims. The ware has been recorded on several sites in north-east Kent, including Canterbury (Frere 1970, fig. 10, no. 21 – no. 179 here), Wingham, Richborough and possibly Reculver (Philp 1957, no. 29); similar wares have also been examined from Dover (Willson 1981, nos. 408, 413, 432, 521, 738, 748, 807, and 858: examination by the present author), Folkestone, and west of Canterbury (see below and Fig. 45). None of these finds need be earlier than the very late second/early third century. The quantified evidence from Canterbury (Appendix 5) suggests that 'Native Coarse Wares' comprised anywhere up to 20 per cent of late second to mid-third century assemblages, with BB2 and grey sandy wares (see below) providing the main competition until the last quarter of the third century when 'late Roman' grog-tempered ware was first produced.

The spatial range of distribution parallels that of the Canterbury grey sandy wares of the Flavian to early Hadrianic periods; it is by no means certain that the grog-tempered ware was produced at Canterbury by either co-ordinated or individualistic concerns, but it can be inferred from the close distributional accord between the two successive wares that this area represented a 'natural trade/exchange zone'. There is no evidence to suggest that coastal trade in either ware was carried out beyond 30 km. of the Wantsum (the marine channel downstream of Canterbury that gave access to the Thames estuary and the Straits of Dover). Indeed, it is possible that all Canterbury grey wares and grog-tempered wares were transported entirely by land. This is in contrast with the industries of Colchester and the lower Thames, which were undoubtedly involved in shipment of pottery both in the Thames estuary and the North Sea (Williams 1977, 211, concluded that products of both the Joyden's Wood (now discounted as a kiln site) and Cooling potteries are represented on Hadrian's Wall in the late second to mid-third century, and the former also occurred at Canterbury). It was the failure to make extensive use of seaborne transport, with the facility to carry bulk cargoes at the cheapest possible rate (Duncan-Jones 1974, Appendix 17) that this mode offered, that was to a large extent responsible for constricting the growth of the Canterbury industry. However, the experience of Colchester's industry suggests that even with a strong coastal trade the industry might not have survived the economic crisis at the end of the second century (Pollard 1983a, 378–83).

The demise of the Canterbury grey ware industry did not lead to the cessation of demand for reduced sandy wares; one of the more numerous elements of third-century pottery assemblages from Canterbury itself (comprising between 10 and 15 per cent of all types) is a wheel-thrown rounded and angular-roll rim, hooked-rim or angular-everted rim necked jar in this ware. This often exhibits similar firing characteristics to the contemporary 'Native Coarse Wares', with a red-scorched or vitrified surface. Moreover, vessels are often decorated with a narrow zone of burnish on the upper shoulder and rim, a feature that also occurs on some 'Native Coarse Ware' vessels and seems to be characteristic of the first half of the third century at Canterbury. Unslipped plain pie- and dog-dishes with erratic facet-burnishing also occur, in small numbers relative to BB2 examples.

These grey sandy wares may have been the products of potters who survived the difficult years of the late second-century industry and found it worthwhile to continue production. The extent of the 'Native Coarse Ware' distribution implies that local potters could still find wide markets, whether operating in a centralised or dispersed manner. Kiln sites of the late second and third centuries are lacking in east Kent, and the grey sandy wares of this period are lacking in idiosyncracies that might enable individual marketing zones to be defined. The pottery is similar to contemporary wares of the Medway-Swale area (see below); a large number of small-scale concerns may be postulated for the whole area east of the Medway in the third century, with little or no co-ordination or centralisation of production and distribution. On the grounds of minor differences in fabric, a local pottery serving Wye may be postulated.

The production of mortaria also continued into the third century. The forms are mostly near-vertical 'hammer-head' flange-rims of rectangular or triangular section (e.g. no. 180 here), though stubby thick-flange-and-bead forms also occur (e.g. Bushe-Fox 1932, no. 357; Williams 1947, fig. 8, no. 12). An oxidised, sometimes sandy, fabric is usual, with flint trituration grit and sometimes a white slip. These appear to have been made from the late second to the late third/early fourth century, and are abundant at Richborough (Hartley 1968, 174, Table 1). Their overall distribution spread at least as far west as the Darent valley, probably during the third century (4.IV.2). It is probable that they were produced somewhere in east Kent, conceivably at Canterbury, though there is no hard evidence for this (cf. Hartley 1981, fabric 3, and no. 386, where a Rhineland derivation of the 'hammer-head' form is proposed).

In addition to Canterbury, Colchester, and 'East Kent', a number of other sources of mortaria are represented in east Kent in the Hadrianic to Severan period (Hartley 1968, 1981, 1982). These include the 'Surrey/Sussex' white ware mortarium (Gillam 1970, Type 272 – see

4.III.2 above) on coastal sites and at Canterbury; wide-flanged vessels from the Verecundus industry (possibly established at Silchester) at Richborough (Hartley 1968, Fabric D, no. 98) of a date in the latter half of the second century; and a rectangular 'hammer-head' flange-rim from the Rhineland at Dover (Hartley 1981, no. 381). A fine, slightly sandy buff (or brown) ware of unknown source, probably in southern Britain or on the Continent, and producing mortaria with rounded or elliptical stubby flanges and near-vertical pendant flanges, is represented at Dover (*ibid.*, nos. 382–5, 387), Wye (unpublished) and Canterbury (Jenkins 1950, nos. 56 and possibly 58; Jenkins 1952, nos. 24 and 26); the type is dated by Hartley (1981) to *c.* A.D. 160–230, but the Canterbury vessels may include mid-third century examples (Jenkins 1952). This type has not been recorded on west Kent sites by the present author, but does occur in the central-northern region (see below).

The range of amphorae in east Kent in this period parallels that in the west, with the addition of the Canterbury ware (see above). Finds of South Spanish wares are confined to unstratified contexts except at Canterbury (Arthur 1986) and Richborough (Callender 1968). Other, unstratified finds include South Gaulish Dressel 30 at Highstead (Arthur forthcoming) and possibly Wye (unpublished), and a wider range of types at Canterbury and Richborough (references as above). These have not been studied by the present author, however.

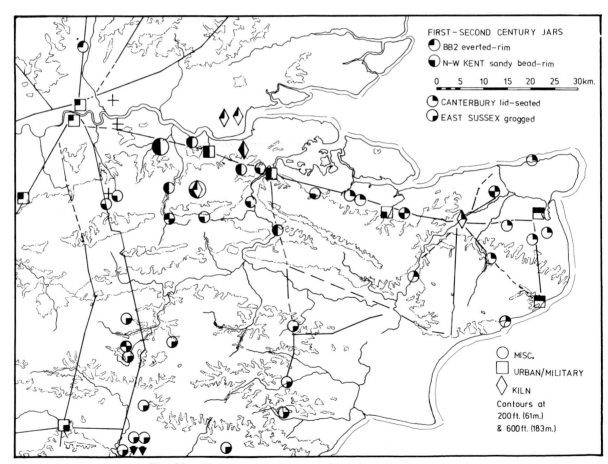

Fig. 30.   First- to second-century jars: Distribution. + = absent.

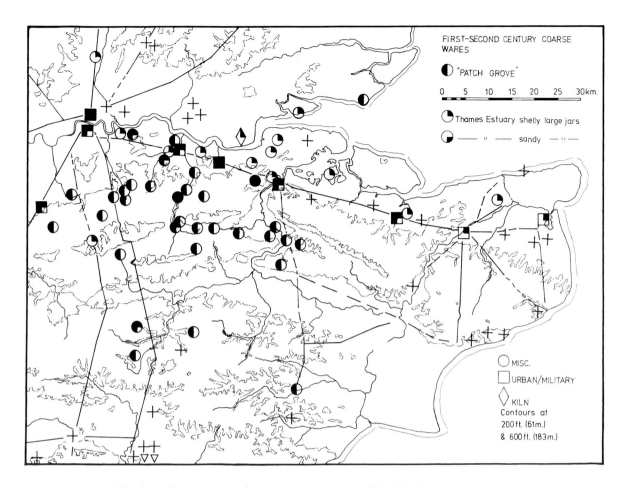

Fig. 31.   First- to second-century coarse wares: Distribution. + = absent.

4. *The Coarse Wares of Central-Northern Kent*

The most common types of the Hadrianic-Severan period in this region are roll-rim necked jars
and jar/bowls and dog-dishes in reduced sandy wheel-thrown ware, and pie- and dog-dishes in
BB2. There is a dearth of useful groups of pottery of Hadrianic to early Antonine date, but the
pit at Radfield (Baxter and Mills 1978) may have been filled in the mid-second century with
material of first- to mid second-century date. This pit included a Dressel 20 amphora handle
with a stamp of *c*. A.D. 120–160 (Peacock in Baxter and Mills 1978); other coarse pottery that
could be second century from this feature includes bead-rim and roll-rim necked jars (*ibid.*, nos.
2 and 6), but characteristic 'Canterbury' forms such as lid-seated jars and flanged bowls are
absent, as is BB2. The scarcity of Canterbury wares in central-northern Kent has been noted
above (4.II.4). Flagons and mortaria possibly from this source have been recovered, the former
particularly in the Ospringe cemetery, which was founded probably in the mid-second century.
The grey sandy wares were probably local products, as BB2 jars of west Kent/Colchester(?)

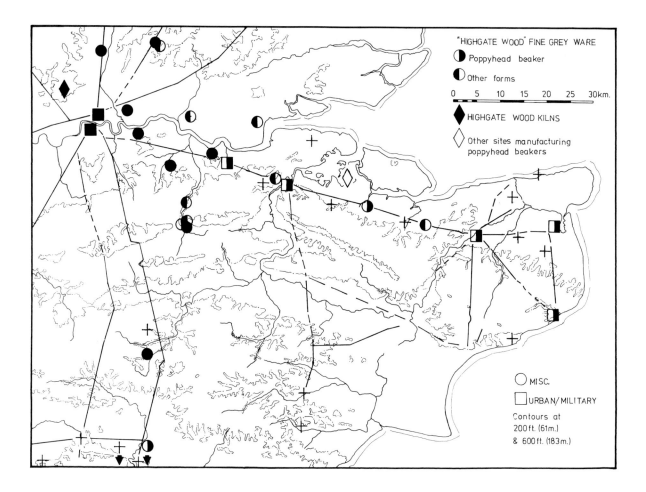

Fig. 32. 'Highgate Wood' fine grey ware: Distribution. + = absent.

origin are also notably rare in this region, (for example there are two vessels only from two large pit groups of late second- to mid third-century date at Brenley Corner, comprising some 4 per cent of contemporary jars), and it would seem unlikely that the plain jars of west Kent were imported, if BB2 jars were not. The sandy wares are usually somewhat finer than Canterbury wares, although there is some overlap. The bead-rim jars (no. 90 here) and decorated necked bowls (Whiting *et al.* 1931, several examples including nos. 420, 512, and 576) provide a typological link with west Kent wares, but the region was on the fringe of the main distribution area for the late second to mid-third century BB2 and burnished wares of west Kent (Figs. 45–48). BB2 nevertheless comprises 22 per cent of pottery from one of the Brenley Corner pits referred to above; the other contained less than 2 per cent BB2, but also included a large first- to mid second-century residual element. The former pit included a few sherds of late first to second century Canterbury grey and oxidised wares, but roll-rim necked jars with angular or rounded rims comprised some 30 per cent, and BB2 plain dishes 27 per cent, of

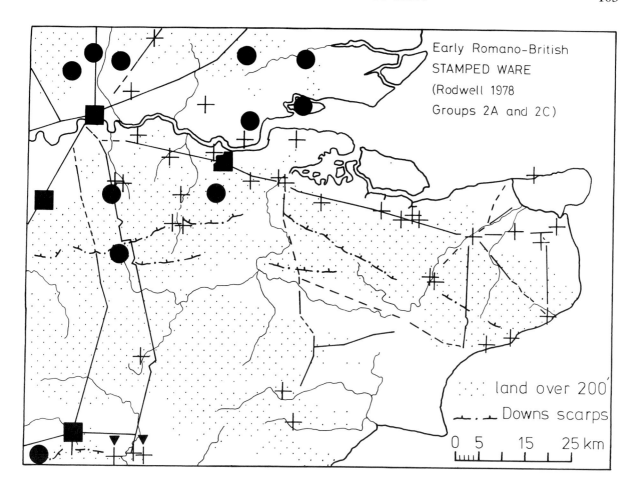

Fig. 33. Early Romano-British stamped ware (Rodwell 1978, Groups 2A and 2C): Distribution. + = absent.

coarse wares. These forms were also represented in the early third-century cellar fill at Faversham (Philp 1968, fig. 26).

The marked increase in usage of BB2 observed at Canterbury is paralleled in the central-northern region, where decorated BB2 dishes, though present (Fig. 25), are rare in comparison to the abundance of plain forms. East Kent high-fired grog-tempered jars are present at Brenley Corner and Ospringe (e.g. Whiting *et al.* 1931, no. 163) but apparently only in small quantities. However, there are several large 'storage' jars used as cinerary urns of third-century date, possibly interred as early as the first half of that century, at Ospringe (e.g. no. 178 here). These are generally facet-burnished and decorated with linear and stick-stabbed motifs and do not exhibit the characteristics typical of east Kent 'Native Coarse Ware' (see above).

Exotic coarse wares, apart from mortaria and amphorae, of the Hadrianic-Severan period are extremely rare in this region. A single 'Patch Grove' ware storage jar (no. 21 here) was recovered from the Ospringe cemetery, and a 'Thames Estuary' shelly storage jar was

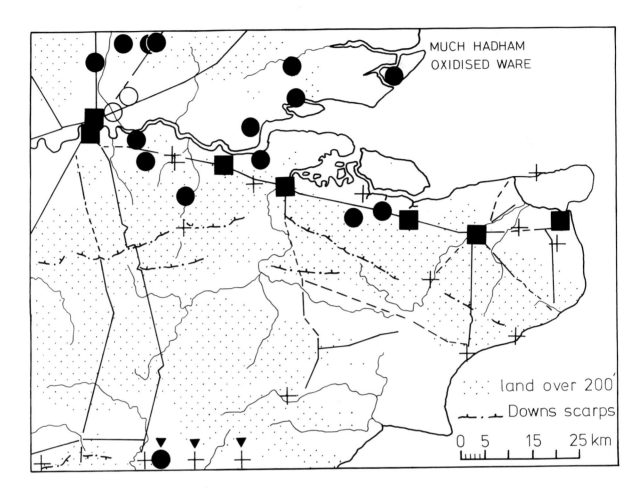

Fig. 34. Much Hadham oxidised ware: Distribution. + = absent.

incorporated in the Faversham cellar fill (Philp 1968, no. 273). BB1 dishes from one of the Brenley Corner pits could be of mid-third rather than Severan date, as may a jar from Ospringe (Whiting *et al.* 1931, no. 402; Gillam 1970, Type 132). A BB1 mug from the latter site (*ibid.*, no. 550; Gillam 1970, Type 65) is from a burial group of possible Severan date, however.

Mortaria of the Hadrianic to Severan period include oxidised and white ware hook-flange types with 'herringbone' stamps, and 'hammer-head' near-vertical flanges, amongst which are grooved-flange types, in white ware and oxidised white-slip 'East Kent' ware (cf. Gillam 1970, Types 273 and 282). A Canterbury or east Kent source may be proposed for most of these, except perhaps the grooved 'hammer-heads'. Exotic mortaria include Hartley's 'Southern Britain/Continent' white ware with flint trituration grit (1981, particularly no. 383 form) at Brenley Corner and Ospringe (both unpublished, the former in a pit fill of the late second to mid-third century), and possibly the grooved 'hammer-heads' (but cf. *ibid.*, no. 386, for which a Kent source is proposed).

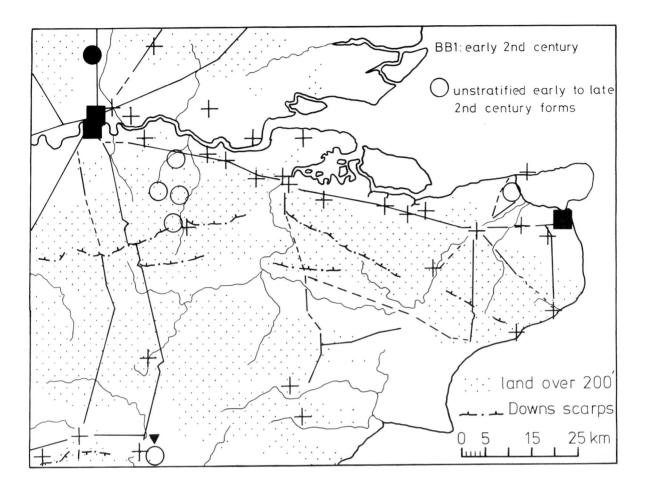

Fig. 35.   Early second-century BB1: Distribution. + = absent.

The Ospringe cemetery provides an unusual example in Kent of the large scale re-use of amphorae as cremation urns. These were not available for study, but it may be deemed probable that the majority were Dressel 20 South Spanish types: five vessels, all globular, were recorded at the nearby Faversham villa (Philp 1968, 82), and the form is also known at Radfield (Baxter and Mills 1978) and Brenley Corner (unpublished). Some of the Ospringe vessels are described as 'wine amphorae' (Whiting 1921, 1923, 1925, 1926; Whiting *et al.* 1931), perhaps reflecting the misunderstanding of the contents of Dressel 20 that was current at that time (cf. Peacock 1978). Thirty-eight instances of amphorae in funerary contexts were recorded at Ospringe, a cemetery founded in the mid-second century and in use until at least the early fourth century. One of these is probably of Tintagel B iv ware (Whiting *et al.* 1931, no. 502; see Peacock 1977d, 298), associated with a second-century glass vessel and a necked roll-rim jar of second- to fourth-century type. Other instances of Dressel 20 in funerary contexts include two from the Lockham walled cemetery to the south-east of Maidstone (Smythe 1883; Jessup 1959)

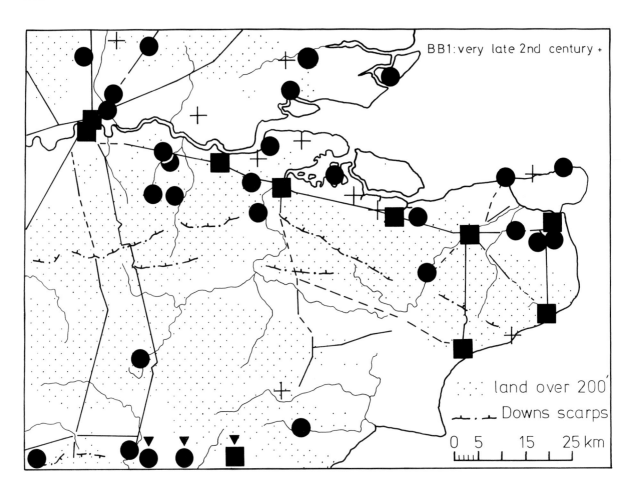

Fig. 36.   Very late second-century+ BB1: Distribution.   + = absent.

and one from Green Street Green, south-east of Bromley in west Kent (Payne 1900, l: Payne 1902, lxiii). No other forms of amphorae can be recognised amongst material examined from the central-northern region of Kent.

The Jaccard correlation coefficients for the Hadrianic-early Antonine and mid-Antonine to mid-third century periods show a general increase in similarity between assemblages of the five sites (Canterbury, Brenley Corner, Ospringe, Radfield and Rochester) studied. Coefficients of 70 per cent or a higher degree are recorded for Canterbury: Brenley Corner in both periods (as in the Flavian period, taking all types studied into account), and for Canterbury:Ospringe and Canterbury:Radfield in the latter. The coefficients for Rochester and the other sites range from 45 per cent to 65 per cent over both periods, somewhat lower than those for Canterbury (50 per cent to 75 per cent). The widespread circulation of imported colour-coated wares, 'Upchurch' fine grey wares, and BB2, and the general adoption of buff and oxidised ware mortaria may provide the main reasons for the increase in similarity of assemblages. The

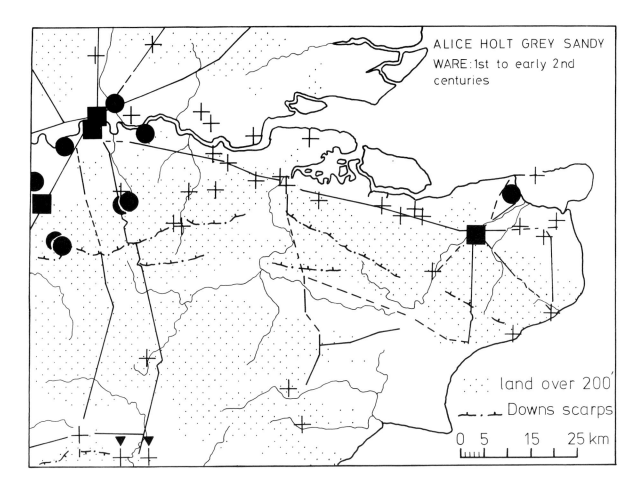

Fig. 37.   First- to early second-century Alice Holt ware: Distribution. + = absent.

occurrence of second-century 'Canterbury' grey and oxidised wares and third-century 'Native Coarse Ware', albeit in small numbers, on sites east of Rochester is in some measure behind the lower coefficients registered by the latter site in comparison to Canterbury. Degrees of similarity between Radfield, Ospringe and Brenley Corner range from 50 per cent to 69 per cent; the proximity of these three sites to one another, and their common location on Watling Street, makes it surprising that higher coefficients have not been computed. The wide range of fine wares and Canterbury wares recorded at Brenley Corner in the Hadrianic-early Antonine period differentiates this site from Radfield (50 per cent similarity). The figures for the later period, taking account also of Ospringe as the cemetery provides a large data base, range from 64 per cent to 69 per cent. Variation between assemblages is more associated with the range of forms present in commonly-occurring fabrics such as fine grey and red wares rather than with markedly different ranges of fabrics.

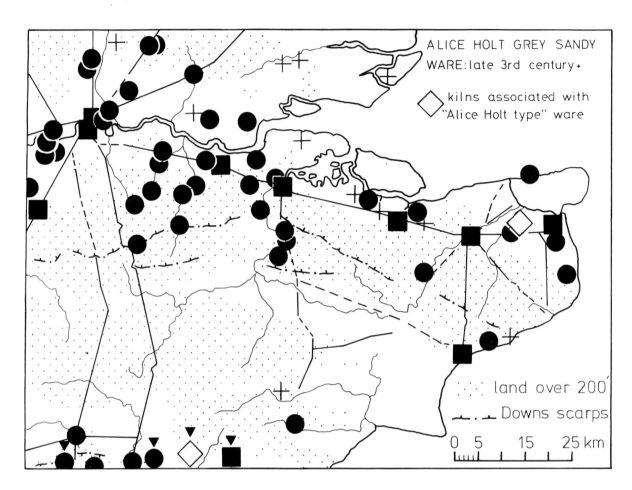

Fig. 38. Late- third-century+ Alice Holt grey sandy ware: Distribution. + = absent.

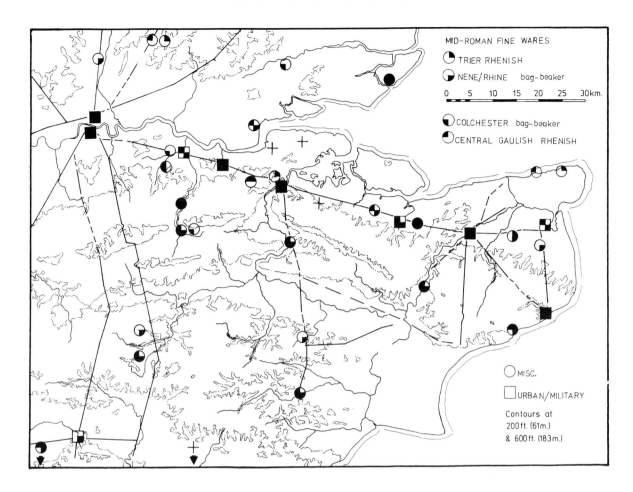

Fig. 39.   Mid-Roman fine wares: Distribution. + = absent.

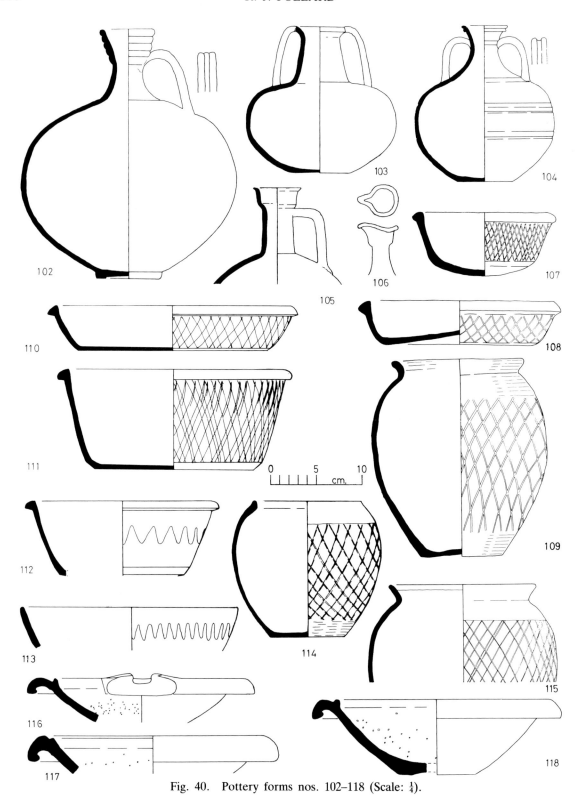

Fig. 40. Pottery forms nos. 102–118 (Scale: $\frac{1}{4}$).

Fig. 40. **102–106**: Otford kiln material; Pearce (1930, 161) describes the fabric as of 'red clay', changing to yellow or brown in the same vessel.

102. Conical-ring-neck flagon, globular body, Pearce 1930, no. K14. **103**. Everted-rim flagon, bulbous body, *ibid.*, no. K12. **104**. 'Pulley-rim' flagon, *ibid.*, no. K2. **105**. Collared-rim cupped-mouth flagon, *ibid.*, no. K7. **106**. Pinched-lip jug, *ibid.*, no. K10.

107–109: Sandy reduced burnished BB2-derived ware.

107. Deep pie-dish, cf. Gillam 1970, Type 222; Detsicas 1966, no. 182.

108. Shallow pie-dish, cf. Gillam and Mann 1970, no. 22; Detsicas 1966, no. 175. **109**. Everted-recurved-rim jar, cf. Gillam 1970, Type 137; Detsicas 1966, no. 125.

110–115: BB2.

110. Triangular-rim pie-dish, Gillam and Mann 1970, fig. 2, no. 22; Pollard 1983b, no. 18, Oakleigh Farm, Higham, kiln. **111**. Rectangular-rim pie-dish, Gillam 1970, Type 222; Pollard 1983b, no. 19. **112**. Triangular-rim pie-dish, Gillam 1970, Type 223; Pollard 1983b, no. 20. **113**. Plain-rim dog-dish, Gillam 1970, Type 328; Pollard 1983b, no. 1. **114**. Bead-rim jar, Gillam and Mann 1970, fig. 2, no. 14; Bushe-Fox 1949, no. 427. **115**. Everted-rim jar, Gillam 1970, Type 137; Pollard forthcoming, b, no. 73.

116–118: Iron-free Gault Clay fabric ('Kent/Colchester cream-buff ware') with flint trituration grit; possibly products of an undetected kiln in the vicinity of Rochester (Hartley 1972).

116. Hooked flange with bead level with top of flange, mortarium, Hartley 1972, no. 35. **117**. Hooked flange with low bead, mortarium, overfired, *ibid.*, no. 32. **118**. Form as no. 116 above, *ibid.*, no. 30.

Dating: 102–106: Late first century. 107–109: Hadrianic. 110–112: *c.* 120–210 (Gillam 1970). 113: *c.* A.D. 130–200 (Gillam 1970). 114: Mid- to late second century. 115: Hadrianic to first half of fourth century. 116–118: *c.* A.D. 100–150.

Fig. 41. **119–123**: Fine reduced ware.

119. Biconical beaker, rouletted, Bushe-Fox 1932, no. 292. **120**. Carinated/sub-biconical bowl, Bushe-Fox 1949, no. 445. **121**. Angular-bead-rim biconical jar, Bushe-Fox 1926, no. 75. **122**. Comb-incised butt-beaker, Cunliffe 1968, no. 541. **123**. Pedestal urn with carinated shoulder, rouletted and 'compass'-incised, Couchman 1924, no. 2.

124: Fabric uncertain; quoit-base pedestal urn, Bushe-Fox 1925, pl. XI, no. 6, from Folkestone (same vessel as Winbolt 1925b, fig. 1B).

125–135: Fine reduced ware.

125. Bead-rim S-jar, Bushe Fox 1932, no. 273. **126**. High-shouldered short-everted-rim beaker, rouletted, *ibid.*, no. 279. **127**. Form as no. 126 above, but globular, *ibid.*, no. 280. **128**. Sub-cylindrical small-everted-rim beaker, 'compass'-incised, Marsh 1978, Type 22.12 type-sherd. **129**. Short-everted-rim 'poppyhead' beaker with barbotine dot panels, Bushe-Fox 1949, no. 417. **130**. Flange-rim segmental bowl, Whiting *et al.* 1931, no. 671. **131**. 'Hammerhead'-flange-rim segmental bowl, Marsh and Tyers 1976, no. 151. **132**. Bead-rim segmental bowl recurved to base, Bushe-Fox 1932, no. 235. **133**. 'Drag. 30'-derived bowl, 'compass'-incised, Mucking, unpublished; drawn by kind permission of Mr T.A. Jones. **134**. 'Drag. 27'-derived cup, Bushe-Fox 1932, no. 225. **135**. Flange-rim segmental bowl with domed basal 'kick' and rouletted flange, Tyers and Marsh 1978, Type VC 1 type-sherd.

Dating: 119–21: Late first to early second century. 122–123: late first century. 124. Coarse Ware Fabric 11A, late first century B.C. to first century A.D.; Fine Ware Fabric 24A, as no. 122. 125. Late first to early (or mid-) second century. 126. Flavian. 127–128. Flavian to Trajanic. 129. Late Flavian to early second century. 130. Late first to second century. 131–134. As no. 125. 135. *c.* A.D. 90–130 (Southwark).

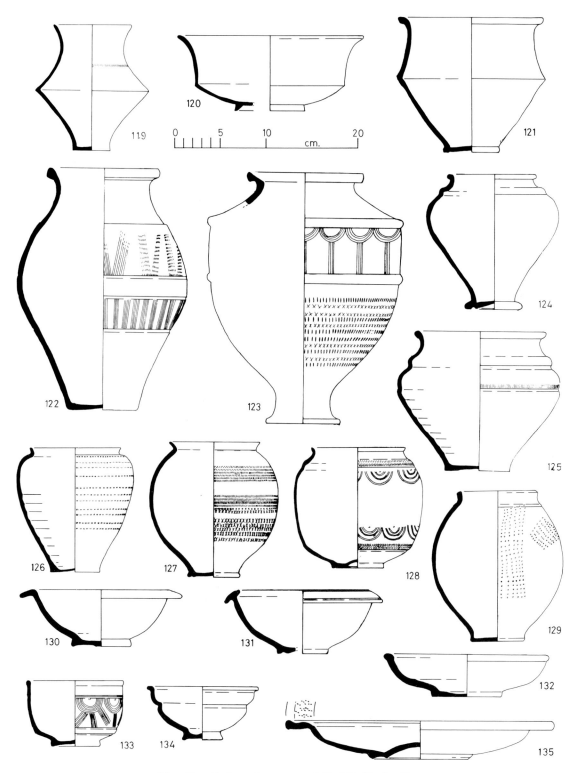

Fig. 41.   Pottery forms nos. 119–135 (Scale: ¼).

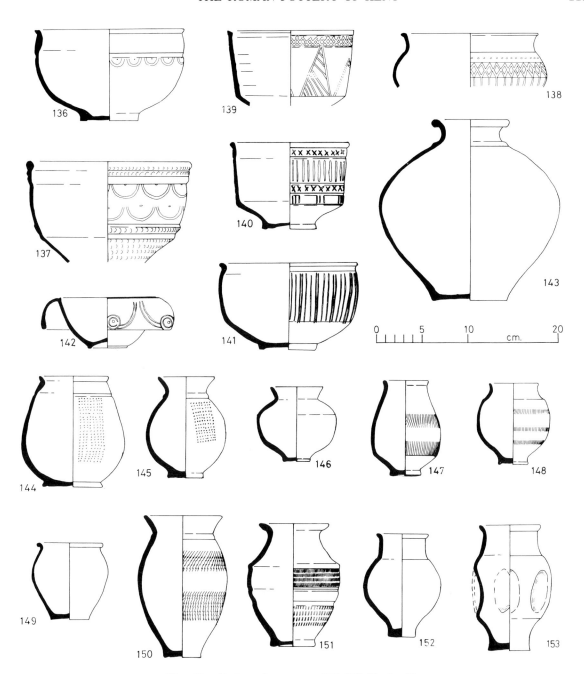

Fig. 42.   Pottery forms nos. 136–153 (Scale: ¼).

Fig. 42.   **136–137**:   Fine oxidised ware.

136. 'Drag. 37'-derived hemispherical bowl, 'compass'-incised, Philp 1963a, no. 17. **137**. 'Drag. 29/30'-derived(?) bowl, rouletted and 'compass'-incised, *ibid.*, no. 18.

138–142:   'Upchurch' painted ware.

138. Oxidised, orange slip, white paint; S-bowl, Springhead, unpublished. **139**. Fabric as no. 138 above; 'Drag. 30'-derived bowl, Springhead, unpublished. **140**. Fabric as no. 138 but with cream paint; form as no. 139 above, Cunliffe 1968, no. 597. **141**. Reduced, orange-pink slip, white paint, carinated bowl, Bushe-Fox 1949, no. 454. **142**. Reduced, purple-red slip, white paint; hemispherical bowl with high hook-flange, *ibid.*, no. 441.

143:   Fine reduced ware, rolled-rim narrow-mouth S-jar, Whiting *et al.* 1931, no. 111.

144:   'Highgate Wood' fine sandy grey ware; bead-everted-rim bag-beaker, barbotine dot panels, Tyers and Marsh 1978, Type IIIE 1 type-sherd.

145–146:   Fine reduced ware.

145. Tall-everted-rim globular 'poppyhead' beaker, barbotine dot panels, Bushe-Fox 1932, no. 307. **146**. Everted-rim carinated 'poppyhead' beaker, Whiting *et al.* 1931, no. 172.

147:   Fine oxidised ware; bead-rim carinated bag-beaker, rouletted, Whiting *et al.* 1931, no. 556.

148–153:   Fine reduced ware.

148. Everted-recurved-rim beaker, rouletted, Whiting *et al.* 1931, no. 380. **149**. Rolled-rim beaker, *ibid.*, no. 89. **150**. Tall-everted-rim elliptical 'poppyhead' beaker, rouletted, *ibid.*, no. 256. **151**. Necked everted-rim 'sugarloaf' bulbous-beaker, rouletted, *ibid.*, no. 373. **152**. Bead-rim tall-necked bulbous-beaker, *ibid.*, no. 65. **153**. Form as no. 152 above, but folded/indented, *ibid.*, no. 629.

Dating: 136–137: Late first to early (or mid-) second century. 138–142: Late first to early second century. 143: (Late first to early second) mid-second to early fourth century. 144. Flavian to Antonine (Southwark); early to mid- second century (Verulamium, Wilson 1972). 145–146: Second to mid- (or late) third century. 147: mid- second to first half third century. 148: As nos. 145–146. 149: Late second to early fourth (?) century. 150–153: Late second to early fourth century.

Fig. 43.   **154**:   Fine reduced ware; plain-rim necked squat bulbous-beaker, rouletted, Whiting *et al.* 1931, no. 15.

155–157:   Fine oxidised ware with white slip.

155. Triangular-lip ring-neck bag-shaped flagon, Whiting *et al.* 1931, no. 549. **156**. Cupped-ring-neck globular flagon, *ibid.*, no. 571. **157**. 'Hammerhead-ringed' bag-shaped flagon, *ibid.*, no. 260.

158–166:   Fine oxidised ware.

158. 'Ring-neck' tall-neck flagon, Whiting *et al.* 1931, no. 283. **159**. Cupped-mouth elliptical flagon, *ibid.*, no. 124. **160**. Conical-mouth flagon, *ibid.*, no. 389. **161**. Cupped-ring-neck bag-shaped flagon, *ibid.*, no. 248. **162**. 'Drag. 38'-derived bowl, *ibid.*, no. 382. **163**. 'Ludowici Tg' grooved-flange-rim segmental bowl, *ibid.*, no. 317. **164**. 'Drag. 36'-derived bowl, *ibid.*, no. 547. **165**. Plain-rim segmental bowl, possibly derived from Drag. 32, *ibid.*, no. 174. **166**. Bead-rim segmental bowl, possibly derived from Drag. 31, *ibid.*, no. 173.

Dating: 154: Late second to early fourth century. 155: Mid- to late second century (?). 156–61: Mid-second to early third century. 162: Late second to third century (?). 163–164: Very late first to early second (possibly mid- second), late second to third century (?). 165: As no. 162. 166: As nos. 163–164.

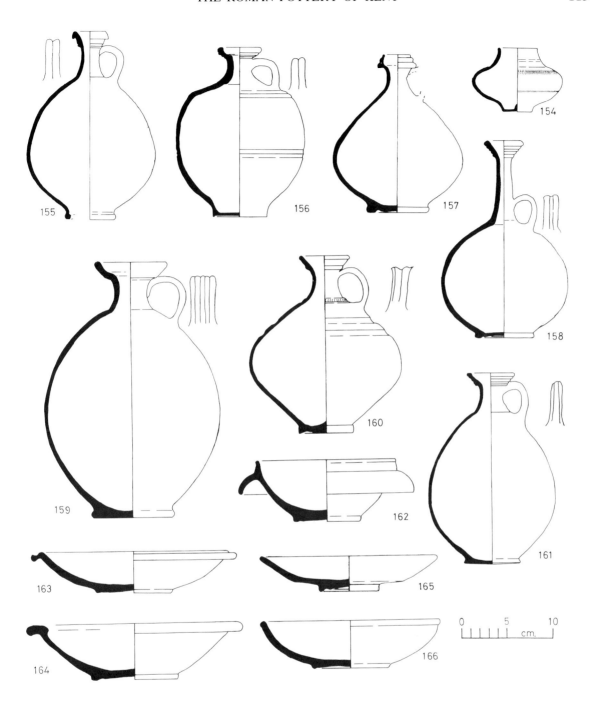

Fig. 43. Pottery forms nos. 154–166 (Scale: ¼).

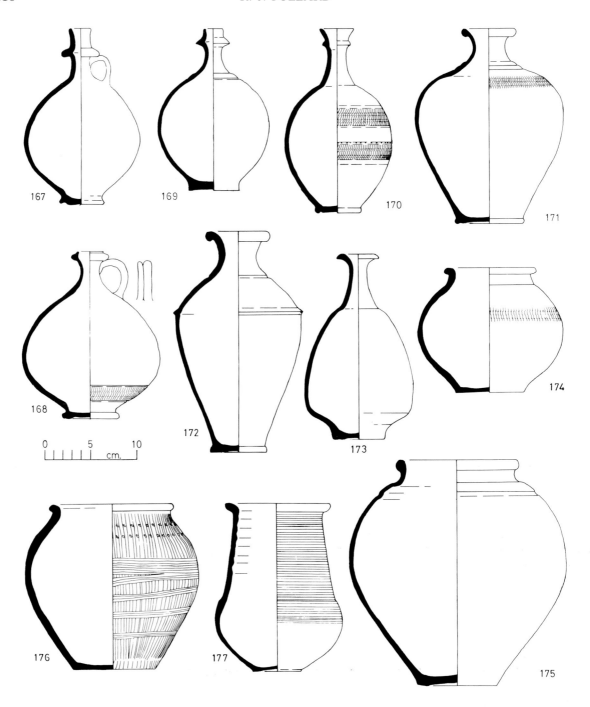

Fig. 44.   Pottery forms nos. 167–177 (Scale: $\frac{1}{4}$).

Fig. 44. **167–169**: Fine oxidised ware.
167. Flanged-neck flagon, Whiting *et al.* 1931, no. 529. **168**. Bead-rim bag-shaped flanged-neck flagon, rouletted, *ibid.*, no. 222. **169**. Flanged-neck flask, *ibid.*, no. 68.

170–175: Fine reduced ware.
170. Flanged-neck flask, rouletted, Whiting *et al.* 1931, no. 185. **171**. Rolled-rim ovoid flask, rouletted, *ibid.*, no. 119. **172**. Rolled-rim ovoid flask, with cordon at girth, *ibid.*, no. 314. **173**. Everted-rim tall-neck bag-shaped flask, *ibid.*, no. 190. **174**. Short-everted-rim necked globular jar, rouletted, *ibid.*, no. 631. **175**. Rolled-rim necked jar, *ibid.*, no. 66.

176: Coarse sandy grey wheel-thrown ware, an import from Gallia Belgica or the lower Rhineland; bead-rim globular jar with stabbed/rouletted shoulder and combed lattice, Dover, unpublished.

177: 'Arras' North Gaulish fine sandy grey wheel-thrown ware; '*vase tronconique*' (Richardson and Tyers 1984): tall-neck everted-rim bulbous-beaker with burnished lines on neck, Tuffreau-Libre 1980b, fig. 13, no. 3.

Dating: 167–169: Late second to early third century. 170–175: Late second to early fourth century. 176: Late second to early/mid- third century. 117: (Late first to early second), mid- second to early third century.

IV. SEVERUS ALEXANDER TO THE BRITANNIC EMPIRE, *c.* A.D. 220–300

1. *The Fine Wares*

The most striking differences between fine ware assemblages of this period and those of the Hadrianic to Severan era are the almost complete absence of known imports from the Continent. The exotic wares that have been recognised came mainly from the East Gaulish region, including samian (e.g. Pryce 1949, 183; Pl. LXXXIV, fig. 1, no. 74), 'Rhenish' ware (*Moselkeramik*; cf. Greene 1978c, 56) from Trier, and mottled colour-coated flagons (Bird 1981, Bird and Williams 1983) from the Rhineland. The Westerndorf factory in Raetia (Fig. 59) also supplied samian to Britain, and it is possible that the East Gaulish kilns at Lavoye and Pfaffenhofen did, too. These four samian industries may have continued to operate into the 260s (King 1981), but may not have been exporting to Britain any later than the 240s (*ibid.*). Westerndorf is represented by a sherd of a Drag. 37 hemispherical bowl from Canterbury of *c.* A.D. 200–250 (Simpson 1970, no. 15), but it is uncertain whether the other sources of samian supplied Kent in this period. Second- and early third-century samian is often encountered in later third- and even fourth-century assemblages; it may be proposed that much of this material remained intact, perhaps with an heirloom status involving only occasional utilisation, throughout the third century. Orton and Orton (1975) have argued that on two sites in the London area samian of all periods had an average life expectancy of some 20–30 years, and this is illustrated by the association of samian with mid/late third- to fourth-century tall-necked bulbous beakers in Oxfordshire colour-coated ware (no. 532) and Oxfordshire/Nene Valley colour-coated ware (no. 233) in burials at Ospringe (Groups CLXV and LXVIII, respectively: Whiting *et al.* 1931). The former group contains a flagon base (no. 531), the latter a Drag. 35 or 36 bowl (no. 234) both in pale pink ware of possibly Central Gaulish origin. More remarkable still is the late second-century samian bowl inscribed with a *Chi Rho* graffito of a style current in the second half of the fourth century, found unstratified in Canterbury (Day 1980, 6). These finds are exceptional, and it is extremely difficult to ascertain the general rate of survival of serviceable samian during the late Roman period in Britain.

The importation of Trier 'Rhenish' ware is thought to have ceased in the mid-third century (Greene 1978c, 56) at a time when the incursions of barbarian raiders wrought considerable damage to the East Gaulish potteries (*ibid.*, 57). Occasional survivals of complete vessels are encountered, however; the votive beaker from Lullingstone (Meates 1979, 36 and Plate Va and b) may be an example. The trade in mottled-slip flagons may have survived the mid-third century. These vessels (see Appendix 2 for description) are dated to the third century in Germany (Gose 1950, Type 262), and occur in contexts of the mid-third century or later in Britain (Bird 1981; Bird and Williams 1983) where dateable. Kent and London would seem to have been the main recipients of these vessels, including finds at Dover, Richborough (Bushe-Fox 1949, no. 379), Ospringe (Whiting *et al.* 1931, no. 263), Lyminge (Kelly 1962: vessel in Maidstone Museum), Eastry (Pollard 1982, no. 12) and Canterbury (M. Green, pers. comm.), the latter in contexts securely dateable to the mid-fourth century A.D. (Green forthcoming). Pitchers in similar ware, probably from the Trier area, are represented by body sherds of two vessels from Canterbury (Bird 1982a; the forms are Gose 1950, Types 277/278/280 and Type 272). These are forms of a late third- to fourth-century date in Germany.

Samian of second- to early third-century date can form a large proportion of the third-century fine wares; for example at Chalk the lowest layer in the third century cellar (Johnston 1972, layer 8) included samian to the sum of roughly one-quarter of the fine wares (Appendix 5 here). However, fine reduced wares are consistently predominant over both Continental and Romano-British colour-coated wares in quantitative terms. Canterbury fine ware assemblages of late second to mid-third, and mid-third to early fourth-century dates include between 50 per cent and 90 per cent of this ware (by vessel rim equivalents), the lower figures reflecting the presence of samian. The proportion of total assemblages of fine and coarse wares that fine reduced wares comprise ranges from 12 per cent to 35 per cent. In west Kent these wares were of less importance relative to others, rarely totalling more than 5 per cent of a complete assemblage, or more than around half of a fine ware assemblage (Appendix 5). This differentiation is in part due to the presence of fine sandy burnished wares of Cliffe peninsula or south Essex origin (Fig. 46), which included flasks and beakers in their range of forms (4.V.2). It is argued that the Upchurch Marshes industry declined in output during the third century, with the Cliffe area taking a major share of the market for finely-finished products in the area between the Darent and the Medway.

The 'poppyhead' beaker, including plain, rouletted and barbotine decorated types (nos. 145, 150 and 146 here), appears to have remained the dominant fine reduced ware form for perhaps the first two-thirds of the century, in company with necked bulbous (nos. 152–4) and bag-shaped beakers (cf. no. 147), flasks (nos. 170–3), everted- and cavetto-rim beakers and jars of BB2 form and decoration, and bead-rim necked jars and bowls (e.g. nos. 143, 174–5). Segmental bowls, often with grooved-flange rims (cf. nos. 130 and 163) occur less frequently, but are present both in east and west Kent. Cordoned bead-rim necked jars and bowls became increasingly important amongst fine reduced wares at Canterbury and possibly also in west Kent, if the evidence from late third-century deposits at Chalk (Johnston 1972: quantification by the present author) is representative. This may have been due to the increasing availability of colour-coated beakers from British industries that is a feature of the last third of the third century, but it is not certain that these types were very much more common than 'Rhenish' (Trier black colour-coated or '*Moselkeramik*' ware) and 'Castor' wares (Nene Valley, Rhineland and Colchester bag-beakers with barbotine or rouletted decoration) were in the earlier years of this century.

The production of red-surfaced fine wares, thought to have begun on the Upchurch Marshes or in the Swale area in the early third century consequent upon the dearth of samian imports, may have continued into the mid-third, although there is little hard evidence for this. Red ware flagons and flasks seem to have declined in popularity, along with white-surface flagons, in the early third century. Vessels of these types produced by subsequent generations of Romano-British potters particularly in the fourth century tend to exhibit reduced or dark brown surfaces (cf. e.g. Fulford 1975a, Types 1–16; Young 1977a, 123, and Types R1–R14; Lyne and Jefferies 1979, Class 8; Howe *et al*. 1980, nos. 13, 14, 63–70), for which inspiration may be sought in the black colour-coated flagons and flasks produced by Trier until the middle of the third century, although not exported to Britain (R. Symonds, pers. comm.). Beakers also tend to have dark surfaces, although this tradition may be traced back to the first-century *Terra Nigra* and rough-cast wares. These preferences help explain the rarity of flasks and beakers in fine oxidised wares in the third century, although other industries such as that at Much Hadham in Hertfordshire, and the establishments responsible for 'streak-burnished' ware found at Canterbury (Green 1981), also produced orange and red closed forms.

The pottery industry at Much Hadham, near Bishop's Stortford in Hertfordshire, became a major supplier of oxidised fine sandy wares to East Anglia, Essex and Hertfordshire during the course of the third century. Little is at present known about the industry, whose products have only become widely recognised since the mid-1970s (e.g. Fulford 1975a, fig. 61; Orton 1977b; Partridge 1981); research currently being undertaken (by C. Going, pers. comm.) will alleviate this deficiency. It is known that fine sandy grey, burnished black, and white-slip wares were manufactured in addition to the burnished oxidised wares. In Kent the white-slip ware is confined, on present knowledge, to sherds probably of a single vessel from late second- to mid third-century contexts in Canterbury (Pollard forthcoming, d). A grey ware bead-and-flange bowl from Chalk, found in a fourth-century context (4.V.2), provides an apparently unique instance of one of the most characteristic forms in this ware in Kent, and it may be that the oxidised ware alone achieved a wide usage south of the Thames. This ware had been adopted in London by the mid-third century (Harden and Green 1978), and was current in north-west Kent at least by the last years of the century, as examples sealed by the collapse of the 'cellar' building at Chalk testify (Johnston 1972: these vessels are unpublished). It is possible that a wider distribution in Kent was achieved by the end of this century (cf. Figs. 34 and 51), but most sherds occur in general mid third- to fourth- or purely fourth-century contexts, and the broader aspects of the trade are more appropriately discussed in the section on the fourth century (4.V.1).

'Streak-burnished' ware, a fine-textured oxidised fabric with discrete facet-burnishing, may be a variant of the fine oxidised ware found at Ospringe, many examples of which exhibit a badly deteriorated surface due to soil action. The date range of the former ware at Canterbury is tentatively placed in the century between *c*. A.D. 275 and 375 (Green 1981). The forms include the tall-necked bulbous beakers, S-profile bead-rim jar, Drag. 38-derived and Drag. 36-derived flanged bowls, plain-rim bowls or dishes, and a flange-neck or disc-mouth flask. Decoration appears to be confined to the use of white paint in simple spirals and possibly other linear motifs. It has so far been recognised only at Canterbury, but sherds with abraded or decayed surfaces may be indistinguishable from other fine oxidised wares. The ware was evidently of minor importance in comparison with colour-coated wares of Oxfordshire and Nene Valley sources.

The second quarter of the third century witnessed considerable changes in the production of colour-coated pottery in Britain. The Colchester industry appears to have fallen into decline, perhaps affected by the general recession postulated by Fulford (1975a, 108–9), Young (1977a, 235–6) and others, and also by the loss of its northern markets (Pollard 1983a, 378–83). Hull (1963) attributes only two kilns to the period c. A.D. 210–260, compared with ten in the preceding half-century or so. In the upper Thames valley, the Oxfordshire potteries may have commenced production of red and brown colour-coated wares as early as c. A.D. 240, and certainly by c. A.D. 270 at the latest (Young 1977a, 237–9). In the lower Nene valley, the potter known as Indixivixvs, thought to be an East Gaulish immigrant (Howe et al. 1980, 9), established himself at Stanground sometime in the first half of the century, where distinctive stamped 'imitation samian' and more conventional bag-beakers were produced (Dannell 1973). The mainstream Nene Valley potteries turned to 'funnel-necked' elliptically-folded beakers (Howe et al. 1980, nos. 38–9, 42–3), this form supplanting bag-beakers during the second quarter of the century. Colchester also introduced this form (Hull 1963, Form 407), but it is not yet clear whether bag-beakers continued to be produced alongside it (as the fill of the mid third-century Kiln 32 suggests; ibid.). With the possible exception of Type C22, defined as a tall-necked bulbous beaker, the Oxfordshire industry does not appear to have manufactured colour-coated beakers before c. A.D. 270, and there is no really close parallel to the 'funnel-necked' plain-lip form of the Nene Valley and Colchester.

This tardiness may be the key to a phenomenon that is becoming increasingly apparent at Canterbury, which is the predominance of Nene Valley/Colchester colour-coated ware, and even Nene Valley buff ware mortaria, over Oxfordshire wares in the middle and late years of the third century. At present the recognition of this trend is more a matter of subjective impression than quantified statistics, owing to the lack of diagnostic rim sherds, but sherd counts support this judgement. A direct trade between the Nene valley and east Kent is possible, for this ware is apparently less common in the west of the county in the third and early fourth centuries. Unfortunately, it has proved extremely difficult to distinguish Colchester from Nene Valley colour-coated ware (cf. Orton 1977b), as there is considerable overlap in the buff to brown fabric range of colours as well as in forms. However, study of material from south-east Essex by the present author suggests that the fine sandy brown fabric of Colchester origin is much more common there (e.g. at Heybridge-on-Blackwater and Little Shelford) than in Kent. Hopefully, research currently being undertaken by H. Toller will clarify this issue. Beakers formed a high proportion both of Nene Valley (Howe et al. 1980, 8) and Colchester (Hull 1963) colour-coated products throughout the third century; the market for colour-coated bowls, except for the Stanground pottery and a single 'Drag. 38-derived' vessel from a kiln of c. A.D. 300 at Colchester (Hull 1963, 162, fig. 93, no. 13, of Form 316), appears not to have been catered for at this time. Colour-coated flagons, small dishes, 'Castor boxes' and wall-sided 'Drag. 45-derived' mortaria were all produced in the Nene valley in the third century (Howe et al. 1980, 8 and nos. 84, 89); the 'Castor box' was also a Colchester form, but is known only from kilns of late Antonine-Severan date (Hull 1963, Form 308). The late second- to late third-century vessel was narrow-based, with an angular profile and ledged shoulder taking a conical upright-rimmed lid, both pieces being rouletted. Later examples are more rounded, with a wider base (Howe *et al*. 1980, 24). Examples found in Kent commonly occur in the coarse white fabric that may have been an exclusively late Nene Valley colour-coated ware, and in buff to orange fabric Nene Valley/Colchester ware. Oxfordshire vessels are much less well-known, but include two examples from Ickham (Young 1977a, Types C87.1–2) of late third- to early fifth-century date. Third-century Nene Valley colour-coated ware in Kent consists mainly of beakers and Castor boxes, although occasional flagons and mortaria at Canterbury may be dated to this time (Green, pers. comm.).

The diversity of sources for beakers marketed in Kent in the third century is reflected in the occurrence of an as yet little-recognised fabric that apparently achieved an extensive distribution. The fabric is fine, hard and sandy, with a white or pink core and grey-white, orange-red or buff surfaces. One form has been recognised, a 'sugar-loaf' tall-necked beaker with chamfered shoulder, bead-everted rim and 'finger-nail shape' rouletted decoration (no. 215 here). Sherds have been noted on several sites in Canterbury, and also at Lullingstone, to which may be added two vessels from the Ospringe cemetery (Whiting *et al*. 1931, nos. 86 and 143). The type also occurs at Corbridge (Gillam 1970, Type 42), Little Shelford in Essex (James and James 1978, no. 10; the settlement is dated from the late second to the late third century, and thus the interpretation of this vessel as a first century 'butt-beaker' is unlikely), and at Etaples in the Pas-de-Calais department of France (Tuffreau-Libre 1980a, 101–2, fig. 33, no. 5, in a fabric *'couleur blanche; pâte blanche, à dégraissant sableux'*). Mme Tuffreau-Libre (*ibid*.) cites parallels in Picardy and Colchester, but as the latter is known to be in colour-coated ware (Hull 1963, Form 395) the former may have a formal similarity only. The dating of the Kent and Little Shelford material fits within the range of *c*. A.D. 200–360 cited by Gillam (1970) at Corbridge, but the Etaples vessel is placed in the second century. A large collection of these beakers has been recovered from the site at New Fresh Wharf, London, in a late second- or early third-century context, and others are known from Beauport Park (East Sussex), Shadwell (east London), Brancaster, and Caister-on-Sea (Norfolk) (Richardson and Tyers 1984). They are thought to hail from the Somme valley, and have a third-century *floruit* (*ibid*., 138), perhaps somewhat later than the 'Arras' grey ware described above (4.III.1) but from the same region and with an overlap in date demonstrated by their mutual association at New Fresh Wharf.

Oxfordshire fine wares are more a feature of the fourth than of the third century in Kent. It is clear from the sealed deposits in the Chalk 'cellar' (Johnston 1972) that red colour-coated ware at least was reaching west Kent by the end of the third century, while a complete Parchment ware bowl from a mid-third century pit at Richborough (Bushe-Fox 1949, no. 460) provides possible evidence of an early trade extending to the Straits of Dover. Two beakers from Ospringe are associated with samian ware in burials (Whiting *et al*. 1931, nos. 233 – possibly from Oxfordshire – and 532). Frere (1970, 107–8) has argued that Oxfordshire red colour-coated ware arrived in Canterbury in the third quarter of the third century, but the body of evidence is small; there is little from the extensive Marlowe Car Park excavations in the city to support this proposition, and a *terminus post quem* in the final quarter of the third or even the early fourth century for large-scale importation of this ware is more probable. Most other sites in all parts of Kent offer little scope for dating the arrival of Oxfordshire wares, despite Young's assertion that Kent was a 'major market' in the third century (1977a, 133). Only one colour-coated ware type is confined to this century, the 'ovolo-stamped' hemispherical bowl (*ibid.*, C58). A single sherd of this has been noted from a site just north of Richborough, from which has been recovered pottery of first- to fourth-century date (Cottington Lane, on the Isle of Thanet; information from N. Macpherson-Grant, pottery identification by the present author). Young published a single example of this type from the Churchill Hospital kiln site in Oxford (1977a, 162–3) within a third-century phase. Negative evidence from mid third-century contexts at Lullingstone (Meates *et al.* 1952, nos. 59–66; the room number has been changed from 15 to 10 for the definitive report, Meates 1979) and Maidstone Mount (unpublished) villas provides some support for the view that Oxfordshire fine wares were extremely rare, if present at all, in most of Kent before the late third century. However, it is clear from the Chalk 'cellar' assemblage that a variety of forms in red colour-coated ware was circulating in the final quarter of the century, including tall- necked bulbous beakers (Young 1977a, C27), 'Drag. 38' flanged hemispherical bowls (*ibid.*, C51 and C109), painted-flange-rim segmental bowls (*ibid.*, C48), and bead-rim hemispherical bowls (*ibid.*, C55). Mortaria of samian 'Drag. 45' derivation (*ibid.*, C97) may have also been used at this time. The Parchment ware bowl from Richborough is apparently a unique example of unequivocally third-century importation of this ware to Kent.

Fine white-surfaced wares are generally uncommon in this century in Kent. Flagons would seem to have been used less than in the preceding centuries. The cupped ring-neck form (no. 161 here) may have lasted into the early decades of the third century, and such vessels usually have a pale buff to white surface. Flange-neck flagons and flasks (nos. 167, 169–170), a more typically late second- to fourth-century form, occasionally have pale surfaces. The popularity of dark-surfaced flagons and flasks has been mentioned earlier in this section. White ware flasks with red paint zonal decoration, possibly from the Nene valley (Howe *et al.* 1980, no. 95), are represented on several sites in contexts of third- to fourth-century date, although in contrast with Nene Valley beakers and mortaria of this period, these occurrences are biased towards the Medway valley (Appendix 3). Other forms are occasionally found with white surfaces, including the carinated bowl in Oxfordshire Parchment ware (Bushe-Fox 1949, no. 460), and a 'Drag. 38' flanged hemispherical bowl in white-slipped fine oxidised ware (from a late second- to mid third-century deposit in Canterbury: unpublished).

Fulford (1975a, 108–9) has suggested that 'the demand for red slipped wares, and possibly all fine, slipped pottery decreased significantly in the third century in comparison with the second'. The basis for this proposition is the low incidence of such wares on British sites subsequent to the cessation of Central Gaulish samian production in the early third century. It is clear from the foregoing discussion that a variety of fine red ware bowls was in use in Kent in the third century, but the small body of quantified data on samian and other fine wares does seem to support Fulford's hypothesis, at least with regard to red bowls. There is no indication of a synchronous decline in the circulation of slipped beakers, although the third-century sources supplying Kent differ to a large extent from those of the Antonine period. The Upchurch Marshes fine ware industry may have waned in the third century, due in part to competition from fine sandy burnished wares produced on the Cliffe peninsula, but possibly also to the slow encroachment of the sea upon the area of the marshes where potting is thought to have taken place (5.II.4). A late third-century resurgence in the production of fine pottery in Roman Britain is indicated by the development of the Oxfordshire and New Forest industries, and at a more local level perhaps also 'streak-burnished' ware in east Kent. Fulford (1975a, 109–11) links this to a general economic expansion connected with the large outlay of public money on projects such as the

'Saxon Shore' fort system and the construction of town walls. Kent was clearly affected by these developments, three forts being built in the late third century (Dover, Port Lympne and Richborough – Cunliffe 1980, 285–7), along with the city walls of Canterbury and possibly Rochester (Frere *et al.* 1982; Pollard 1981a). On present evidence the use of fine pottery in Kent did not increase markedly in this period, despite the importation of Oxfordshire wares; a more modest expansion in the fine ware market is plausible, however, at least in terms of the ratio of fine to coarse pottery consumption.

2. *The Coarse Wares of West Kent*

The most striking feature of the coarse pottery of west Kent in the middle and later years of the third century is the high degree of conservatism expressed. The region is dominated by coarse and fine sandy, fine sandy burnished and BB2 wares, for which kiln sites are known on the Cliffe peninsula. Other wares of probably local origin are confined to a handful of 'Patch Grove' and grog-tempered storage jars, and a small quantity of grog-tempered jars and dishes. The importation of coarse wares may have begun in the final quarter of the century, comprising grey fine sandy slipped ware from the Alice Holt forest (Surrey-Hampshire border) and BB1 from Dorset. It is possible that some fine grey sandy wheel-thrown jars were also imported from north of the Thames. Mortaria were also imported from Oxfordshire and, possibly, also east Kent and the Surrey-Sussex region. With the collapse of the trade in amphorae with southern Spain at the end of the second century, the acquisition of coarse pottery either as containers or for the vessels' intrinsic worth appears to have ceased for a century or more.

The range of pottery produced by the kilns of the Cliffe peninsula, including Higham (Catherall 1983, Kilns B and C) and possibly Cooling (Pollard forthcoming, b), and also on the Essex side of the lower Thames (Mucking – Jones and Rodwell 1973, Kilns IV, V and possibly III), underwent little augmentation in the period under review. The late second-century forms described above (4.III.2) continued to be produced, with the notable exceptions of the pie-dish, decorated dishes, and lid-seated jar (no. 201 here). The middle years of the third century apparently witnessed a 'phasing-out' of the plain pie-dish (and also of its decorated counterpart, if this had not already been discarded) in favour of the bead-and-flange dish. The latter form is absent (in BB2) from Carpow, a fort on the River Tay in eastern Scotland which received BB2 apparently until its military abandonment *c.* A.D. 215/216 (Wright 1974; information on the pottery from J. P. Gillam), but is present in quantity in the Chalk cellar material of the last quarter of the third century, where it outnumbers pie-dishes by between 9:1 and 15:1 (Johnston 1972, layers 8 and 7, respectively, nos. 32 and 34; quantification by the present author). At Lullingstone it is absent from the late second- to mid third-century context in Room 10 (Pollard 1987, Group XVII) where pie- and dog-dishes were apparently common (Meates *et al.* 1952, nos. 44–58); two vessels of uncertain fabric, but Cliffe peninsula/Mucking form (*ibid.*, nos. 63–4) occur in a later third-century group along with a coin of Severus Alexander, samian of *c.* A.D. 200, and a late second- to early fourth-century cavetto rim folded jar (no. 192 here), the deposit being sealed by a mid fourth-century level (Meates 1979, 50–1, and fig. 10). It is possible that the plain dog-dish increased in usage during the middle of the third century in relation to other dish forms, but the Chalk evidence suggests that this may have been short-lived.

Bead-and-flange dishes are known from kiln sites at Higham (Pollard 1983b, Gross Form V;

nos. 189–190 here) and Mucking (Jones and Rodwell 1973, Types C and D), and at Cooling in groups possibly to be interpreted as kiln discards (Pollard forthcoming, b; no. 188 here). With the exception of Mucking Type D, which is in a coarse sandy ware, these vessels are all in BB2, which apparently continued to be produced throughout the third century, although possibly declining in amounts relative to other wares (Appendix 5). Cavetto-rim jars in BB2, and angular roll-rim/everted-rim necked jars (nos. 197, 199 here) in grey sandy ware, were the standard jar forms of this period, with folded jars being of minor quantitative importance. Unburnished ware fabrics of the later third century are often finer than Antonine-Severan examples, and both these and BB2 can exhibit a russet-coloured 'scorching' possibly the result of improved technology enabling higher firing temperatures to be reached. This phenomenon is also seen on sandy wares in east Kent of third-century date (4.IV.3). One jar form which emerged in the later third century in north-west Kent has a finely-moulded 'swan's-neck' pendant-bead rim (no. 203 here). This form occurs infrequently in north-west Kent, but is seemingly abundant in the Roding valley, for example at Chigwell Little London (unpublished), and fairly common at Old Ford (e.g. Sheldon 1971, fig. 8, nos. 32–5; Sheldon 1972, fig. 8, nos. 30–2, 38, fig. 10, no. 6). A vessel from Aldgate, London (Chapman and Johnson 1973, fig. 17, no. 253) is dated to the late second to early third century. This type usually occurs in a fine sandy ware, and is known from third-century kilns at Higham (Pollard 1983b, no. 64), Mucking (Jones and Rodwell 1973, no. 47, plus a narrow-necked jar no. 79) and Orsett (Rodwell 1974, no. 62), as well as from kiln sites further afield (e.g. Ecton, Northants.: Johnston 1969; Alice Holt–Farnham on the Surrey-Hampshire border: Lyne and Jefferies 1979, Class 3C 8–9).

On the strength of the distribution of BB2 bead-and-flange dishes, it would appear that the lower Thames kilns maintained their marketing zone in Kent throughout the third century (Fig. 46, 'flanged bowl'; see also 4.IV.3–4). However, there is some evidence to suggest minor fluctuations in supply, or at least in the cost of products. A mid third-century rubbish deposit from the Maidstone Mount villa (unpublished), which includes a large quantity of BB2 and other reduced sandy wares, also contains sherds in grog-tempered ware, amounting to 11 per cent of the total assemblage. The forms are mostly recurved everted-rim jars and dog-dishes, plus an everted necked jar. There is no reason to suppose that these are not contemporaneous with the deposit, but the quantity is unparalleled on other sites of the third century in west Kent; for example, only a single rim sherd has been recorded from the sealed 'cellar' deposits at Chalk, and they were apparently absent from the filling of the west drain at Darenth (Philp 1973, 152–3 and fig. 45, nos. 420–440). Meates and his colleagues published a 'Patch Grove type' everted necked jar from the later third-century group in Room 10 (originally Room 15) at Lullingstone (Meates *et al.* 1952, no. 65; Pollard 1987, Group XXV). This pottery would appear to be chronologically distinct from the grog-tempered ware of fourth-century date found throughout Kent. The Maidstone site lies only some 25 km. from the Cliffe peninsula kilns, and is easily accessible by river. It is plausible that the pottery represents a short-lived 'household product' (cf. 6.II) made to supplement sandy ware and BB2 imports during a period when the latter were unable to meet local demand at a satisfactory cost. The unusually small quantity of fine wares from the rubbish deposit and the presence of the grog-tempered ware contrast with the wealth manifested in the alterations carried out on the villa prior to the accumulation of this rubbish, leading to the suggestion that the latter comprises kitchen waste. Other non-sandy wares of third-century date are confined to occasional sherds of storage jars in grog-tempered ware (e.g. the 'wedge' used to support Bust II in the late third-century reorganisation of the 'Deep Room' at Lullingstone: Meates *et al.* 1952, no. 38; not necessarily a 'first century survival' as Meates [1979, 36] has postulated) and 'Patch Grove' ware (e.g. Meates *et al.* 1952, no. 66; Johnston 1972, no. 1). The possibility that the latter continued to be produced in storage jar forms into the third century should not be overlooked.

BB1, probably from Dorset, was imported from the end of the second or the early third century into west Kent, but occurs with an irregularity suggestive of a sporadic rather than continuous trade. It is present in contexts probably of the late second to mid-third century at Springhead and Cobham Park but absent from the Maidstone Mount rubbish deposit and the lowest layer in the Chalk 'cellar' (Johnston 1972, layer 8). One rim possibly in Dorset BB1 from the latter site (layer 7) suggests that this trade was operating in the late third century also, but it is conceivable that it ceased entirely in the middle years of the century (see also the following section).

There is no certain evidence for Alice Holt grey wares reaching Kent before the fourth century, although undiagnostic sherds may be represented in the Chalk 'cellar' groups of the late third. Lyne and Jefferies (1979, 56) have observed a marked increase in this ware in London from around A.D. 290, subsequent to the revitalisation of the industry around A.D. 270 that involved a much enlarged scale of production and the introduction of a thick slip firing to white, grey or black, which is the single most characteristic feature of late Alice Holt ware. As in the late first century, the capture of the London market did not signal a massive influx of pottery into Kent, but the ware is frequently encountered in mixed later third- to fourth-century assemblages, so that a late third-century trade in west Kent cannot be ruled out. There seems little likelihood that any such commercial activity overlapped with the importation of 'Surrey-Sussex' white sandy ware mortaria, as these are conventionally dated to *c*. A.D. 150–250 (Hartley 1973a; *q.v.* 4.III.2), although it is possible that they continued to be imported to Kent up to the end of their production.

The trade in mortaria may have slackened in the first half of the third century. Thick-hook-flange and 'hammer-head' white ware vessels may have been procured from Colchester, where they were produced as late as the middle of the century (Hull 1963, Forms 498–9), but the two vessels from Darenth (Philp 1973, nos. 345 and 353) may be Antonine-Severan in date. Two 'hammer-head' flange vessels from Snodland may represent importation of 'east Kent' oxidised ware in the mid- to late third century (Cook 1928, no. 5; Ocock and Syddell 1967, no. 21), and others of this type occur on third-fourth century sites at Otford (the 'Progress' site), Maidstone Mount, and Springhead, in both sandy and untempered wares (4.IV.3). The expansion of the Oxfordshire potteries in the mid-third century (Young 1977a, 237–9) led to a much wider circulation of white ware mortaria than this source had achieved in the second and early third centuries (*ibid.*, 61–8), bringing Kent into its marketing sphere for the first time. The tall bead-wide-flanged form M17 (*ibid.*, 72–4), dated *c*. A.D. 240–300, is found on a number of sites in Kent, including the Otford 'Progress' and Charne sites, Maidstone Mount, Dartford, Chalk and Lullingstone in the west. It is possible that this circulation was achieved during the third quarter of the century, prior to the marketing of colour-coated wares on a significant scale (see above). Other third-century Oxfordshire mortaria also occur in west Kent, adding Joyden's Wood and Springhead to the list of recipients in this century (Appendix 3); Nene Valley buff ware reeded-flange mortaria occur only at Lullingstone in west Kent (Meates 1953, no. 146; Pollard 1987, Fabric 42) but in unstratified deposits. In east Kent they occur in deposits of later third- to mid fourth-century date (see below).

The termination in the trade with Baetica in amphorae carrying olive oil, possibly a result of Severus' confiscations following his victory over Albinus (Callender 1965, xxix; but cf. Todd 1981, 168 and 191), brought an end to large-scale importation of amphorae to Britain. However, Peacock (1977d, e) has recently demonstrated that some late Roman amphorae do occur in Britain, including Tunisian vessels and Mediterranean vessels of uncertain origin. Sherds of the latter have been recorded by Peacock from the Chalk 'cellar' (1977d). The tumulus burial at Holborough, Snodland (Jessup *et al.* 1954) included five amphorae, one of which may be of South Spanish origin (Callender 1965, 47–8); the pottery from the burial included late second- to fourth- and mid to late fourth-century dishes in BB1 (Jessup *et al.*, 1954, fig. 14, nos. 2, 4 and 7) and glass vessel fragments also of a possible third-century date. It is to be hoped that the amphorae will be subjected to petrological analysis in an effort to shed some light on their origins (see Peacock 1977e).

3. *The Coarse Wares of East Kent*

The study of pottery of the mid- to late third century in east Kent leans heavily on the evidence from Canterbury. The Saxon Shore forts at Reculver, Dover and Port Lympne, other occupation sites, and earlier phases at the first three sites have so far produced very little in the way of published third-century assemblages, although a large body of third-century pottery is undoubtedly incorporated in the Richborough reports in unstratified or disturbed deposits (for example, the fills of the mid third-century triple-ditched fortlet – Bushe Fox 1929; 1932). Other sites are dateable solely by parallels with Canterbury or with reference to the widest possible date-ranges of imported wares; of these sites, a third-century group may be recognised at Wingham, and wells including material of this date from Birchington (Wells 2 and 15, unpublished). The following survey is effectively one of the pottery from Canterbury, with some reference being made to material from other sites.

The bulk of the pottery from the middle years of the century shows little change from that in use in the first two decades (4.III.3). The main developments comprise the introduction of the bead-and-flange dish in BB2, and the increasing use of BB1, probably from Dorset, in a volume suggestive of a regular trade rather than the occasional importation that took place in late second to early third century. Some change in the supply of mortaria is also discernible, involving the cessation of importation of Colchester and possibly also 'Surrey-Sussex' wares, and the acquisition of Nene Valley and Oxfordshire vessels from perhaps the third quarter of the century, supplementing the probably indigenous oxidised flint-trituration-gritted ware. Towards the end of the third century a hand-made, grog-tempered ware begins to appear which is in all probablity the product of local, scattered household industries (cf. 6.I). A second indigenous ware of this kind of production unit may be represented by a BB1 fabric that first appears in the very late third or early fourth century, and is visually distinguishable from designated Dorset (Wareham/Poole Harbour) ware. Dorset-type BB1 continued to be imported, however, and represents the only cooking ware for which a non-Kent derivation is certain that is present in mid- to late third-century deposits in Canterbury. 'Swan's neck' pendant-bead-rim jars occur very rarely, and may be imports from north-west Kent or Essex. The high-fired grog- and grog-and-sand tempered 'Native Coarse Ware' may have declined in usage during the second half of the century, but sherds are found in many fourth-century assemblages suggesting that production did not entirely cease.

The most common wares throughout the second and third quarters of the century are, as in the Severan period, in sand-tempered wheel-thrown fabrics. Burnished unslipped fine and coarse wares and BB2 predominate, with plain sandy ware somewhat less. Scorched and vitrified sherds occur not infrequently, but are in a small minority. The predominant unslipped form is the necked jar; variants with short-everted, rounded, angular-rolled (cf. nos. 197 and 199 here), and pendant "swan's neck" (no. 203) rims all occur, the latter so rarely as to suggest importation rather than local production (cf. Fig. 45). Most of these necked vessels are undecorated, except for burnishing; the narrow burnished zone on the shoulder is apparently confined to the first half of the century, later vessels as well as some contemporaries exhibiting a broader zone. A narrow rilled zone on the shoulder is a rare feature, recalling the more commonplace usage in Essex and Hertfordshire (cf. Mucking: Jones and Rodwell 1973, no. 45; Old Ford: Sheldon 1971, fig. 8, no. 28; Sheldon 1972, fig. 8, no. 13; McIsaac et al., 1979, no. 102). Plain vessels also occur. Unslipped sand-tempered wheel-thrown wares comprise between 35 per cent and 45 per cent of coarse wares. Everted-rim neckless jars, burnished dog-dishes and, in the mid- to late third century bead-and-flange dishes, are occasionally encountered in these wares. The range of 'north-west Kent' fine sandy burnished wares are rare finds in east Kent (Fig. 46), which as in the late Antonine-Severan period was probably a peripheral area in the marketing of all Cliffe peninsula wares, except for BB2 (and fine grey micaceous wares, if these are to be attributed in part to this source).

BB2 in east Kent occurs mainly in dish forms. The typological development of these forms may parallel that discernible in west Kent, as is to be expected if BB2 was predominantly an import from the Cliffe peninsula and south Essex kilns. However, it seems possible that pie-dishes may have been used in greater numbers in the middle and later years of the third century in Canterbury than on west Kent sites such as Chalk, Maidstone and Rochester. The assemblage from the 'black earth' that was the highest Roman level on Frere's theatre sites (1970, Trench DIII, layer 39) included plain pie-dishes and bead-and-flange dishes in a ratio of c. 3:1, in comparison with west Kent ratios for mid- to late third-century groups in the order of 1:1.3 to 1:15 (4.IV.2). It is certainly possible that some of the pie-dishes from layer 39 are residual early third-century pieces, but even so the ratio would be at odds with that of 1:9 from Chalk (the lowest fill of the 'cellar', layer 8 [Johnston 1972] which included undoubted early third-century and earlier residual pottery). The 'black earth' includes several fabrics only introduced to Canterbury in the final quarter of the third century, including Oxfordshire red colour-coated ware and 'late Roman' grog-tempered ware, and a coin suite dated to not later than c. A.D. 290–300 plus one issue of c. A.D. 330–335 (Kraay in Frere 1970, 108, footnote 13); the BB2 group contrasts with fourth-century groups from Canterbury, wherein pie-dishes are extremely uncommon and bead-and-flange dishes considerably more common (4.V.3). One solution to this paradox might be that Canterbury BB2 was not primarily acquired from west Kent/south Essex, but from Colchester, where the plain pie-dish was manufactured at least until the middle of the third century (Hull 1963, Form 38, from Kiln 32; Kilns 27–28 are misdated by Hull, and should be attributed to the late second to early third century, cf. Harden and Green 1978), without apparently being supplanted by the BB2 bead-and-flange dish. Williams (1977, 212) has claimed that Colchester BB2 was imported to Canterbury in the late second to early third century. Local east Kent production is also plausible (ibid., heavy mineral analysis Group XVIII, and XX, no. 4).

Bead-and-flange dishes do, however, occur widely in east Kent (Fig. 46, 'flanged bowl'), albeit in small numbers. They are more frequent than cavetto-rim jars, which comprised a very small proportion of BB2 in east Kent throughout the second to fourth century, perhaps for reasons discussed above (4.III.3). Dog-dishes are second to plain pie-dishes in quantitative importance. Taking all forms together, BB2 comprised up to one-quarter of third-century Canterbury assemblages (up to half of the coarse wares), quite possibly with similar quantities in use in both early and later years.

The third coarse ware frequently encountered in early third-century deposits, 'Native Coarse Ware' (*q.v.* 4.III.3), continued to be used throughout the century, probably declining in importance in the latter half (to under 5 per cent of total assemblages). The forms – mostly jars, but occasionally including bowls (e.g. Jenkins 1952, no. 34) and dog-dishes – exhibit no discernible typological development. They occur at Wingham and possibly Reculver (Philp 1957, nos. 22–3, 29 have profiles and scoring suggestive of this ware) in mid- to late third-century levels, as well as at Canterbury. Other, unstratified, examples in east Kent could also be of later third-century date (cf. Fig. 45).

BB1 is a regular occurrence in Canterbury deposits of the mid- to late third century, generally comprising up to 9 per cent of total assemblages and 20 per cent of coarse ware assemblages (by vessel rim equivalents). Vessels are usually bead-and-flange dishes (Gillam 1970, Type 228) and decorated dog-dishes (*ibid.*, Type 329), or more rarely jars with rims of wider diameter than the body (the 'oversailing' rim, *ibid.*, Types 147 and 148; e.g. Jenkins 1952, no. 21). The jars, and the bead-and-flange dish, are dated to the late third century onwards in the northern military zone (*ibid.*), and the dog-dish (Gillam Type 329) from the late second century onwards. There is no reason to suppose that these forms reached the south-east any earlier than they did the north (Williams 1977); in consequence, it may be supposed that the major period of importation to east Kent began in the last third of the third century. Williams has demonstrated that some BB1 from Dorset certainly reached Canterbury (*ibid.*), including two bead-and-flange dishes that may be dateable to the late third century (Williams 1947, fig. 8, nos. 4 and 9; although the excavator dates their contexts to the fourth century, the coins and other finds do not rule out a third-century date for the fills, and this is certainly more likely on ceramic grounds). On the basis of visual inspection under a hand-lens, it is possible to ascribe most BB1 from third-century contexts to a Dorset source. Canterbury, and other settlements throughout Kent including Wingham and Reculver (Philp 1957, no. 7, and unpublished vessels from the foreshore), were evidently sought out by the Dorset distributors in a general intensification of trade with the south-east of Britain (Figs. 35 and 36 here) subsequent to the reduction in the scale of the northern region's consumption (Williams 1977, 204–5). The coincidence of this trade with the development of the Saxon Shore defensive system in the English Channel, Straits of Dover and North Sea is of interest, particularly in view of the presence of oolite stone on several sites in Kent (Williams 1972, fig. 9 and Appendix 3). More research into the dating and sources of this stone is required before it is possible to provide good evidence to support the attractive hypothesis that the Dorset BB1 was imported as a by-product of the transportation of Portland oolite stone. Purbeck Marble may also have been shipped up the Channel in the late Roman period (*ibid.*, citing Hull 1958, 96). This kind of commerce might accord with Fulford's hypothesis (1981, 202–3) that Dorset BB1 was distributed over long-distances as a 'make-weight' in cargoes of more important commodities. The imposition of a system of taxation in kind on the south-east as well as in the north and west in the third century (cf. Hopkins 1980, 116 ff.) may have occasioned a restructuring of the tax collection system that resulted in an increase in Channel traffic, with a concomitant improvement in the opportunities for shipping pottery from the south-west to the south-east. Late third- and fourth-century New Forest fine wares also exhibit a distribution along the Channel coast (Fulford 1975a, figs. 44 to 53), which may have been influenced by the siting of the Saxon Shore forts in Sussex and Kent (*ibid.*, 120), although these apparently utilised only small amounts of New Forest ware (*ibid.*, fig. 55). Several external factors can thus be adduced in order to explain the expansion of the Dorset BB1 trade to Kent in the late third century.

The increased importation of BB1 appears to have spawned a number of imitators in the south-east. Williams (1977, 206) has isolated non-Dorset BB1 in late fourth-century levels at Portchester and Verulamium; an earlier fabric is macroscopically distinguishable from Dorset ware in Canterbury and also at Wye, by virtue of the absence of the white quartz and sparse rounded shale characteristic of Dorset, in place of which is a suite of abundant clear and translucent colourless and brown quartz, plus sparse flint and black iron ore (Pollard forthcoming, d, fabric (ii)). This fabric was made in the same forms as contemporary Dorset BB1, with the addition of an angular-flanged bead-and-flange dish, a type common to several late Roman industries (e.g. Alice Holt: Lyne and Jefferies 1979, Class 5B.8; Howe *et al.* 1980, no. 79). It is dateable broadly to the very late third to mid-fourth century at Canterbury; the slightly later date of introduction supports the hypothesis that it was produced in response to the importation of Dorset BB1.

A second hand-made fabric that first appears in east Kent in the late third century is conventionally termed 'Late Roman grog-tempered ware' (Pollard forthcoming, d). This ware is tempered with abundant grogs of ill-assorted size, with minor inclusions of quartz, iron ore, mica and flint sometimes present. It is invariably facet-burnished or wiped smooth, and jars may be decorated with burnished linear motifs, usually lattices or oblique strokes. Core and surface are usually grey to drab brown, occasionally oxidised, and usually soft and 'soapy' to the touch. Forms are almost wholly confined to recurved rim jars (sometimes with a shoulder offset), dog-dishes, and bead-and-flange or grooved-flange dishes (nos. 204–8, 210–11 here), but everted-rim jars possibly derived from the thickened BB1 form (Gillam 1970, Types 146 and 148; no. 209 here; cf. Green 1980, 78 for parallels of hand-made non-sandy ware exhibiting a BB1 influence) also occur. This ware is absent from a third-century group from 5 Watling Street, Canterbury (Jenkins 1952, Key Deposit 3; additional unpublished material from this group has also been examined), which contains a late third-century-plus BB1 jar (*ibid.*, no. 21) and a coin of Salonina (A.D. 253–268), but is present in the 'black earth' on Frere's theatre site (1970, Trench DIII, layer 39, with late third-century coins plus one of *c.* A.D. 330–335) in the order of 9 per cent of the assemblage (vessel rim equivalents; 11 per cent of coarse wares), and in a late third/early fourth-century redeposition of flood silt on the Marlowe Car Park (Pollard forthcoming, d) as some 3 per cent (12 per cent of coarse wares). It is not possible on present evidence to date its introduction on other sites, but there is no reason to disbelieve that broadly contemporary dates apply throughout east Kent. West of the Medway, however, the ware may not have been produced or imported until the fourth century (4.V.2). Late Roman grog-tempered ware may conceivably have been produced alongside 'Native Coarse Ware', but the lower firing temperature and wider range of forms mitigate against such a circumstance. Its introduction seems to coincide with a contraction in the numbers of 'Native Coarse Ware' vessels in use at Canterbury, suggesting that in some sense the latter was superseded by 'Late Roman' grog-tempered ware.

The supply of mortaria to east Kent underwent similar changes to those described in west Kent (4.IV.2). Mid- to late third-century examples of the probably indigenous oxidised ware have been recovered from Canterbury (Williams 1947, fig. 8, no. 12; Jenkins 1952, nos. 27 and 30), and it is highly likely that some vessels from other sites, such as the complete 'hammer-head' flanged example from the hypocaust flue on the Wye Harville site (unpublished; information from J. Bradshaw) and many of the 114 examples of 'Kent' mortaria cited by Hartley (1968, Table 1) from Richborough, belonged to this period. Two pale pink/white sandy pendant-flange-and-bead vessels from Canterbury, of a type probably manufactured in southern Britain or on the Continent (Hartley 1981, nos. 382–5, 387), may be ascribed to the mid-third century (Jenkins 1952, nos. 24 and 26). Nene Valley buff ware mortaria, with characteristic ironstone trituration grit and reeded-flange or 'hammer-head'-flange rims (Hartley 1960, fig. 3, nos. 10–11), and Oxfordshire white ware mortaria with pink and clear quartz trituration grit, are both widespread in east Kent in the later third century. The former is more common in east than west Kent on present evidence, being found at Canterbury (e.g. Jenkins 1952, nos. 23 and 31, the latter in a fourth-century context), Richborough, and Birchington. Oxfordshire white wares of mid- to late third-century date (Young 1977a, Types M17–21) have a wider distribution, including the civitas capital, all four Saxon Shore forts and the Wingham aisled building (unpublished). It is possible that these imported mortaria were marketed mainly to higher status sites, in the latter case at least in the third century. However, body sherds and the third- to fourth-century form M22 (*ibid.*; this form is mainly fourth century in date) in Oxfordshire white ware have been recovered from other sites (see Appendix 3). There is insufficient evidence to refine the period of introduction of these two wares to east Kent beyond a 'mid- to late third-century' range. As in west Kent, it is conceivable that the Oxfordshire white ware began to circulate in the east before colour-coated ware from the same industry achieved a market share of more than modest proportions. The latter ware was also manufactured in mortaria forms, broadly derived from late Central and East Gaulish Drag. 43 (perhaps fortuitously) and Drag. 45 types (Young 1977a, Types C97–100). The 'Drag. 45' derivatives, produced from the mid-third century onwards, appear to have been used in east Kent, if not in the west (where positive evidence is lacking), before the end of the third century (Frere 1970, fig. 11, no. 28). Hartley (1973a, fig. 6) notes a group of sites in east Kent from which mortaria of the Mancetter-Hartshill industry (1973b) have been recovered. To these may be added Port Lympne (Cunliffe 1980, fig. 27, no. 2, illustration published inverted). Mrs. Hartley places the six Richborough examples in the fourth century (1968).

The comments on amphorae importation given above (4.IV.2) apply also to east Kent. At the time of writing, nothing is known of later Roman importation to east Kent; it is to be hoped that Arthur's report on the amphorae from Canterbury (Arthur 1986) will clarify the situation.

4. *The Coarse Wares of Central-Northern Kent*

The pottery from this region exhibits a high degree of similarity with both east and west Kent, as is reflected in Jaccard's correlation coefficients (see below). The dating of sites is tentative, but the presence of sherds of Oxfordshire red colour-coated ware (including C26, a form introduced to the repertoire *c.* A.D. 270 (Young 1977a)) in two pits and of Oxfordshire white ware mortaria suggest that domestic occupation continued at least into the final quarter of the third century at Brenley Corner, alongside the possible temple or shrine the coin suite from which

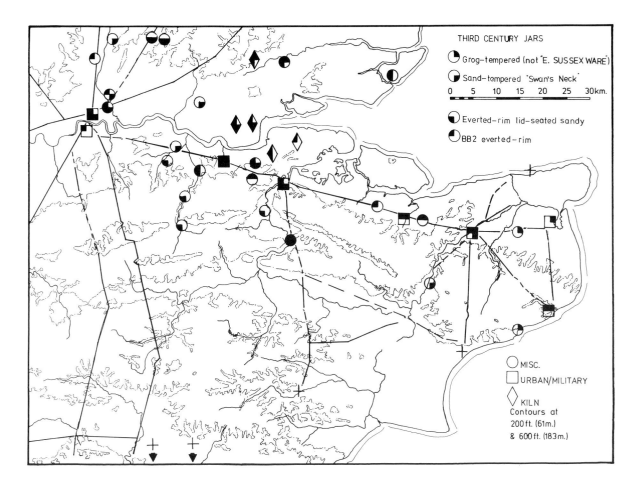

Fig. 45. Third-century jars: Distribution. + = absent.

included issues up to the third quarter of the fourth century (Jenkins 1973; 1974). Late third- to fourth-century fine wares and mortaria are also present at Radfield and Ospringe.

It is probable that reduced sandy wheel-thrown wares and BB2 remained the dominant wares for most, if not all, of the third century. The necked jar, as elsewhere in Kent, is the major type in the former ware, and both it and the burnished dog-dishes that also occur may have been made locally. A cracked waster of a necked jar containing a ritual burial possibly of third-century date has been recovered from the Upchurch Marshes (Noël Hume 1956, 164–5, no. 3), and some very coarse sandy small necked jars were buried in the Ospringe cemetery (e.g. Whiting *et al*. 1931, nos. 496 and 518). 'Swan's neck' jars (no. 203 here: 4.IV.2) have not been recorded in this region. BB2 bead-and-flange dishes occur at Radfield, Brenley Corner and Ospringe, the last-named including one (*ibid*., no. 217) associated with a late third-century-plus Nene Valley beaker (no. 216 – cf. Howe *et al*. 1980, no. 52). The presence of these dishes implies that, as in east Kent, BB2 from north-west Kent or south Essex continued to be

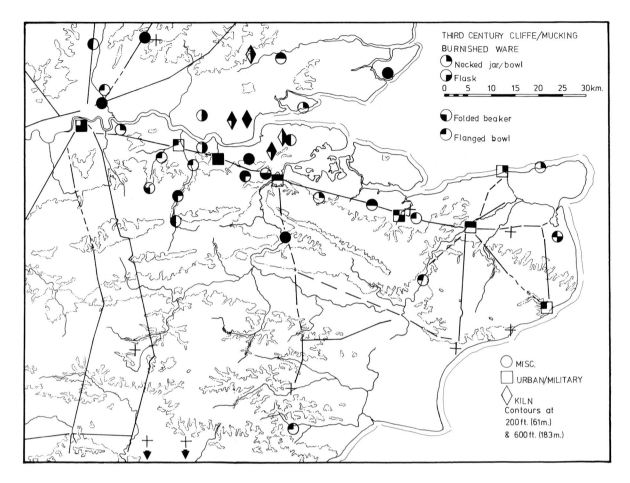

Fig. 46. Third-century Cliffe peninsula/Mucking—south Essex burnished wares: Distribution. + = absent.

imported into the latter half of the third century at least. Fine burnished wares of north-west Kent type (Fig. 46) are less frequently encountered than BB2, but the Ospringe cemetery does include several flasks (e.g. Whiting *et al.* 1931, nos. 48, 530, 534, and 615) and bulbous tall-necked beakers (*ibid.*, e.g. nos. 110 and 403) amongst which are vessels in burials dateable to the late third or fourth century.

'Native Coarse Ware' occurs at Ospringe and Brenley Corner; two cinerary urns from the former site (*ibid.*, nos. 41 and 337), with tooled linear decoration, were interred not earlier than the last quarter of the third century, as they are associated with colour-coated ware beakers of forms originating in that period (no. 43 in Nene Valley ware, cf. Howe *et al.* 1980, no. 53; and no. 339, an Oxfordshire C27 – Young 1977a). The absence of late Roman grog-tempered ware from Brenley Corner may be indicative of an introduction of this ware very late on in the third century, if not in the fourth; the main period of domestic and industrial activity on this site appears to have ended by the turn of the third century on the evidence of pit fills. If this date is

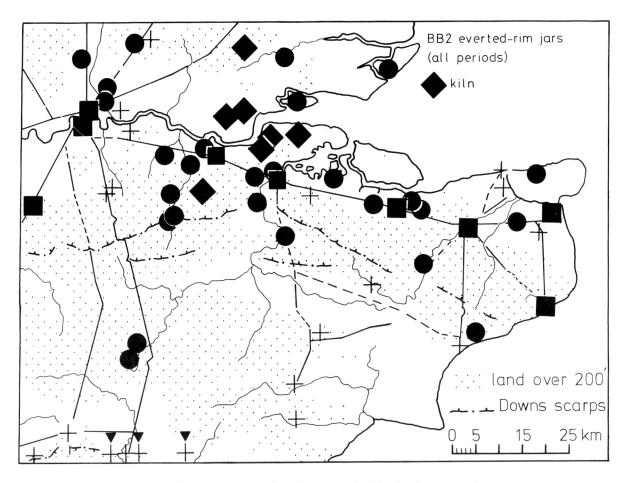

Fig. 47. BB2 everted-rim jars (all periods): Distribution. + = absent.

correct, it would correlate with west Kent dating rather than the slightly earlier period of introduction deduced at Canterbury (see above). The hypothesis of a temporal diffusion of this ware or the concept of its production is attractive, but at present there is too little evidence to put this model to the test.

BB1 from Dorset may have been imported to the central northern region from the late third century onwards as part of the major expansion of that industry's trade in the south-east discussed above (4.IV.3), but there is insufficient data to allow quantitative judgements to be made. Four of the six BB1 vessels in the Ospringe cemetery (Whiting *et al.* 1931, nos. 402, 462, 473, and 550) may be of third-century date, including a mug dated to *c.* A.D. 140–300 in the north (Gillam 1970, Type 65), and a jar (*ibid.*, Type 146) of late third-century origin. BB1 is also present at Brenley Corner, where the lack of diagnostic fourth-century wares suggests that the vessel concerned (*ibid.*, Type 329) was imported in the late second to third century. A second jar of late third-century-plus form has been recovered from the Upchurch Marshes (*ibid.*, Type

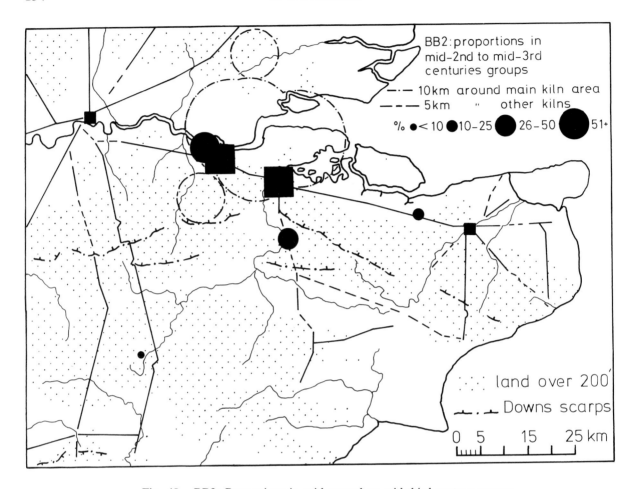

Fig. 48.   BB2: Proportions in mid-second to mid-third-century groups.

146; Noël Hume and Noël Hume 1951, no. 1). The ?local 'Canterbury' BB1 (4.IV.3) has not
been recognised, but may possibly have been overlooked.

The range of mortaria that may be attributed to the mid- to late third century in this region
includes a painted 'hammer-head' flange-rim Nene Valley buff ware vessel from Radfield, white
ware and oxidised 'east Kent' 'hammer-head' vessels with flint trituration grit from Radfield,
Brenley Corner and Ospringe, and a possible third century Oxfordshire white ware form
(Young 1977a, Type M19) from Brenley Corner. The third to fourth century Type M22 (*ibid.*)
in the same ware is present on all three sites. The Ospringe cemetery material includes a rare
example of an east Mediterranean amphora of a type better known as 'B iv ware' from
fifth-century contexts in the south-west (Peacock 1977d, 298); the vessel (Whiting *et al.*, 1931,
no. 502) was associated with a second-century glass vessel and a second- to mid fourth-century
necked bead-rim jar. This fabric of amphora is also known from a Roman cellar of uncertain
date at Burham, on the right bank of the Medway near the Eccles villa (Jessup 1956; the
amphora is noted in Peacock 1977d, 298).

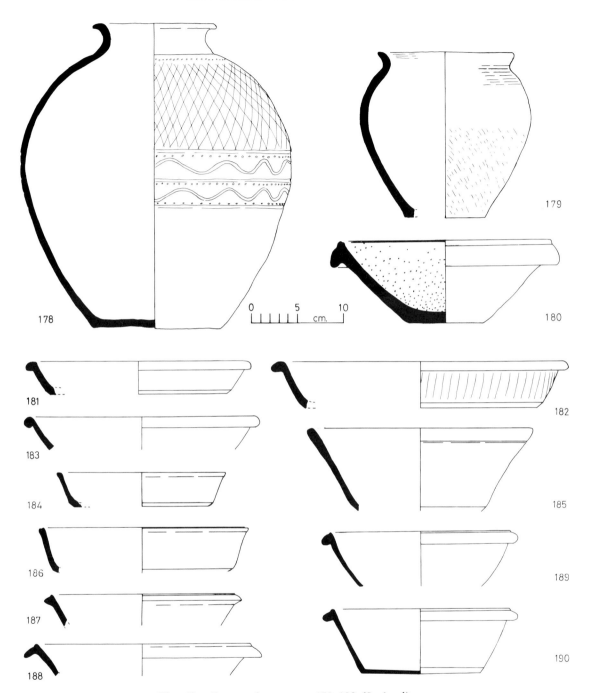

Fig. 49. Pottery forms nos. 178–190 (Scale: ¼).

Fig. 49. **178–179**: 'Native Coarse Ware'.
178. Everted-rim necked storage jar, tooled lattice, grooved wavy lines and stick-stabbed decoration, Whiting *et al.*, 1931, no. 193. **179**. Bead-everted-rim jar, burnished upper and wiped or knife-trimmed ('scarred') lower exterior, Frere 1970, fig. 10, no. 21.

180: 'East Kent' untempered oxidised ware, flint trituration grit, grooved-bead and 'hammerhead'-flange mortarium, Jenkins 1952, fig. 5, no. 30.

181–190: BB2
181. Rectangular-rim pie-dish, Gillam 1970, Type 313, Pollard forthcoming, b, no. 54. **182**. Form as no. 181 above, decorated, Gillam 1970, Type 313, Pollard 1983b, no. 12, **183**. Rolled-rim pie-dish, Pollard forthcoming, b, no. 57. **184**. Shallow plain-rim dog-dish, Pollard 1983b, no. 5. **185**. Deep dog-dish with high groove, cf. Gillam 1970, Type 319, *ibid.*, no. 8. **186**. Dog-dish with groove on rim-top, *ibid.*, no. 11. **187**. Pie-dish with groove on rim-top: 'nascent bead-and-flange', *ibid.*, no. 27. **188**. Bead-and-wide-flange dish, Pollard forthcoming, b, no. 59. **189**. Bead-and-heavy-flange dish, Pollard 1983b, no. 25. **190**. Form as no. 189 above, *ibid.*, no. 24.

Dating: 178–179: Late second to early fourth century. 180: Late second to third century. 181: Very late second to mid- third century. 182: Late second to early/mid- third century (wide vessel). 183: As no. 181. 184: (Hadrianic), mid- second to first half fourth century. 185: (Hadrianic to mid- second), late second to first half fourth century. 186: Late second to third, (to first half fourth century). 187–190. Mid- third to first half fourth century.

Fig. 50. **191**: BB2; cavetto-rim pear-shaped jar, Gillam 1970, Types 143/144, Tester 1961, no. 41.
192–193: Sandy reduced wheel-thrown ware.
192. Form as no. 191 above, folded/indented and burnished, Meates *et al.* 1952, no. 59. **193**. Everted-rim S-bowl, combed-rouletted decoration, Tester and Caiger 1954, no. 20.

194–196: BB2.
194. Bead-rim S-bowl, Noël Hume 1954, fig. 3, no. 6, from Hartlip (?) (possibly same vessel as Monaghan 1983, no. 32): a waster. **195**. Rolled-rim flask, Jones and Rodwell 1973, no. 90. **196**. Bead-and-flange-rim narrow-mouth jar, Pollard 1983b, no. 31.

197–203: Sandy reduced wheel-thrown ware.
197. Angular-bead-rim necked jar, Pollard forthcoming, b, no. 77. **198**. Form as no. 197 above, with 'lead-seating' on rim, Pollard 1983b, no. 41. **199**. Form as no. 197 above, Noël Hume 1956, fig. 1, no. 1. **200**. Everted-rim lid-seated bowl, possibly globular, Pollard 1983b, no. 44. **201**. Everted-rim lid-seated jar, Jones and Rodwell 1973, no. 25. **202**. Bead-rim necked storage jar, stabbed decoration, Whiting *et al.* 1931, no. 378. **203**. 'Swan's neck' pendant-rolled-rim necked jar, Johnston 1972, no. 21.

Dating: 191: (Hadrianic to mid- second), late second to first half fourth century. 192. Late second to third, (to first half fourth century). 193: Mid- second to early third century (?). 194–196: (Mid- second), late second to early fourth century. 197–199: (Mid- second), late second to fourth century. 200–201: Second half second to mid- third century. 202. Third to early fourth century. 203: Third to fourth century.

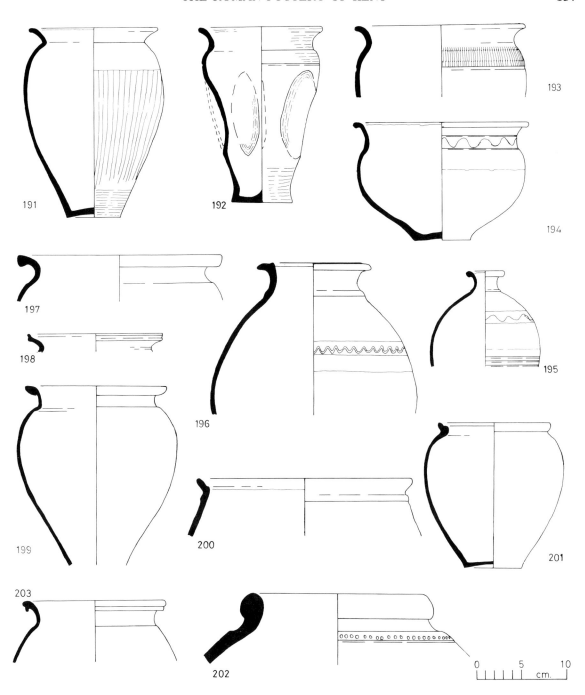

Fig. 50. Pottery forms nos. 191–203 (Scale: ¼).

A high range of correlation coefficients obtained from applying Jaccard's measure to pairs of sites taking Canterbury, Rochester, Radfield and Ospringe into consideration has been recorded. With the exception of a similarity figure of 63 per cent for Ospringe:Radfield, all six permutations of pairs show a degree of similarity of 66.6 per cent or higher. The figures for Brenley Corner are markedly lower, between 48 per cent and 59 per cent, possibly a reflection of the hypothesised termination of domestic occupation on that site before the end of the third century. Canterbury has the largest range of fabrics and forms, as befits the civitas capital, but it should also be borne in mind that the city has been investigated by archaeologists more intensively than the other four sites in this survey, notwithstanding the excavation of the Ospringe cemetery. The pottery assemblages are qualitatively more or less subsets of the total Canterbury assemblage. There are quantitative differences between Rochester and Canterbury (Appendix 5) that are interpreted as indicating two marketing zones for coarse pottery, but these zones overlap, with the result that to some extent wares from north-west Kent were distributed throughout east Kent and vice versa, with the central northern region acquiring pottery from both sources as well as indigenous products of widely fashionable types and exotic imports with a county-wide distribution.

V. THE FOURTH AND EARLY FIFTH CENTURIES

1. *The Fine Wares*

The fine pottery of late Roman Britain, both indigenous and imported, has been the subject of intensive research over the past decade, encompassing studies of individual industries (e.g. Fulford 1975a; Young 1977a; Galliou *et al.* 1980) and of the competitive interaction of those industries (e.g. Fulford 1977a, 1977b, 1978c; Green 1977). It is now recognised that a wide variety of fine wares from numerous sources were current in Kent in this highly competitive trade, of which Oxfordshire wares were the predominant participant.

The main features of fine pottery developments in this period in Kent are the demise of local grey wares; increase in the volume of Oxfordshire wares; an increase in the importation of fine wares from the Continent, and the diversity of Romano-British sources represented. A high degree of standardisation at a generalised level can be detected, with red-surfaced open bowls, dark tall-necked beakers, and red or dark dishes, flagons and flasks predominating, white bowls and beakers providing the bulk of the remaining styles.

The decline in Upchurch Marshes fine ware production may have begun in the third century, despite or perhaps because of the evident resurgence of the Romano-British fine pottery industries (Fulford 1975a, 109–11). The increasing availability of colour-coated wares from Oxfordshire, coupled with the established importation of Nene Valley wares, may have squeezed the Upchurch industry to the point where competitive productivity was no longer feasible. It may be significant that many of the late third- to fourth-century fine grey ware vessels are necked jars of quite large sizes (nos. 174–5 here), forms which were not in direct competition with most of the imports. Flasks and tall-necked bulbous beakers (e.g. Jenkins 1950, nos. 61, 71) may also have continued into the fourth century, along with 'Drag. 38' and flange-rim segmental bowls (cf. nos. 162–4 here); no new forms are encountered, however. Fine grey wares are absent from the fourth-century soil accumulation in the Chalk 'cellar' (Johnston

1972, layers 5 and 6), and comprise less than 2 per cent (vessel rim equivalents) of the pottery from a large 'flood silt' deposit of the middle years of that century at Canterbury (Pollard forthcoming, d; Appendix 5). Body sherds only are present in late fourth- and early fifth-century deposits at Canterbury, in very small numbers, and the ware is entirely absent from the recorded assemblages from the late fourth- to early fifth-century destruction and post-destruction deposits at Lullingstone (Pollard 1987), the early to mid fourth-century site at Bexley Maxim Road, and the fourth-century pits at Richborough. It is probable that few vessels were in use throughout Kent later than the early fourth century.

Oxfordshire red/brown colour-coated ware producers were the main beneficiaries from the probable closure of the Upchurch potteries. The quantities of this ware at Chalk and Canterbury more than trebled as proportions of fine wares between the late third and the late fourth centuries. Over 50 per cent of the fine wares from the third- to early fifth-century 'black earth' deposit at Rochester (Flight and Harrison 1978) were of this ware, and the remainder included 39 per cent fine grey wares, which on analogy should include a large residual element. The Wye pit group, from the upper Great Stour in east Kent (Pollard forthcoming, a), includes over 45 per cent Oxfordshire red/brown colour-coated ware. The fine wares from the late destruction and post-destruction deposits at Lullingstone are all in Oxfordshire wares, including a Parchment ware bowl sherd. Sherd counts of late fourth-century and early fifth-century deposits at Canterbury reveal this colour-coated ware to have been the second most common ware after grog-tempered coarse ware, but the proportions by vessel rim equivalents are depressed partially due to the small numbers of fine ware rims recovered (Pollard forthcoming, d). In this late period, Oxfordshire ware quantities also increased in relation to other wares at Portchester (Fulford 1975b, 285–6) and possibly also in southern Essex (Drury 1977, 40), although the reverse may be true in East Sussex (Green 1977, 177–8). The typological fossilisation of Oxfordshire wares that occurred after the mid-fourth century (Young 1977a, 240) renders isolation of late vessels on unstratified sites very difficult, but it is clear that the red/brown colour-coated ware was ubiquitous in Kent in the fourth century as a whole (Fig. 51).

The sandy white, red-painted Oxfordshire Parchment ware (Young 1977a, 80–92) is a much rarer find than its colour-coated counterpart (cf. Appendix 5), but is nevertheless widespread in Kent as elsewhere within the Oxfordshire industry's marketing area (Appendix 3). The carinated, moulded rim bowl (Young 1977a, P24) is the most common form, but other bowls and globular beakers also occur in Kent. There is no reason to think that this ware did not continue to be exported to Kent throughout the fourth century, although it is absent from late fourth- and early fifth-century deposits at Canterbury. Oxfordshire white-slip wares (ibid., 117–22) in Kent are predominantly in mortaria forms, which are widely distributed. The carinated bowl form (ibid., Type WC3) has been recorded at Richborough (ibid.) and possibly at Otford (the 'Progress' site, unpublished), but flagons and jars were apparently absent from Kent.

The Nene valley was the source of the second major group of colour-coated wares marketed in Kent in the fourth century. Late fabrics of this industry include a quite coarse-textured white ware, grey and orange wares. Slips are thick, ranging from orange to black, and often exhibit a lustrous sheen (Howe et al. 1980, 8–9). The main forms found in Kent comprise tall-necked bead-rim bulbous beakers (cf. nos. 152–3 for forms) including vessels with circular and/or narrow 'slit' vertical folds (Howe et al. 1980, nos. 49–57; e.g. Ospringe: Whiting et al. 1931, nos. 43, 214, and 216), incurved-rim dog-dishes and angular-flanged bead-and-flange dishes (*ibid.*, nos. 87 and 79), 'Castor boxes' (4.IV.1), flagons often with a slight pouring lip (*ibid.*, nos. 63–8) and short-necked angular-rim wide-mouth jars (*ibid.*, nos. 75–7). It is apparent that there is some degree of differentiation between colour-coated ware forms from Oxfordshire and the Nene valley that were exported to Kent. The dish, 'Castor box' and jar forms were all produced by the former industry (Young 1977a, Types C93–4, C87, C18) but appear to have been rare in eastern Britain, though more common in Oxfordshire and the Severn valley (*ibid.*). The Oxfordshire pinched-lip flagon (*ibid.*, Type C12) is rare throughout Britain. In contrast, bowls and mortaria from the Nene valley, including samian 'derivatives' (Howe *et al.* 1980, nos. 80–4) and a 'hammer-head' flange-rim conical open bowl (*ibid.*, no. 88) are infrequently encountered in Kent, though a wide range of forms has been recovered from Canterbury (M. Green, pers. comm.). Oxfordshire colour-coated bowls and mortaria are both diverse and abundant throughout Kent (Fig. 51), being by far the most common ware in which red-surfaced bowls of the late third- to early fifth-century are found (cf. Fig. 51). Beakers were the main form in which the two industries were in direct competition, but production of these in the Nene valley 'appears to have declined during the fourth century and it is possible that the percentage made of the whole output after the middle of the century was very low' (Howe *et al.* 1980, 8); in Kent at least this left Oxfordshire with a virtual monopoly of the market for beakers in the late fourth century. The ratio of Oxfordshire to Nene Valley colour-coated ware quantities at Canterbury does seem to shift in favour of the former over the course of the fourth century, implying that this industry was more able to make use of the coastal trade routes around the Thames estuary and Straits of Dover. A regression analysis studying the percentage of Oxfordshire wares as proportions of assemblages throughout southern Britain (Fulford and Hodder 1974) has provoked the hypothesis that the Thames estuary was of especial significance in the distribution of these wares; comparative statistics concerning Nene Valley wares have not as yet been published. It is probable that the latter continued to reach Kent to the end of the fourth or even into the fifth century. The industry itself was almost certainly 'in full production' at the beginning of the fifth (Howe *et al.* 1980, 10), and sherds have been recovered from deposits of this date at Lullingstone and Canterbury.

A number of other Romano-British fine ware industries achieved some share of the trade in Kent in the fourth century (Figs. 57–8), but only on a regional level. The Much Hadham industry is the most important, quantitatively, of these, having the advantage of an established commerce dating back to the third century (4.IV.1). The oxidised ware is found throughout north Kent (Fig. 34), but is proportionally more common in the north-west, particularly at Springhead and Chalk. Jars, including wide- and narrow-necked types sometimes with 'pie-crust' pendant frills on the rim and ring-stamped decoration on the body (e.g. at Canterbury), are widespread, but bowls are mainly confined to the north-west (Fig. 51). Mortarium sherds occur at Springhead. Relief-moulded zoomorphic decoration has been recorded on a bead-rim bulbous bowl at Chalk (unpublished), and dimple-and-boss motifs on a similar form from Highsted, near Sittingbourne (Jessup 1935, fig. 3, no. 1). This vessel is now lost, but the description suggests a Hadham source. The motifs are part of a style commonly termed 'Romano-Saxon', from the contentious belief that the tastes of Germanic mercenaries in fourth-century eastern Britain influenced the Romano-British potters' designs. This hypothesis was formulated by Myres (1956), and has been adopted by other authors in more recent papers (e.g. Rodwell 1970a; Hurst 1976, 290–2); however, Gillam (1979) has argued strongly against the association of the style with Germanic mercenaries, and the present author finds himself sympathetic with his opinions. Be that as it may, 'Romano-Saxon' as a style, including oblique tooled slashes as well as bosses and dimples, is rare in Kent in comparison with Essex, both in Much Hadham oxidised ware and various sandy reduced wares. In addition to the Highsted vessel, instances may be cited at Darenth (Philp 1973, no. 419) and Springhead (unpublished) with slash and ring-stamp motifs in reduced ware; boss and comb-stamp motifs occur on a reduced ware sherd from Bexley Maxim Road (unpublished; cf. Drury 1977, fig. 9, no. 36); bosses occur at Lullingstone and Canterbury (Pollard 1987, Fabric 19; *id.*, forthcoming d, no. 223, respectively) on narrow-neck pendant-frill-rim jars, the former in oxidised, the latter in reduced ware; a dimpled bulbous bowl from Richborough is of uncertain fabric (Hurst 1976, fig. 7.2, no. 4). Much Hadham wares may have been used in Kent throughout the fourth century, but closely-dateable occurrences are rare. There is little dating evidence for 'Romano-Saxon' styles in Kent, but it is probable that all were of late third-century or later occurrence.

There is little positive evidence for Colchester wares in fourth-century Kent, and the fine ware industry may well have been restricted to a local market at this time, if it had not been closed down altogether (Hull 1963). 'Streak-burnished' oxidised ware (4.IV.1) is thought to have been used at Canterbury for most, if not all, of the fourth century, with a possible decline in the later years (Green 1981). It has not been identified on other sites. New Forest colour-coated ware (Fulford 1975a) is restricted to the civitas capital and Saxon Shore forts (*ibid.*; Young 1980; M. Green, pers. comm.), in very small quantities. Sherds have also been recorded in London (Fulford 1975a) and Southwark (Fulford in Bird *et al.* 1978b, 125). The lustrous orange-to-purple-slipped grey ware tall-necked bulbous beakers (Fulford 1975a, Fine Ware Types 27–43) are distinctive, but a flange-neck flagon (*ibid.*, Fine Ware Type 11) in this ware, and bowls in red-slip ware (*ibid.*, fabric 1c) and white Parchment ware (*ibid.*, fabric 2; Young 1980, 277) have also been recorded. 'Pevensey' red colour-coated ware, a very hard dark orange fine-textured fabric with uneven surfaces (Fulford 1973a) thought to have been produced in East Sussex mainly in the mid-fourth to early fifth century, has been recorded on only two sites in Kent, Wye (Pollard forthcoming, a) and Port Lympne (Young 1980, 278). The latter find may reflect activity between this Saxon Shore fort and Pevensey fort, but the former is enigmatic, although it is within 15 km. of Port Lympne (Fig. 51). One apparently local red ware of the fourth century has been identified in west Kent. This is a coarse sandy orange-red to brown ware with burnished surfaces, found at the Otford 'Progress' site, Twitton Hospital (unpublished) and the Chalk 'cellar' (unpublished). The first site has produced fragments of several vessels, including hemispherical bowls with combed wavy line and stabbed decoration (Pearce 1930, 163, nos. D.31 and D.43), and roll-rim necked jars with externally-grooved rims. Single sherds of hemispherical bowls alone have been found on the other two sites. The concentration of finds in the upper Darent valley suggests a source in the interior of west Kent, but clearly this allocation must be tentative.

The range of Continental, or possibly Continental, fine wares in Kent is as wide as that of Romano-British wares, and covers a diversity of sources (Figs. 60–61). The most frequently-encountered provenanced ware is Argonne ware from the Franco-Belgian border between the Meuse and Aisne (Fig. 61). This is usually in an orange fabric with orange-red slip, probably developed from the samian industry of the second century (Fulford 1977a). The forms are primarily hemispherical bowls, sometimes with a stub-flange on the lower exterior (Jenkins 1950, no. 89), but mortaria also occur (e.g. at Canterbury). Roller-stamped decoration on the lower exterior is characteristic of the flangeless bowls, but plain vessels also occur and may be slightly earlier in date (Fulford 1977a). British finds may all be of fourth-century date, but there are as yet insufficient closely-dateable finds from Kent to enable refinement of this dating to be attempted. Argonne ware is widespread in Kent (Fig. 51), with a possible bias towards eastern sites; it is also found with some frequency in Essex, the London area, and central southern Britain (Fulford 1977a). The pale oxidised 'marbled' slip 'à l'éponge' ware probably from the Poitiers region (Fig. 61) has, in Britain, mostly been recorded in Hampshire and along the Channel coast, with secondary concentrations in the lower Severn and east Kent/lower Thames regions (Fulford 1977a; Galliou *et al.* 1980, fig. 2; Fig. 51 here). In Britain the forms are confined to hemispherical bowls with deep flanges, and biconical bead-rim bowls (Fulford 1977a), but beakers are known on the Continent (Galliou *et al.* 1980, fig. 4). Again, only a general fourth-century date can be applied. A handful of sherds are known from Kent, and this is the only import for which a western Gaulish origin can be surmised.

Fine wares of this period of German derivation are extremely rare, but include mottled-slip pitchers and two-handled flagons (4.IV.1) of third- to fourth-century date (Bird 1981, 1982a; Bird and Williams 1983) and possibly brown colour-coated flagons with white paint decoration, found at Canterbury (Blockley and Day forthcoming) and paralleled at Oudenburg in Flanders (Mertens and van Impe 1971, Grave 128, Pl. XLV, no. 1a; Grave 141, Pl. XLVII, no. 3). A fine buff-fabric red-slipped ware with 'cut-glass' incised decoration is represented by sherds in fourth-century contexts at Canterbury (Blockley and Day forthcoming) and Richborough (unpublished, Pit 303). The form and source are uncertain, but a bead-everted rim ovoid beaker with an identical fabric and decoration has been published from Oudenburg (Mertens and van Impe 1971, Grave 93, Pl. XXIX, no. 1). The fine white rouletted beakers described above (4.IV.1; no. 215 here) may also have been in use in the fourth century, providing further evidence of cross-Channel trade in fine wares (cf. Fulford 1977a).

One ware that has not been described up till now in the present volume is 'African Red Slip'. A synthesis of this ware in Britain has recently been published (Bird 1977), in which it has been shown that occurrences date from the later first to the late fourth or early fifth century. Bird has proposed that these vessels 'are likely to have entered with their owners, probably traders, or craftsmen' (*ibid.*, 272). To her catalogue may be added a foot-ring base with internal grooving of the body from the Chalk 'cellar' (unpublished, layer 8), in a sandy orange fabric with orange-red semi-matt slip, and a sherd from Canterbury (Bird 1982a); both of these may be of late third- or fourth-century date.

The range of flagons in colour-coated ware has been described above. Flagons and flasks generally seem to have been uncommon in the south-east in the fourth century, and most are in dark- or red-surfaced wares, sometimes painted or rouletted. Apart from the colour-coated wares, these include fine grey and fine sandy grey-slip wares plus Alice Holt neutral-slip sandy grey ware (see the following two sections). It has been observed that there is a greater percentage of pewter and glass vessels against pottery in the second half than in the first half of the fourth century in the Winchester Lankhills cemetery (Clarke 1979), and this increasing availability of non-ceramic vessels may have had repercussions for the fine pottery industries of Roman Britain. Fulford (1975a, 134) has observed that decorated beakers and closed forms in New Forest colour-coated ware tend to decline before red slipped bowls, and Howe *et al.* (1980, 8) have proposed a marked decrease in the production of beakers in the Nene valley. However, the flagons of the Nene Valley and Alice Holt industries, and both flagons and beakers from the Oxfordshire kilns, show no such trends. There is insufficient evidence from funerary contexts in

Kent to provide comparable statistics to those from Lankhills, but the establishment of a pewter works at Ickham, between Canterbury and Richborough, must have provided competition for the pottery importers (Young 1975).

It is important to distinguish between pottery imported as objects of trade and as items of personal possession. There can be no doubting the existence of an extensive trade network encompassing Oxfordshire, Nene Valley, Much Hadham and Argonne wares in Kent. However, as with 'African Red Slip' ware, the possibility that the rarer wares were purchased elsewhere in Britain or on the Continent and brought into Kent amongst personal baggage should not be overlooked. A large volume of traffic between Britain and the Continent is implied by Ammianus Marcellinus' reference (xviii, 2, 3) to a regular movement of corn from Britain although this may have been an exclusive cargo (Fulford 1978c); movement of troops into Britain through Richborough is also attested in A.D. 360 under Lupicinus (Ammianus, xx, 1; xx, 99) and in A.D. 368 under Theodosius (Zosimus, iv, 35, 5). The Saxon Shore forts also presumably generated a considerable amount of coastal trade, to which the extended distribution of New Forest and Pevensey colour-coated wares in the Straits of Dover and beyond may in some measure be ascribed (cf. Young 1977b); it is becoming clear that these bases were not inhabited solely by military personnel, but by others as well (Cunliffe 1977), and large extra-mural settlements could also be attached to the forts (e.g. at Brancaster: Edwards and Green 1977). BB1 from Dorset was also exported up the Channel to south-east Britain (see the following section), and is one of several late Romano-British wares to have been recorded on the Continent (Fulford 1977a; 1978c). It is noticeable that several of these sites receiving Romano-British pottery are military bases as well as civilian settlements including Oudenburg, Boulogne and Alet. However, this may reflect a recovery bias towards sites of this type; in Britain, Canterbury appears to have played a significant part in receiving Continental fine wares, but the city is not known to have had any military functions other than those appropriate to any walled town. It seems more likely, therefore, that both military personnel and civilians played a part in the private importation of fine pottery for their own use, and that the distribution of the rarer wares may be a reflection of the places in which these mobile individuals chose to live.

2. *The Coarse Wares of West Kent*

The fourth century witnessed a number of changes in the supply of pottery to west Kent, which in sum amounted to a radical transformation from the situation that had appertained since the late Hadrianic period. Three main factors may be defined; the demise of BB2 and fine sandy burnished ware production, both in north-west Kent and, seemingly, in southern Essex; a synchronous increase in the importation of exotic coarse pottery, mainly of slipped grey fine sandy ware from the Alice Holt-Farnham industry on the borders of Hampshire and Surrey, but also of coarse buff sandy ware from the same source, dense, buff Mayen ware from the Rhineland, BB1 from Dorset, and grey fine sandy ware from Much Hadham in Hertfordshire; and thirdly, the re-emergence of a hand-made, grog-tempered, ware in widespread use for jars and dishes, after a period of some two hundred years since the disappearance of hand-made, non-sandy wares as a regular feature of coarse pottery assemblages (storage jars apart). These three factors all mark a break with the traditions and commercial practices of the third century (4.IV.2) and, although the rapidity of the changes cannot be closely monitored in the assemblages studied, it is reasonably clear that all were complete by the second half of the fourth century. Certain elements of continuity with the late third century can be detected, in particular the intensive utilisation of reduced sandy wheel-thrown plain necked jars, and the predominance of Oxfordshire wares amongst the mortaria, achieved with the wane of 'East Kent' oxidised wares in the late third (or possibly early fourth) century. However, it seems possible that consumption of both mortaria and sandy wheel-thrown plain wares declined in the late fourth century.

The study of west Kent pottery in this period is inhibited by the dearth of fourth-century assemblages uncontaminated by residual material. Springhead and Rochester have only provided deposits of a broad third- to early fifth-century date (S. Harker, pers. comm.; Flight and Harrison 1978), the latter covered by medieval layers. The build-up of material within the 'cellar' at Chalk over the late third/early fourth century collapse (Johnston 1972, layers 5 and 6) includes some samian (unpublished). Lullingstone villa material is mostly unstratified, but two pits (Meates *et al.* 1950, 18–19, Group III – Room 8 has been renumbered 15 (Meates 1979); Meates *et al.* 1952, nos. 82–90, from Room 14, renumbered 11 (Meates 1979)) include quantities of mid fourth-century coins (Meates 1979, 56–7, 87–8) associated with small pottery assemblages (Pollard 1987, Groups XLVI and XLV), and the pottery from destruction and post-destruction levels in particular of the 'Deep Room' and bathing establishment would appear to be free of contamination from material at least of residual third- to early fourth-century date (*ibid.*, Groups LI, LII, XXXVII). Further evidence of the range of pottery in use in the fourth century is provided by a small assemblage from Bexley (Tester 1963) associated with coins from A.D. 222–235 to 337–341; the pottery does not include BB2 or third century 'north-west Kent' fine sandy burnished ware, suggesting that it is dateable to within the final century of the Roman occupation of Britain. Varying quantities of material of late third- to fourth-century type have been recovered from numerous other sites in unstratified contexts (cf. Figs. 7 and 8). No fourth-century kilns are known in west Kent.

The quantified pottery sequences from Chalk, Springhead and Rochester allow very broad trends in the consumption and discard of wares in the third and fourth centuries to be detected (Appendix 5). On this basis a decline in BB2 can be postulated; the 'fourth century' accumulation in the Chalk 'cellar' incorporated some 30 per cent BB2 (vessel rim equivalence) which comprises 31 per cent of the coarse wares alone, a lower proportion than was present in the late third-century layers, wherein BB2 comprised over 44 per cent of the coarse wares. Comparisons of the figures from late second to mid-third and third- to fourth-century assemblages from Rochester, and mid-second to mid-third and mid-third to fourth-century assemblages from Springhead, also show an overall fall in the amounts of BB2. There is no evidence for any additions to the formal range of this ware in west Kent later than the mid-third century adoption of the bead-and-flange dish. It is quite conceivable that BB2 continued to be produced into the first half of the fourth century; indeed, there is no evidence to conflict with this view. However, the absence of the ware from the Bexley group, and apparently from both Lullingstone pits (this pottery could not all be traced by the present author – Pollard 1987; there is no obvious BB2 in the original publication, except perhaps Meates *et al.* 1950, no. 14), suggests that it was passing out of usage in the second quarter of the century or thereabouts. The pottery attributable to the destruction and post-destruction groups of late fourth to early fifth century from Lullingstone, and to an occupation level close to the Temple-Mausoleum on its south side (Pollard 1987, Group XL, associated with three coins of Magnentius and two copies of the '*Fel. Temp. Reparatio*' series, dateable to A.D. 350–353 and *c.* A.D. 354–364, respectively (Casey 1980, 44)) excludes BB2, which supports the hypothesis that use of this ware had ceased by the latter half of the fourth century. Clearly more dating evidence is needed, if this hypothesis is to be verified. The absence of fine sandy burnished wares of late second- and third-century 'north-west Kent' types from Bexley and the Lullingstone deposits suggests that these and BB2 disappeared from use contemporaneously. It is possible that pressure from the expanding Alice Holt industry, which also sought to market fine slipped reduced wares in west Kent, played a major part, as BB2 itself may have done in the late second-century decline of the Canterbury grey ware industry. However, as with the Canterbury situation, the discontinuation of production of certain wares cannot be equated with a total abandonment of production of grey sandy wares, for such wares, from whatever source, continued to comprise a significant element in later fourth-century coarse pottery assemblages.

The differentiation, and allocation to sources, of fourth-century grey sandy pottery is no less a problem than in earlier periods; it has, however, been brought into sharp focus by the detailed studies of the late Roman grey ware industries of Oxfordshire (Young 1977a), the New Forest (Fulford 1975a) and Alice Holt-Farnham (Lyne and Jefferies 1979). Attempts to distinguish the grey ware products of the New Forest and Alice Holt-Farnham potteries have so far proved unsuccessful (Peacock 1967; Fulford 1975b), but this is of less importance to Kent (where the extreme rarity of New Forest colour-coated wares carried the implication that grey wares of that industry would also have been rare, if not unknown) than to Sussex and more westerly regions (e.g. Green 1977, 157). The occurrence of Oxfordshire grey wares in Kent is also most improbable (Young 1977a, 207–8). However, grey wares from the Much Hadham kilns may have been distributed south of the Thames, and it is likely that production of such pottery also continued within Kent (see also the following section). The fourth-century accumulation in the Chalk cellar incorporated some 39 per cent unslipped reduced sandy wheel-thrown wares (42 per cent of coarse wares, by vessel rim equivalence), plus 14 per cent (16 per cent) slipped 'Alice Holt-Farnham' grey wares. The former included a single characteristic Much Hadham grey ware type, a bead-and-flange dish with a wavy line tooled on the upper interior (unpublished). The great majority of the grey wares are of fine or medium coarseness (cf. Orton 1977a), and additional Much Hadham grey ware vessels may also be represented. The 'swan's neck' pendant roll-rim jar (cf. no. 203 here) is, however, absent, as it is from the Bexley and Lullingstone groups (cf. 4.IV.2). Unslipped grey wares may also have been exported to Kent from the Alice Holt-Farnham industry, where fine sandy angular and hooked-rim necked jars were manufactured until *c.* A.D. 330 (Lyne and Jefferies 1979, Class 3C.2, 4–8). If the North Kent industry continued to function until the mid-fourth century, it is probable that plain sandy necked jars, produced alongside BB2 as in earlier centuries, satisfied the bulk of the local demand up until the discontinuation of production of the parallel Alice Holt forms.

The majority of grey sandy unslipped wares in west Kent in the fourth century (at least in the first half) may well be local products therefore. The forms are mostly necked round or angular roll-rim jars (e.g. Philp 1973, nos. 394, 402, 408 and 410 from Darenth), with lesser numbers of everted recurved and necked burnished jars, dog-dishes and bead-and-flange dishes. These also occur at Bexley, where BB2 and third-century North Kent fine sandy burnished wares are absent, and Alice Holt-Farnham slipped ware present. There is also a number of slipped and unslipped 'Drag. 38' flanged bowls in Kent which do not belong either to Alice Holt-Farnham or the third century north-west Kent/south Essex industries, including an example from Lullingstone in a post-destruction deposit in the 'Deep Room' (late fourth-early fifth century: Pollard 1987, Group LII, fig. 76, no 173). These may be Kent products, or from kilns north of the Thames. Burnished bead-and-flange dishes also occur in the aforementioned Lullingstone deposits. These are in a finer fabric than the formally similar vessel found in Kiln III at Mucking, ostensibly the latest of the six kilns on that site and possibly operating in the fourth century (Jones and Rodwell 1973, no. 18; the dating published therein has since been challenged – M.U. Jones and V. Swan, pers. comm.), and may thus not emanate from that site. It is impossible to ascertain how important unslipped grey sandy wares were in Kent in the late fourth century, but they were almost certainly used for some time after the disappearance of BB2. Much Hadham oxidised wares are rare throughout this region (*q.v.* the preceding section), partially at least as a result of the strength of competition from Oxfordshire colour-coated ware. The ratios of oxidised to grey Much Hadham wares on sites in Hertford-shire and north Essex need to be established before discussion of the issue of Much Hadham grey ware export to Kent can usefully proceed. At present, it may be proposed that local kilns continued to supply the bulk of the plain grey pottery of north Kent for the greater part, if not the whole of, the fourth- to early fifth-century period. These wares were the coarsest of the grey wares, dispensing as they did with the labour-consuming processes of slipping and burnishing, and by virtue of their lack of refined finishing and bulky shapes may have been the most uneconomical to import from Alice Holt-Farnham, Much Hadham or elsewhere (see below, this section, however). The burnished bowls and dishes may indicate that some marketing headway could be made against fine grey imports also, at least by unslipped wares.

Exportation of Alice Holt-Farnham white, black and grey slipped grey wares to Kent may have begun in earnest in the final decade of the third century, or slightly later (cf. 4.IV.2). The 'rim counts' percentages published by Lyne and Jefferies (1979, Appendix 3) may be suspect on theoretical grounds (cf. Orton 1975; 1980, 156–67; Hinton 1977), but the figures from Lullingstone villa and Springhead are in harmony with those calculated by the present author using vessel rim equivalents; these reveal Alice Holt-Farnham slipped grey ware to have provided 8–10 per cent of all wares in the third to fourth century at Springhead and Rochester, and 14 per cent of all wares in the fourth-century 'cellar' infill at Chalk. The proportion of coarse ware assemblages alone is in each case some 2 per cent higher. These are minimum estimates, as the slipped Alice Holt ware was not manufactured before *c.* A.D. 270 (Lyne and Jefferies 1979, 35; M. Millett, pers. comm.), and significant quantities of pre- A.D. 270 wares are certainly present in the first two assemblages at least. The ware reached every fourth-century site studied in west Kent with the possible exception of Cooling (Fig. 38) where only tiny quantities of late pottery were found (Pollard forthcoming, b). The numbers of types of this ware, and of the buff coarse sandy 'Portchester "D"' ware with which it was imported from *c.* A.D. 325/330 (see below), appear to be similar on a number of different sites, the variations exhibited being possibly functions of the amount of fourth-century pottery recovered and the length of occupation of sites rather than of site type or location (Fig. 11). East of the Medway both the range of types and the proportions of fourth-century assemblages which they comprise fall off, however (see the following section). The most frequently occurring types in west Kent are everted rim jars (Lyne and Jefferies 1979, Class 3B.10–13), bead-and-flange dishes (*ibid.*, Class 5B.4–10), dog-dishes (*ibid.*, Class 6A.8–10, 12–13), heavy-bead rim storage jars (*ibid.*, Class 4.42, 4.44–45), flange rim necked jars (*ibid.*, Class 1.32–33), moulded rim necked storage jars (*ibid.*, Classes 1A.14–20, 1C.2–5), and flagons (*ibid.*, Class 8.11–14). It has been suggested (*ibid.*, 97–8) that the storage jars were exported as filled containers, whose contents covered the cost of transportation and indirectly created a suitable climate for the long-distance marketing of other forms. Alice Holt-Farnham slipped grey ware may have been exported to west Kent throughout the fourth century. A handful of vessels can be allocated to the destruction and post-destruction deposits at Lullingstone, including two storage jars (Meates *et al.* 1952, nos. 91–2), whilst other vessels probably of this ware occur in the mid fourth-century pits on the same site (Meates *et al.* 1950, nos. 12–13; Meates *et al.* 1952, nos. 87–8). At least one vessel was recovered from the mid fourth- to early fifth-century cemetery at Chalk (Allen 1954, no. 28).

'Portchester "D"', a name originally applied to a distinctive coarse sandy buff wheel-thrown ware, often with a sooted black exterior, identified at Portchester Castle (Fulford 1975b, 299–301), has so far been positively demonstrated to have been produced by only one industry, Alice Holt-Farnham, and there only on the outlying kiln sites at Tilford (Lyne and Jefferies 1979), despite claims for additional production elsewhere (*ibid.*, 35, 61). Production of this ware began in the first third of the fourth century (Fulford 1975b, 299–301; Lyne and Jefferies 1979, 35; Millett 1979, 125), with three forms predominating: the hook-rim necked jar with horizontal-grooved ('rilled') decoration (Lyne and Jefferies 1979, Class 3C.10–19), the bead-and-flange dish (*ibid.*, Class 5B, undecorated), and the convex-sided dog-dish (*ibid.*, Class 6A.11). An essentially identical ware, but with a grey colour, was used for hook-rim necked rilled jars from a somewhat earlier date, around the turn of the third century (*ibid.*, 35, 45: Class 3C.9,11). Both the buff and grey wares (the latter here termed 'Tilford' ware for convenience, although both wares were produced at this site) were widely marketed in Kent (Fig. 52), but are much less common than slipped fine grey Alice Holt-Farnham wares. The buff ware is absent from the Chalk 'cellar', though two dishes appear to have been interred in the nearby late cemetery (Allen 1954, nos. 19 and 26; these could not be located in the museum collection), and is also absent from Bexley. The buff ware does, however, comprise over 4 per cent of the third- to fourth-century Springhead assemblage and nearly 2 per cent of the broadly contemporary Rochester assemblage (Appendix 5), and the grey 'Tilford' ware some 3 per cent of the latter. Several buff ware vessels occur in the latest Lullingstone deposits (e.g. Meates *et al.* 1950, no. 29; Meates *et al.* 1952, no. 93), suggesting that this ware, if not the grey 'Tilford' ware, continued to be imported to the end of the fourth century at least.

Alice Holt-Farnham grey wares, and 'Portchester "D"' buff ware are quantitatively the most significant designated coarse ware imports to west Kent in the fourth century as a whole. A number of other sources are represented by small amounts of pottery, evincing a complexity in the coarse pottery trade the like of which had not been experienced in earlier centuries. BB1 from Dorset and conceivably elsewhere (*q.v.* 4.IV.3 and 4.V.3), of late second- to fourth-century date, is widely distributed throughout Kent (Fig. 36). These occurrences include several examples of the late third- to fourth-century bead-and-flange dish (Gillam 1970, Type 228), including one in a mid fourth-century pit at Lullingstone (Meates *et al.* 1952, no. 89), and less frequent examples of the wide-rimmed everted jar of similar date (Gillam 1970, Types 146–8). The mid fourth-century-plus plain dog-dish (*ibid.*, Type 330) has only been positively recognised on two sites in west Kent, Rochester (unpublished) and Snodland (Jessup *et al.* 1954, 50–1, nos. 3–7, three of which bear the 'Redcliffe' motif which may be a late fourth-century feature to judge from its absence in the north of the province; cf. Williams 1977, 175 and 205), although examples may have gone unnoticed as rim sherds are indistinguishable from the late second-century to fourth-century decorated form (Gillam 1970, Type 329). Nevertheless, it seems probable that Dorset BB1, and perhaps also local 'derived' products (of which the undecorated bead-and-flange dishes from Cobham Park and Rochester may be examples, as Dorset vessels are generally decorated) were out of use by the last years of the fourth century; none can be ascribed to the destruction and post-destruction deposits at Lullingstone, and this hypothesis is in accord with the Canterbury evidence (see the following section). In total, BB1 comprised under 3 per cent of the third- to fourth-century Rochester assemblage (under 4 per cent of coarse wares), and 1 per cent of the Chalk 'cellar' fourth-century accumulation. A single vessel of a type current in this century (Gillam 1970, Type 329) has been recorded in the third- to fourth-century deposits at Springhead, a point which emphasises the rarity of BB1 in west Kent in the last century of Roman occupation.

In contrast with BB1, late Roman shelly wares (Sanders 1973) may have arrived in Kent only in the last third of the fourth century and perhaps into the fifth (*q.v.* the following section). There is no positive dating evidence from west Kent, but earlier examples from the London area are extremely rare (e.g. McIsaac *et al.* 1979, fig. 18, no. 112, of the first half of the fourth century), as is also the case in Essex (Drury 1976a, 46). The ware is soft, black to brown, with abundant shell inclusions, and wheel-thrown. The most common form in Kent and the London area is the angular hook-rim necked rilled jar (no. 212 here), though bead-and-flange dishes also occur (no. 213 here), and other forms are known in the east Midlands, where the centres of production are most likely to have been located (cf. Sanders 1973). Parallels can be drawn with 'Portchester "D"' (cf. Lyne and Jefferies 1979, 59–61); both wares comprise three main forms – the hook-rim rilled jar, bead-and-flange dish, and dog-dish–, all executed on a wheel and buff-fired often with a blackened surface. The jar is the most frequently-encountered form in both wares in Kent and the London area, both areas lying outside the primary areas of distribution (Sanders 1973; Lyne and Jefferies 1979, fig. 52, where a distinction is made between 'Portchester "D"' and an ill-defined 'Surrey buff ware' which the present author has elected to ignore). The shelly ware was evidently less common in Kent and London than 'Portchester "D"' (Appendix 5), although it achieved a considerable dispersal in north-west Kent (Fig. 52).

The phenomenon of long-distance importation of course wares to Kent in the fourth century finds its apogee in 'Mayen' ware, thought to have been produced in the Eifel mountains in the angle of the Rhine and Moselle, Germany (Fulford and Bird 1975). This ware is wheel-thrown, yellow to brown or purple in colour, and extremely dense with inclusions of volcanic glass being particularly distinctive. The forms include jars with a thick everted rim and internal rim projection (*ibid.*, no. 3), hemispherical and carinated bowls with an internally-thickened rim (*ibid.*, nos. 6–7) and conical-sided dishes with an inwardly-everted rim (*ibid.*, nos. 9–10). Jugs, handled narrow jars, and lids are also known (*ibid.*, nos. 1, 2 and 11). The jars are the most frequently-encountered form in Britain, but bowls and dishes also occur widely, and other forms more rarely. The ware is found mainly in south-east Britain. Examples in Britain date to the fourth or early fifth century (*ibid.*, 179; Pollard forthcoming, d), including a bead-rim bowl (Fulford and Bird 1975, no. 6 type) from a post-destruction level above the House-Church at Lullingstone (Pollard 1987, Group LII, fig. 77, no. 204), a deposit possibly as late as the second decade of the fifth century or even somewhat later (Meates 1979, 41–2). Six sites in west Kent from which 'Mayen' ware has been recovered have been recorded (Fig. 52, to which a vessel from Joyden's Wood of jar form – Tester and Caiger 1954, no. 42 – in grey ware with volcanic inclusions may be added), all of which were occupied in the fourth century. There is no clear evidence of differential distribution of the ware according to site function or location (cf. Fulford and Bird 1975, 179–81). It is possible that 'Mayen' ware was exported to Britain in ships involved in delivering grain to the Rhineland that had been collected as part of the *annona militaris* (corn requisitions) in Britain (Ammianus Marcellinus, xviii, 2, 3), in much the same way as BB1 from Dorset may have been transported to the northern military zone of Britain through the Irish Sea (Fulford 1981, 202–3). The commerce between Britain and the Rhine was intensified by the emperor Julian in A.D. 359, when a large fleet was built to supply the imperial campaign in the lower Rhine (Frere 1974, 390). Glass vessels may also have been exported to Britain from the lower Rhineland (Price 1978, 75–7), but it is thought that this trade may have declined in volume in the late fourth century (*ibid.*). The high proportion of the total number of 'Mayen' vessels in Britain that jars comprise has been used to support the hypothesis that these vessels were imported laden with some commodity (Fulford and Bird 1975, 181). This is an interesting possibility, but it would be necessary to compare vessel ratios in Britain with those in the area of production, and recognise some differentiation between the two regions, before this piece of evidence can be considered valid to the testing of the hypothesis. The predominant rôle of the jars over other forms in Britain bears a close resemblance to the patterns exhibited by 'Portchester "D"' and late Roman shelly ware; while it is possible that these were also imported for their contents, all three patterns may also be a reflection of an especial esteem in which high-quality, often very hard-wearing, jars were held. In Kent at least, local production of sandy ware jars may have failed to fulfil the demand for such vessels in the middle and late years of the fourth century, encouraging importation to fill the void (see the following section). Slipped Nene Valley necked jars (*q.v.* the preceding section; Howe *et al.* 1980, 9 and nos. 70, 75–7) may also have taken a part in this trade.

Late Roman grog-tempered ware (4.IV.3) may have been the main local competitor with these imports in the late fourth century throughout Kent. It evidently emerged in west Kent somewhat later than in the east of the county, perhaps not becoming a significant element in pottery assemblages until the second or third quarter of the fourth century. Only one out of some 38 vessels represented at Bexley is in this ware, all of these vessels conceivably being of fourth-century date. Five out of the ten vessels published from one of the mid-fourth century pits at Lullingstone are grog-tempered jars (Pollard 1987, Group XLV, Fabric 75; *q.v.* Meates 1979, 56–7); several vessels are also represented in the destruction and post-destruction deposits of the villa, and in the occupation level south of the Temple-Mausoleum. A mid-fourth century development of large-scale importation and/or local production (it is at present not possible to differentiate between these two modes of distribution) would be concomitant with the apparent rarity of the ware at the Cobham Park and Maidstone villas, where occupation may have ended at this time (Tester 1961, 97; the Maidstone evidence has been assessed by the present author in consultation with the excavator, Mr D. Kelly). It would also help explain the low proportion of grog-tempered ware in the Chalk 'cellar' infill accumulation (Appendix 5; the figure of 6 per cent is under half that for this ware in the third-fourth century Rochester deposit, and one-quarter that of the Springhead deposit of the same date). The layer containing most of the pottery (layer 6), was sealed by a 'nearly sterile' layer (5) prior to the deposition of building material (layer 4) *c.* A.D. 395 (Johnston 1972, 120). Deposition of the Rochester and Springhead material may have continued into the fifth century (Redfern 1978, 54; the Springhead coin list from the *temenos* area includes several late fourth- to early fifth-century issues: Penn 1959, 1960, 1962; Pollard 1983a, fig. 64), as did the destruction/post-destruction sequence at Lullingstone (Meates 1979, 41–2). The development of grog-tempered ware, thought to be a 'household industry' product requiring the minimum of labour, skill, and equipment (*q.v.* 6.I.) may have been a reaction to a decline in the output of potters producing sandy wheel-thrown, kiln-fired ware, which itself might have resulted from some changes in landlord-tenant relations and in the economic climate, which proved detrimental to labour-intensive, specialist industries. This line of thought is pursued elsewhere (Pollard 1983a, 519–35).

The Oxfordshire kilns appear to have achieved an almost complete monopoly of the market for gritted mortaria in west Kent in the fourth century. The vessels from the mid fourth-century Lullingstone pits (Meates *et al.*, 1950, no. 21; Meates *et al.* 1952, no. 90) and occupation level south of the Temple-Mausoleum (Pollard 1987, Group XL, Fabric 35) are all in Oxfordshire white ware, while the five vessels found on the latest floor of the 'Deep Room' at Lullingstone include three in this ware and two in Oxfordshire white-slipped ware (Meates *et al.* 1952, nos. 39–43). Vessels from the destruction and post-destruction deposits are also predominantly in Oxfordshire wares, including a red colour-coated vessel possibly used as a receptacle for paint (*ibid.*, no. 61; Meates 1979, 54). One Nene Valley buff ware mortarium may also have come from this sequence of deposits (Meates 1953, no. 146). The vessels from layers 5 and 6 at Chalk are solely Oxfordshire products, as were all of the mortaria from the third- to fourth-century layers at Springhead and Rochester that could, on the adducement of parallels from Canterbury and elsewhere, be ascribed to the mid-fourth century or later, with the exceptions of a handful of oxidised Much Hadham ware sherds. The main form used in Kent in the fourth century has a high bead and short, thick flange folded back onto itself or moulded (Young 1977a, M22, WC7 and C100). 'Wall-sided' Oxfordshire red colour-coated ware vessels derived from the samian form Drag. 45 (*ibid.*, C97) also occur, and 'East Kent' vessels (4.IV.3) may have been used in the early part of the century. Although Oxfordshire wares predominate amongst mortaria with trituration grit, it is conceivable that vessels without this feature may also have been used for similar functions. The hemispherical flanged bowl of 'Drag. 38' type is formally well-suited to the task if the mortarium was cradled in the arm, and Oxfordshire vessels of this form (Young 1977a, C51–2) sometimes exhibit marked abrasion of the interior slip. A heavily built, hand-made sandy red-black 'Drag. 38' vessel from the uppermost post-destruction level above the bathing establishment at Lullingstone (Pollard 1987, Group XXXVII(c), Fabric 59) could well have performed this function; perhaps significantly, it was burnished only on the exterior. Conversely, gritted mortaria might be used for purposes other than food preparation. The 'paint-pot' from Lullingstone, a broken vessel mended with rivets prior to its final use, has already been mentioned; in addition, Meates (1979, 39) has proposed that the five vessels found on the floor of the 'Deep Room' may have been used as balers for the well in the floor.

There is virtually no information on fourth- to early fifth-century amphorae in west Kent. A rim sherd from layer 3 at Chalk (Peacock 1977d, 298, no. 6) may represent a late import of unknown origin, whilst the presence of Dorset BB1 dishes of mid-fourth century-plus form in the Holborough tumulus (Jessup *et al.* 1954, fig. 14, nos. 4 and 7) suggests that the amphorae were interred in this period but not that they necessarily were imported in the fourth century. The rim of a hollow-foot amphora was recovered from Lullingstone (Pollard 1987, Fabric 80).

3. *The Coarse Wares of East Kent*

Fourth-century pottery has been recovered from a considerable number of sites in east Kent

(Figs. 7, 8), but rarely in securely stratified deposits. The most important assemblages studied comprise a handful of pit-groups (for coarse wares, Pits 37, 54: Bushe-Fox 1932; 69: Bushe-Fox 1949; and 303: Cunliffe 1968) from Richborough; a mid-late fourth century pit group from Wye (Pollard forthcoming, a), the bulk of the material from Professor Cunliffe's excavations at Port Lympne (Cunliffe 1980; Young 1980), and that from the sequence of structures and levels excavated by the Canterbury Archaeological Trust (Blockley and Day forthcoming; Pollard forthcoming, d) in Canterbury itself. A detailed study of the last-named assemblage has enabled the construction of an absolute chronology for the pottery of the civitas capital to be attempted, with an abundance of coins providing the vital independent dating medium. It is to be hoped that the extensive excavations of the Dover Saxon Shore fort under the direction of Brian Philp will provide a second ceramic sequence in east Kent; unfortunately, the pottery recovered could not be made available to the present author at the appropriate time.

The early years of the fourth century witnessed a continuation of ceramic trends apparent in the late third century at Canterbury (4.IV.3): steady usage of reduced sand-tempered wheel-thrown wares, slight increases in the volume of late grog-tempered ware and BB1, and decreases in BB2 and high-fired sand-and-grog tempered wares. The undesignated BB1 fabric (thought not to have come from Dorset) introduced in the very late third century (*ibid.*) may have partially eclipsed Dorset ware in the first half of the fourth. Several wares emerged during the course of the century, including a BB2 variant and a hand-made flint-and-sand tempered fabric of probably local origin, and imports from the Alice Holt-Farnham industry and the Rhineland (Mayen ware). Other imports are also occasionally encountered, including shelly ware from north of the Thames, and possibly Much Hadham reduced ware. Grog-tempered ware dominates assemblages of the latter half of the century and, with the possible exception of reduced sand-tempered wheel-thrown ware, may have been the sole indigenous product in the final decades. Throughout the century gritted mortaria were supplied almost exclusively by the Oxfordshire industry, as has been observed in west Kent (in the preceding section), with minor quantities of other imports also circulating.

The reduced sand-tempered unslipped wheel-thrown wares exhibit the high degree of conservatism that characterises them in the third century. Angular and round roll-rim, and everted, necked jars continued to be the most common forms, comprising over half of the total in this ware in the Canterbury sample. Other forms include cavetto-rim jars of BB1/BB2 style, dog-dishes and bead-and-flange dishes, lids, and flanged hemispherical bowls of 'Drag. 38' derivation (e.g. two vessels, unpublished, from Richborough, Pits 54 and 303). Burnished vessels are more common than scorched/vitrified or plain examples, particularly in fine sandy wares. Reduced sand-tempered unslipped wheel-thrown wares as a group comprise between 15 per cent and 35 per cent of early fourth-century assemblages at Canterbury (vessel rim equivalents, all wares), an identical range to that estimated for the preceding period (4.IV.3). The problems encountered in isolating imports in this ware group in west Kent (4.V.2) are relevant also to east Kent. Slipped grey wares of forms alien to Alice Holt have been recognised, for example at Wye (Pollard forthcoming, a) where bead-rim jars (*ibid.*, nos. 44–6) and a 'Drag. 38' bowl occur. Two burnished black necked jars with a pendant frill to the rim, one with bosses pressed out on the shoulder, from Canterbury (Pollard forthcoming, d, no. 223) may be imports from the Essex-Hertfordshire region to judge from their style (e.g. Myres *et al.* 1974). 'Swan's neck' pendant-bead rim necked jars (cf. no. 203 here) are extremely uncommon, however, only one vessel having been recorded from the sampled fourth-century assemblages at

Canterbury, plus one from a mixed third- to fourth-century deposit. Much Hadham oxidised wares do occur in east Kent (4.V.1), but are less common than in the north-west of the county, where grey wares of this source may have been little-used (4.V.2). It follows, therefore, that the latter would have been still rarer in east Kent. The proportional representation of reduced sand-tempered unslipped wheel-thrown wares is lower in mid fourth-century assemblages from Canterbury than in those of the early part of the century, comprising around 10 per cent– 20 per cent of all wares. The mid- to late fourth-century group from Wye has also given a figure within this range. It is impossible on present evidence to say whether a gradual decline in production, or a relatively abrupt termination of the activity of most potters working in this medium, occurred. However, by the end of the fourth century virtually no pottery in these wares appears to have been used: from Canterbury figures of only 5 per cent of a late fourth-century group, and 3 per cent of an early fifth-century group have been recorded (proportions of total assemblages; coarse ware proportions are 7 per cent and 4 per cent, respectively) (Pollard forthcoming, d).

One probable kiln producing grey wares has been excavated in east Kent on a rural site, at Preston-near-Wingham (Dowker 1878; 1893). The pottery found in this feature is described as of 'coarse blue ware. . .partially burnt. . .of a red colour' (Dowker 1878, 47), two vessels being illustrated by the excavator. One of these has been traced by the present author (Maidstone Museum registered as 5.PW.3), and is in a fine sandy grey ware with white slip, practically identical to Alice Holt ware. The form is similar to Alice Holt products (Lyne and Jefferies 1979, Class 3B.12), and the kiln structure – apparently a double flue type – is paralleled at Alice Holt, Farnham and Tilford (ibid., 1), all sites of the Alice Holt industry, and at Arlington in East Sussex (Holden 1979). Sandy wares in 'Alice Holt' forms, but of a somewhat coarser fabric and darker colour, have been recorded at Richborough (e.g. Bushe-Fox 1932, nos. 329 and 345, from Pit 37) and with considerable frequency at Canterbury (Pollard forthcoming, d) (see also the following section). The total of this grey ware variant in the fourth-century assemblages studied from the latter site is very close to that of Alice Holt pale grey fine sandy ware, and there is no clear chronological differentiation in intensity of usage of 'Alice Holt type' ware and Alice Holt grey ware. A neutral grey, black or white slip has been identified on both wares, and the formal ranges are similar. 'Alice Holt types' have been defined as occurring in forms known from Alice Holt, but only part of that range is at all common in east Kent, and it is this part that the former ware mostly reflects. Bead-and-flange dishes (Lyne and Jefferies 1979, Class 5B.8) are predominant, comprising some two-thirds of Alice Holt and one-half of 'Alice Holt type' ware in the Canterbury sample. Other forms common to both wares include the pointed-rim straight-sided dog-dish (ibid., Class 6A.12, undecorated) and the cavetto-rim elliptical or globular jar (ibid., Class 3B.11–14). The latter has also been recognised at Richborough (see above) and Ospringe (Whiting et al. 1931, no. 499), as well as in the Preston kiln. The bead-and-flange dish variants (Lyne and Jefferies 1979, Classes 5B.5 and 6C.1) have been recorded in 'Alice Holt type' ware, but not Alice Holt ware, at Canterbury (Pollard forthcoming, d). The angular-flanged '5B.8' is one of the most frequently-encountered Alice Holt ware forms throughout east Kent, sharing this distinction with the late flagons with bead or 'ring-neck' rim (Lyne and Jefferies 1979, Class 8.10–14). Storage jars (ibid., Classes 1A.16–20, 1B.3–4, 1C.3–6, 4.42–45), incurved rim dog-dishes (ibid., Class 6A.9), and horizontal- or depressed-flange-rim necked jars (ibid., Class 1.32–35) appear to have had a more restricted distribution (cf. Lyne and Jefferies 1979; Pollard forthcoming, a, d. Fig. 38 illustrates the overall distribution of Alice Holt grey ware). The range of forms in Alice Holt wares that occurs on sites in east Kent is generally narrower than that in the west, with the exception of Richborough (Fig. 11). At Canterbury, both Alice Holt and 'Alice Holt type' grey wares appear to have been in use mainly in the mid- to late fourth century, although present in late third- to early fourth- and early fifth-century contexts also. They comprise 3 per cent and 5 per cent respectively of all wares (3.5 per cent and 7 per cent of coarse wares) in the large mid fourth-century 'flood-silt' assemblage (Appendix 5), and generally account for less than 10 per cent each of groups of that century; the Wye pit group contained 6 per cent of the former ware (7 per cent of coarse wares). It should be emphasised that the identification of the variant 'Alice Holt type' is somewhat tentative, and that it may represent one end of the fabric range of Surrey-Hampshire border wares rather than a product of some other source, whether in east Kent or elsewhere. The possibility of emigrations of potters from the Alice Holt-Farnham-Tilford complex to sites close to major civil/military population nuclei is discussed below (6.VIII).

Coarse sandy wares from Tilford in west Surrey occur infrequently in east Kent, and mainly at Canterbury and the Saxon Shore forts (Fig. 52). The grey 'Tilford' and buff 'Portchester "D"' ware (described in the preceding section) from this eastern outlier of the Alice Holt industry are found mainly in angular-rim necked jar forms, though lid-seated jars and, in the latter ware, bead-and-flange dishes (Lyne and Jefferies 1979, Class 5B. 6, 8–10) and incurved-rim dog-dishes (*ibid*., Class 6A. 11) also occur. 'Portchester "D"' may have been introduced to east Kent in the middle years of the fourth century (Pollard forthcoming, d), somewhat later than its first appearance at Portchester Castle (Fulford 1975b, 299–300), from which its date of origin is taken. It comprises less than 5 per cent of Canterbury assemblages, but may well have been in use up to the end of the Roman period, as in west Kent. The extent of 'Tilford' ware usage is uncertain, but the ware seems to have been imported alongside 'Portchester "D"' and may have a similar history to the latter.

Four varieties of black-burnished ware may be isolated in east Kent, two each of BB1 and BB2 style. BB1 comprises probable Dorset vessels, and the more coarsely-tempered but finer-finished fabric thought to have emerged in the last years of the third century (4.IV.3). Both BB1 fabrics are extremely uncommon, if not entirely absent, in assemblages dateable to the second half of the fourth century (e.g. Canterbury: Jenkins 1950, the well; Pollard forthcoming, d; Wye pit: Pollard forthcoming, a), and they comprise a mere 1 per cent and 2 per cent respectively of the total mid fourth-century 'flood-silt' assemblages from Canterbury (1.5 per cent and 2.5 per cent of coarse wares; Appendix 5). In the late third and first half of the fourth centuries these proportions are somewhat higher, but usually each fabric comprises less than 5 per cent of all wares. It is possible that the undesignated fabric partially eclipsed Dorset imports during the second quarter of the fourth century at Canterbury. This fabric has tentatively been recognised at Birchington (unpublished; Well 2) and in the Saxon Shore fort at Port Lympne (Young 1980, nos. 32–34; examination by the present author), but not in west Kent.

BB2 is found in somewhat larger amounts than BB1 in deposits of early to mid fourth-century date at Canterbury, generally comprising between 3 per cent and 8 per cent of all wares. Dog-dishes and bead-and-flange dishes predominate, with cavetto-rim jars a minor component. 'North-west Kent/south Essex' dish forms are widespread, but outside of Canterbury it is impossible to assign occurrences with confidence to the fourth rather than the third century. However, a range of variant dish forms has been isolated in the civitas capital which may represent a local fourth-century development. These include dog-dishes with pointed rims and an external groove (cf. Lyne and Jefferies 1979, Class 6A.4), bead-and-stub-flange dishes (*ibid.*, Class 6C.1) and bead-and-angular-flange dishes (*ibid.*, Class 5B.8), forms not recognised in BB2 in west Kent or at Mucking. They comprise some 35 per cent of the BB2 in the mid fourth-century 'flood-silt', and lesser proportions in other deposits of early to mid fourth-century date. BB2 of all forms was apparently little-used in the late fourth century, and production may have been discontinued altogether. BB2, Dorset and undesignated (east Kent?) BB1, reduced sand-tempered unslipped wheel-thrown ware, and flint-and-sand tempered ware (see below) all apparently declined in use in the third quarter of the century, in contrast with a marked increase in quantities of grog-tempered ware. The number of pottery production units in operation in east Kent may have dropped, therefore, but it is equally plausible that this period saw an intensification of production of grog-tempered ware involving an increase in the numbers of potters. This may reflect a change in fashion, but it should be remembered that in all of these wares the range of forms comprised jars, dog-dishes and bead-and-flange dishes, with others such as lids accounting for small proportions of the output. The economies of production, rather than fashion, may have dictated the course of fabric development in the late fourth century; technologically, the grog-tempered ware was less accomplished than these other wares (excepting flint-sand ware), with wheel-throwing and trimming not practised, and vessels presumably demanded less time to produce, rendering it a ware suitable for 'spare-time' production by 'household industries'.

Local east Kent wares using tempering agents additional to, or in place of, sand may be divided into four groups: grog/sand-and-grog-tempered 'Native Coarse Wares' (*q.v.* 4.III.3), late grog-tempered ware (4.IV.3), flint/flint-and-sand tempered ware, and wares with miscellaneous tempers. The first-named may have continued in production into the mid-fourth century on a very small scale. It had evidently fallen into decline in the late third (4.IV.3), but sherds occur sporadically in fourth-century contexts in Canterbury (e.g. Jenkins 1950, no. 99), including 2 per cent in the mid fourth-century 'flood-silts' (Appendix 5). Differentiation between this ware and high-fired 'late Roman grog-tempered' ware is often arbitrary, however, as there is some formal overlap particularly in the jar range. Late Roman grog-tempered ware comprises between 5 per cent and 25 per cent of assemblages of the first half of this century at Canterbury, exhibiting a steady increase in quantities which accelerated in the latter half, when up to 75 per cent of the pottery of east Kent was in this ware (Appendix 5: at Canterbury both sherd counts and vessel rim equivalents have generated this statistic). Bushe-Fox's impression of the pottery from the Temples site at Richborough (1932) would seem to be in accord with this proportion. By the end of the fourth century grog-tempered ware may have been virtually the only coarse ware in use on most sites in east Kent.

The last two local wares to be described appear to have had a restricted regional distribution, in contrast with the widespread 'Native Coarse Ware' and grog-tempered ware. The flint-and-sand tempered ware has been recognised at Canterbury in several contexts (Pollard forthcoming, d), at Wye in the pit group (Pollard forthcoming, a, coarse ware fabrics II and III) and as a single sherd at Birchington (unpublished: Well 2). It is hand-made, often with uneven surfaces, reduced, with inclusions of flint in moderate amounts (up to 5 mm. in size) and ill-assorted quartz also in moderate quantities (*c.* 0.25–3 mm. in size); minor inclusions range from naturally-occurring mica, iron ore and chalk to grog and, in one sherd, pink mortar. Most vessels are facet-burnished, and rims occasionally exhibit signs of trimming. The forms comprise necked angular roll-rim, and everted-rim, jars, a bead-and-flange dish, and dog-dishes including a vessel with an exterior burnished lattice decoration. The ware is mainly found in mid fourth-century deposits at Canterbury, including 6 per cent of the 'flood-silts' assemblage (8 per cent of coarse wares), and could conceivably have been the product of a single generation of potters, probably operating in the vicinity of Canterbury itself. It is possible that these artisans sought to take advantage of the demise of BB1 and sandy wheel-thrown wares at this time.

A hand-made reduced ware heavily tempered with miscellaneous inclusions of mudstone, chalk, flint and grog has been described by Young at Port Lympne (1980, 281, Reduced-ware 8). The formal range is practically identical to late Roman grog-tempered ware (nos. 204–11 here), and comprises over half of the sherds found in the recent excavations on the Saxon Shore fort. One vessel, a biconical bowl (Young 1980, no. 47) with abundant white inclusions, exhibits moderate grass striations on all surfaces. The form, and the presence of these lacunae, suggest a Saxon rather than late Roman vessel, but too little is known about the pottery of either period in this part of Kent for the attribution to be certain. The fabrics of the remainder of 'Reduced-ware 8' are not closely paralleled by material from other sites in Kent known to the present author, but a general similarity to late 'East Sussex Ware' from Bishopstone (Green 1977) is apparent. Young (1980, 281) has expressed the opinion that the Port Lympne ware did not come from East Sussex, however. The date range of this ware is uncertain, owing to the dearth of stratified deposits at Port Lympne. Cunliffe (1980, 288) has postulated an abandonment of c. A.D. 350, which would imply that the inhabitants of this part of Kent used a much higher proportion of hand-made non-sandy coarse ware in the first half of the fourth century than did their counterparts in north-east Kent. The coarse pottery assemblage of Port Lympne, couched in these terms, bears a closer resemblance to that of Bishopstone in East Sussex (Green 1977) than to Canterbury.

Alice Holt wares and Dorset BB1 are the only exotic coarse wares that are thought to have achieved a significant share of the market in east Kent, apart from mortaria, in the fourth century. However, Mayen ware (see the preceding section) is widely distributed (Fig. 52), being found on several classes of site in small quantities. This import may have been first introduced to Canterbury in the mid-fourth century (Pollard forthcoming, d), continuing in use up to the end of the Roman period. The everted 'lid-seated' jar (Fulford and Bird 1975, Form 3) is the form most frequently encountered, as in west Kent, but lids, bowls, dishes, a jug, and a handled jar are also known. Richborough and Canterbury exhibit the widest ranges of forms (Fulford and Bird 1975; Pollard forthcoming, d), but this may be a reflection of the extent of excavations on these sites in comparison with the remainder of east Kent (excepting Dover, the material for which has not been studied by the present author). Late Roman shelly wares from the Midlands or East Anglia have only been recorded at Richborough, Dover (Willson 1981, no. 599) and Canterbury, and in very small quantities. The sherds from the last-named site derive from late fourth-century contexts. A single shelly ware vessel from further north – a Dales ware jar from the north Midlands or south Yorkshire – has been recorded, from Richborough (Loughlin 1977, 110; Bushe-Fox 1928, no. 147). This is very much of a 'stray' find, far away from the main area of distribution (Loughlin 1977) and its appearance may be a result of the movement of shipping between the Kent military base and the coast of north-east Britain.

The mortaria of the fourth century in east Kent were predominantly from the Oxfordshire kilns, including red- and white-slipped wares and plain white ware, as in west Kent. These three wares are found on all classes of site throughout the region (cf. Young 1977a). Nene Valley colour-coated and buff wares, Mancetter-Hartshill white ware, and Argonne red colour-coated ware also occur; Hartley's map (Hartley 1973a, fig. 6) implies that Mancetter-Hartshill wares were also widely distributed, and may be confined to the fourth century, in east Kent (Hartley 1968). One fragment of Argonne ware, from Port Lympne, can only be given a broad later second- to fourth-century date (Young 1980, 277). Hartley (1968) has recorded a New Forest ware vessel at Richborough, but this find is not confirmed by Fulford (1975a). The late fourth-century pottery groups from Canterbury are not large enough to enable any decline in mortarium usage (cf. the preceding section) to be detected. There is no reason to disbelieve that Oxfordshire wares at least were imported throughout the fourth and into the early fifth century.

There is no information on the importation of amphorae to east Kent known to the present author at the time of writing. The report on Canterbury amphorae of the late Iron Age and Roman periods prepared by Arthur (1986) may change this situation.

4.   *The Coarse Wares of Central-Northern Kent*

The evidence of fourth-century pottery from this region is derived from small collections of funerary material from Milton, Sittingbourne and Faversham, a handful of burial groups from Ospringe, and unstratified sherds from Radfield, Brenley Corner and Ospringe. The ascription of coarse pottery to this century is dependent upon the association with externally-dateable fine wares, mostly colour-coated vessels from Oxfordshire and the Nene valley. These can generally only give a late third- to fourth-century date-range, although fourth-century forms have been found on most sites, excepting Faversham and Brenley Corner, the latter having produced fourth-century coins, however.

The presence of these fine wares implies that this region participated in the extensive trade in ceramics in the fourth century. This is underlined by the occurrence of Alice Holt grey ware flagons at Ospringe and Sittingbourne, and a 'Portchester "D"' jar at Milton. Two dishes from the Ospringe cemetery are of fourth-century form (Gillam 1970, Type 330) and may both be in Dorset BB1 (see also 4.IV.4 above). Local production of reduced sand-tempered wheel-thrown wares may have continued, although there is no direct evidence of this. Several examples of 'Alice Holt type' grey sandy ware globular jars (Lyne and Jefferies 1979, Class 3B.11) have been recorded, from Ospringe (Whiting *et al.* 1931, no. 499), Milton and Sittingbourne, the Milton vessels being apparently unslipped. Fine grey sandy slipped tall-necked bulbous beakers from Milton and Faversham are of uncertain origin, but could conceivably be from a Kent source. One possible 'east Kent' BB1 vessel (4.IV.3, 4.V.3) a bead-and-flange dish, is in an unstratified collection of sherds from Ospringe. Grog-tempered wares are ubiquitous, but as with other late fabrics in this region their date of introduction cannot, at present, be ascertained (4.IV.4). Vessels in this ware include jars from burials at Ospringe and Milton and from an unstratified level at Radfield, and dog-dishes from burials at Milton and Faversham. Mortaria are mostly from the Oxfordshire industry, but a painted Nene Valley vessel has been recorded at Radfield. The one possible fourth-century amphora, from Ospringe, has been discussed above (4.IV.4).

There are insufficient data to allow Jaccard's correlation coefficients to be calculated. It should, however, be noted that fourth-century Continental imports have yet to be positively identified in this region, although a wide range of Romano-British imports are present (cf.

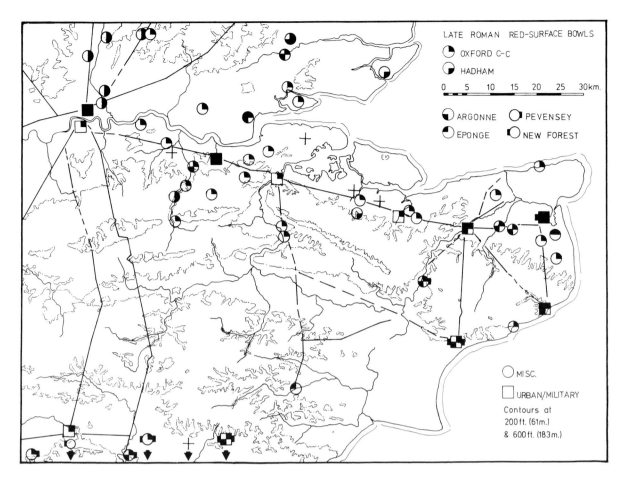

Fig. 51. Late Roman red-surface bowls: Distribution. + = absent.

4.V.1, and above). The small volume of data collected does not allow any inferences to be drawn from negative evidence, especially as the 'small town' site of Ospringe has only received attention to its sepulchral remains of this period (Fletcher and Meates 1969; 1977; Whiting *et al*. 1931).

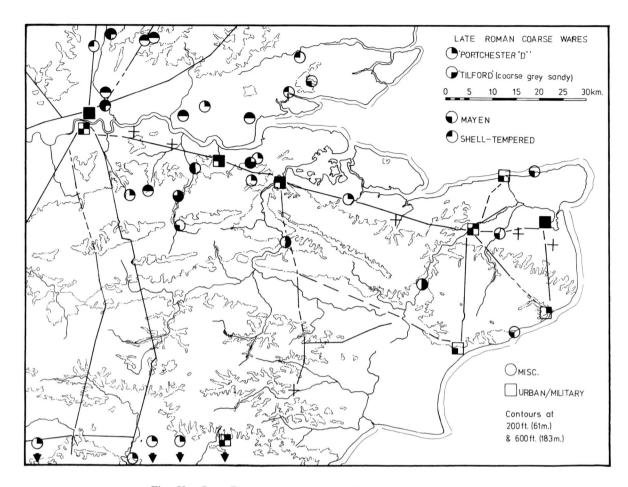

Fig. 52.   Late Roman coarse wares: Distribution.   + = absent.

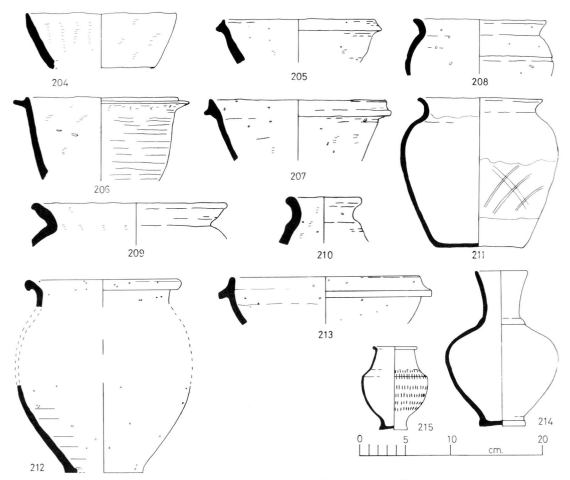

Fig. 53.   Pottery forms nos. 204–215 (Scale: ¼).

Fig. 53.   **204–211**:   Late Roman grog-tempered ware.

204. Plain-rim dog-dish, Pollard forthcoming a, no. 24. **205**. Triangular-rim ('vestigial bead-and-flange') dish, *ibid.*, no. 27. **206**. Bead-and-flange dish, *ibid.*, no. 29. **207**. Triangular-bead-and-flange dish, *ibid.*, no. 26. **208**. Everted-rim jar; the girth-groove is atypical of this ware, *ibid.*, no. 7. **209**. Bead-everted-rim jar, possibly derived from BB1 (Gillam 1970, Type 146), *ibid.*, no. 14. **210**. Everted-rim narrow-mouth ?storage jar, *ibid.*, no. 2. **211**. Everted-rim jar with tooled lattice, Jenkins 1950, no. 76.

212–213:   Late Roman shelly ware.

212. Hooked-rolled-rim necked jar, Orton 1977b, nos. 253 and 257. **213**. Bead-and-flange hemispherical bowl or dish, *ibid.*, no. 258.

214:   Fine orange-buff ware with dark-brown colour-coat, possibly a Nene Valley product; ovoid beaker with very tall everted 'trumpet' mouth, Whiting *et al.* 1931, no. 560.

215:   Fine sandy pink/white ware, probably an import from northern Gaul (Richardson and Tyers 1984), everted-rim tall-necked bulbous-/pentice-moulded beaker, rouletted, Gillam 1970, Type 42, Whiting *et al.* 1931, no. 86.

Dating: 204–211: Late third to early (or mid-) fifth century. 212–213. (Early to mid- fourth), late fourth to early fifth century. 214: Fourth century (?) 215. Late second to third (or early fourth) century.

VI. THE END OF ROMAN POTTERY IN KENT

The end of the fourth century would appear to have seen eight fabrics in large-scale usage in Kent, five imported and three local or possibly local. The former were Oxfordshire red- and white-slip, and plain white wares, Nene Valley colour-coated ware, and Alice Holt neutral-slip grey ware; the latter, late Roman grog-tempered, 'Alice Holt type' sand-tempered grey ware (in east Kent) and miscellaneous sand-tempered grey wares (possibly more common in west and central districts than in the east). Of these, the most abundant were Oxfordshire red colour-coated and late Roman grog-tempered wares, which together may have comprised up to 80 per cent of pottery assemblages in east Kent, perhaps somewhat less in the west (Appendix 5). Other wares in quite extensive use included Much Hadham, Argonne, 'Portchester "D"' and Mayen, all imports (Figs. 34, 51, 52, 61 and 68). Thus, quite a wide range of wares from a number of different industries would appear to have been available in the final decades of the diocese in Kent. The disappearance of this pottery, and its eventual replacement in the archaeological record by Germanic styles, presents one of the great enigmas of Roman pottery studies in the south-east of Britain.

There is very little evidence that can be adduced to show the contemporary usage of 'Romano-British' and 'Germanic' pottery in Kent. Occasionally, Roman vessels have been found in Germanic cemeteries, for example a second-century ring-necked flagon in the Bifrons cemetery (Maidstone Museum), or vice versa; a Germanic beaker of a style known as 'Anglo-Frisian' (a term now considered to be obsolete: Mainman, pers. comm.) from the site of the Roman cemetery at St. Sepulchre's in Canterbury (Kelly and Myres 1973), and two vessels from Preston-near-Wingham (Myers 1944, nos. 1 and 2) may be cited. However, it is by no means certain that these extraordinary coincidences are not the result of temporally separate interments, rather than of the cohabitation of Roman and German or the use of one's pottery by the other. The two cemeteries of Roman origin containing Germanic material were open in the late third-fourth, if not the early fifth, century (Brent 1861, no. 11; Dowker 1893, no. 7), and their location may have thus been known to fifth-century inhabitants of these areas. At least three other sites east of the Medway have revealed both Roman and Germanic pottery: Canterbury (e.g. Frere 1966; Mainman forthcoming), Wingham (Myres 1944; Jenkins 1965; 1966b; 1967) and Hartlip (Myres 1944). Anglo-Saxon *Grübenhäuser* of varying dates have been found elsewhere, for example at Darenth and Keston in west Kent (Philp 1973) and Dover (Philp, undated). Some of the Wingham pottery came from within the aisled building, but may represent nothing more than a re-occupation of a partially-upstanding structure offering some shelter, as happened in Canterbury.

Stylistically and technologically, there is little overlap between Romano-British and Germanic pottery in Kent. The earliest Germanic pottery in Canterbury is sandy, sometimes with a moderate or abundant admix of chalk, possibly reflecting the exploitation of local brickearths (Mainman forthcoming). Although hand-made and probably fired in a clamp or bonfire, and thus having some similarities with late Roman grog-tempered ware, the forms are different, including bead-rim and biconical jars, often with grooved chevrons or grouped vertical lines (*ibid.*, and Frere 1966, fig. 18). The squat globular recurved-rim jar is common to both late Roman grog-tempered and Germanic sand/chalk-tempered ware, but this form is so simple that this may be fortuitous. The use of grog is virtually unknown in Saxon period wares from Canterbury, implying a fundamental technological change from late Roman practice. A single vessel from Preston-near-Wingham (Myres 1944, no. 2) that has been examined by the present author is grog-tempered, however, and possibly finished on a wheel. This may represent a transitional stage between Roman and Germanic pottery, as the form is not closely paralleled by known late Roman grog-tempered vessels from Kent (e.g. nos. 204–11 here; Bushe-Fox 1932; Jenkins 1950, nos. 76–80; Meates *et al.* 1952, nos. 82–6; Whiting *et al.* 1931, nos. 60, 99, 112, 311, 337, 387, 397, 496). Germanic pottery from west Kent has not been examined by the present author, but published descriptions of material include everted-rim jars in 'hard dense ware' from Keston (Philp 1973, nos. 464–7, 470) associated with 'grass-tempered' shallow bowls or dishes (*ibid.*, nos. 468–9) and sherds with stamp-and-groove and dimple-and-groove decoration in the former ware (*ibid.*, nos. 471–2). Vessels from Dartford are in 'grass-tempered ware', including everted-rim jars, open bowls or cups, and a triangular-everted-rim jar with combed grooves and stabbing from one site (Tester 1956a), and an everted-rim jar with stamp-and-groove decoration from a burial in association with a fifth-century glass bowl (Walsh 1980). 'Grass-tempered' pottery in Canterbury is at present thought to have had a *floruit* in the eighth century (Mainman forthcoming).

The stylistic parallels between Romano-British and Germanic wares that have been interpreted as representing the influence of Germanic mercenaries upon Romano-British potters (Myres 1956; Rodwell 1970a) have more recently, and convincingly, been argued to be fortuitous (Gillam 1979). In any event, this so-called 'Romano-Saxon' pottery of the Roman period is extremely rare at Canterbury, where numbers of Germanic sherds exhibiting the motifs under discussion have been found (e.g. Frere 1966, fig. 18, nos. 1, 7, 11, 18–26).

It may be reasonably proposed, therefore that, in Kent, there is no clear sign of a 'transitional' fifth-century ceramic tradition linking Romano-British and Germanic pottery, with the possible exception of a single unstratified vessel from Preston. The question arises as to what became of the Romano-British pottery industries active in the late fourth century. Students of the major industries exporting pottery to Kent have been unable to shed any light on their termination, other than to speculate on the economic causes such as the loss of markets, the disruption of communications, or the breakdown of the monetary system of exchange (Young 1977a, 240–1; Fulford 1979, 128–9; Lyne and Jefferies 1979, 60–1). It is generally accepted that Romano-British pottery manufacture had ceased by *c.* A.D. 450 at the latest (Fulford 1979, 120), but that the major industries of Oxfordshire (Young 1977a, 240), the Nene valley (Howe *et al.* 1980, 10) and Alice Holt (Lyne and Jefferies 1979, 60–1) were still strong at the beginning of the fifth century. These conditions almost certainly pertain also to the late Roman grog-tempered ware industries of Kent, and also of Hampshire (Fulford 1975b), although perhaps not to the hand-made 'East Sussex Ware' potteries to the south of Kent (Green 1977, 177).

The evidence for the conditions of the pottery trade in Kent in the late fourth and early fifth centuries in Kent is not strong, but certain observations may be made. The distribution of Oxfordshire red colour-coated ware types thought to have been introduced around A.D. 350 suggests that there was still considerable interaction between town and country, for these types; in particular, the flagons C11, C13 and C14, the 'Drag. 38' flanged-bowl C52, and the cordoned bowls C84 and C85 have been found on a diverse number of sites of urban, military and rural nature throughout the modern county (Young 1977a; Appendix 3 here). Late Roman shell-tempered ware, dating probably to the late fourth century in Kent, has also been recorded on urban, military and rural sites, although in east Kent it is only known at Canterbury,

Richborough and Dover (Fig. 52). If, as Fulford (1977a) suggests, the bulk of Continental pottery was imported in the latter half of the fourth century, then the distributions of Argonne, 'à l'éponge' and Mayen wares (Figs. 51 and 52) provides further evidence of the continuance of extensive commercial activity in later fourth-century Kent. In contrast, the number of potteries operating within Kent may have diminished, or at least the range of wares produced did. The Upchurch fine ware and Cliffe peninsula BB2 industries are both thought to have been terminated in the first half of the fourth century (4.V and 5.II.4), whilst the east Kent local variants of BB1 and BB2, and the flint-and-sand ware of that region, do not seem to have been produced beyond the middle of the century. Reduced sand-tempered wheel-thrown wares also declined relative to grog-tempered ware, in east if not west and central-northern Kent, in this period. The absolute volume of pottery consumed in the late fourth century may or may not have declined from that in use in the early and middle thirds of that century, but the range of local wares almost certainly did. In west Kent, however, grog-tempered ware may have been little-used before the second half of the century, and some imports may have only arrived in quantity in the latter period, providing some counter-balance to the indigenous reduction of wares produced.

The present evidence from Kent does not conflict with Fulford's view that the pottery industry and trade as a whole were in a state of decline in the later fourth century (1979, 121–2). No new wares or forms appear to have been introduced either by importers or local producers in the last third of the century, with the possible exception of shelly ware (which throughout Kent occurs in only very small amounts). The presence of large quantities of Theodosian coinage, and less frequent issues of Honorius and Arcadius, in 'black earth' abandonment deposits at Rochester (Redfern 1978) and Canterbury (Reece 1972) implies continued activity in the two major towns of Kent up to the end of the fourth and possibly into the fifth century, while Richborough was also held at this time (Cunliffe 1968). The late coins published from Springhead exhibit a temporal distribution in harmony with Reece's model (1972), suggesting that commercial life continued to flourish in this 'small town', if not in the Ospringe settlement (Pollard 1983a, fig. 64). The excavations of villas at Lullingstone and Hartlip have also revealed late coins (Reece 1972; Roach Smith 1852). It would appear, then, that considerable activity involving the use of money was still taking place in Kent at the end of the fourth century (Pollard 1983a, 519–35), although, of course, this need not all have been of a commercial nature, and certainly not all involving the marketing of ceramics. The diminution of consumption of the products of the centralised industries, for whatever reason, may have led to the continuation of production becoming an economically unviable proposition (Fulford 1979, 128–9), this position being reached apparently in the early fifth century. These industries may have been inextricably tied to a coin-using economy (*ibid*.), but it is perhaps surprising that the more localised grog-tempered industries did not outlive them by more than a few years, for this certainly seems to have been the case in Kent. Fulford has speculated that 'Pagan Saxon' pottery supplanted 'Romano-British' because for the former 'manufacture was less specialised from the start and village or craft-potting was customary' (*ibid*.). It has been observed that the technology of late Roman grog-tempered ware and Germanic ware in Kent has certain similarities, including hand-manufacture and firing without a special kiln. There is no pressing reason to disbelieve that the former was produced primarily for neighbourhood consumption with inter-settlement exchange a secondary function, at least in areas away from the towns and forts. The collapse of the coin-using economy may have precipitated a more general breakdown of the social order, but it is not clear how extensive the use of coinage was on rural sites even in the late fourth century, when ceramic trade appears to have still flourished. In short, late Roman grog-tempered ware production and distribution may have partially operated outside of a coin-using system within the Roman period, and may have been the output of a mode of production similar to that hypothesised for the Germanic wares. Its disappearance from the archaeological record during the first half of the fifth century is probable, for sites have not been found in Kent wherein this ware was used in the absence of products of the centralised industries, a situation that might appertain if grog-tempered ware outlived these industries by more than, say, a quarter of a century. The lack of late fourth- to fifth-century stratification on most rural sites prohibits the pursuit of this line of argument, as does discussion of the effect of the Germanic migrations upon rural life in Roman Britain. At present it seems as likely that the breakdown of social order precipitated the abandonment of potting in the Romano-British tradition for local consumption as that broader economic factors such as the loss of urban markets and the collapse of the monetary system were responsible (see also Pollard 1983a, 519–35).

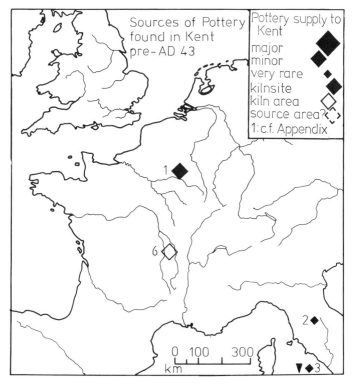

Fig. 54.   Sources of pottery found in Kent: Europe, pre-A.D. 43.

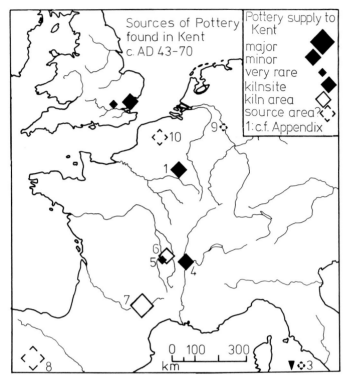

Fig. 55.   Sources of pottery found in Kent: Europe, *c.* A.D. 43–70.

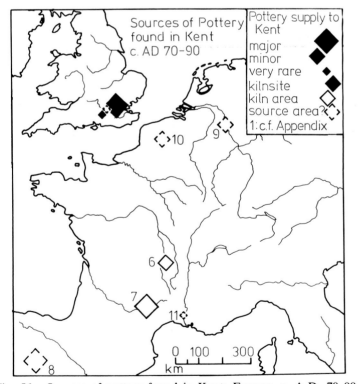

Fig. 56.   Sources of pottery found in Kent: Europe, *c.* A.D. 70–90.

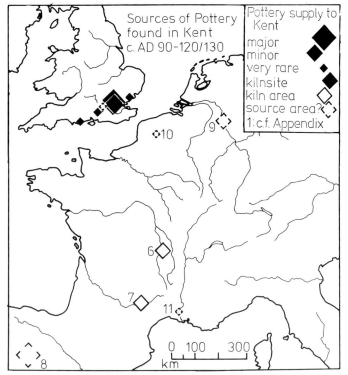

Fig. 57.   Sources of pottery found in Kent: Europe, *c.* A.D. 90–120/130.

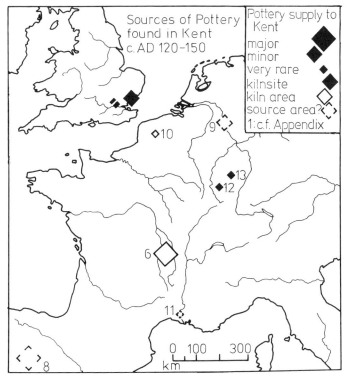

Fig. 58.   Sources of pottery found in Kent: Europe, *c.* A.D. 120–150.

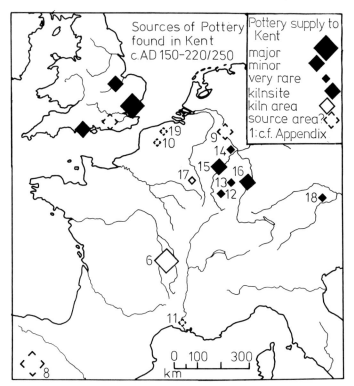

Fig. 59.   Sources of pottery found in Kent: Europe, *c.* A.D. 150–220/250.

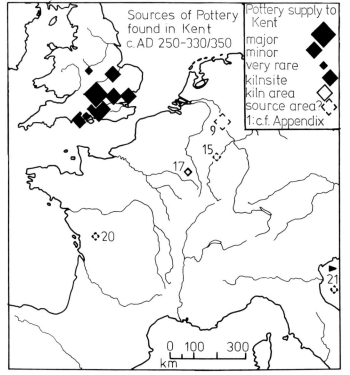

Fig. 60.   Sources of pottery found in Kent: Europe, *c.* A.D. 250–330/350.

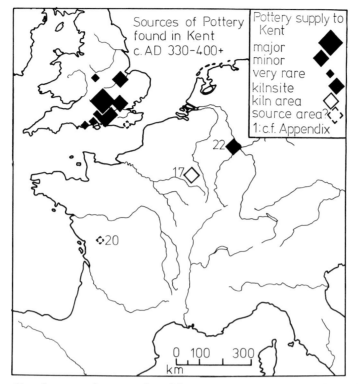

Fig. 61.   Sources of pottery found in Kent: Europe, *c.* A.D. 330–400+.

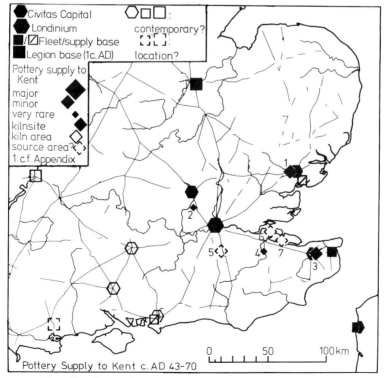

Fig. 62.   Pottery supply to Kent: Britain, *c.* A.D. 43–70.

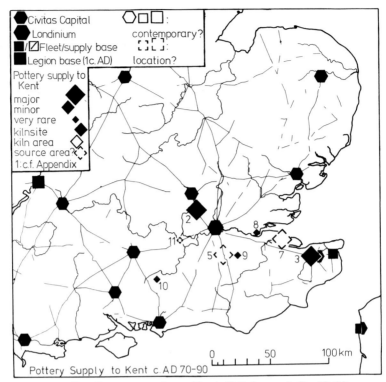

Fig. 63.   Pottery supply to Kent: Britain, *c*. A.D. 70–90.

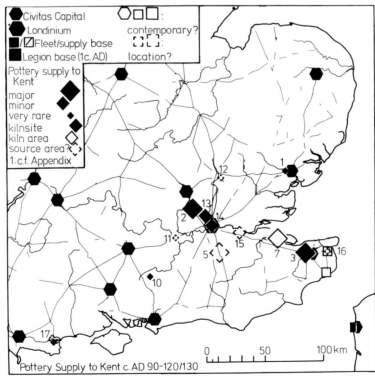

Fig. 64.   Pottery supply to Kent: Britain, *c*. A.D. 90–120/130.

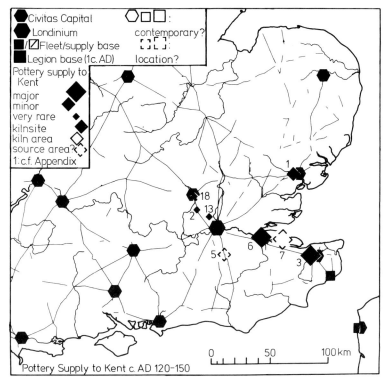

Fig. 65.   Pottery supply to Kent: Britain, *c.* A.D. 120–150.

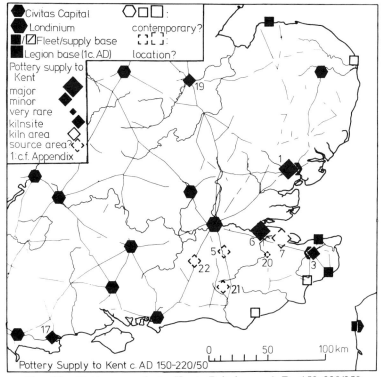

Fig. 66.   Pottery supply to Kent: Britain, *c.* A.D. 150–220/250.

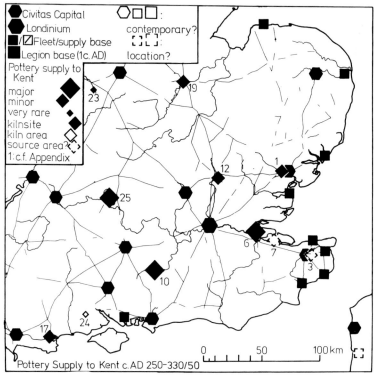

Fig. 67.   Pottery supply to Kent: Britain, *c.* A.D. 250–330/350.

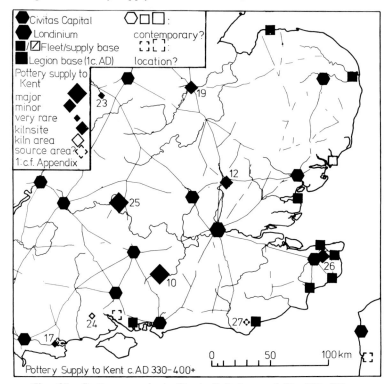

Fig. 68.   Pottery supply to Kent: Britain, *c.* A.D. 330–400+.

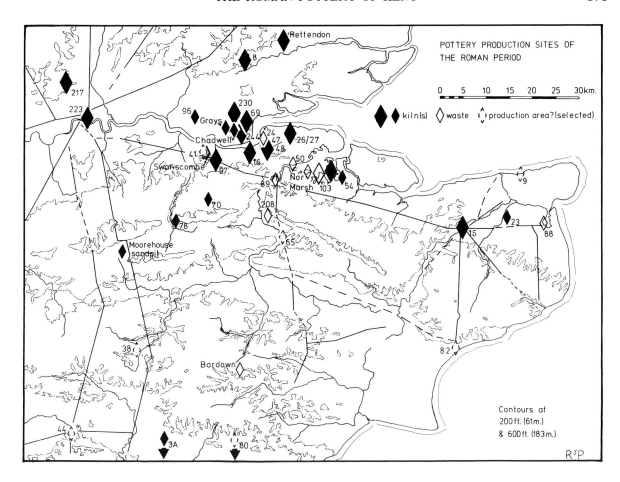

Fig. 69.   Pottery production sites of the Roman period (see Appendix 1 for gazetteer). Distribution.

CHAPTER 5

THE PRODUCTION OF POTTERY IN KENT: HISTORY

I. INTRODUCTION

An exhaustive gazetteer of production sites in Roman Britain lists 67 sites in Kent (Swan 1984, 387–421). Twenty-four of these lay in the Upchurch Marshes, mostly poorly recorded by nineteenth- and twentieth-century antiquaries. A further ten sites are known along the southern fringes of the Medway estuary, nine on the Cliffe peninsula and Isle of Grain, and 12 along the floodplain of the Thames between Swanscombe in the west and Higham in the east. Canterbury is ringed by seven sites, the only other east Kent location being at Preston-near-Wingham, above the mouth of the Little Stour. Two sites at Ash-cum-Ridley (New Ash Green, between the rivers Darent and Medway), and one each at Otford (near Sevenoaks, south-west Kent) and Eccles (in the Medway valley) complete the picture. Two hypothesized kiln sites, at Joyden's Wood, Bexley, and at Stone Wood, Stone near Dartford, are discredited, whilst a third at Dymchurch (Wheeler 1932) fails to merit even a dismissal.

The studies of the distribution of pottery wasters and of wares can add some generalized areas of production to the sites catalogued by Swan (see below, 5.IV and 6.III.2). It is to be expected that in a county whose Iron Age traditions of potting were as strong as those in Kent, pottery manufacture was a widespread, though by no means ubiquitous activity. Two regions stand out, however: that between Swanscombe and the Upchurch Marshes, and the environs of Canterbury.

II. THE POTTERY INDUSTRY OF NORTH KENT: THAMESIDE, THE CLIFFE PENINSULA AND THE MEDWAY MARSHES

1. *Background*

The southern marshes of the Medway estuary, around Rainham and Upchurch, were the scene of some of the earliest searches for Roman pottery in Britain. The sea level has risen since the Roman period, inundating the second-century and later sites (Evans 1953), and areas such as Otterham Creek, Rainham, formerly one of the richest 'veins' of pottery, are now practically sterile. The antiquarian collectors have left little record of their finds (Monaghan 1987, 242–3), even the pots themselves often having been lost or separated from indications of their provenance (e.g. Monaghan 1983), and one is forced to conclude, with Monaghan, that 'it is best to disregard all work prior to . . . 1954 and start afresh' (Monaghan 1982, 31; Noël Hume 1954).

The western part of the north Kent potteries has also suffered at the hands of man. Kiln sites have been recorded in general either in salvage work or rescue excavations in advance of industrial activities (e.g. Jessup 1928; Allen 1954; Catherall 1983) or of tidal erosion (Swan 1984), or during investigations by individuals where enthusiasm in the field has sadly not been matched by that at the desk. John Gillam's recognition of a black-burnished ware (BB2) tradition strong in northern Britain but emanating from south-eastern potteries (Gillam 1960; 1973; Gillam and Mann 1970) has focused attention on the north-west Kent industry (e.g. Farrar 1973; Williams 1977), whilst Monaghan has taken up the challenge of unravelling the mysteries of 'Upchurch ware' and the Medway marshes industry in a broader study of the Upchurch and Thameside industries (Monaghan 1982; 1983; 1987).

Excavations in south Essex have revealed a number of sites, including Thurrock, Mucking, Orsett, and Billericay (e.g. Drury 1973; Jones and Rodwell 1973; Rodwell 1974, Toller 1980; Goodburn 1978), where pottery akin to the products of the Thameside and Cliffe peninsula was made. Without exception, interim reports alone have been published at the time of writing (Spring 1985); pending full publication of these sites, this history must be accepted as an interim statement.

2. *Origins*

The earliest known production dates to within later first century B.C. to mid-first century A.D. parameters, the climate of opinion favouring the upper end of this range (Noël Hume 1954; Monaghan 1982; Swan 1984). The sites lie on the Upchurch Marshes (Noël Hume 1954; Jackson 1962; 1972/3) and are associated with coarse flint-tempered reduced ware jars often with oblique furrowing. These are broadly contemporary with a hand-made sandy ware found in quantity during trenching for a gas pipeline across Broomhey Farm, Cooling, on the Cliffe peninsula, in 1978. The fabric is hard, and harsh to the touch, sand-gritted with lesser amounts of shell, grog, water-worn gravel, iron ore and mica. It is fired brown or grey, with brown, grey or buff surfaces often patchy in colour. The forms (nos. 1–9; from Pollard forthcoming, d, to be published with a report on excavations by Miles – Miles 1973; Miles and Syddell 1967 – on a neighbouring site) are utilitarian, but the combination of ?knife-trimmed bead rim and rilled body (e.g. nos. 2, 3) is sufficiently distinctive to enable a distribution to be plotted (Fig. 20 "Cooling" sand-and-shell) suggestive of manufacture on the Cliffe peninsula or the Medway marshes. Contacts were extensive enough for one vessel to come to rest at Canterbury (Bennett *et al.* 1982, no. 296). Shelly wares were produced on the north side of the Thames in the mid- to late first century A.D. (at Mucking: Jones 1973, and Tilbury: Drury and Rodwell 1973) with an exchange area confined in the main to southern Essex (Jones 1972; Fig. 20, Essex 'graffito' in the present volume).

The potteries so far described were essentially household concerns (6.III) making 'kitchen' utility wares. A large group of white-slipped vessels, mostly flagons, found on the Medway estuary at Hoo (Blumstein 1956) has been taken to imply a 'probable pottery kiln nearby' working in the Claudio-Neronian period (Swan 1984, 403). The vessels represent an intrusive element in local traditions, and immigrant craftsmen may be suspected, as in the Medway valley above Rochester at Eccles (Detsicas 1977a).

'Upchurch ware' is a term which has been interpreted in many ways in relation to the pottery of the north Kent industry (Monaghan 1982). Throughout its history, however, it has been applied consistently to the fine reduced ware so characteristic of the collections of antiquaries such as Woodruff (Monaghan 1983, Fabric II). The dating of the inception of production of this ware, and its less common oxidised and white-slipped counterparts, is complicated by the suspected presence of a rival concern in east Kent (4.II.1) and by the 'London Ware' industry in the provincial capital (Marsh and Tyers 1976; Marsh 1978). A late first-century origin for all three potteries is certain, that at London possibly post-dating the others by a decade or so (4.II.1; Pollard 1983a, 311–17).

The reduced sandy ware industries are still more difficult to date, due in part to the conservative, and widespread, range of jars, bowls and dishes that were their main lines. A biconical bowl from Bedlam's Bottom (4.II.4; Pollard 1983a, 319–20) and a necked jar or bowl from Slayhills Marsh (*ibid.*) dateable to the late first or earlier second century, may be amongst the earliest vessels produced by the eastern potters in this ware, whilst vessel typology suggests an early to mid second-century dating for the Chalk kiln site (cf. nos. 95, 110, 111, 113, 115, 182, 191; Allen 1954, 1959; Pollard 1983a, 320). The earliest forms (nos. 90–94 here) could date back to the later first century in wheel-thrown, reduced sandy wares, however (4.II.2).

The contexts for the emergence of the Thameside-Medway industry have been discussed above (4.II-III), and their organisation, so far as it can be deduced, below (6.IV-V in particular). The Upchurch Marshes fine ware industry in its earliest (late first to early second century) phase, it can be argued, drew on a wide range of sources for its inspiration, including Gallo-Belgic, indigenous 'Belgic' (Aylesford-Swarling) and samian wares. White-slipped wares are generally rare, as indeed are flagons in general, in this phase, so that it cannot be said with confidence that the Upchurch industry grew out of the pre-Flavian 'Hoo' workshop.

3. *Developments in the second Century*

The repertoire of the Upchurch Marshes fine ware industry concentrated upon beakers, with apparently smaller output of jars, necked and open bowls, and flasks (4.II.1, 4.III.1, 4.IV.1). Segmental bowls (nos. 130–132), early third-century samian derivatives (nos. 162–166) and combed butt- and pedestal beakers (e.g. nos. 122–123) appear to have been more a feature of the putative east Kent industry (see also Green 1981). Painted ware was a minor product of the late first to early second century (nos. 138–141) with a local distribution (Fig. 26). The Hadrianic period witnessed a marked reduction in the range of types in the industry, with reduced ware beakers and oxidised and white-slipped ware flagons (e.g. nos. 155–161) dominant amongst Upchurch-type fine wares in north Kent. It cannot be positively demonstrated that the flagons were products of the Medway, rather than of more easterly, potters, but the beakers, of which the 'poppyhead' is the most common (e.g. nos. 145, 146, 150), certainly were (Tyers 1978; Monaghan 1983, nos. 40–58).

The reduced sandy wares of the Thames-Medway area as a whole in the first instance almost certainly adopted the forms of their 'Aylesford-Swarling' antecedents (nos. 91–94). The introduction of the black-burnished ware style to the south-eastern potteries is something of a mystery, since the Dorset progenitor (BB1) occurs only occasionally here until the very end of the second or even the third century and then mostly in London and its suburbs (Tyers and Marsh 1978). Farrar (1973, 202) suggested that BB2 represented a 'Romanised offshoot of the

Dorset industry', while Williams (1977, 208) tentatively proposed that the Purbeck marble trade brought BB1 or a description of its forms to the south-east. The development of BB2 in Kent has been described above (4.III.2, 4.IV.2, 4.V.2), where a Hadrianic inception is argued for. The jars and dishes of the second century (nos. 110–115) were produced alongside the established bead-rim jars and necked bowls (4.III.2) on Thameside and Cliffe peninsula potteries; BB2 does not appear to have been made on the Upchurch Marshes (Monaghan 1982, 45), but fine beakers and jars in the BB2 style do appear there. Conversely, the fine wares of the latter area have not been recognised amongst the products of the western potteries.

Two groups of potteries can thus be demonstrated for the Hadrianic-Antonine period, both producing reduced sandy wares, but with mutually exclusive ranges of 'finer' wares. A third element at this time may be represented by a group of mortaria from Rochester studied by Hartley (1972, nos. 30, 32, 35; nos. 116–118 here). These are in the fine cream fabric used extensively at Colchester and Canterbury (cf. Hartley and Richards 1965), and include one 'distorted and almost certainly unsaleable waster which should indicate the presence of a kiln in the area' (Hartley 1972, 136). The forms are of mid- to late second-century date. No other evidence of mortarium production has been reported in north Kent, though across the Thames mortaria and flagons were made at Thurrock (Drury 1973).

4. *Diversification and Decline: from the late second Century onwards*

The rising sea level seems to have engulfed the northern marshes of Slayhills and Milfordhope, below Upchurch, around the turn of the second century (Noël Hume 1954, 79–80). Thenceforth potting may have continued on the banks of Otterham Creek, Rainham, throughout the third century. Beakers remained the dominant form in fine reduced ware, their shapes reflecting developments in contemporary colour-coated wares, notably Nene Valley, Colchester, and 'Rhenish' (Trier) types (4.V.1; e.g. nos. 145, 147, 148, 150–154). Flasks supplanted flagons (e.g. nos. 159, cf. 161, 167, 168), with white-slipped wares falling from favour. Production on the Upchurch Marshes undoubtedly declined in the third century, in the face of increasing competition from British colour-coated wares and from the western potteries of the north Kent industry. The Upchurch fine ware potteries are unlikely to have outlived this century.

The range of slipped, burnished reduced wares featured in Thameside and Cliffe peninsula kiln site groups was expanded in the last quarter of the second century, most elements being found both north and south of the Thames (Pollard 1983b, 134–8; 4.III.2; e.g. nos. 181–92, 194–6). Beakers were apparently produced for the first time (cf. no. 152).

North Kent BB2 is thought to have found an important market in the northern frontier zone (Williams 1977, 211) at the end of the second century and, in all probability, expanded its trade in the south-east as well. The export of BB2 to the north continued into the mid-third century (Gillam 1973), and the Thameside and Cliffe peninsula industry probably maintained its marketing zone in Kent throughout the third century (4.IV.2). Plain reduced sandy wares in a variety of jar and bowl forms (4.III.2, 4.IV.2; Pollard 1983b) were produced alongside the decorated vessels.

A typological fossilisation (cf. Fulford 1979, 121–2) set in throughout the industry in the middle years of the third century, and by the middle of the fourth century at the latest the slipped, burnished types, including BB2 as defined by Farrar and Gillam, had disappeared (4.V.2). The situation in Essex is unclear, but it is worth noting that the fourth-century site at

Rawreth is apparently devoid of BB2 (Drury 1977, 40). The loss of long-distance markets, coupled with increasing pressure from the Alice Holt industry to the west and from the competitive hand-made grog-tempered ware to the east, evidently proved fatal for the north Kent potteries. Their decline may well have set in earlier in the third century, for from then on the kiln sites themselves disappear from the archaeological record: the latest kiln known of is Kiln A at Oakleigh Farm, Higham (Catherall 1983), dated to the mid-third century.

III. THE CANTERBURY POTTERY INDUSTRY

1. *Introduction*

The existence of potters at Canterbury was first demonstrated in 1939, when a kiln was excavated under salvage conditions during the construction of a wartime shelter (Webster 1940). Since that time another six industrial sites around the city have been recorded under salvage or rescue conditions (Swan 1984, 390–3), from which a history of the industry can be deduced covering the first 150 years of the province. The Canterbury potteries are a classic example of an urban industry, but despite this have received little or no attention in standard works on Romano-British pottery (e.g. Webster 1976; Swan 1975a).

2. *Origins*

Two groups of potters can be recognised in pre-Flavian Canterbury. Salvage excavations to the south of the city at Stuppington Lane (Bennett *et al*. 1980) recorded a kiln associated with coarse sandy ware jars and bowls of essentially late Iron Age inspiration. This ware comprises between 5 per cent and 13 per cent of pre-Flavian assemblages from the Marlowe Car Park sites in Canterbury (Pollard forthcoming, d), but has not been recognised beyond the city. It may have developed from local 'Aylesford-Swarling' grog-tempered ware, kiln sites for which remain undetected. The latter ware has been found within one kiln, but it cannot be certain that it was fired therein rather than being incorporated in backfill or even as baffles (Jenkins 1956a, fig. 8, nos. 27–29, 31–32).

The second group of potters is known to have worked on two sites, at Reed Avenue (unpublished; noted in Jenkins 1966a; and Swan 1984, 392) and at St. Stephen's Road, Area II (Jenkins 1956a). The grey wares and misfired flagons (nos. 47–57) find close parallels in the Gallo-Roman pottery of the Nord/Pas-de-Calais region of France (Tuffreau-Libre 1980a; Richardson and Tyers 1984, '*vases tronconiques*'; 4.I.3 above), but are absent from Camulodunum (cf. Hawkes and Hull, Form 242, however), and from first-century legionary sites in the Midlands and West, which are associated with Rhineland-derived forms (Greene 1973; Frere and St. Joseph 1974; Bidwell 1977; Darling 1977). The 'Hofheim' flagon (no. 56) is an exception, being ubiquitous in pre-Flavian Britain and the Rhineland (Gose 1950, Types 362–364; Greene 1973; cf. Hawkes and Hull 1947, Forms 136 and 140). It seems likely that this pottery was produced by craftsmen who migrated to Kent during the reign of Nero, attracted by the new markets Canterbury and the military supply base at Richborough (see Pollard forthcoming, d, for further discussion). They achieved a similar market share in the city to the Stuppington Lane potters, though their operations may have extended into the Flavian period, up to *c*. A.D. 80.

3. *Expansion and Standardisation: the Flavian to early Antonine Period*

The massive expansion of the Canterbury pottery industry in the late first century has been described above (4.II.3). Products included reduced and oxidised coarse sandy wares, and buff to off-white wares (nos. 63–84) and were marketed throughout east Kent and, occasionally, further afield, mortaria having been recognised at Lullingstone (Pollard 1987, Fabrics 44–45) and Boulogne (4.II.3). The evidence for continuity between the North Gaulish and Stuppington Lane potters and their mid-Flavian heirs is inconclusive. The differences in form outweigh the similarities (in flagons and jars), but this reflects developments in contemporary industries in Britain with an urban orientation (cf. 6.VII), and there is no reason to think that the industry did not grow directly from Neronian roots. The names of Juvenalis and Valentinus have been linked with the Canterbury industry (4.II.3, 4.III.3) in the second century, both stamping mortaria (e.g. no. 71), and Juvenalis amphorae, also.

The kiln sites of this period include Dane John Gardens (Webster 1940), Whitehall Road (now Rheims Way) (Jenkins 1956b), Whitehall Gardens (Jenkins 1960), North Lane (Bennett *et al.* 1978), and St. Stephen's Road, Area I (Jenkins 1956a). North Lane may be the earliest, with Flavian-Trajanic pottery, whilst Dane John and kiln III at Whitehall Gardens are Antonine, as may be the Whitehall Road kiln associated with mica-dusted face-jars, and other forms including pie-dishes (Swan 1984, 391).

One kiln site not mentioned so far in this account is that off Stour Street (*ibid.*, 390, Site 3). Provisional assessment is that the three kilns are of mid first-century date, and perhaps belonged to the same group of potters as the Reed Avenue and St. Stephen's Road Area II sites.

The range of forms and fabrics produced by the Canterbury industry underwent little change throughout this period (4.II.3, 4.III.3), though a diverse range of flagons was found on the Dane John site (e.g. nos. 60, 75, 76, 78–84 here). The high degree of standardisation exhibited by the industry as a whole in the second century is a phenomenon widespread in Romano-British potteries of the period, and may be interpreted as reflecting stability in producer-consumer relations as local monopolies were carved out.

4. *The Decline of the Canterbury Industry in the second half of the second Century*

The shifting fortunes of the Canterbury industry have been charted above (4.III.3). BB2 became increasingly common in the city itself during the latter part of the second century and may have captured coastal markets such as Dover and the waning port of Richborough as early as A.D. 130–150. The hypothesized production of BB2 in east Kent is likely to have accounted for only a small proportion of the emergent ware's market share in the region, with Colchester and Thameside potteries providing the bulk. The range of reduced and oxidised sandy ware forms found in Canterbury diminishes towards the end of the second century, as the characteristic forms of the industry at its peak were discarded. This may have been a reaction to the pressures of competition (cf. Fulford 1975a, 133–4). The jar, bowl and dish forms of late Antonine-Severan Canterbury are far less distinctive than many of those they supplanted, rendering definition of the putative 'late' industry's markets much more difficult on typological grounds than in early periods.

The city of Canterbury continued to witness building construction in the later second and early third centuries (Williams 1947, 68–87; Frere 1970; Blockley and Day forthcoming). The paradox of an industrial decline coinciding with an apparently stable urban condition is not easily resolved. The surmised economic problems of the period (Young 1977a, 235–6) may have affected those with commercial interests more severely than those whose wealth lay in property and agrarian investments. No kiln sites in east Kent can be ascribed a post-Antonine date except for the enigmatic site at Preston-near-Wingham (6.VII). Fulford (1977b) has observed that urban potteries in Roman Britain are generally a feature of the first two centuries of the province rather than of the later years. On balance, it seems unlikely that a co-ordinated, nucleated industry existed in the vicinity of third-century Canterbury, although individual concerns may have functioned at the household industry or individual workshop level (Chapter 6), each supplying a small but possibly quite widespread market within east Kent.

IV. OTHER PRODUCTION SITES

1. *Known Kilns*

Publication of the four isolated kiln sites identified in Kent (5.I) is either inadequate (Preston, Otford) or of an interim nature (Ash-cum-Ridley, Eccles). They are discussed in the following chapter, and their wares described in greater detail in the preceding one.

2. *Sites suggested by Wasters*

In addition to kilns and substantial dumps of wasters, a small number of imperfect vessels has been published from occupation sites, including a blistered late second- to early fourth-century jar/bowl from Hartlip (?) (Noël Hume 1954, 86 and fig. 3, no. 6; no. 194 here), and a warped late first- to early second-century jar/bowl from West Wickham Fox Hill (Philp 1973, fig. 22, no. 159). To these vessels may be added the wasters from around the Medway estuary published by Noël Hume (1954) and Monaghan (1982; 1983; 1987), the possible kiln rejects from Cooling (Miles 1973; Pollard forthcoming, b; noted by Swan 1984, 397–8), and an enigmatic group from Richborough excavated by Bushe-Fox but not published.

The Richborough material comes from a box labelled 'Sec. 47 15'–19' b. datum "Kiln Waste"' in Dover Castle (Department of the Environment store). This section was cut across the face of the causeway across the Claudian ditches (Area XVI: Bushe-Fox 1949). The pottery (the range is illustrated by nos. 85–88 here) is in a coarse sandy wheel-thrown ware, mostly grey but occasionally red to purple, with some differential colouration of joining sherds. This, and the adhesion of pale green globules of glassy vitrified clay on both surfaces and fractures, implies either shattering (due to extremely high temperatures) in the kiln or secondary firing. No pottery kiln has been recorded at Richborough, but the fact that some sherds are buckled suggests that kiln waste may be represented. Typologically, the vessels belong to the late first to early/mid-second century.

3. *Areas of Production suggested by Distribution of Wares*

The potential locations of certain household industries, defined thus by the character of their wares, have been discussed elsewhere (Chapters 4; 6.III.2). The domestic site at Greenhithe

(Detsicas 1966) has been considered to be in the immediate neighbourhood of a pottery producing early BB2 (Williams 1977), or a modest imitation of that ware (4.III.2), which is found in some abundance in Hadrianic-early Antonine levels on the site (e.g. nos. 107–109 here).

'Upchurch ware' is a term which has been interpreted in many ways in relation to the pottery of the north Kent industry (Monaghan 1982). Throughout its history, however, it has been applied consistently to the fine reduced ware so characteristic of the collections of antiquaries such as Woodruff (Monaghan 1983, Fabric II). The dating of the inception of production of this ware, and its less common oxidised and white-slipped counterparts, is complicated by the suspected presence of a rival concern in east Kent (4.II.1) and by the 'London Ware' industry in the provincial capital (Marsh and Tyers 1976; Marsh 1978). A late first-century origin for all three potteries is certain, that at London possibly post-dating the others by a decade or so (4.II.1; Pollard 1983a, 311–17).

The reduced sandy ware industries are still more difficult to date, due in part to the conservative, and widespread, range of jars, bowls and dishes that were their main lines. A biconical bowl from Bedlam's Bottom (4.II.4; Pollard 1983a, 319–20) and a necked jar or bowl from Slayhills Marsh (*ibid.*) dateable to the late first or earlier second century, may be amongst the earliest vessels produced by the eastern potters in this ware, whilst vessel typology suggests an early to mid second-century dating for the Chalk kiln site (cf. nos. 95, 110, 111, 113, 115, 182, 191; Allen 1954, 1959; Pollard 1983a, 320). The earliest forms (nos. 90–94 here) could date back to the later first century in wheel-thrown, reduced sandy wares, however (4.II.2).

The contexts for the emergence of the Thameside-Medway industry have been discussed above (4.II-III), and their organisation, so far as it can be deduced, below (6.IV-V in particular). The Upchurch Marshes fine ware industry in its earliest (late first to early second century) phase, it can be argued, drew on a wide range of sources for its inspiration, including Gallo-Belgic, indigenous 'Belgic' (Aylesford-Swarling) and samian wares. White-slipped wares are generally rare, as indeed are flagons in general, in this phase, so that it cannot be said with confidence that the Upchurch industry grew out of the pre-Flavian 'Hoo' workshop.

3. *Developments in the second Century*

The repertoire of the Upchurch Marshes fine ware industry concentrated upon beakers, with apparently smaller output of jars, necked and open bowls, and flasks (4.II.1, 4.III.1, 4.IV.1). Segmental bowls (nos. 130–132), early third-century samian derivatives (nos. 162–166) and combed butt- and pedestal beakers (e.g. nos. 122–123) appear to have been more a feature of the putative east Kent industry (see also Green 1981). Painted ware was a minor product of the late first to early second century (nos. 138–141) with a local distribution (Fig. 26). The Hadrianic period witnessed a marked reduction in the range of types in the industry, with reduced ware beakers and oxidised and white-slipped ware flagons (e.g. nos. 155–161) dominant amongst Upchurch-type fine wares in north Kent. It cannot be positively demonstrated that the flagons were products of the Medway, rather than of more easterly, potters, but the beakers, of which the 'poppyhead' is the most common (e.g. nos. 145, 146, 150), certainly were (Tyers 1978; Monaghan 1983, nos. 40–58).

The reduced sandy wares of the Thames-Medway area as a whole in the first instance almost certainly adopted the forms of their 'Aylesford-Swarling' antecedents (nos. 91–94). The introduction of the black-burnished ware style to the south-eastern potteries is something of a mystery, since the Dorset progenitor (BB1) occurs only occasionally here until the very end of the second or even the third century and then mostly in London and its suburbs (Tyers and Marsh 1978). Farrar (1973, 202) suggested that BB2 represented a 'Romanised offshoot of the

Dorset industry', while Williams (1977, 208) tentatively proposed that the Purbeck marble trade brought BB1 or a description of its forms to the south-east. The development of BB2 in Kent has been described above (4.III.2, 4.IV.2, 4.V.2), where a Hadrianic inception is argued for. The jars and dishes of the second century (nos. 110–115) were produced alongside the established bead-rim jars and necked bowls (4.III.2) on Thameside and Cliffe peninsula potteries; BB2 does not appear to have been made on the Upchurch Marshes (Monaghan 1982, 45), but fine beakers and jars in the BB2 style do appear there. Conversely, the fine wares of the latter area have not been recognised amongst the products of the western potteries.

Two groups of potteries can thus be demonstrated for the Hadrianic-Antonine period, both producing reduced sandy wares, but with mutually exclusive ranges of 'finer' wares. A third element at this time may be represented by a group of mortaria from Rochester studied by Hartley (1972, nos. 30, 32, 35; nos. 116–118 here). These are in the fine cream fabric used extensively at Colchester and Canterbury (cf. Hartley and Richards 1965), and include one 'distorted and almost certainly unsaleable waster which should indicate the presence of a kiln in the area' (Hartley 1972, 136). The forms are of mid- to late second-century date. No other evidence of mortarium production has been reported in north Kent, though across the Thames mortaria and flagons were made at Thurrock (Drury 1973).

4.   *Diversification and Decline: from the late second Century onwards*

The rising sea level seems to have engulfed the northern marshes of Slayhills and Milfordhope, below Upchurch, around the turn of the second century (Noël Hume 1954, 79–80). Thenceforth potting may have continued on the banks of Otterham Creek, Rainham, throughout the third century. Beakers remained the dominant form in fine reduced ware, their shapes reflecting developments in contemporary colour-coated wares, notably Nene Valley, Colchester, and 'Rhenish' (Trier) types (4.V.1; e.g. nos. 145, 147, 148, 150–154). Flasks supplanted flagons (e.g. nos. 159, cf. 161, 167, 168), with white-slipped wares falling from favour. Production on the Upchurch Marshes undoubtedly declined in the third century, in the face of increasing competition from British colour-coated wares and from the western potteries of the north Kent industry. The Upchurch fine ware potteries are unlikely to have outlived this century.

The range of slipped, burnished reduced wares featured in Thameside and Cliffe peninsula kiln site groups was expanded in the last quarter of the second century, most elements being found both north and south of the Thames (Pollard 1983b, 134–8; 4.III.2; e.g. nos. 181–92, 194–6). Beakers were apparently produced for the first time (cf. no. 152).

North Kent BB2 is thought to have found an important market in the northern frontier zone (Williams 1977, 211) at the end of the second century and, in all probability, expanded its trade in the south-east as well. The export of BB2 to the north continued into the mid-third century (Gillam 1973), and the Thameside and Cliffe peninsula industry probably maintained its marketing zone in Kent throughout the third century (4.IV.2). Plain reduced sandy wares in a variety of jar and bowl forms (4.III.2, 4.IV.2; Pollard 1983b) were produced alongside the decorated vessels.

A typological fossilisation (cf. Fulford 1979, 121–2) set in throughout the industry in the middle years of the third century, and by the middle of the fourth century at the latest the slipped, burnished types, including BB2 as defined by Farrar and Gillam, had disappeared (4.V.2). The situation in Essex is unclear, but it is worth noting that the fourth-century site at

CHAPTER 6

THE PRODUCTION OF POTTERY IN KENT: ASPECTS OF ORGANISATION

I. MODES OF PRODUCTION

Peacock, on the basis of extensive ethnographical research, has provided a series of models of production systems that might have operated in the Roman Empire (1982, 6–11). These are, starting with the simplest, household production, household industry, individual workshop, nucleated workshops, and manufactory. Two variants are also proposed, estate production and official production, the latter including military output. Three of these models are of particular relevance to pottery production in Roman Kent: household industry, individual workshop and nucleated workshops. Their characteristics as defined by Peacock may be summarised as follows (see also van der Leeuw 1977).

Household Industry: A secondary, part-time, non-essential means of livelihood, commonly associated with impoverished farming communities seeking to supplement their income and practised in the spare time that the farming calendar allowed. Any aids to production will be simple; for example, a turntable and oven or crude kiln, and permanent industrial sheds are unnecessary. Products tend to be coarse kitchen wares, often of a high resilience and are aimed at all types of community within a confined area which may nonetheless be of considerable size. Long-distance marketing is also sometimes practised.

Individual Workshop: A major source of subsistence, essential to the livelihood of the potter but often only part-time. The use of kilns and potter's wheels is usual. Permanent industrial sheds need not be built, although it is usual for a wheel to be housed under cover (Rudling 1986). Rural tenant potter-farmers may have manned the bulk of individual workshops, working singly or with a small group of assistants in a sedentary existence, and perhaps adopting an itinerant mode in order to serve dispersed communities and produce cumbersome or very low-value items without incurring inordinately high transport costs. The distribution from any one kiln site is usually extremely restricted, and may be oriented towards the most lucrative markets. In the Romano-British context 'grey wares' are particularly characteristic products, along with storage jars and ceramic building materials. Fine wares are seldom produced. A rural location is usual, as the existence of a large population nucleus is likely to encourage aggregation.

Nucleated Workshops: The primary means of subsistence, any other activities being wholly subsidiary. The highest available technology will be exploited and drying sheds may be built in order to extend the potting season into colder, damper months. Wheel-houses are also constructed. A wide variety of types of ware, conforming to set standards of forms and fabrics, is common, with some specialisation of individual workshops in particular forms and/or fabrics. The focus for nucleation may be an urban centre or a rural area, supplying widespread markets.

The boundaries between these modes of production are blurred: the turntable characteristic of the household industry can, if heavy enough, be used for finishing pots in a manner more commonly associated with the wheel, and both modes are engaged in coarse 'kitchen' ware production. The scattered kiln sites along the Thames Estuary producing BB2 and other grey wares resemble individual workshop concerns, perhaps peripatetic, but their marketing patterns are more akin to those of nucleated industries.

The lowest level of production has been termed *household production*, a mode geared towards the self-sufficiency of the individual household with little exchange of vessels between households. Technology is low, and may leave no archaeological record other than the completed pots themselves. The recognition of this mode of production in an archaeological context must rest on detailed fabric and construction analyses in the hope of demonstrating contrasts between sites and correspondences between fabric compositions and locally available materials. The chances of this mode being recognisable from the kind of analysis conducted by the present author on Roman pottery in Kent are thus slim.

The manufactory by way of contrast was, in the western Empire, the preserve of the giant fine ware industries particularly of Gaul and northern Italy. The essence is the association of a large number of individuals under a supervisor, often with a 'production line' organisation. The proprietor/slave relationship attested by stamps of the Arezzo industry mark this industry out as the most likely contender for the title of manufactory (Peacock 1982). The largest Romano-British industries, including those of Oxfordshire, are considered by Peacock (*ibid*.) to fall within the category of 'nucleated workshops' rather than manufactories.

Estate production is likely to have been geared primarily towards ceramic building materials for intra-estate consumption, with a commercial rôle developing in time. The production of ceramics by the estate itself must be distinguished from production by tenants for their own purposes, commercial or otherwise.

II. HOUSEHOLD PRODUCTION

The practical problems of recognising this mode in the archaeological record are exacerbated by the apparent existence of a villa-estate economy over most of the Roman period in the valleys and coastal plain of north-west Kent at least, if not throughout the county. The differentiation of estate from household products may lie in the nature of the pottery itself, fine and specialised types being produced under orders from the owner or his agent, and coarse utilitarian wares on the initiative of the workers for their own immediate needs. The mid third-century grog-tempered ware from the Maidstone Mount villa (4.IV.2) may be one example of a household product.

III. HOUSEHOLD INDUSTRIES

1. *Known Kilns*

The simple kilns recorded by Ian Jackson on the Upchurch Marshes (Jackson 1962; 1972/3; Swan 1984) were associated with pottery described as 'hand-made', flint-and grog-tempered. A localised distribution of flint-tempered ware in the mid-first century A.D. around the Medway estuary and western Swale has been plotted (Fig. 17; 4.I.2), which with the evidence of kilns and the fabrics themselves is suggestive of a household industry.

2. *Postulated Household Industries: regional Traders*

The study of Romano-British pottery in Kent has brought to light a number of coarse wares whose fabric characteristics and distribution patterns are consistent with the model of household industry production. The bulk of this pottery is datable to the first and to the late third to early fifth century, but the intervening period is nowhere devoid of such material. The wares include, in the early period, shelly, sandy and 'Patch Grove' wares in west Kent and grog- and flint-tempered wares in central and east Kent (Chapters 3, 4.I–II). Grog-and flint-tempered pottery is also a feature of the late Roman period, the latter primarily at Canterbury, the former throughout Kent at least from the Cray Valley eastwards (4.IV, 4.V). Such pottery tends to be fairly soft and either coil-built or at least of an appearance suggestive of construction on a turntable. Storage jars and smaller jars are particularly common, the former occurring in non-sandy, non-wheel-thrown wares throughout the Roman period in all parts of Kent (and also in southern Essex). Platters, necked bowls, cups and flagons are forms mainly of the first century and dishes mainly of the late period. Two kiln sites in Essex may be linked with the production of shelly and sandy wares in the late first century A.D. (Mucking: M.U. Jones 1974; and Tilbury Gun Hill: Drury and Rodwell 1973) but, apart from the Upchurch kilns, no production centres have been recorded in Kent. A handful of 'Belgic' grog-tempered vessels were recovered from the furnace of a kiln at Canterbury dateable to the mid-first century A.D. (Jenkins 1956a, fig. 8, nos. 27–29, 31–2), but it is more likely that they were incorporated in the backfill (St. Stephen's Area II kiln). Whilst it is possible that kilns for the firing of 'Patch Grove', late Roman grog-tempered and the other wares listed above may yet be discovered, it is at least equally likely that they were fired in clamps or bonfires, leaving little archaeological trace.

Extensive patterns of distribution have been uncovered for several of these wares (e.g. Figs. 17, 20, 31, and 45), with a high intensity of usage of any one ware on sites several kilometres apart (Appendix 5). These could reflect itineracy of production or peddling of vessels manufactured at one place, or other mechanisms of dispersal (6.X, and Pollard 1983a, 415–417). The isolation of the Essex 'graffito' jars (Jones 1972) as a group within the southern Essex/west Kent/east Surrey 'shelly bead-rim jar' tradition carries the implication that in at least one instance a 'household industry' ware was produced by a number of different potters working to the same or similar specifications at a distance from one another rather than by a single community with extensive exchange connections. Other examples of 'local variations' on a tradition include the Thanet fine sandy and Medway marshes flint-tempered versions of the 'Aylesford-Swarling' furrowed ware (4.I.3), and the Port Lympne 'grog plus miscellaneous inclusions' ware of 'late Roman grog-tempered ware' tradition (4.IV.3). In this context, it is worth noting that Fulford's characterisation of Portchester late Roman grog-tempered ware revealed no less than four fabric groups (1975b).

The petrological analysis of Iron Age pottery has revealed that mechanisms could have existed for the dispersal of products from a single source or group of sources over quite extensive areas (Peacock 1968, 1969; Drury 1978, 58). The wares studied include one which may be termed 'coarse' (Malvernian ware) and two 'fine' (Glastonbury ware and glauconite-rich 'foot-ring bowls'). It is conceivable that the 'Aylesford-Swarling' fine ware of Kent, particularly the east Kent grog-tempered platters and flagons, was subject to centralised production, but their high quality compared with contemporary wares suggests that the potters responsible for them functioned at a level higher than that of the 'household industrialist'. 'Patch Grove', 'Thames Estuary shelly' and East Kent comb-stabbed storage jars are more plausible candidates for the status of household industry products. The distribution of the first two is figured (Fig. 31), whilst the last-named, a first-century A.D. type, has been recorded on seven sites in east Kent (Brenley Corner, Canterbury, Highstead, Richborough, Eastry, Wye and Dover: e.g. nos. 28 and 46 here). The 'Thames Estuary shelly' type alone of Kent storage jar types has been recorded with any frequency outside of the area in which its fabric group predominates.

3. *Postulated Household Industries; localised Traders*

The household industries that have been postulated appear for the most part to have satisfied regional demand only, foregoing the theoretical option of long-distance trade. Three examples may be cited of pottery potentially from household industries (on fabric grounds) being confined almost entirely to one settlement. Two of these come from Richborough in the first century and one from Canterbury in the fourth.

The Richborough examples concern two styles of decoration. The first is the impression of a tool, perhaps a short length of cord, in a series of oblique marks on the shoulder of jars 'hand-made' in grog-tempered ware (e.g. no. 45 here; Bushe-Fox 1949, no. 385; Cunliffe 1968, no. 589). Two examples of this style have been recorded in the neighbourhood of Richborough, at Birchington and at Eastry (where the 'cord-ridges' are absent), both unpublished. Parallels can be drawn with jars from Dragonby in Lincolnshire (Elsdon 1975, fig. 6, nos. 21–2; fig. 18, no. 13 and Plate IIa) but none closer to east Kent are known to the present author. Ettlinger has published examples from Vindonissa, Switzerland (1977, fig. 52, nos. 8–13) and argues for diverse origins. The former parallel is given a *terminus ante quem* in the early first century, whilst the latter is broadly Claudian-Trajanic in date. It is possible that the east Kent examples derive from a potting camp-follower of Claudius' legions, but further research on the pottery of their military bases occupied prior to the invasion of Britain is needed. A local east Kent man adapting his products to copy jars brought into Richborough in quarter-masters' stores is a second hypothesis.

The grog-and-sand tempered comb-stabbed small jars (or beakers) of Richborough (e.g. nos. 39–40 here) are paralleled at Colchester (Hawkes and Hull 1947, Form 108), where they became the predominant form of this class in the Flavian period. Sandy, possibly wheel-thrown vessels of this style have been found in ones and twos on several sites south of the Thames (e.g. Canterbury; Rochester; Eastry: Pollard 1982, no. 19; Southwark: Bird *et al.* 1978b, nos. 557 and 798) as well as at Richborough, but the fabric variant with grog is known only at the last-named site and may represent a local potter working in an alien tradition to take advantage of the market offered by the military base and embryonic 'small town'. Colchester vessels also include examples in both 'native brown ware' (equivalent to the Richborough grog-sand ware) and 'pure Roman [i.e. sandy wheel-thrown] fabric' (Hawkes and Hull 1947, 237). Two other forms with this motif are also recorded solely at Richborough so far as Kent is concerned, a small narrow-necked vessel (unpublished; cf. Hawkes and Hull 1947, Form 119C) and a flask with a carinated shoulder (Bushe-Fox 1949, no. 387). The former at least is also in a grog-and-sand ware, which bears comparison with the Stuppington Lane pottery from Canterbury (Bennett *et al*. 1980). The fact that the latter was associated with a kiln suggests that the Richborough ware may also have been kiln-fired and an individual workshop or household industry status is thus equally plausible.

The third example, that from fourth-century Canterbury, is of the flint-and-sand tempered hand-made coarse ware described and discussed above (4.V.3), which occurs in small numbers within the city and in one or two instances beyond it. This ware was produced in a tradition ultimately inspired by black-burnished ware dishes, with standard plain necked or everted-rim jars complementing these forms (cf. Pollard forthcoming, d).

IV. INDIVIDUAL WORKSHOPS

1. *Kiln Sites within Nucleations*

The two nucleated industries of Kent (6.V) both seem to have experienced formative phases when potters operated in comparative isolation from one another in organisational terms. The Thameside and Cliffe peninsula zone of the Thames-Medway rural nucleation may have been the province of individual workshops from the inception of wheel-thrown sandy ware production up to the late second century, around A.D. 180. BB2 production in this period has not been attested on a scale comparable with that of the late second and third centuries: 'early' sites, including Chalk (Allen 1954, 1959) and Higham Kiln C (Catherall 1983), functioned at a time when Colchester is thought to have played a dominant role in the supply of BB2 to Scotland and London (Williams 1977, 211–12). The north Kent potters' sights in contrast were fixed on local markets.

Canterbury's earliest, 'North Gaulish' pottery kilns are associated with flagons and utility vessels of types which occur almost solely in the city itself and at the supply base of Richborough. The jars in particular (e.g. no. 49 type) not infrequently exhibit misshapen rims indicative of an attitude of 'quantity not quality' prevailing in the industry. The small scale of the industry as measured by the proportion of its wares in contemporary assemblages (between 3 per cent and 17 per cent: Pollard forthcoming, d), and its orientation towards potentially the most lucrative, 'Romanised' markets, are suggestive of individual workshops. The crude 'Stuppington Lane' ware, recognised only at Canterbury, might belong either to this model or that of the household industry. The hypothesized post-Antonine local potteries supplying Canterbury with grey wares would also fit the individual workshop model.

2. *Isolated Kiln Sites*

These sites are associated with villa-estates, small towns or, in one possible instance, a military base. The fine/specialised products of Otford and Eccles are considered under the estate model

(6.VI); the remaining sites produced, so far as can be inferred, grey wares for local markets. The kilns at Springhead (Southfleet) and Swanscombe may have operated within the Thameside-Cliffe peninsula rural nucleation, at its western extremity, or as a separate group or succession of sites serving the small town and religious complex at *Vagniacae*. The New Ash Green (Ash-cum-Ridley) kilns lay close to a villa centre, but on high ground some distance from the River Darent and thus in geographical isolation from the Thameside potteries. Kiln 1 (Swan's notation, 1984) lay within a possible field system (cf. Mucking: Jones and Rodwell 1973) and may have fired BB2 as well as grey wares. Kiln 2 was adjacent to, but antedating the stone phase of, a villa outbuilding. Neither is thought to post-date the second century.

Richborough has been cited already as the *raison d'être* for various potteries known and putative (6.III.2, 6.IV.1). The kiln site at Preston, it is argued below (6.VIII), existed at least in part to capitalise on the potential custom of the garrison of the Saxon Shore fort and its *vicus*. The enigmatic group of pottery 'kiln waste' (5.IV.2) would seem to represent a dependent individual workshop within the early military supply base or perhaps the small town 'port of entry' that succeeded the base. In view of the strong indigenous potting tradition in east Kent, it is unlikely that the army or fleet would have taken any direct rôle in pottery manufacture, and a civilian concern can be postulated with confidence. The existence of another individual workshop just across the county boundary, near Titsey in Surrey, is also worth noting (Swan 1984, 627, Tatsfield).

V. NUCLEATED WORKSHOPS

1. *The Thames-Medway Industry*

The model of four elements of this industry – the Thameside and Cliffe peninsula grey wares, the Hoo flagons, the Rochester mortaria, and the Medway estuary grey and fine wares – has been introduced above (5.II). It has been proposed that up to the late Antonine period the first of these operated as a series of individual workshops in mutual contact but with an essentially localised custom for a range of forms common to all sites. The evidence for the Hoo and Rochester potteries rests solely with the vessels themselves, products of workshops assuredly, but at what level of organisation? The lack of other evidence for mortarium production in this part of Kent is suggestive of an individual workshop, though mortaria were made at Thurrock along with flagons and utility vessels (Drury 1973). The relationships between Thurrock, Rochester, Canterbury and Colchester in the second century remain to be explained. Swan (1984, 403) considers that at Hoo the 'range of vessels may imply production geared mainly to military markets', a theory favoured also for the possibly contemporary kiln sites at Otford and Eccles (*ibid.*, 406, 389, respectively). A pre-Flavian military presence at key points of communication on the rivers of Kent has yet to be identified, though Eccles may have had military connections (Detsicas 1976, 162). The military/estate models are examined below.

The fine ware potteries of the Upchurch Marshes may have nucleated from their earliest years. Their location may have been determined in no small measure by the development of the villas at Hartlip and Boxted within the first century A.D. in an area which exhibits signs of considerable wealth at this time, as is also reflected by the number of rich early post-Conquest burials around Milton Creek, Sittingbourne (Roach Smith 1852; Wheeler 1932, 96–8; Kelly 1964). The social stratum that the villas and interments represent may well have been instrumental in establishing, or at least encouraging, the fine ware industry, with Rochester, the Thames estuary and Watling Street providing a strong potential distribution network. Second-century 'poppyhead' beakers from this industry were exported to the northern frontier (J. Monaghan, pers. comm.) and distribution in south-east Britain may have been widespread (cf. Monaghan 1982). Potting may not have been 'the primary means of subsistence', and the existence of such indicators of an intensive investment in production as drying sheds may never be proved. However, given the proximity of contemporary villas, it is worth considering whether landlord-tenant relationships might have played a part in the organisation of the industry, the villa patrons determining the nature of the output and controlling its marketing with an eye to profit. The comparatively high value of a fine ware such as 'Upchurch ware' may have rendered the pottery acceptable as rent payment in kind. The Hartlip villa was certainly an important consumer of 'Upchurch ware'.

There is evidence for a differentiation of production between Thameside and the Cliffe peninsula on the one hand, and the Upchurch Marshes on the other, in the second century. It would appear that fine pottery manufacture was generally confined to the latter (although 'very glossy black jars' are noted by Monaghan (1982) from a supposed kiln site near Cliffe (Hutchings 1966) and BB2 to the former (Monaghan 1982, 45). Coarse sandy wares were made in both districts and include virtually identical necked jars with tooled linear decoration on the shoulder.

The involvement of villa-estates in the Thameside and Cliffe peninsula potteries is less discernible than on the Upchurch Marshes; although the Chalk sites do lie close to a nucleus of buildings (Johnston 1972; Harker 1975), no evidence of substantial buildings has been found around the peninsula itself. However, Williams (1977, 21) considered that 'by the late second or early third century, a number of small kilns situated in Kent were also supplying BB2 vessels to the northern military garrisons', including Cooling (the Joyden's Wood site has since been generally discounted as a production locus by Detsicas (1977b, 239, and 1983, 156–7), Monaghan (1982, 33–7) and Swan (1984, 387). Results of analysis of Oakleigh Farm, Higham samples were not available at the time of publication (Catherall 1983). The presence of a small group of fine, untempered, reduced necked bulbous beakers (cf. no. 152) amongst the dumps of BB2 and sandy grey ware waste material at Cooling suggests that the virtual monopoly of production of fine ware forms held by the Upchurch Marshes potteries may have been eroded in the late Antonine to Severan period. The expansion in both marketing and repertoire permits the classification of the Thameside-Cliffe peninsula industry as a rural nucleation from around the reign of Commodus into the Severan era, if not beyond.

2. *Canterbury*

The intensification, and diversification, of pottery manufacture in the industrial quarters of the civitas capital in the mid-Flavian years represents a classic example of the development of an urban nucleated industry along the lines hypothesized by Peacock (1982) and conforms to a broad pattern of first to second century urban-orientated potteries discerned by Fulford (1977b). The expansion coincided broadly with the construction of the theatre (around A.D. 80–90: Frere 1970), and with Agricola's reforms of the Imperial tax collection system, which would have promoted industrial development (Tacitus, *Agricola*, xix–xx; Fulford 1981, 200; Hopkins 1980, 103). The relationship between the Canterbury industry and the mortarium factories of Q. Valerius Veranius and his colleagues (Hartley 1977, Group 2) is unknown, but at least one potter can be assigned circumstantially to Canterbury in the early years of the nucleation, Juvenalis, who stamped both mortaria and amphorae, and whose products are found in both Britain and Gaul (4.II.3). The dearth of known villas in mainland east Kent (discounting Thanet) suggests that estates were directed from the city. The white clays used for flagons and mortaria may have been quarried from the Gault Clay deposits situated below the escarpment of the North Downs and shipped down the Great Stour in barges, since the Brickearths available around Canterbury are iron-rich.

The Canterbury potters would undoubtedly have benefited from the formalisation of trading that the establishment of the Forum, presumably synchronous with that of the theatre (cf. Wacher 1975, 180–1), would have represented. Their repertoire included types such as *tazze* and *unguentaria*, which found particular favour in towns and villas as opposed to lower status rural sites, and a limited range of fine wares, notably mica-dusted vessels (Jenkins 1956b). The concentration of the kilns to the west of the Stour implies an element of town planning (the Dane John site, though within the later city walls, lies to the south of the domestic quarter), but the direct involvement of city patrons cannot be demonstrated either in the pottery or tile industries. It is tempting to invoke the existence of a collegium of potters which, *ex officio*, co-ordinated production and distribution of their wares. Guilds were supposed legally to confine themselves to social and charitable activities, but it is difficult to believe that they did not provide a forum for discussion of industrial affairs (cf. A.H.M. Jones 1974, Chapter II).

VI. ESTATE PRODUCTION

1. *Otford*

The isolated location of the Otford kiln would appear to be incompatible with its association with flagon production (nos. 102–106), which is found normally in nucleated industries. Activity may have antedated the Lullingstone villa (a Flavian foundation imposed on an existing farmstead) as well as the stone villa on the Otford site itself (Swan 1984, 406). The kiln type is unique in Kent, conforming to Swan's H5 or 6 (*ibid.*). It may be surmised that the kiln was built to serve the needs of the local community rather than a wider custom, but whether this comprised military consumers (as Swan, 1984, favours) or civilians alone, can only be a matter for speculation.

2. *Eccles*

Pottery production at Eccles, attested by a waste dump, would appear to have preceded the construction of the villa by perhaps five years (Detsicas 1977a, 28–9). The excavator felt unable to comment on the relationship between pottery manufacture and pre-villa occupation, but it may be surmised that the extraordinary range of forms, drawing on Gallo-Belgic, Lyon and other imported traditions, is related in some way to the authority that commissioned the villa *c.* A.D. 65. Detsicas has observed that the circular *laconicum* of the early villa (Room 32:

Detsicas 1964, 122–3) is normally a feature of military establishments; a parallel at Ashtead villa in west Surrey (Lowther 1927; 1929; 1930), dated to the later first century, is associated with a major tilery whose products were distributed throughout Surrey and to places as distant as Verulamium and Chelmsford, perhaps by peripatetic craftsmen, in the Flavian period (*id.*, 1948). Eccles ware has not been recorded away from the villa itself (Greene 1979a, 85), but local consumption at Rochester and elsewhere need not be detectable in the extremely small pre-Flavian assemblages extant from the town and the Medway valley. Potential military consumers, supplied via the Medway, are postulated by Swan, as at Otford (1984, 389). Peacock (1982, 10) envisaged a commercial rôle for estate production, and it may be that both Otford and Eccles represent estate interests.

3. *Other Estates*

The potential involvement of villa owners or managers in pottery manufacture has been surmised in several cases above (e.g. 6.V.1). It must be stressed that the organisation of the estates themselves is subject to speculation. Production directed from the villa authority may be inferred in particular where the repertoire is of a specialised nature or where long-distance trade is indicated, that is to say where the potential for profits is greatest, but cannot be attested positively in any instance. The cases of Otford and Eccles apart, it is considered that workshop models, individual or nucleated, are best applied to the kiln- and wheel-using potteries in Kent.

VII. RELATIONSHIPS BETWEEN POTTERIES IN KENT AND BEYOND: STYLISTIC CONSIDERATIONS

Close affinities in ranges of types can be recognised between the Thameside-Cliffe peninsula BB2 and grey ware potteries and those of south Essex and Colchester (Pollard 1983b, 134–8). The kiln sites of south Essex have yet to be published in detail, with the exception of Mucking (Jones and Rodwell 1973), the conclusions drawn from which have subsequently been revised (M.U. Jones, R. Birss, R. Jefferies, pers. comms.). The south Essex sites were not included in Williams' programme of petrological analysis of BB2 (1977), or in Monaghan's neutron activation analysis of BB2 and grey wares (1982). It is likely, pending full publication, that south Essex and north Kent potters were in direct communication, but operated within mutually discreet circuits of itinerary (see below). Farrar (1973, 101) has suggested that a merchant concern – a *negotiator artis cretariae* – was involved in the trade up the North Sea coast (cf. Fulford 1981), and it may have been this middleman activity that provided the link between the potteries of the Thames and Colchester and ensured that, for the 'export' market at least, they produced a common range of types.

The mechanisms that determined the styles of pottery produced in Roman Britain are understood very imperfectly. The influence of popular wares such as samian or BB1 is often invoked when the derivations of forms are discussed, and military preferences are also popular determinants. The 'new wave' of fashion defined as BB2 is held commonly to have been derived from BB1, presumably under the stimulus of the latter's success in capturing northern markets, although in south-eastern Britain BB1 is extremely rare until the third century. This implies either a degree of awareness amongst potters of their colleagues' activities, or the intervention of an entrepreneur. The Flavian expansion of the Canterbury industry involved the adoption of a style, which can be seen in part or whole in several other late first-century urban-orientated industries, including Brockley Hill, London, Silchester, and Leicester. The reeded rim bowl is a ubiquitous element (no. 70), but forms of jar, flagon, jug and dish (e.g. nos. 64, 68–70, 73, 74) can also be found in some or all of these industries (Pollard 1983a, 365–83). It is more likely that these all responded to an external stimulus than that they were in direct contact with one another. The fact that this 'urban style' was not universally adopted (cf. Fig. 24) demands the rejection of a simple diffusion model for the spread of fashions in pottery forms.

VIII.   THE MIGRATION OF POTTERS: ITINERACY AND SINGLE MOVEMENTS

The recognition of a considerable number of small settlements and farmsteads, associated with small groups of kilns producing identical wares over a century and more, around the Thames estuary has led to the proposition that the activity of professional itinerant potters is here represented (Rodwell 1974, 35). This hypothesis was forwarded with specific reference to material from Orsett and Mucking, two sites only 2–3 km. apart on the Thurrock gravel plateau. The hypothesis was supported by the evidence of roller-stamps of very similar, if not the same, die being used at both sites. Such stamps were not apparently used at other kiln sites, such as Higham, Cooling and Billericay, although in the latter case at least this may be a function of the time-span of production. While this negative evidence and the typological differences also observed between Kent and Essex wares (Pollard 1983a; 1983b, 134–8) should not be taken as invalidating the hypothesis, it suggests that any such peripatetic activity was conducted only at a parochial level, respecting the natural boundary of the Thames to the south and east. Peripatetic production has also been adduced by Drury (1976b, 258) in respect of the 'Rettendon' sand-flint tempered wares of the late third to early fifth century in mid-Essex, kiln sites producing which are scattered over an area of eastern-mid Essex some 25 km. in length. Drury has observed minor typological differences between the sites, which might be a function of space, time or both factors.

Peacock (1982, 9) has observed that peripatetic production is particularly useful to individual workshop potters serving dispersed markets and also to potters producing cumbersome, low-value items such as storage jars or ceramic building materials. The former seldom carry distinctive stamps, although basic motifs such as finger-tip decoration ('Patch Grove' ware) and combed herringbone, chevron and wavy line patterns interspersed with zones of slip (Alice Holt) can often be recognised and might be interpreted as a deliberate expression of identity of source. Bricks and tiles are often stamped, however, and itineracy has not infrequently been proposed to explain dispersed distribution (e.g. Lowther 1948; McWhirr and Viner 1978, 369–71). The movements of mortaria and samian manufacturers are well-attested by stamps, although movements in one direction only tend to be the rule rather than circuit-tours (cf. Hartley 1973a; 1976; 1977).

There are no clear examples of possible itineracy within Kent itself, although the potters of the Q. Valerius Veranius and Q. Valerius Se. . . groups of first-century mortaria may have moved to Kent from Gallia Belgica (Hartley 1977). The Thames Estuary kiln sites produced very similar pottery, but stamps were not used and typological similarities of form could equally well be explained by personal contact between potters (the main area of production in the western Cliffe peninsula is only 10 by 5 km. in extent) or standardisation imposed by a middleman or other vested interest (see above). However, the site of a possible kiln at Preston-near-Wingham presents an intriguing case of long-distance movement by potters producing grey sandy wares to lucrative markets. The feature represented can be interpreted as a double-flue kiln, with no surviving interior furniture (Dowker 1878). Corder (1957, 23) has noted that the 'double stokehole' kiln type is 'confined in the main to the Farnham district', and more recent work has not wholly invalidated this statement (Swan 1984, 117–20). The New Forest kilns were wholly of single-flue type (Fulford 1975a, 13–16), while of 21 kilns of the Oxfordshire industry only one was twin-flued (Young 1977a, 40). Hull published only two double-flue kilns out of some 30 known structures at Colchester (Hull 1963, 3–9, Kilns 10 and 11).

The Preston feature is the only known possible double-flue kiln in Kent. The double-flue kiln at Arlington (Holden 1979) is also unique, as the only pottery kiln of any type recorded in East Sussex: kiln production is suspected at Great Cansiron (Cawood 1986) and Hassocks, and 'Pevensey' ware should be kiln-fired and could well have been produced in East Sussex. The two kilns differ in structural detail, but they are similar in location and, so far as can be determined, in products. The Arlington kiln lies within 1 km. of a Roman road to Pevensey (Margary 1939, 37–44; Holmes 1979, 61) which is some 16 km. to the east, while that at Preston is within 10 km. of Richborough via Watling Street or perhaps via the Little Stour and Wantsum. Holmes (*ibid.*) has noted the similarity between Arlington pottery and Alice Holt/Farnham grey wares, particularly those from Overwey (Clark 1949) where the three kilns are all double-flue types. The single vessel known to be associated with the Preston feature, the cremation(?) vessel blocking one flue entrance, is virtually identical to Overwey 27 (*ibid.*, fig. 7) in form, fabric and decoration (ref.: Maidstone Museum reg. 5PW.3); furthermore Overwey Kilns 1 and 2 are simple bowl ovens, as Preston would appear to have been. Holmes has suggested that the Arlington kiln represents the work of a Farnham potter seeking to cash in on the construction of the Saxon Shore fort at Pevensey; it would seem reasonable to apply the same hypothesis to the Preston kiln also, the potter there being attracted by the re-establishment of the Richborough garrison in the Saxon Shore fort. The dates of these two potters' migrations may also be broadly similar: Pevensey may have been constructed in the wake of Constans' visit to Britain in A.D. 342–3 (Johnson 1976, 144) and Richborough would seem to have witnessed a marked intensification of activity sometime in the A.D. 330s–340s after a quiet spell in the early fourth century (Reece 1968). The Overwey group of kilns and an associated dump are dated by Lyne and Jefferies to *c.* A.D. 350 on the basis of pottery typology (1979, 10–11). Double-flue kilns at Farnham date back to the third century, however (*ibid*). Recent studies of pottery from Saxon Shore forts (Young 1977b, 1980; Pollard 1983a, 304–6) have expressed the view that individual forts sought out their own pottery supplies without recourse to large-scale contracts or 'military' production. Fulford has suggested a connection between the injection of large sums of money into the construction of the Saxon Shore forts and of civilian defences, and the development of the massive potteries of Alice Holt, Oxfordshire, the New Forest and others in the late third century (Fulford 1979). The migration of potters producing wares of a value, which might be considered to be modest to locations closer to lucrative markets such as the forts, would seem a logical development and the resulting production accords well with Peacock's 'individual workshop' model (1982, 9).

IX. THE ASSOCIATION OF POTTERY PRODUCTION WITH OTHER INDUSTRIES

In the preceding section, pottery manufacture has been treated in isolation from other industries. In terms of co-operation in production, as opposed to vulnerability to socio-economic fluctuation, this may to a great extent reflect the situation in which the potter worked. However, it would be misleading to overlook evidence for the joint operation of potteries with at least two other industries, both of which shared with the potter the basic skills of working the clay medium: brick and tile manufacture and salt-winning.

The similarities between pottery and tile manufacture and salt-winning are two-fold. First, all three require warm, dry weather, for the drying of ceramics and the evaporation of salt. The creation of an artificial climate by constructing drying sheds is not attested either ethnographically or archaeologically for the household industry and individual workshop models of ceramic production hypothesized for the north Kent potteries, implying summer seasonal activity only. The second similarity arises from the first: the industries are compatible with farming, as they occupy the slack part of the agricultural cycle (Bradley 1978, 67–9).

1. *Brick and Tile Manufacture*

The intensity with which this aspect of Roman industry has been studied in recent years is reflected in the number of publications readily accessible to the researcher. The task of the present author has been made much simpler by the works of Brodribb (1969, 1979), McWhirr and Viner (1978), McWhirr (1979a), Peacock (1977b) and others.

Kilns producing ceramic building materials have been found on only three sites in Kent, two outside Canterbury (Jenkins 1956a, 1960) and one close to the Eccles villa (Detsicas 1967, 170–4). Monaghan (1987, 28) records 'a probable tile kiln' on the Medway Marshes. In addition, military stamps of the *Classis Britannica* are known from a number of military and industrial sites and one villa (Folkestone) in Kent, East Sussex and the Pas-de-Calais (Peacock 1977b) and of the *Cohors I Baetasiorum* from Reculver (Hassall 1977). Peacock has suggested that his fabric 2 *Classis Britannica* bricks and tiles were produced in the south Romney Marsh-Camber area (Peacock 1977b, 242). A tile kiln and pottery wasters have been excavated at Great Cansiron in the central Weald (Rudling 1986; Cawood 1986).

The association of building ceramics and pottery production in a military context is known at several sites in Britain, such as Holt (Grimes 1930), Brampton in Cumbria (McWhirr 1979a, 111–19) and Grimescar, Yorks (*ibid.*, 182–3). However, there is no evidence for, and circumstantially weighty evidence against, military pottery production in association with tileries in Kent.

In civilian contexts the production of both classes of ceramics on a single site has been suggested for several sites: these include Park Street (Herts.), Little Hadham (Herts.), Colney Street (Herts.), Minety (Wilts.), Eccles and Canterbury (McWhirr 1979a) as well as Great Cansiron. Canterbury is unique on two counts: first, it is the only place where co-operation in production, if not production by the same individual, is firmly attested. The Area I site at St. Stephen's Road comprised a pottery kiln and a tile kiln/drying chamber sharing a stokehole pit (Jenkins 1956a, 41–50). The use of tiles and bricks in the construction of pottery kilns is commonplace, but need not imply the same level of co-operation. The second feature unique to Canterbury is the proximity of tileries to the town itself, Kiln II at Whitehall Gardens (Jenkins 1960, 154–6) and that at St. Stephen's Road both lying within 1 km. of the later walled area. The evidence of brick-making in London (Merrifield 1965, 189, 227) is purely circumstantial. Indeed, evidence for production of building ceramics even in the general vicinity of towns is extremely rare, as Peacock (1977b, 8–9) has observed. McWhirr (1979a, 125–9) has dismissed Hull's suggestion that Kilns 17 and 31 at Colchester (Hull 1963) were used for tiles, leaving only the enigmatic Kiln 7 as a possible tilery; the Lexden kilns produced no published evidence of associated products (McWhirr 1979a, 129–32). The Park Street and Black Boys Pit tile kilns lie close to Verulamium, but only a single kiln is known from each site (ibid., 141–7), while evidence from Little London, Silchester, suggests a brickworks, perhaps under Imperial jurisdiction, some 3 km. beyond the Roman walls (Karslake 1926; Boon 1974a, 101 and 277–9; a full gazetteer of evidence of tile-production will be found in McWhirr and Viner (1978), updated and amended by McWhirr (1979a)). The evidence of municipal involvement in brick/tile production afforded by the RPG (? *Res Publica Glevensium*) and PR BR LON stamps from Gloucester and London respectively (Peacock 1977b, 9) is not paralleled at Canterbury or elsewhere in Kent. The present author has suggested that a *collegium* under local patronage may have unofficially represented the potters of second-century Canterbury (Chapter 7) and by extension perhaps the tileworkers also; there is no hard evidence to support this, however, nor Peacock's suggestion that some of the kilns around urban sites may have been under estate control (Peacock 1977b, 9).

The Eccles tilery may have been an estate concern, as Peacock (*ibid.*) has proposed; the present author has argued for estate interest in the pre-Flavian pottery works (Detsicas 1977a; 6.VI.2 above). It is not at present possible to ascertain whether this tilery was engaged in supplying other sites in the area; the approximate period of its construction (*c.* A.D. 180–290: Detsicas 1967, 174) covers also the construction phases 2 and 3 of the villa at Snodland Church Field (Ocock and Syddell 1967) and construction phases 2 and 3 (if not also 1) of the Maidstone 'Mount' villa (D.B. Kelly, pers. comm.; ceramic dating by present author), both on the banks of the Medway within 10 km. of Eccles. The town of Rochester is also readily accessible by river, and was involved in town defence building in the early third century (Pollard 1981a), from which other construction may be inferred as such defences could rarely be sited without some demolition of property.

Peacock (1982) has observed that in addition to estates, the individual (rural) workshop model of production is particularly well-geared to brick and tile production, with peripatetic operation commonplace. Nineteenth- and twentieth-century brickworks were widespread in north Kent, using the creeks to export products along the coast and the Thames. It is worth observing that the villa at Plaxtol produced a number of tiles with Lowther's die 31 which was not recorded by Lowther from any other site in southern Britain (1948), although more recently one find has been made at the Darenth villa (Philp 1973); three of Lowther's dies (41–43) were recorded only from Canterbury. Associations with Essex tiles are provided by Lowther's die 16 (Canterbury, Chelmsford), 29 (Canterbury, Alresford) and 32 (Canterbury, possibly Hartlip, and Great Chesterford) and with London tiles by dies 9 (Richborough, London) and 27 (Dover, London). The Ashtead industry's associated dies have not been recorded at all from Kent by Lowther, although die 5 has been recorded from several sites in east Surrey, and 5A from Great Cansiron, East Sussex (Rudling 1986). The sample from Kent is small, however. Long-distance associations between dies found in Kent and elsewhere include die 16 (Wall, Staffs.), 9 (Cobham, Surrey; Leicester), 27 (Silchester), 32 (Boxmoor, Herts., Beckley, Oxon.), and 38 (Hartlip, Silchester) (data from Lowther 1948).

Lowther's research was conducted specifically on flue-tiles; the dating evidence available to
him suggested the main period of production to be *c.* A.D. 80–150. The use of tiles in the
construction of the pre-Flavian kiln at St. Stephen's Road (Jenkins 1956a) implies an early start
for the Canterbury industry, while the filling of the stokehole pit of the pottery and tile kilns on
Area I at this site is given a *terminus post quem* by two pieces of later second-century samian
(ibid., 50); the filling of the vertical flues of the tile kiln at Whitehall Gardens included a coin of
Geta (*c.* A.D. 211–12; Jenkins 1960, 155). The Canterbury tileries lasted at least as long as the
structurally-attested pottery industry, therefore, from the pre-Flavian to the Severan periods.
Structural evidence from within Canterbury suggests that tiles were used in building construc-
tion into the fourth century (Blockley and Day forthcoming). The links between Canterbury
and Essex are of interest in that they reflect the strong typological links binding the pottery of
Kent and Essex; however, these links are primarily with west Kent and the military bases of the
Channel, rather than with Canterbury itself. Colchester mortaria and BB2 are attested at
Canterbury in the second century. Drury has suggested that Chelmsford derived most of its tile
from the Ashtead area (quoted in Johnston and Williams 1979, 384). Small quantities of early
Alice Holt wares are also found at Chelmsford as are fourth-century Alice Holt wares. The
absence of attested Ashtead flue-tiles from Kent may be compared with the rarity of Surrey
pottery of first- to mid third-century date in the latter county, excluding what is now Greater
London. It is not suggested that Ashtead tiles and Alice Holt pottery were necessarily
transported and sold together, much less that their production was in the same hands.
Nevertheless, the evidence of the two industries is mutually supporting in implying a lack of
movement from west Surrey to Kent of low value industrial products in the first two centuries
A.D. The comparative insularity of the Canterbury pottery industry of Flavian to Antonine date
is also paralleled by the evidence of flue-tiles (dies 41–43). It is perhaps significant that the
Classis Britannica elected to manufacture its own tiles in Kent and/or East Sussex rather than
rely solely on purchases from Canterbury, as the pottery evidence shows that, at Dover,
Canterbury grey wares were also spurned from at least the mid- to late second century (4.III.3),
while they never gained a foothold in East Sussex markets.

2. *The Salt Industry*

The main areas of 'red hills', mounds of fire-reddened debris of the salt industry, in Kent
coincide with those of pottery manufacture – the western part of the Cliffe peninsula and around
the Medway estuary (Miles 1975), although this is not the case in southern Essex (Rodwell 1979,
151). Rodwell has considered that the Thames-mouth salt industry 'was organised in small,
compact units' (*ibid.*, 161) associated in Kent with black-burnished pottery production and in
Essex with 'a distinctive type of very coarse shell-tempered storage jar', presumably of the type
here termed 'Thames Estuary' (Rodwell 1966a, fig. 7, no. 1; no. 16 here). The latter is
associated with kiln debris at Tilbury Gun Hill (Drury and Rodwell 1973), but not elsewhere.
Rodwell speculates that these vessels may have been 'made cheaply on site, for the storage and
transportation of crystalline salt' (1979, 161) alongside *briquetage* evaporating pans. This
hypothesis would certainly fit the observed distribution of this type of storage jar (Fig. 31;
cf. Pollard 1983a, 279–81), including, as it does, a number of sites accessible by creek or river from the
Thames but also a handful of sites well inland, where salt must have been at a premium (e.g. Great
Cansiron in the Weald, and Coulsdon and Otford on the line of the North Downs scarp).

Rodwell has argued that the salt industry of south-east Essex was imposed on the landscape by Roman state intervention (1979, 160–6), and by the implications of a coincident emergence of the industry on the Kent side of the Thames (in the later first century A.D.) and the extension of rectilinear systems of land division across the Thames from the Grays-Thurrock area to Cliffe; this must, by the logic behind the argument, apply also to parts of north Kent (though this is not explicitly stated). The theory is untestable against present evidence; the 'imperial estate' has often been seized upon as an explanation for voids in villa distribution, and for the expansion or creation of extractive industries and, in consequence, its validity as a concept has been undermined.

3. *Other Industries*

A fourth major industrial activity attested in the archaeological record concerns the extraction and working of iron. The extractive processes are also best carried out in dry weather, but tend to occur in areas of low agricultural value, such as the High Weald of Kent and Sussex.

There is no conclusive evidence to suggest the combination of pottery-making with iron extraction in the Weald. However, the coarse, low-technology 'East Sussex Ware' could have been produced on iron-extraction sites or centres such as Bardown (cf. Cleere 1970) and Garden Hill without leaving any archaeological trace. The evidence for both pottery and iron-working industries at Wakerley, Northants. (Jackson and Ambrose 1978) suggests that these two industries did co-exist on rural sites alongside agricultural activities, although the dating evidence for iron-working at Wakerley is insufficient for contemporaneity with potting to be confirmed. A bloomery is known to lie in the vicinity of the tile kiln and grey ware pottery wasters excavated at Great Cansiron Farm, East Sussex (Rudling 1986).

X. RELATIONSHIPS BETWEEN PRODUCER AND CONSUMER

A variety of exchange mechanisms may have operated in distributing the products of the pottery industries of Roman Britain (Renfrew 1977, 9). The potter's home or workshop, a permanent market place such as a *forum* or *macellum*, a rural fair or a religious centre all have the potential to act as places of formal exchange involving pottery. The identification of such a place in the archaeological record is problematic, however; the two clear examples in Britain are at Wroxeter (Atkinson 1970) and Colchester (Hull 1958), in the *forum* and shops respectively (cf. Pollard 1983a, 417–22). The concept of a middleman has been introduced above (see also Hassall 1978); he may have taken on the task of trading the pots at the exchange places, or taken them directly to the customer, for example a military quartermaster. The potter himself may have peddled his wares during the course of a peripatetic production circuit or in special journeys (cf. Fulford 1975a, 122 and fig. 55). It would be impossible to distinguish itinerant peddling from itinerant production in the archaeological record, if the commodities being distributed did not require permanent equipment to produce them, and peddling from a series of production sites established in itinerant fashion is also feasible (see Pollard 1983a, 422–73 for extensive analysis of patterns of distribution in Kent). Renfrew's fifth model, that of the producer taking his wares to some central agency, which assigns him goods in exchange (1977, 10), might be adapted to fit the hypothesis of a tenant paying his rent in pots, wherein the 'goods' are his fields and possibly equipment. The use of pots as containers for traded commodities such as wine, luxury foods, and salt introduces a further factor in producer-consumer relationships; the case for salt transportation has been put by Rodwell (1979, 161), whilst Loughlin (1977, 88) has suggested that Dales ware jars were used as containers for unspecified traded commodities.

CHAPTER 7

CONCLUSIONS

The preceding chapters have presented a description and analysis of the trends in the development of production, importation and dispersal of pottery in Kent from the first to the fifth century A.D. The patterns that have been propounded evince complex networks of trade/exchange connections both within the region and between it, neighbouring and more distant regions, which change in directions and intensity several times during the course of the period. These changes may be gradual, as with the expansion of the Oxfordshire industry's market during the third century, or abrupt, such as the flood of samian that entered Britain in the Flavian period. Certain elements of the network remain comparatively stable over a period of centuries, such as the parallel development of forms and fabrics in north Kent and south Essex, the apparent dominance of the Upchurch industry of the market for beakers, and the isolation of east Kent from west Kent in coarse ware exchange.

The principle adopted in defining the various elements in these networks has been to work from known production units, whose styles are frequently quite distinct from one another. These units – the Canterbury sandy ware kilns, the 'BB2'/grey ware kilns of the lower Thames area, the Brockley Hill-Verulamium kilns, for example – form a framework for discussion of many aspects of production, importation and dispersal, but they only produced a part of the total pottery found in Kent. The remainder has been divided on the grounds of fabric and form into 'wares' such as 'Patch Grove', early shelly, and late grogged. The system is not dissimilar to that employed by Cunliffe (1978) in his work on Iron Age pottery. In this, Cunliffe argues that 'the only value to be gained from defining minor regional variations [the style-zones] is to provide a broad framework for descriptive purposes' (346). The style-zones are not, he is at pains to point out, representations of significantly different cultures. This pessimistic view of Iron Age pottery study is echoed by Lambrick (1978, 112): 'It is doubtful how significant purely pottery groupings may be in reflecting more general trading patterns and areas of contact, let alone more fundamental cultural, social or political relationships'. The contrast with Peacock's view of pottery studies in general is marked; he has written (1977a, 23) that 'pottery can and has been used to establish directions of the main trade currents, to investigate marketing arrangements and to give an indication of social questions such as the function of a site or its wealth and prosperity'. It is worth pointing out that much of Peacock's own work has been on pottery of the Iron Age (Peacock 1968, 1969, 1971; Drury 1978, 58–9). Roman scholars tend to be more optimistic about the value of pottery as an indicator of broader trends; this view may be presented in a qualified form, as Fulford proposed in a paper comparing medieval pottery trade and medieval documentation for trade with Britain's late Roman trade (1978c). Here, and in an earlier paper on the evidence of coins and pottery for Britain's late Roman trade (1977a), the conclusion reached is that while the evidence of pottery can be used to demonstrate the existence of trade links, the greater abundance of one type rather than another cannot necessarily be used as evidence of the relative importance of source areas in the volume of real trade in the total range of commodities, which is largely concealed in the archaeological record.

The question of the value of pottery as an indicator of economic patterns and trends is crucial to the assessment of the validity of the study here presented. It is generally recognised that pottery comprised a relatively unimportant element of industry and commerce in the Roman world. Very few of the wrecks investigated in the Mediterranean contain a cargo solely of pottery, although the Pudding Pan Rock wreck in the Thames estuary carried a large consignment of Central Gaulish fine wares and roofing-tiles, and traders specialising in fine pottery are known from the epigraphic and documentary records (Hassall 1978; Middleton 1979). The products of agriculture and mining were of far greater importance to the economy of the Roman Empire (A.H.M. Jones 1974, Chapter 2), both on a regional and inter-provincial level. If pottery can only be adduced as evidence of the trade and exchange in pottery, it must be asked if the effort expended in producing pieces of research such as this presented here is justified. In the first place, it cannot be asserted that pottery is unrepresentative of any other traded commodity, for in some cases it is clearly the carrier of other commodities, and these, particularly wine, olive oil and sauces, may be considerable profit-generators. Amphorae are an exceptional form of pottery, however, and the lack of relevant petrological work published at the time of writing has necessitated the restriction of discussion on their sources and distribution patterns. In the second place, Hopkins (1980) has proposed that manufactured goods, including pottery, formed an integral part of the balance of tax and trade flows that helped support the economy of the whole empire. Clearly, the evidence for trade and exchange that is presented by pottery has to be interpreted with some caution; but the volume of that evidence demands that it be examined.

The geographical location and evident prosperity of Roman Kent enabled its population to tap most of the ceramic trade routes from the Continent throughout the period. The Rhineland (du Plat Taylor and Cleere 1978) and northern Gaul (Rigby 1973; Peacock 1977c) were both important sources of pottery, including local products and exports in transit from further afield. Kent's location was less favourable with regard to the Atlantic/Biscay trade from Spain and western Gaul than was that of the Channel *civitates* (the Regni, Belgae and Durotriges in particular), but this appears to have been a disadvantage only in the acquisition of imports of low trade volume (notably '*A l'éponge*' ware from the Loire area: Fulford 1977a; Galliou *et al*. 1980), with no bearing on that of the more massive trade in South Gaulish samian and South Spanish amphorae. However, the Cantiaci did not gain their own wealth from the exporting of pottery in any great measure, BB2 alone achieving a wide market (Williams 1977) (cf. Monaghan 1987, 211–13; 220; 224–6; 233) that may have included the Channel coast of Gaul at a restricted level (Fulford 1977a). If there was a direct, reciprocal trade from Kent to the Continent, then it must have involved agricultural produce, particularly cereals, and the sale of corn in the years after the Agricolan reforms and before the imposition of the *annona militaris* may also have been the main generator of the wealth of the *civitas*, or at least of its magnates (cf.

Detsicas 1983). BB2 probably represents the tip of the iceberg with regard to commerce flowing from Kent to the north of Britain and into London. Agricultural produce and Kentish rag (Greensand building stone), would also have found a ready market in London (a Roman barge found in London contained a cargo of rag, and it is known from Roman buildings in the city: Marsden 1966; Williams 1971, 172). Rag was also used at Colchester (*ibid.*), a Kentish source being likely in view of the relative ease of sea and river transport. The mineral wealth of the Weald may have been exploited in part by men of the Cantiaci under Imperial licence (Cleere 1974, 181). It has been suggested (Pollard 1983a, 251–88) that pottery flowed in a reciprocal trade between north Kent and London on the one hand and the Wealden ironworks on the other. The existence of a trade in raw materials, minerals or agricultural products between the Midlands and Kent is less easy to envisage, and it may, therefore, be the case that the pottery from Oxfordshire and the Nene valley is representative solely of trade in manufactured goods, if not confined to pottery alone. It is nevertheless clear from the evidence of Kentish rag, and from the implications of the assumptions of a high corn yield from the *civitas* and of its involvement in Wealden iron ore extraction, that pottery does reflect broader trade networks. This concept has also been imposed upon the seaborne trade along the west coast of Britain (Fulford 1981) and may be applied to the Channel also, where monumental stone and worked or unworked shale may have accompanied Dorset BB1 and New Forest fine wares in extensive commerce.

Pottery production in any form is subject to changes in the economic background, but this is a feature particularly characteristic of 'urban' and fine ware industries or any industry whose well-being depends upon long-distance trade. In the Roman period it was these kinds of industry which developed most rapidly in the first century A.D., supplying not only the military market but also civilian populations. It seems reasonable to equate the advancement of these concerns with the expansion of cash as a means of exchange, for the army and towns were undoubtedly the main agencies through which money was channelled. Rural industries were apparently less susceptible to economic changes; apart from the growth of 'Patch Grove', there is no clear indication of any development in the rural wares of Kent, beyond the experimentation with sand tempering, until the early second century. The same can be said of south Essex, and 'East Sussex ware' never developed beyond the production and distribution level of its late Iron Age antecedents so far as can be judged (Green 1980). When the rural industries of north-west Kent and south Essex did develop in the early second century, villas may already have been in existence (in west Kent at least) for several decades. These industries in due course showed themselves to be more resilient to the general depression of pottery production in the late second to early third century than did their urban counterparts at Canterbury, Brockley Hill-Verulamium, Highgate Wood (whose market must have been dominated by London) and elsewhere. This resilience is common also to the Oxfordshire and Alice Holt coarse ware industries (Young 1977a; Lyne and Jefferies 1979). It is remarkable that 'urban' industries did not undergo a general expansion corresponding with that of the large rural industries (e.g. Alice Holt, Oxford, New Forest) in the later third century. This phenomenon has been discussed by Fulford (1977b) and the present author (Pollard 1983a, 365–83).

The evidence (presented in Pollard 1983a, 474–535) strongly suggests that pottery production and trade on the whole reflect the economic fortunes of the province(s) in general, within certain limitations of sensitivity applying particularly to rural coarse ware concerns. Thus, even if the directions of trade flow exhibited by pottery do not represent those of other commodities (and this negative proposition does not necessarily hold true), the production patterns and trade intensity can be representative of wider trends. The equation of urban and fine ware industries with a cash-using economy, while tentative, allows the developments of that most characteristic feature of the Roman Empire to be monitored at an intra-provincial level providing a complement to the military frontier situations.

The trade flows that are represented by pottery distribution patterns suggest that exchange systems operated independent of the *civitas* system, as a ware can be found in more than one *civitas* without occurring throughout its 'home' *civitas*. The function of the *civitas* system was in no small part geared to the maintenance of tax-levying. This might imply that the whole of one *civitas* population was economically tied to its capital or, more properly, its tax-collecting decurions. The extent of the *civitas* of the Cantiaci is not known – the maps of Roman Britain that preface many notable works represent only speculation (Rivet 1964, 131–7). It is a paradox that London, the provincial capital, was not a *civitas* capital. Frere (1974, 235) has considered that it must, therefore, have been a *municipium* or a *colonia* and may thus have possessed a *territorium* (but cf. Rivet 1964, 138). This may have been extensive in area in order to compensate for the low population density of the London Clay basin (Sheldon and Schaaf 1978), and, if it existed, would surely have included part of the area usually ascribed to the *civitas Cantiacorum*. It is tempting to see in the distribution of pottery such as Brockley Hill, Highgate Wood, and Copthall Close type coarse wares a reflection of the *territorium* in Kent through the marketing of these wares in the city to its dependent population. Clearly these wares were also dispersed outside of the London area (Brockley Hill is closer to Verulamium than London, incidentally) and much coarse pottery entered London from well outside that area (e.g. Colchester BB2, Dorset BB1, Alice Holt grey wares). It can at least be fairly stated that west Kent, in terms of its industrial output and input, was linked more closely with London than with the *civitas* capital at Canterbury (cf. Pollard 1983a, 251–306). The sale of west Kent surpluses to London is not incompatible with the payment of taxes (and rents) to the decurions of Canterbury, however. The lack of integration of west and east Kent into a single coarse ware exchange network may be seen to date from at least as early as the first century B.C. to the second or even third century A.D. It has been noted (*ibid.*, 63–5) that the coinage of Tasciovanus, Dubnovellaunus (Kent), Eppillus and others exhibits a marked bias in distribution either towards west Kent and Essex or towards east Kent. This fragmentation is reflected in Allen's (1971) type L *potin* coins, but was apparently overcome by coins of types O and P and issues of Cunobelin. The apparent independence of west from east Kent in pottery is thus reflected in Iron Age coins; although this need not indicate political autonomy, the system of obligation that Iron Age gold coins are believed by some authorities (e.g. Haselgrove 1979) to represent would appear to have involved separate networks east and west of the Medway up until the A.D. 20s.

The generation of hypotheses concerning matters beyond those merely of ceramics must be an important function of pottery studies in general, if these are to be developed to their full potential. Here two hypotheses have been examined: that pottery industries of an urban or fine-ware producing type are synonymous with a cash-using economy; and that the pottery of west Kent reflects industrial, and perhaps political, independence of east Kent, with London as a candidate for administrator of at least the westernmost part (perhaps west of the Cray valley) of the modern county. The provision of a description of pottery developments within Kent also provides a solid basis for the making of value judgements on the social status and wealth of sites in the region: this function of pottery was envisaged by Peacock (1977a, 23–4), who bemoaned the lack of investigation conducted into the economics of ceramic production. This aspect of the study owes much to that author's more recent work on the ethnography of pottery production (Peacock 1982). On the whole, coarse pottery does not reflect differential site status (Pollard 1983a, 444–61), except that towns and military bases are distinctive in the variety of wares of minor quantitative importance that tend to be included in assemblages. The cases of the selective marketing of BB2 in the early second century to the more prosperous sites, and of pre-Flavian Canterbury sandy wheel-thrown ware to the city and military base(s), are rare exceptions to this rule. Others may be obscured by the inadequacies of chronological refinement. Higher value wares may, in their proportions relative to coarse wares, provide information on site prosperity; occasionally, a limited distribution, such as those of pre-Flavian colour-coated wares and third-century *Moselkeramik*, may reflect selective marketing to (or purchase by) wealthier individuals or communities.

It is the present author's belief that the regional study of the whole network of pottery production, importation and distribution is a valid approach in archaeology. How then might future studies be conducted? It is plain that the quantification of assemblages is of vital importance to the furtherance of such studies. The initiative must come from post-excavation teams, for much material that lies in museums is patently worthless so far as quantification is concerned. Hodder's '30 sherd threshold' was, it would seem, adopted in the absence of a more appropriate measure to test his theories against available evidence. Hodder's (1974b) own reservations on the assemblages with which he was dealing, and the low value accorded to sherd-count statistics by Orton (1975; 1980, 156–67) imply that this technique is a poor substitute for the full, or statistically sampled, quantification of recovered assemblages prior to disposal. The application of well-funded sampling strategies to post-excavation sorting should also pay dividends in time saved and in producing comparable data. A third improvement will be aided by sampling; it is important that a greater number of assemblages be examined from each site if inter-site comparison is to be made, in order to level out possible biases due to assemblage-differentiation according to place-function within each site.

A regional study must be followed up by the asking of specific questions: D.F. Williams' work on petrological characterisation of BB1 and BB2 (1977) and Monaghan's study of 'Upchurch' wares (1982) are excellent examples of the kind of issue that can be pursued. Mainman's (forthcoming) petrological work on late Roman and Saxon coarse wares in Canterbury provides a third case-study, and serves to highlight the need for fabric and technological analysis as well as form-decoration studies, if the thorny problem of the transition from 'Romano-British' to 'Saxon' pottery is ever to be solved (Chapter 4.VI). The fabric groups defined on visual examination by the present author also need to be examined in more detail; in particular, it would be of interest to learn whether there are any consistent differences in inclusion-composition between Canterbury, Swale, Cliffe and Mucking grey wares that might confirm the visual isolation of a 'Canterbury' group from the remainder. Other aspects of the present study that should be worth following up are the cross-Channel trade in coarse pottery (cf. Fulford 1977a and Chapter 4 above); the movement of Nene Valley wares southwards along the Anglian coast to east Kent and its relationship to the development of the Saxon Shore system (cf. Young 1977b; 1980), and the general trade along the Channel coast of Britain (cf. e.g. Williams 1971; Cleere 1974; Fulford 1975a, 1975b; Williams 1977). The latter topic would shed some light also on the mutual isolation of Sussex and Kent that is apparent (Pollard 1983a, 251–306). The two regions have much in common – physical geography, the early development of villas, and the incorporation into the Saxon Shore system; were they 'parallel worlds' independent of one another, similar merely because of a common environment, or did the shared connections with iron-extraction and the Imperial fleet serve to integrate them to some extent? The similarities suggest that there was little that one could offer that the other did not have already, and thus that economic relationships were unnecessary to the well-being of either; but this must be a proposition to be tested, not an assumption.

The overall conclusion to be drawn from the present study is that pottery can provide insight into a wide variety of issues that are of significance to the archaeology of Britain and the Roman Empire; enthusiasm must be tempered with a realisation of the limitations of the material evidence. In the final analysis, pottery evidence is only as good as the context from which it is derived.

APPENDIX 1

THE SITES (Figs. 2–9)

Data listed in the following order:
1 = site gazetteer number. Abridge – site location (modern). Essex – county, if not in Kent. TQ 474978 – 4- or 6–figure National Grid Reference (*c*. = approximate or general location). V – site type, following system described in Chapter 2. III. L1–4 – period of occupation, A.D. unless stated otherwise.* Followed by publication references and (1978–80) location of material where known. The following abbreviations for institutions holding pottery have been used:

BM	–	British Museum
BtM	–	Battle Museum
BEM	–	Bexley and Erith Museum
CM	–	Canterbury Royal Museum
ChM	–	Chelmsford and Essex Museum
CAT	–	Canterbury Archaeological Trust
DM	–	Dartford Museum
DOE	–	Department of Environment stores, Dover Castle
FM	–	Folkestone Museum
GM	–	Greenwich Museum
KARU	–	Kent Archaeological Rescue Unit, Dover Castle
LM	–	Barbican House Museum, Lewes
MM	–	Maidstone Museum
OM	–	Orpington Museum
P-CM	–	Powell-Cotton Museum, Birchington
P-EM	–	Passmore-Edwards Museum, Stratford, London
RL	–	Ramsgate Library
RM	–	Rochester Museum

*E = early, M = middle, L = late, ½ = first half, (etc.)

I. *Sites studied at first-hand*

1. Abridge, Essex TQ 474978 V L1–4 Wilkinson 1977 P-EM.
2. Allington *c*. TQ 738578 VIII L1BC-M1+2. Thompson 1978; 1982, 578–9 MM.
3. Arlington, Chilver Bridge, East Sussex *c*. TQ 535065 VII M2–4 Holden 1979 (note) LM.
4. Aylesford *c*. TQ 7359 IX 1–2 Jessup and Taylor 1932 MM.
5. Bayford *c*. TQ 913639 IX L1–3/E4 Payne 1886 BM.
6. Bearsted, Crismill Farm TQ 8055 IX M1–2 Whiting 1927c MM.
7. Bexley TQ 510744 III/VII L3–M4 Tester 1963 BEM.
8. Billericay, Essex *c*. TQ 6793 VIII; XI 1BC-1, L2–4; L2–E3 Goodburn 1978, Myres *et al.* 1974 S. Weller, Billericay.

9A. Birchington, Minnis Bay TR 284697 VII 1BC-4 Powell-Cotton and Pinfold 1939; Thompson 1982, 617–24 P-CM.

9B. Birchington, Oyster Bay *c*. TR 293700 VII 1-E3 unpublished P-CM.

9C. Birchington, Epple Bay *c*. TR 307699 VIII 1BC–1 Anon. 1924; Thompson 1982, 625–7 P-CM.

10. Bodiam, East Sussex TQ 783251 (III)/VII L1–4 Lemmon and Hill 1966 BtM.

11. Boxted TQ 852663 V ½c? Jessup and Taylor 1932 BM.

12. Brenley Corner TR 043597 VII;IV 1–E4; 2–L4 Jenkins 1973, 1974 CM.

13. Bridge *c*. TR 1854 IX 4 Jenkins 1956b CM.

14. Buckland Hill, Hawthorndene near Maidstone VII M–L1 unpublished MM.

15. Canterbury *c*. TR 1457 I;XI L1BC–E5; M1–L2 Bennett *et al*. 1978, 1980, 1982; Blockley and Day forthcoming; Frere 1954, 1970; Jenkins 1950, 1952, 1956a, 1960, 1966a; Pollard 1981b; forthcoming, d; Rady forthcoming; Webster 1940; Whiting 1927d; Williams 1947 CM; CAT; F. Jenkins, Canterbury.

16. Chalk TQ 690732 XI M–L2 Allen 1954, 1959, 1970 MM.

17. Chalk TQ 677729 (V)/VI L2–E5 Johnston 1972 MM; D. Johnston, Southampton University.

18. Chalk TQ 690732 VIII 2;L4–E5 Allen 1954 MM.

19. Charlton TQ 418787 VII 1–L2 Elliston Erwood 1916, 1923, 1951 GM.

20. Chatham *c*. TQ 7566 IX 2 unpublished BM.

21. Chatham/Rochester, Fort Borstal *c*. TQ 7366 IX 3? Payne 1897 BM.

22. Cheriton TR 193369 VIII L1BC–E2 Tester and Bing 1949; Thompson 1982, 670–1 FM.

23. Chigwell, Little London, Essex *c*. TQ 4595 III/VII L1–E5 unpublished P-EM.

24. Cliffe-at-Hoo *c*. TQ 708771 VII E2–E3 unpublished MM.

25. Cobham Park TQ 683693 VII;V M–L1; L1–M4 Tester 1961 MM.

26. Cooling, Broomhey Farm TQ 765766 VII, X, (XI) L2–3 Miles and Syddell 1967; Miles 1973, 1975 MM.

27. Cooling, Broomhey Farm *c*. TQ 765766 VII, X, (XI) 1BC–4+ Pollard forthcoming, b; Thornhill and Payne 1980 RM.

28. Cranbrook, Little Farningham Farm TQ 809358 VI, X M2–M3 Cleere 1974, 195–196 Cranbrook Museum.

29. Crayford TQ 528773 IX M–L2 Balls 1958 BEM.

30. Dartford *c*. TQ 5574 V M2–M3. unpublished Dartford and District Archaeological Group.

31. Dover *c*. TR 3241 VII; II M1–E2; E2–L3 Philp 1981; Rahtz 1958; Murray Threipland and Steer 1951; unpublished KARU, Dover Museum, MM.

32. East Studdale TR 320495 IX M–L2 unpublished BM.

33. Eastry TR 298562 VII L1–L3 Ross 1968, Ogilvie 1982; Pollard 1982 BM.

34. Eltham *c*. TQ 4475 IX E3+ Rigden 1974 GM.

35. Faversham *c*. TR 0161 IX M3–4 unpublished BM.

36. Folkestone TR 242370 V M1–E3, 4(E-M?) Winbolt 1925a; Rigold 1972 FM.

37. Folkestone *c*. TR 2237 IX M1–E2 Winbolt 1925b FM.

38. Garden Hill, East Sussex TQ 444319 VII/X 1BC–M3 Money 1977; Pollard forthcoming, c J. Money, Tunbridge Wells.

39. Gaynes Park, Essex *c*. TL 477013 VII M3–4 unpublished P-EM.

40. Great Cansiron, East Sussex TQ 447383 X E2–M3 Tebbutt 1972 LM.

41. Greenhithe TQ 583732 VI/VII 2–M1BC, L1–M2 Detsicas 1966 DM.

42. Ham Saltings *c*. TQ 849696 ? M1–M3 unpublished BM.

43. Hartlip TQ 829641 V M1–M3 (coins to L4–E5) Roach Smith 1852; Myres 1944 MM.

44. Hassocks, East Sussex *c*. TQ 2915 III/VIII M1–M3 Couchman 1925 LM.

45. Herstmonceux Castle, East Sussex TQ 650104 IX E–M1 Norris 1956 LM.

46. Heybridge, Essex *c*. TL 865075 III M2–4 Wilson 1973 ChM.

47. Higham, Oakleigh Farm TQ 725743 XI M2–M3 Catherall 1983; Pollard 1983b RM.

48. Higham *c*. TQ 7570 ?;VIII/IX L1–L2; L2 unpublished; Roach Smith 1877 MM; RL.

49. Highstead TR 215661 II/VII 1/1–3(4) Tatton-Brown 1976 CAT.

50. Hoo TQ 783708 VII M1 Blumstein 1956 MM.

51. Hornchurch, Corbets Tey, Essex TQ 558847 VII, IX M–L1 Marshall 1963 P-EM.

52. Horton Kirby *c*. TQ 5768 IX? L1–M2 unpublished MM.

53. Hythe *c*. TR 1634 VII L1–4 unpublished MM.

54. Iwade *c*. TQ 687887 XI E2 Ocock 1966 Maidstone Area Archaeological Group.
55. Joyden's Wood TQ 501708 VII, XI L1–M4 Tester and Caiger 1954 BEM.
56. Kemsing TQ 544587 VI 2–4 Evans 1950 DM.
57. Larkfield/East Malling *c*. TQ 704589/*c*. TQ 7058 VIII M1–2+ Jessup and Taylor 1932 MM.
58. Leyton, Essex TQ 376867 VII L3–L4 Greenwood 1979 P–EM.
59. Little Shelford, Essex *c*. TQ 980905 VII, IX L2–L3 James and James 1977, 1978 Foulness AWRE Archaeological Group.
60. Longfield *c*. TQ 6069 IX M1 unpublished DM.
61. Loose, Quarry Wood TQ 765515 Hillfort 1BC–1 Kelly 1971; Thompson 1982, 773–5 MM.
62. Lower Halstow *c*. TQ 862765 VII M2–M3 unpublished BM.
63. Lullingstone TQ 529651 VII; V M–L1; L1–E5 Meates 1953, 1979; Pollard 1987; Meates *et al.* 1950, 1952 DOE (Lullingstone and temporary storage).
64. Lullingstone Park TQ 524639 VII E–M1 Horner 1965, 1966, 1967 G. Horner, Sidcup.
65. Maidstone, The Mount TQ 755564 V L2–M4 Charles 1847; Miles 1972 MM.
66. Margate (?–Rowe Bequest) (*c*. TR 3570) (VI, VII) M1–L3/4 unpublished; Thompson 1982, 780–1 ('Belgic' material) BM.
67. Milfordhope *c*. TQ 8669 VII M1–M2 unpublished CM, MM.
68. Milton Regis, Bex Hill *c*. TQ 910646 VIII/IX L3–4 Payne 1874 BM.
69. Mucking, Essex TQ 673803 VII; VIII; XI 1–5; 2–E4; M–L1, L2–E4 Jones 1968, 1972, 1973, 1974; Jones and Rodwell 1973 Thurrock Museum.
70. New Ash Green TQ 607649 VII, IX, XI –M–L2– Cockett 1976 Fawkham and Ash Archaeological Group.
71. Northfleet TQ 6174 V 2–3 Jessup and Taylor 1932; V. Smith 1979; the late S. Harker, Gravesend.
72. Offham *c*. TQ 6657 IX M1–2? Thompson 1982, 790 MM.
73. Orpington, May Avenue TQ 468675 IX M2 Palmer 1975 OM.
74. Orpington, Poverest Road TQ 468675 VI L2–L4 Tester 1969; Palmer 1975 OM.
75. Orpington, Ramsden School TQ 471663 VII 1–E2 unpublished OM.
76. Ospringe *c*. TQ 9961 VII/III, VIII M1–E5, M2–E4+ Whiting 1921, 1923, 1925, 1926, 1927b; Whiting *et al.* 1931 BM, CM, DOE (including Maison Dieu, Ospringe).
77. Otford, Charne Building Site *c*. TQ 5360 VII E2–E3 Meates 1954 DM.
78. Otford, 'Progress' TQ 536593 V L1–E2, L3–4 Pearce 1927, 1930 BM, DM, MM.
79. Petley Wood, East Sussex TQ 764716 X L2–M3 Cleere 1974, 198 BtM.
80. Pevensey, East Sussex TQ 6404 VII; III 2+; M4–E5 Salzmann 1908, Johnson 1976 LM (Eastbourne Museum not examined).
81. Pippingford, East Sussex TQ 446313 X M1 Tebbutt and Cleere 1973 LM.
82. Port Lympne TR 118342 II?; II 2–M3?; M3–M4 Cunliffe 1980.
83. Preston *c*. TR 2460 VIII/IX; XI? 1, 4–5; 4 Dowker 1878, 1893 CM, MM, RL.
84. Radfield TQ 939628 VII 1–E4 Baxter and Mills 1978 Sittingbourne Area Archaeological Group.
85. Rainham, Essex *c*. TQ 544810 VII E2, 4 Goodburn 1978 P–EM.
86. Ramsgate *c*. TR 375643 IX L1? Couchman 1924 RL.
87. Reculver *c*. TR 229693 II, VII L2–M4 unpublished CM.
88. Richborough TR 324602 II, III, II M–L1, L1–M3, M3–E5 Bushe-Fox 1926, 1928, 1932, 1949; Cunliffe 1968 DOE.
89. Rochester *c*. TQ 7468 I 1BC–E5 Chaplin 1962; Flight and Harrison 1968; Pollard 1981a G. Horner, Sidcup; RM.
90. Sandon, Essex TL 752043 VII L1–4 Drury 1976b ChM.
91. Sedlescombe, East Sussex TQ 772198 X 1–E3 Cleere 1974, 194 BtM, LM.
92. Sittingbourne *c*. TQ 915640 IX 1–E2 Payne 1877, 47 BM.
93. Sittingbourne *c*. TQ 906640 IX? M2–4 unpublished BM.
94. Slayhills Saltings *c*. TQ 7086 IX 3–4 Noël Hume 1956 BM.
95. Snargate TQ 979283 VII 1BC Kelly 1968; Thompson 1982, 822 MM.
96. South Ockendon, Essex TQ 582831 VII M–L1 Chaplin and Brooks 1966 P–EM.
97. Springhead *c*. TQ 6172 III 1–4/E5 Wilson 1970, 1971, 1972, 1973; Frere 1977; Goodburn 1978, 1979; the late S. Harker, Gravesend.

98.   Strood *c.* TQ 7369 VII M1–M3 Pollard unpublished J. Preston, Rochester.
99.   Strood *c.* TQ 735693 VIII E2–L4 Roach Smith 1842 BM, MM.
100.   Teston TQ 698532 VII 1BC Ocock 1974; Thompson 1982, 842 MM.
101.   Twitton *c.* TQ 516594 VII 2–3 Godwin 1931 (Ward 1968) DM.
102.   Uckfield, East Sussex TQ 479222 VII 1 Tebbutt and Norris 1968 LM.
103.   Upchurch Marshes *c.* TQ 8670 VII/(XI) L1–3 Jessup and Taylor 1932; Monaghan 1983, 1987; Noël Hume 1954, 1956; Roach Smith 1847, 1868; Wright 1852 BM, RM.
104.   West Ham, Essex *c.* TQ 418823 VII L1–E3 unpublished P-EM.
105.   West Wickham *c.* TQ 3866 IX M–L1 Cook and McCarthy 1933 MM.
106.   Westgate *c.* TR 3169 VII 2–4 unpublished BM.
107.   Wickford, Essex *c.* TQ 762937 III/VII L2–L4 Rodwell 1966b, 1968, 1970b, ChM.
108.   Wingham TR 240572 VII; V M1; L1–E5 Dowker 1882, 1883; Jenkins 1965, 1966b, 1967; Myers 1944 MM; F. Jenkins, Canterbury.
109.   Woolwich *c.* TQ 4579 VIII/IX L3–4 Jessup and Taylor 1932; Rigden 1974 GM.
110.   Worth TR 336554 IV E–M1, L3–4 Klein 1928; Stebbing 1937 BM, Deal Museum (Deal Castle, Town Hall).
111.   Wrotham Hill *c.* TR 6160 IX E–M2 unpublished DM.
112.   Wye, Harville TR 048465 VI 1–E4 Bradshaw 1972 J. Bradshaw, Challock.
113.   Wye TR 049475 X 1–E4 Bradshaw 1970 J. Bradshaw, Challock.
114.   Wye TR 048473 VII L1(–E2) Bradshaw 1970 J. Bradshaw, Challock.
115.   Wye TR 049461 VII M–L4 Bradshaw 1972; Pollard forthcoming, a, J. Bradshaw, Challock.

II. *Sites studied through publications, within the main study area*

Note: An 'A' suffix denotes a settlement area also studied at first-hand, listed in section I above; individual sites studied both in the hand and in publication are not thus suffixed

3A.   Arlington Chilver Bridge, East Sussex TQ 530074 XI 4 Holmes 1979 LM.
4A.   Aylesford TQ 730592 VIII 1BC–1 A. J. Evans 1890; Thompson 1982, 588–602 Ashmolean Museum; BM.
200.   Barham Downs TR 236475 VII M–L1 Philp and Philp 1974 KARU.
7A.   Bexley TQ 506734 VII E–M1 Caiger 1958; Thompson 1982, 609–10 DM.
201.   Bigbury TR 117575 Hillfort 2–1BC Jessup 1932; Jessup and Cook 1936 MM.
202.   Bishopstone, East Sussex TQ 468007 VII 1BC–L4 Bell 1977 LM.
13A.   Bridge Hill TR 189538 VII 1BC–1 Watson 1963.
203.   Bromley Common TQ 419664 VII M1–M3(?) Philp 1973 KARU.
15.   Canterbury *c.* TR 1457 I 1–7 Brent 1861; Frere 1966; Jenkins 1951; Kelly and Myres 1973; Whiting 1927e; Whiting and Mead 1928; Williams 1946; Williams and Frere 1948; Williams 1975 CM, MM.
204.   Tonbridge, Castle Hill TQ 608439 (Hillfort) VII 1 Money 1975.
17.   Chalk TQ 677729 (V)/VI 3–E5 Peacock 1977d.
18.   Chalk TQ 690732 VIII L4–E5 Allen 1954.
205.   Chilham, Juliberrie's Grave TR 077533 IX M1 Jessup 1939; Thompson 1982, 742–3.
24A.   Cliffe-at-Hoo *c.* TQ 7075 VIII 1–4 Payne 1911 RM.
29A.   Crayford TQ 510751 VII 2BC–1 Ward-Perkins 1938; Thompson 1982, 684 DM.
206.   Darenth TQ 564707 (V)VI M2–L4 Philp 1973 KARU.
30A.   Dartford TQ 543740 VII/III 1–2 Dale 1971.
30B.   Dartford TQ 551749 VII M–L1 Tester 1956b.
30C.   Dartford TQ 546746 VII 6–7 Tester 1956a.
31A.   Dover *c.* TR 3241 II 1–4 Murray Threipland 1957; Murray Threipland and Steer 1951; Rahtz 1958; Philp 1981 Dover Museum KARU.
207.   Downe TQ 398611 VII M1–E2 Philp 1973 KARU.
208.   Eccles TQ 722605 XI M1 Detsicas 1977a A. P. Detsicas, Icklesham.
209.   Enfield, Middlesex TQ 341959 (III)/VII L1–4 Gentry *et al.* 1977 P. Tyers unpublished archive.
210.   Ewell, Surrey TQ 218621–222630 VII, III ?2BC–L4 Frere 1942/43; Lowther 1946/47; Pemberton 1973 Bourne Hall Museum, Ewell.

211. Farningham, Calfstock Lane TQ 550678 VII 1 Philp 1973 KARU.
212. Farningham 'Villa II' TQ 545667 V L1–M4+ Meates 1973 DM.
35A. Faversham TR 021617 VII; V L1BC–L1; ?L1–M3+ Philp 1968; Thompson 1982, 696–9 KARU.
213. Fawkham, Eastwood TQ 589647 VII, IX 1 Philp 1963a, 1973, 1980 KARU.
214. Green Street Green *c*. TQ 4563 ? 1–2 Payne 1900, 1902 RM.
215. Hayes, Baston Manor TQ 409646 VI L1–M2 Philp 1973 KARU.
216. High Rocks, East Sussex TQ 561382 Hillfort, VII –M1 Money 1968 Tunbridge Wells Museum.
217. Highgate Wood, Middlesex TQ 283891 XI M1–M2 Brown and Sheldon 1974 Museum of London.
218. Highsted *c*. TQ 907617 IX L3–M4 Jessup 1935; Kelly 1978.
219. Hothfield *c*. TQ 9744 IX 1BC–E1; M–L2 Brinson 1944; Gaunt 1974; Thompson 1982, 738–9, Ashford Archaeological Society.
220. Keston, Warbank TQ 413633; TQ 414639 V; IX 1–4; M1–E2 Mynott 1977; Philp 1969, 1973; Piercy Fox 1955 KARU.
221. Little Chart TR 939458 VII:(VI) 1–L2;(4) Eames 1957.
59A. Little Shelford, Essex TQ 980905 IX L2–L3 James and James 1978.
222. Lockham, near Sutton Valence *c*. TQ 8149 VII –2– Smythe 1883 MM.
223. City of London *c*. TQ 3281 I M1–E5 Chapman and Johnson 1973; Harden and Green 1978; Marsden 1975; Marsh and Tyers 1976; Orton 1977b; Tatton-Brown 1974 Museum of London..
224. Minepit Wood, East Sussex TQ 522338 X 1–E2 Money 1974.
225. Minster, Thanet *c*. TR 3064 IX L1–M2 Whiting 1924.
226. Newhaven, East Sussex TQ 446013 (V) M1–2 Bell 1976 LM.
227. Northbourne TQ 329527 VIII M3–M4 Philp 1978 KARU.
228. Old Ford, Essex *c*. TQ 370837 III L1–E5 Sheldon 1971, 1972; McIsaac *et al.* 1979.
229. Oldbury *c*. TQ 5856 Hillfort 1BC–1 Ward Perkins 1939, 1944 MM.
74. Orpington, Poverest Road TQ 468675 VI L2–L4 Tester 1969 OM.
230. Orsett, Essex TQ 654814 VII, XI L2–3 Rodwell 1974.
78. Otford 'Progress' TQ 536593 XI L1–E2 Pearce 1930 alleged at BM.
231. Rainham *c*. TQ 8269 IX M1–2 Wood 1883.
103A. Rainham (Upchurch Marshes, Otterham Quay) *c*. TQ 8267 VII/(XI) L1–3 Roach Smith 1847; Monaghan 1987.
232. Ranscombe Hill, East Sussex TQ 432089 VII 1–L4 Bedwin 1978 LM.
233. Rawreth, Essex TQ 774929 VII L3–4/E5 Drury 1977 Southend Museum.
87. Reculver *c*. TR 229693 II M1;L2–M4 Thompson 1953; Philp 1957, 1958, 1959 –;KARU.
89. Rochester *c*. TQ 7468 I 1–M3 Harrison 1972; Harrison and Flight 1968 RM.
234. Sanderstead, Surrey TQ 352608 VII, IX M1–M2 Little 1961, 1964; Philp 1973 –;KARU.
235. Sittingbourne *c*. TQ 923642 VIII 1–2? Payne 1876 BM.
236. Slonk Hill, East Sussex TQ 226065 VII L1–4/E5 Hartridge 1978 Brighton Museum.
237. Snodland, Holborough TQ 698627 IX 3–4 Jessup *et al.* 1954; Farrar 1973, 90; Peacock 1977e MM.
238. Snodland, Church Field TQ 708620 V M1–4 Cook 1928; Ocock and Syddell 1967 MM (fire-damaged).
239. South Benfleet, Essex TQ 765863 VII 1BC–4 Rodwell 1976b Benfleet Historical Society, Southend Museum.
240. Southwark, Surrey *c*. TQ 326800 I M1–E5 Sheldon 1974; Bird *et al.* 1978b Southwark and Lambeth Archaeological Excavation Committee.
241. Stone, near Greenhithe *c*. TR 561748 IX E–M2 Cotton and Richardson 1949 DM.
242. Stone, near Greenhithe TR 561748 VIII/IX L1BC–M1 Cotton and Richardson 1941; Thompson 1982, 831–2 DM.
243. Swarling TR 135534 VIII lBC–1 Bushe-Fox 1925; Thompson 1982, 834–42 BM.
244. Tilbury, Gun Hill, Essex TQ 655778 VII –2BC–1+ Drury and Rodwell 1973 Thurrock Museum.
245. Titsey, Surrey TQ 408561 IX L1–2 Philp 1973 KARU.
246. Tong *c*. TQ 9364 VII(IX) M1 Whiting 1927a.
103B. Upchurch Marshes (including Milfordhope, Slayhills) *c*. TQ 8569 VII;XI 1–3; M1 Noël Hume 1954; Roach Smith 1842, 1847, 1868; Jackson 1962, 1972/3 BM; I. Jackson, Upchurch.
247. Waltham, Anvil Green *c*. TR 109496 ? 1 Payne 1902 RM.
248. Waltham Holy Cross, Essex TQ 379976 VII 4 Huggins 1978.

249A.   West Wickham, Fox Hill TQ 386641 VII L1–M2 Philp 1973 KARU.
249B.   West Wickham, North Pole Lane *c.* TQ 402641 VII L1BC–M2 Philp 1973 KARU.

III.   *Major sites outside of the main study area*

250.   Braintree, Essex TL 7523 III 1–E5 Drury 1976a.
251.   Braughing, Hertfordshire *c.* TL 392243 I 1–4 Partridge 1977.
252.   Brentford, Middlesex TQ 172772 III (1) 2–4 Laws 1976.
253.   Chichester, West Sussex SU 8604 I 1–E5 Down 1974, 1978, 1981; Down and Rule 1971 Chichester Museum.
254.   Colchester, Essex TL 9925 I E1–E5 Dunnett 1966, 1971; Hawkes and Hull 1947; Hull 1958, 1963 Colchester and Essex Museum.
255.   Fishbourne, West Sussex SU 8304 V 1–4 Cunliffe 1971 Chichester Museum; Fishbourne Villa.
256.   Rapsley, Surrey TQ 080415 V L1–M4 Hanworth 1968.
257.   St. Albans (Verulamium), Hertfordshire TL 1307 I 1–E5 Anthony 1968; Corder 1941; Frere 1972 Verulamium Museum.
258.   Wiggonholt, West Sussex *c.* TQ 065176 M1–L4 Evans 1974 Worthing Museum.

APPENDIX 2

THE FABRICS: DATE-RANGES; REGIONS WITHIN STUDY AREA; REFERENCES TO DESCRIPTION AND DISCUSSION

I. *Fine Wares*

1. African Red Slip: Various, very rare; Chapter 4.V.1 Bird 1977.
2. Argonne ware: Fourth century; throughout; Chapter 4.V.1 Fulford 1977a.
3. Central Gaulish wares: A. Lead-glazed: pre-Flavian; throughout; Chapter 4.I.1 Greene 1973, 1978b, 1979a.
    B. 'Lezoux' rough-cast: pre-Flavian; high-status sites mainly, very rare; Chapter 4.I.1 Greene 1973, 1979a.
    C. Colour-coated white ware with barbotine motifs: late first to early second century; rare, mainly urban, overall; Chapter 4.II.1 Greene 1978a.
    D. Samian: late first century – very rare, urban; second to early third century – overall; Chapter 4.II.1, III.1 Hartley 1969, 1972; Johns 1971.
    E. 'Rhenish' black slip: second half second century; throughout; Chapter 4.III.1 Brewster 1972; Greene 1978a.
4. Colchester colour-coat: A. Rough-cast, pre-Flavian; Essex. Greene 1978a.
    B. Miscellaneous, mid-second to mid-third century *floruit*; Kent, Essex, London area; Chapter 4.III.1, IV.1 Hull 1963; Orton 1977b. Fig. 39 here depicts sites with the brown fabric only, as paler fabrics can be confused with contemporary Nene Valley ware.
5. East Gaulish wares: A. 'Lower Rhine' pre-Flavian rough-cast: pre-Flavian; very high-status sites Greene 1979a.
    B. 'Lower Rhine' colour-coat: late first to mid/late second century (rough-cast), mid-second to early third (barbotine, rouletted); mainly urban late first, throughout in second and third; Chapter 4.II.1, III.1. Anderson 1980 Lower Rhine Fabric 1; Greene 1978c.
    C. Samian: early second to mid-third century; throughout in second, third-century distribution unclear; Chapter 4.III.1, IV.1 Hartley 1969; Johns 1971; Greene 1978c.
    D. Trier 'Rhenish' black slip (*Moselkeramik*): early to mid-third century; throughout, possibly mainly urban and villas; Chapter 4.IV.1 Greene 1978a, 1978c.
    E. Mottled colour-coat: third to early fourth century; mainly Kent and London; Chapter 4.IV.1 Bird 1981, 1982a; Bird and Williams 1983. Fine cream-buff fabric containing large inclusions of pale-brown clay, sparse;

covered with dark-brown through orange to buff 'mottled' slip. Flagons. Can be given white paint decoration.

F. Miscellaneous fine wares: third and fourth centuries? Mainly Kent and London? Chapter 4.V.1 Green forthcoming. Fig. 53, 214 (Possibly Nene Valley rather than East Coast).

6. *A L'éponge* ware:

Fourth century; throughout; Chapter 4.V.1. Fulford 1977a; Galliou *et al.* 1980.

7. Gallo-Belgic:

A. *Terra Nigra:* Augustan to late first century; throughout; Chapter 4.I.1 Detsicas 1977a; Rigby 1973, 1981.

B. *Terra Rubra* and colour-coats: Augustan to mid-first century; throughout; Chapter 4.I.1. Rigby 1973, 1981.

C. White wares: early to mid-first century; throughout; Chapter 4.I.1.

8. 'Hardham' ware:

Late first to mid-second century?; Sussex, Surrey; Pollard 1983a, 269–70; Green 1976.

9. 'Highgate Wood' fine sandy grey ware:

Early to mid-second century; mainly London area, in west Kent Trajanic-Hadrianic; Chapter 4.II.2. Brown and Sheldon 1974; Orton 1977b; Tyers 1977a; Tyers and Marsh 1979. Fig. 29, 95–96; Fig. 42, 144.

10. London area wares:

A. 'Ring-and-dot beakers', buff ware: Flavian: mainly London area; Chapter 4.II.1. Green 1978b.

B. 'London' grey ware: late first to early second century; London area? Chapter 4.II.1; Pollard 1983a, 262–73; Marsh and Tyers 1976; Marsh 1978.

C. Mica-dusted ware: (as 10.B).

D. 'Marbled': late first to early second century; mainly London area; Chapter 4.II.1; Pollard 1983a, 262–73; Marsh 1978.

E. 'London-Essex' stamped: late first to early second century; London area, west Essex, north-west Kent; Chapter 4.II.1; Philp 1980; Rodwell 1978.

F. 'Eggshell' ware: (as 10.D).

11. Lyon colour-coat:

Pre-Flavian; throughout, mainly high-status sites; Chapter 4.I.1. Greene 1979a.

12. Much Hadham:

A. Oxidised ware: mid-third to fourth century; mainly London area, Essex, north-west Kent; Chapter 4.IV.1. Orton 1977b.

B. White-slip ware: early third century at Canterbury, one vessel, nowhere else south of Thames known; Chapter 4.IV.1.

13. Nene Valley:

A. Colour-coat: late second to early fifth century; throughout; Chapter 4.III.1, IV.1, V.1. Hartley 1960; Dannell 1973; Howe *et al.* 1980; Orton 1977b. Fig. 39 here maps white-ware beakers, which may include Rhineland imports (Fabric 5A, barbotine, and rouletted).

B. White ware, painted: late second and third centuries? throughout? Howe *et al.* 1980.

14. New Forest:

A. Colour-coat: late third and fourth centuries; Sussex, east Kent (high-status sites); Chapter 4.V.1. Fulford 1975a, Fabric 1; Green forthcoming.

B. 'Parchment': late third to fourth century; one example in Kent, at Canterbury: Green forthcoming; Fulford 1975a, Fabrics 2a, 2b.

15. North Gaulish wares:

A. Colour-coat: late first to mid-second century; high-status sites at least; Chapter 4.II.1. Anderson 1980, North Gaul Fabric 1; Pollard 1981b; Green in Blockley and Day forthcoming.

B. White ware ('Gillam 42'): late second to early fourth century? Kent and east coast mainly; Chapter 4.IV.1. Oxidised vessels of identical form have been found in Canterbury (Green forthcoming) and London (Richardson and Tyers 1984) and are known also on the Continent in North Gaul, mainly in the Somme basin (J. Alain, J. Barbieux, pers. comms.).

16. Oxfordshire wares:

A. Red colour-coat.

B. White-slip.

C. Parchment: A–C all mid-third to early fifth centuries; throughout, but rare in Essex prior to mid-fourth, and rare in Sussex after mid-fourth; Chapter 4.IV.1, V.1. Young 1977a.

17. 'Pevensey' ware: Fourth century; south-east Kent, Sussex, mainly east; Chapter 4.V.1. Fulford 1973a; Green 1977.

18. 'Pompeian Red' wares: Mid-first to early third centuries; throughout; Chapter 4.I.1, III.1. Peacock 1977c.

19. 'Romano-Saxon' style (including Much Hadham wares): Mainly fourth century in Kent, possibly wider date-range in Essex; Chapter 4.V.1, VI. Rodwell 1970a; Gillam 1979.

20. South Gaulish wares:
A. Samian: mid- to late first century; throughout, though pre-Flavian mainly high-status sites; Chapter 4.I.1. Hartley 1960; Johns 1971.
B. Colour-coat: pre-Flavian; very rare, high-status sites. Greene 1973, 1979a. (as 20.B).

21. Spanish colour-coat:

22. 'Staines' lead-glazed: Late first to early second century; London area, Kent, Essex; Chapter 4.II.1. Arthur 1978.

23. 'Streak-burnished' oxidised: Mid-third to mid-fourth century; Canterbury; Chapter 4.IV.1; Green 1981, forthcoming.

24. 'Upchurch' types:
A. Reduced: late first to early fourth century in Kent, second to early third in south Essex and Weald(?); Chapter 5.II. A variety of grey, grey-brown and black wares without temper, often micaceous with a high iron ore content. Exterior surfaces (closed forms) or all surfaces (open forms) may be burnished to a high gloss, or slipped grey or black. Difficult, if not impossible, to distinguish in the hand from fine ware 10.B (above). Monaghan 1982, 1983, 1987. Fig. 41, 119–135; Fig. 42, 143, 145–146, 148–153; Fig. 43, 154; Fig. 44, 170–175.
B. Oxidised: late first to late third or early fourth century; Kent; Chapters 4.II.1, III.1; 5.II. Oxidised version of 24A (above), ranging from pink through red to orange, often with a reduced core. Fig. 42, 136–137, 147; Fig. 43, 158–166; Fig. 44, 167–169.
C. Painted: late first to early second century; north Kent; Chapter 4.II.1. Fabric as 24B, with cream paint decoration, or cream-slipped with red paint decoration. Fig. 42, 138–142.
D. White-slipped: mid-first to late-second/early third century; Kent; Chapter 4.I.1, II.1, III.1. Fig. 43, 155–157.

25. West Kent red burnished: late third to fourth century? west Kent, mainly Darent valley; Chapter 4.V.1.

II. *Coarse Wares*

1. Alice Holt-Farnham grey sandy ware: Late first to early second century, Surrey, London, north-west Kent mainly; late third to early fifth century, throughout but rare in Essex; Chapter 4.II.2, IV.2, V.2. Lyne and Jefferies 1979; Millett 1979; Orton 1977b; Tyers and Marsh 1978. Fig. 29, 97–99.

2. 'Alice Holt type' grey sandy ware: Fourth century; mid- and east Kent; Chapter 4.V.3.

3. BB1
A. Dorset: early Hadrianic – London area, occasionally elsewhere on high-status sites; late second to mid-fourth century – throughout; Chapter 4.III.2, 4.IV, 4.V. Farrar 1973; Williams 1977. Fig. 29, 100–101.
B. 'East Kent': very late third to mid-fourth century; east Kent; Chapter 4.IV.3.

4. BB2: Hadrianic to the first half of the fourth century; mainly west Kent, London

			area, Surrey, Essex in Hadrianic-Antonine, east Kent rare; common in all these regions (except west Surrey) in third century, rarer in fourth; Chapters 4.III.2, III.3, V.3; 5.II. Farrar 1973; Monaghan 1982, 1987; Williams 1977. Fig. 40, 110–115; Fig. 49, 181–190; Fig. 50, 191–192, 194–196.
5.	Brockley Hill-Verulamium buff sandy ware:		Pre-Flavian to late second century in London, mainly Flavian to Hadrianic in west Kent; uncertain dating in Surrey and Essex; Chapter 4.II.1–2, III.1–2. Orton 1977b; Tyers and Marsh 1979.
6.	Canterbury sandy wares:	A.	'Stuppington Lane' sandy: mid-first century; Canterbury; Chapter 5.III. Pollard forthcoming, d.
		B.	'North Gaulish' grey sandy: Neronian to Vespasianic; east Kent high-status sites; Chapter 5.III. Pollard forthcoming, d. Fig. 16, 47–55, 57–59.
		C.	'Canterbury' reduced and oxidised sandy: Vespasianic to late second century; east Kent, very rare in mid-Kent; Chapters 4.II.3, 5.III. Fig. 16, 60; Fig. 28, 63–70, 72–84.
7.	Dales ware:		One vessel from Richborough, third or fourth century; Chapter 4.V.3. Loughlin 1977.
8.	'East Sussex ware':		First century B.C. to early(?) fifth century; east Sussex, very rare in south Kent. Pollard 1983a, 259–61; Green 1976, 1977, 1980; Hamilton 1977; Pollard forthcoming, c.
9.	'Aylesford-Swarling' flint-tempered:		Mid-first century B.C. to mid-first century A.D.; east Kent; Chapters 3.III, 4.I.3.
10.	Late Roman flint-sand-tempered:		Mid-fourth century; east Kent; Chapter 4.V.3. Pollard forthcoming, a, d.
11.	Grog-tempered wares:	A.	'Aylesford-Swarling': mid-/late first century B.C. to late second century A.D. in east Kent, early(?) to late first century A.D. in west Kent; Essex and London area also, dating uncertain; Chapters 3.III; 4.I.2–3. Birchall 1965; Hawkes and Hull 1947; Rodwell 1976a *inter alia*. Fig. 13, 22–24; Fig. 14, 25–31; Fig. 15, 32–38, 42–43, 45–46.
		B.	'Late Roman': late third to fifth century in east (and mid-?) Kent, mainly mid-fourth to fifth in west Kent; Chapter 4.IV.3, 4.V.2. Pollard forthcoming, a, d. Fig. 53, 204–211.
		C.	'Port Lympne': late third to fourth century; south-east Kent; Chapter 4.V.3. Young 1980, Reduced Ware 8.
12.	Mayen ware:		Fourth century; throughout; Chapter 4.V.2. Fulford and Bird 1975.
13.	Micaceous jars (Hawkes and Hull 1947, Form 262):		Early to mid-first century; high-status sites mainly north of Thames, plus Canterbury; Partridge 1981; Pollard forthcoming, d.
14.	'Much Hadham' reduced ware:		Fourth century? west Essex, north Kent and London area? Chapter 4.V.2–3.
15.	'Native Coarse Ware':		Late second to early fourth century; mid- and east Kent; Chapter 4.III.3; Pollard forthcoming, d. Fig. 49, 178–179.
16.	North Gaulish grey sandy – 'Arras' ware:		Mainly mid-second to early-third; east Kent and Thames estuary; Chapter 4.III.1. Tuffreau-Libre 1980a; Richardson and Tyers 1984; Fig. 44, 177.
17.	Otford ware:		Late first century; Otford (upper Darent valley); Chapter 4.II.1. Pearce 1930. A group of flagons from a kiln on the Otford 'Progress' villa site. Fig. 40, 102–106.
18.	'Patch Grove' ware:		Mid-first to early second century, storage jars up to early third; east Surrey, west Kent, occasionally London and mid-Kent; Chapter 4.I.2. Fig. 13, 17–21.
19.	'Portchester "D"' ware:		Early/mid-fourth to early fifth centuries; throughout; Chapter 4.V.2. Fulford 1975b; Orton 1977b.
20.	'Rettendon' flint-sand-tempered ware:		Late third to early fifth century; Essex, mainly central; Pollard 1983a, 289–92; Tildesley 1971; Drury 1976b.

21. 'Richborough' grey sandy ware: Late first to early second century? Richborough; Chapter 4.II.3. Fig. 29, 85–88.

22. Miscellaneous Kent grey sandy wares:
   A. West Kent, late first to early second century; Chapter 4.I.2, II.2. Fig. 29, 89–94.
   B. Lower Thames products; early second to fourth century; west and mid-Kent mainly; Chapter 4.III.2, IV.2, V.2, 5.II. Includes ware produced alongside BB2. Fig. 29, 90; Fig. 40, 107–109; Fig. 50, 192–193, 197–203; Forms nos. 194–196 (slipped) also in this ware.
   C. Unprovenanced, east Kent; late second to mid-fourth century; Chapter 4.III.3, IV.3, V.3. Pollard forthcoming, d.

23. Shelly wares:
   A. West Kent, Surrey, Essex, London area: late first century B.C. to late first century A.D., possibly later in Lea valley; Chapters 4.III, 4.I.2. Includes shell-and-sand-tempered ware. Fig. 12, 1–15.
   B. 'Thames Estuary' storage jars: mid-first to late second/early third century A.D.; east Surrey, London area, south Essex, west Kent plus outliers in Weald, east Kent (and North Sea coast). Fig. 12, 16.
   C. 'Late Roman': mainly late fourth to early fifth century in Kent, south Essex and London area; Chapter 4.V.2. Sanders 1973; Orton 1977b; Drury 1976a. Fig. 53, 212–213.

24. 'Thanet' buff fine sandy: Mid-first century A.D.?; Isle of Thanet mainly; Chapter 4.I.3.
25. 'Tilford' coarse grey sandy: Fourth century; distribution as 'Portchester "D"' (above); Chapter 4.V.2.
26. Urmitzer(?) ware: Late second to mid-third centuries; Lullingstone; Chapter 4.III.2.

III. *Mortaria*

1. Brockley Hill-Verulamium sandy wares: Late first to late second/early third century; throughout, particularly in late first and early second centuries, occasional later; Chapter 4.II, III. Castle 1972, 1976; Hartley 1982, Fabric 8.

2. Canterbury oxidised sandy wares: Late first to third century; east and mid-Kent mainly, rare in west Kent and London; Chapters 4.II.3, III.3, IV.3, 5.III. Hartley 1982, Fabrics 2A, 2E. Fig. 28, 71.

3. 'East Kent' oxidised ware: Late second to third/early fourth century; east Kent mainly, rarely in west and mid-Kent; Chapter 4.III.3. Hartley 1982, Fabrics 2C, 2D. Fig. 49, 180.

4. 'East Sussex' ware: Mid-second to mid-third century?; east Sussex; Pollard 1983a, 278–9.

5. Kent-south Essex-Colchester cream-buff ware: Hadrianic to early third century in Kent; throughout except Sussex; Chapter 4.III.2. Hartley 1963, 1973a; 1982, Fabrics 1B, 1D. Fig. 40, 116–118.

6. Mancetter-Hartshill: Very rare in third century, mainly late third to fourth century in east Kent; Chapter 4.V.3. Hartley 1973a, b.

7. Much Hadham oxidised ware: (as fine ware 12A, but only in Essex, west Kent and London area).

8. Nene Valley buff ware: Mid-third to fourth century? east Kent and London area mainly; Chapter 4.IV.3. Hartley 1982, Fabric 5.

9. Oxfordshire wares:
   A. White ware: mid-third to early fifth century; throughout; Chapter 4.IV, V. Young 1977a; Hartley 1982, Fabric 3.
   B. Colour-coated and white-slipped (as fine ware 16, Young 1977a; Hartley 1982, Fabric 4).

10. Rhineland wares (Kreis Düren): Second half of second and first half of third centuries; high-status sites in Kent, Essex(?) and London area; Chapter 4.III.2–3. Hartley 1973a; 1982, Fabrics 6 and 7.

11. Southern Britain/North-east Gaul iron-free wares:
   A. Mid-first to early second centuries; throughout except pre-Flavian – high-status sites only; Chapter 4.I, II. Hartley 1977; 1982, Fabrics 1A, 1B, 1C. Fig. 16, 61; Fig. 28, 62.

B. Second half of second and first half of third centuries; mid- and east Kent, (elsewhere?); Chapter 4.III.3. Hartley 1981, nos. 382–385, 387.

12. Surrey/Sussex white sandy   Later second to mid-third centuries; throughout; Chapter 4.III.2. Hartley
     ('Gillam 272'):   1973a, Evans 1974.

APPENDIX 3

THE FABRICS: CORPORA OF KNOWN EXAMPLES WITHIN THE MAIN STUDY AREA

Note that publication references are here given only for material not examined by the present author at first-hand. Where standard type-series of wares, or significant collections, exist in print, the forms in which these wares occur may be referred to these publications. Forms produced by the 'grey ware' industries of the Cliffe peninsula, Canterbury and so forth are only isolated where this is required by the mapping of these forms. Site numbers refer to Appendix 1: sites not therein listed are only recorded here in the cases of extremely rare wares. Fabric numbers refer to Appendix 2. Certain ubiquitous wares, such as samian (excluding pre-Flavian) and undesignated grey wares, have been omitted. (See also Green forthcoming; Pollard 1987).

I. *Fine Wares*

1. African Red Slip. Sites: 15 (Young and Bird 1982). 17 (Bird 1977, Fabric a, e or f, bead-foot open form with 3 concentric grooves on interior base; from Layer 8 and thus third century or earlier). 31 (Bird 1977). 223 (*ibid.*). 228 (*ibid.*). 240 (*ibid.*). Shadwell, east London (*ibid.*).
2. Argonne ware. Sites: 15. 46. 69. 80. 82. 88. 97. 107. 108. 115. 206 (Philp 1973, no. 396). 223 (Orton 1977b, 42). 232 (Green 1978a). 233 (Drury 1977). 240 (Bird *et al.* 1978b, 336, no. 152).
3A. Central Gaulish lead-glazed. Sites: 9B. 14. 15. 88. 89. 97. 105. 223 (Greene 1978b). 234 (Little 1961, no. 3). 240 (Bird *et al.* 1978b, nos. 598–560). Bapchild (Greene 1978b, Form 2.3).
3B. Lezoux rough-cast. Sites: 15 (from Frere 1970, unpublished, from Neronian layer 3, Trench DII). 88 (Bushe-Fox 1926, no. 12; Bushe-Fox 1932, no. 298). 202 (Green 1977, no. 38e). 223 (Greene 1979a, fig. 20).
3C. Central Gaulish colour-coat. Sites: 12. 78. 88. 223 (Tatton-Brown 1974, fig. 31, no. 278). 240 (Bird *et al.* 1978b, no. 949).
3D. Central Gaulish samian, pre-Flavian. Site: 240 (Bird *et al.* 1979, nos. 11, 12).
3E. Central Gaulish 'Rhenish'. Sites: 9 (Quex Park, unpublished). 10. 12. 15. 23. 25. 30. 31. 36. 38. 46. 55. 59. 63. 65. 69. 76. 77. 84. 88. 89. 97. 112. 113. 223 (Tatton-Brown 1974, fig. 28, no. 58). 236 (Fulford 1978b). 240 (Bird *et al.* 1978b, 532).
4B. Colchester colour-coat (brown fabric). Sites: 1 (Hull 1958, Form 408). 7. 8 (*ibid.*, Forms 391A – rough-cast; 408/409). 9A (*ibid.*, Form 360/363). 9B. 10 (*ibid.*, Form 391B – barbotine). 12 (*ibid.*, Forms 391, 408/409). 15 (including *ibid.*, Forms 391, 407). 17 (beaker, barbotine scales). 25 (beaker, barbotine scales). 31 (*ibid.*, Form 392). 35A (*ibid.*, Form 391, rouletted; Philp 1968, no. 272). 38 (Hull 1958, Form 391). 39 (*ibid.*, Form 391, rouletted). 46 (including *ibid.*, Forms 391, 392, 407B). 55 (*ibid.*, Form 391, barbotine zoomorphic). 56. 58. 59 (*ibid.*, Forms 392, 406, 407, 408/409). 63 (*ibid.*, beaker, barbotine zoomorphic; Form 406/407). 65 (*ibid.*, Form 391A, barbotine; 391/392, rouletted). 69 (*ibid.*, Form 395). 76 (*ibid.*, Form 409, painted; 391, barbotine zoomorphic – Whiting *et al.* 1931, 'associated with no. 616'). 77 (*ibid.*, beaker, barbotine). 78 (Hull 1958, Forms 391, 407/409). 84 (*ibid.*, Form 407). 88 (*ibid.*, Form 157). 89 (*ibid.*, Forms 391, rouletted and plain; 392, rouletted). 96. 97 (*ibid.*, Forms 391/392, rouletted; 406/407). 98 (*ibid.*, Form 396). 107 (*ibid.*, Forms 391/392, 407B). 115 (*ibid.*, Form 391, rouletted). 223 (Orton 1977b).

228 (Hull 1958, Form 391; Sheldon 1971, fig. 9, no. 17). 233 (Drury 1977, 41). 240 (Hull 1958, Forms 391 (plain, barbotine scrolls), 392 (rouletted), 408/409; Bird *et al.* 1978b, nos. 275, 276, 1159, 1305, 1690, 1746).

5A.   'Lower Rhine' pre-Flavian. Sites: 15. 88 (Greene 1979a, fig. 23; Bushe-Fox 1949, no. 412).

5B.   'Lower Rhine/Cologne' colour-coat, rough-cast. Sites: 10. 12. 15. 17. 19. 25. 31. 36. 38. 40. 41. 53. 63. 69. 77. 78. 88. 89. 97. 98. 113. 209 (P. Tyers, unpublished archive, Pit F.50). 223 (Orton 1977b, no. 59). 226 (Green 1976, no. 287). 228 (?-Sheldon 1972, 127). 238 (Ocock and Syddell 1967, nos. 11, 32). 240 (Bird *et al.* 1978b, nos. 1158, 1632, 1633, 1670; see Greene 1978c, 58 for re-assessment of these pieces).

5D.   Trier 'Rhenish'. Sites: 1. 12. 15. 17. 25. 31. 36. 46. 59. 63. 66. 88 (Bushe-Fox 1949, no. 461). 89. 97. 98. 108. 206 (Philp 1973, 138, 'white slip' sherds). 223 (Orton 1977b, 42). 236 (Fulford 1978b). 240 (Bird *et al.* 1978b, no. 1376).

5E.   German mottled colour-coat. Sites: 15 (Bird 1981b; Green forthcoming; Jenkins 1950, fig. 14, no. 62). 31 (Bird 1981). 33 (Pollard 1982, no. 12). 63. (see also Bird and Williams 1983.) 76 (Whiting *et al.* 1931, no. 263). 82 (Young 1980, 277). 88 (Bushe-Fox 1949, no. 379). 223 (Bird 1981). 240 (Bird *et al.* 1979, no. 1867). Lyminge (Kelly 1962; Maidstone Museum).

6.   *A l'éponge* ware. Sites: 10. 15. 31. 80 (Galliou *et al.* 1980, 276). 82 (*ibid.*, 277). 88. 97. 110. 223 (*ibid.*). 240 (Bird *et al.* 1978b, no. 1866). Canvey Island, Essex (Galliou *et al.* 1980, 277).

7A.   *Terra Nigra.* Sites: 7A (Central Gaulish) (Caiger 1958, no. 4). 9B. 9C. 15. 31. 35A (Philp 1968, nos. 195, 198). 84. 88. 89. 97. 105B (Philp 1973, no. 215). 107. 108. 110. 202 (Green 1977, no. 104a). 208 (Detsicas 1977a, no. 4). 223 (Chapman and Johnson 1973, no. 108; information from Museum of London). 226 (Green 1976, no. 94). 232 (Green 1978a). 240 (Bird *et al.* 1978b, 532).

7B.   *Terra Rubra* (Rigby 1973, Fabrics 1 and 2). Sites: 15. 88. 89. 97. 107. 108. 223 (information from Museum of London). 226 (Castle Hill: Bell 1976, 271).

7C.   Gallo-Belgic white wares (forms mapped on Fig. 18 only). Sites: 2. 9B. 9C. 15. 35A (Philp 1968, no. 217). 37. 38. 43. 45. 61. 63. 69. 81. 88. 89. 96. 97. 105B (Philp 1973, no. 211). 107. 108. 110. 208 (Detsicas 1977a, no. 1). 210 (Lowther 1946/47, fig. 24, no. 3). 223 (Chapman and Johnson 1973, no. 115). 246 (Whiting 1927a). Deal (Deal Castle Museum; Birchall 1965, no. 97).

8.   'Hardham' ware. Sites: 44 (Green 1976, 266). 202 (Green 1977, 154). 210 (Lowther 1946/47, 24). 226 (Green 1976, nos. 55–61). 236 (Fulford 1978b, no. 1).

9.   'Highgate Wood'. Sites: 1. 12. 15. 19. 23. 31. 38. 41. 53. 55. 63. 69. 77. 78. 85. 88. 89. 92. 97. 98. 99. 101. 104. 209 (Tyers 1977b, Fabrics A1, A2). 217 (Brown and Sheldon 1974). 223 (Orton 1977b, 32–5). 226 (Green 1976, fig. 37, no. 2a). 240 (Tyers and Marsh 1978, 535). Possible published occurrences (not on Fig. 32): 203 (Philp 1973, no. 278). 210 (Lowther 1946/47, fig. 25; Pemberton 1973, fig. 8, no. 14). 215 (Philp 1973, nos. 240, 245).

10A.   'Ring-and-dot' beakers. Sites: 9B. 14. 15. 88. 97. 210 (Lowther 1946/47, fig. 19, nos. 6–7). 223 (Green 1978b). 240 (Tyers and Marsh 1978, Type IIIB.1). Deal (Deal Castle Museum).

10C.   'London' mica-dusted. Sites: 15 (March 1978, Type 24, possibly Canterbury source). 19 (*ibid.*, Type 24). 38 (*ibid.*, Type 21 body sherd). 55 (*ibid.*, Type 3). 63 (*ibid.*, Types 21/23, 23, 24/26 (base)). 71 (*ibid.*, Type 24). 78 (*ibid.*, Type 12). 84 (*ibid.*, Types 26 and 37). 89 (*ibid.*, Type 34. 7/10). 97 (*ibid.*, Types 19–23.3, 24). 209 (P. Tyers, unpublished archive; *ibid.*, Types 1/2, 24, Ditch F.4). 210 (Lowther 1946/47: Marsh 1978, Type 24). 223 (Marsh 1978). 240 (Marsh 1978). Possible occurrences (not on Fig. 21): 17 (Johnston 1972, no. 54: Marsh 1978, Type 24 with tripod feet). 88 (*ibid.*, Type 21). 108 (*ibid.*, Type 24, but fabric suggests a Canterbury source).

10D.   'London' 'Marbled'. Sites: 88 (foot-stand base). 97 (Marsh 1978, Type 11/44 rim, foot-stand base). 223 (Marsh 1978). 240 (Marsh 1978).

10E.   'London-Essex' stamped. Sites: 8 (Rodwell 1978). 23 (*ibid.*). 44 (*ibid.*, Group 2C; block-stamp 2, ring-stamp 3.2A/10). 69 (*ibid.*). 97 (*ibid.*). 105 (site unspecified: Philp 1980). 107 (Rodwell 1978). 209 (*ibid.*). 210 (*ibid.*). 213 (Philp 1980). 217 (Rodwell 1978). 223 (*ibid.*). 236 (Fulford 1978b, nos. 21, 22). 245 (Rodwell 1978). Canvey Island, Essex (*ibid.*). Nazeing, Essex (*ibid.*).

10F.   Buff 'Eggshell' ware. Sites: 5 (Marsh 1978, Type 13). 15 (Marsh 1978, Type 13.6, and Type 13 variant with oval indentations: Macpherson-Grant 1982, no. 247). 63 (Marsh 1978, Type 22.6). 88 (Marsh 1978, Type 11: Cunliffe 1968, no. 613; Marsh 1978, Type 12.1/2). 209 (foot-stand base: Tyers 1977b, no. 9). 223 (Marsh 1978). 240 (*ibid.*).

11. Lyon colour-coat. Sites: 14. 15. 35 (Greene 1979a, 42; site unrecorded). 88. 89. 97. 108. 208 (*ibid.*). 223 (*ibid.*). 240 (Bird *et al.* 1978b, 529).

12A. Much Hadham oxidised. Sites: 1. 15. 17. 23. 34. 39. 46. 58. 59. 63. 65. 66 (not on Fig. 34 as source of Rowe Collection uncertain). 69. 76. 78. 84. 85. 88. 89. 97. 109. 202 (Green 1977, no. 175). 209 (Tyers 1977b, nos. 15, 21.1, 21.9, 21.16, 23). 218 (Jessup 1935, fig. 3, no. 1). 223 (Orton 1977b, 37; Harden and Green 1978). 233 (Drury 1977, nos. 23–29). 239 (Rodwell 1976b, no. 88). 240 (Bird *et al.* 1978b, no. 303). 248 (Huggins 1978, nos. 7, 12, 13, 21–23, 66, 68, 87, 89). Possible occurrences: 18 (Allen 1954, no. 29). 206 (not on Fig. 34: Philp 1973, nos. 401, 406). 228 (McIsaac *et al.* 1979, nos. 169, 209).

13A(i). Nene Valley/Rhineland white ware colour-coat: bag-beakers, plain or with roulette and/or barbotine. Sites: 10. 12. 15. 28. 30. 31. 33. 36. 38. 40. 44. 59. 63. 65. 69. 76. 78. 84. 88. 89. 97. 108. 113. 209 (P. Tyers, unpublished archive, Pit F.69). 223 (Orton 1977b, 41). 236 (Fulford 1978b, no. 33). 240 (Bird *et al.* 1978b, nos. 1160–1162, 1276).

13A(ii). Nene Valley white ware colour-coat: late third- to early fifth-century forms. Sites: 1. 9A (Howe *et al.* 1980, cf. no. 68). 12 (closed form). 15 (various; see Young and Bird 1982, Green forthcoming). 17 (Howe *et al.* 1980, cf. no. 79). 46 (*ibid.*, cf. nos. 38/39, 42/43, 77, 86 plain, 88). 55 (*ibid.*, cf. no. 89). 58 (*ibid.*, cf. nos. 75/76, 89). 59 (*ibid.*, cf. nos. 49/53, 75/77). 63 (various; including *ibid.*, cf. nos. 49/57, 66, 70, 72, 75/77, 79, 87, 89). 76 (*ibid.*, cf. no. 79). 82. 84 (*ibid.*, cf. nos. 75/77). 88 (*ibid.*, cf. nos. 63 (rim form), 64/65, 79, 87, 89). 89 (*ibid.*, cf. nos. 49/57, 79 or 87 (base)). 90 (*ibid.*, cf. nos. 77, 79, 80). 97 (*ibid.*, cf. nos. 42/43). 98 (*ibid.*, cf. no. 89). 108. 115 (*ibid.*, cf. no. 49). 206 (*ibid.*, cf. no. 54/57: Philp 1973, no. 318). 209 (Howe, *et al.* 1980, cf. nos. 75/77: Tyers 1977b, no. 21. 15). 223 (*ibid.*, cf. nos. 49/57, 66, 79, 83, 89: Orton 1977b, respectively, nos. 313–315, 307, 309, 310, 133 and 139, plus 'jars', nos. 318–319; Marsden 1975 figures a triangular-rim conical-sided dish or bowl possibly in this ware – no. 199). 228 (*ibid.*, cf. no. 79: Sheldon 1971, fig. 5, no. 19; cf. nos. 66, 79; beakers with white barbotine dots: Sheldon 1972, respectively, fig. 11, no. 32, fig. 10, no. 4; cf. nos. 49/57, 68, 85, 87, fig. 9, nos. 16–17: McIsaac *et al.* 1979, respectively, nos. 69, 250, 222, 227). 233 (*ibid.*, cf. nos. 80, 87, 89: Drury 1977, respectively, nos. 21, 22, 20). 239 (*ibid.*, cf. no. 87: Rodwell 1976b, no. 96). 240 (*ibid.*, cf. nos. 49/53, 63, 66, 79, 87, 89: Bird *et al.* 1978b, respectively nos. 277, 838 (pedestal base), 837, 371, 839, 1366). 248 (*ibid.*, cf. nos. 87, 89: Huggins 1978, respectively nos. 10, 9 and 49).

13B. Nene Valley (?) white ware, painted. Except where specified, the sherds recorded represent rounded closed forms with exterior horizontal bands of red-brown paint (cf. Howe *et al.* 1980, no. 95). Sites: 17. 24. 25. 46 (hemispherical bowl with internal paint). 84. 93 (cf. Hull 1963, Form 369; possibly a flagon). 206 (hemispherical plain-rim bowl with external and internal paint: Philp 1973, no. 337, cf. Young 1977a, Type P18). 228 (double-bead rim closed form with ?scroll externally: Sheldon 1972, fig. 10, no. 13).

14A. New Forest colour-coat. Sites (from Fulford 1975a, unless otherwise specified): 10 (*ibid.*, Type 27; pers. observ.). 15 (*ibid.*, Types 27, 30, 33: M. Green forthcoming). 44 (*ibid.*, Types 27, 44). 80 (*ibid.*, Types 27, 39, 42, 63, 67). 82 (*ibid.*, Types 27, 30, 42: Young 1980). 88 (*ibid.*, Types 11, 27, 36, 39, 41, 77). 202 (*ibid.*, Types 8, 1/26: Green 1977, respectively, nos. 185, 186). 223 (body sherd, Fabric 1a: Orton 1977b, no. 380). 228 (*ibid.*, Type 27 – from Bow: Fulford 1975a). 236 (*ibid.*, Type 30, plus body sherd in Fabric 1b or 1c: Fulford 1978b, respectively, no. 63 and unfigured). 240 (body sherd, Fabric 1a: Bird *et al.*, 1978b, 125). West Blatchington, East Sussex (*ibid.*, Types 27, 67).

14B. New Forest 'Parchment'. Sites: 15 (Fulford 1975a, Type 89 variant: Green forthcoming). 80 (*ibid.*, Type 102 mortarium: Fulford 1975a). 82 (*ibid.*, Type 89: Young 1980). 202 (*ibid.*, Type 88/89: Green 1977, no. 71). West Blatchington (*ibid.*, Type 103 – mortarium: Fulford 1975a).

15B. North Gaulish white ware necked beakers. Sites: 15 (Whiting 1927d, no. 700, and unpublished). 59 (James and James 1978, no. 10). 63. 76 (Whiting *et al.* 1931, nos. 86, 143). Possible occurrence: 33 (Ogilvie 1982, body sherd). (See also Richardson and Tyers 1984).

16A. Oxfordshire red-brown colour-coat. (i) all types except those with a date-range restricted to *c*. A.D. 350+ (Young 1977a): Sites: 1 (*ibid.*, Types C.44/46, 83). 5 (*ibid.*, Type C51). 7 (*ibid.*, Types C45, ?C64). 8 (*ibid.*, Type C83/84/85 base). 9A (*ibid.*, Types C8, 45/46, 46, 82). 10 (*ibid.*, Type ?C22). 12 (*ibid.*, Types ?C2/15 (painted), C26, bowl with internal rouletting). 15 (*ibid.*, Types C8, 22, 23, 27, 28, 31, 45, 46, 47, 51, 54, 55, 68, 69, 70, 71, 75, 77, 78, 79, 81, 82, 83: Young 1977a, Young and Bird 1982; see also Green forthcoming). 17 (Young 1977a, Types 23, 26, 27, 28, 48, 51, 55 (undecorated), 75, 82, 109). 18 (*ibid.*, Types C3, 12: Allen 1954, nos. 24, 17, respectively). 23 (*ibid.*, Types C45, 68 variant or 81/83 – demi-rosette stamp; C47: Young

1977a). 25 (*ibid.*, Types C51, 82, bowl with external and internal rouletting and bowl with stamps cf. 73.1). 31 (*ibid.*, Type C51: Young 1977a). 33 (*ibid.*, Types C51, 51/52 (abraded)). 35 (*ibid.*, Type C22). 35A (*ibid.*, Type C51: Philp 1968, no. 247). 36 (*ibid.*, Types C8, 51, 79, plus plain-rim bowl with demi-rosette stamps, possibly Oxford). 38 (flagon handle and neck, possibly Oxford). 44 (*ibid.*, Types C29, 47). 46 (*ibid.*, Types C46, 50, 51, 79). 48. 49 (*ibid.*, Type C51: others present, not examined). 51 (*ibid.*, Type C44/46). 55. 56 (closed form, rouletted). 58 (*ibid.*, Types ?C23, C46, 51, 54, 75, ?78, 81). 63 (*ibid.*, Types C3, 5, 16, 18, 20, 23, 24, 26, 27, 28, 29/31, 37, 45, 46, ?48, 50, 51, 71, 72, 77, 78, 81, 82, 83, 87). 65 (*ibid.*, Type ?C51). 66 (*ibid.*, Types C51, 107.1, bowls with white paint and rosette stamps). 68 (*ibid.*, Type C22). 69 (*ibid.*, Types C24, 45, 49, 50, 51, 71, 75, 78, 81, 82, 83: Young 1977a). 70 (carinated bowl with rosette stamp). 76 (*ibid.*, Types C8, 10, 12, 22, 23, 27, 51, 75, 81, plus rosette-stamped bowls). 78 (*ibid.*, Types ?C23, C45/46, 51, 69 or 78, 70, 77 or 83, 82). 80 (*ibid.*, Types C22, 23, 27, 28, 45, 47, 49, 51, 68, 75, 77, 78, 81, 116: Young 1977a and pers. observ.). 82 (*ibid.*, Types C18, 22, 26, 29, 34, 45, 47, 51, 55, 75: Young 1977a). 84 (beaker base). 85 (*ibid.*, Type C44/46). 88 (*ibid.*, Types C1, 8, 10, 18, 22, 23, 25, 26, 27, 30, 38, 40, 41, 44, 45, 46, 47, 48, 49, 50, 51, 55, 56, 64, 68, 69, 70, 71, 72, 73, 75, 77, 78, 79, 81, 82, 83, 94, 105, 111, 115: Young 1977a and pers. observ.). 89 (*ibid.*, Types C20, 23, 26, 45, 50, 51, 75 plus curved-wall bowl with paint). 97 (*ibid.*, Types C1/15, 23, 27, 28, 30, 46, 48, 51, 69 or 82, 70 or 83, 75, 78, 79, 81, ?82, ?88: Young 1977a and pers. observ.). 98 (*ibid.*, Type C23). 99 (*ibid.*, Type C8). 106 (*ibid.*, Type C48 or 50, ?Oxford). 107 (*ibid.*, Types C22, 24, 27, 38, 44, 45, 47, 49, 51, 68, 75, 78, 79, 81, 82: Young 1977a). 108 (*ibid.*, Types C49, 51, 83). 109 (*ibid.*, Types C16, 40, 81). 110 (*ibid.*, Types C40, 77). 112 (body sherds including white-painted). 113 (*ibid.*, Types C51, 75 and unclassified beaker rim). 115 (*ibid.*, Types C8, 27, 28, 50, 51, 75, 78). 202 (*ibid.*, Types C38, 51, 75, 81, 109: Young 1977a). 206 (*ibid.*, Types C27, 46, 50, 51, 81: Philp 1973, respectively nos. 399, 405, 444, 389 and 390, 393 and 409). 209 (*ibid.*, Types C55, 78: Tyers 1977b, respectively nos. 21.11, 21.9, 21.10; C9, 46, 50, 51, 75, 82: Young 1977a). 212 (*ibid.*, Type C82 and rosette-stamped bowl: Meates 1973, nos. 30 and 31). 223 (wide range: see Young 1977a). 226 (*ibid.*, Type C22 rim, ?Oxford: Green 1976, no. 288). 227 (*ibid.*, Types C23, 27, 51: Philp 1978, respectively nos. 18, 7, 4). 228 (*ibid.*, Types C24, 27, 30, 45, 50, 51, 55, 68, 69, 72, 75, 77, 78, 81, 83: Young 1977a). 232 (demi-rosette stamped bowl: Green 1978a, no. 37, plus 'two plain bowls and a jar'). 233 (*ibid.*, Types C23, 27, 51, 75: Young 1977a; C117: Drury 1977, no. 18). 236 (*ibid.*, Type C24 and rouletted bowl: Fulford 1978b, no. 97 and not illustrated). 239 (*ibid.*, Type C113 plus beaker and bowl with internal rouletting: Rodwell 1976b, respectively nos. 98, 97, 99). 240 (wide range: see Young 1977a, Bird *et al.* 1978b). 248 (*ibid.*, Types C18, 44, 45, 51 plus beaker rim and white painted body sherd: Huggins 1978, respectively nos. 24, 50, 88, 62, 85). Canvey Island, Essex (*ibid.*, Types C22, 45, 51, 75, 81: Young 1977a). Ickham, Kent (wide range: see Young 1977a). Sandling, near Maidstone, Kent (*ibid.*, Type C77). West Blatchington, East Sussex (*ibid.*, Type C23: Young 1977a).

16A. (ii) types with date-range *c.* A.D. 350–400+ (Young 1977a). Sites: 4 (*ibid.*, Type C21: Young 1977a). 7 (*ibid.*, Types C13, 84). 13 (*ibid.*, Type C13). 15 (*ibid.*, Types C14, 52, 63, 84: Young 1977a, Young and Bird 1982). 17 (*ibid.*, Type C84). 18 (*ibid.*, Types C14, 85: Allen 1954, respectively nos. 27 and 31, 25). 36 (*ibid.*, Type C84). 46 (*ibid.*, Type C84). 58 (*ibid.*, Types C52, 84). 63 (*ibid.*, Types C13, 84). 68 (*ibid.*, Type C13). 69 (*ibid.*, Types C52, 84: Young 1977a). 80 (*ibid.*, Types C52, 60, 84: Young 1977a). 88 (*ibid.*, Types C11, 13, 52, 84, 85: Young 1977a). 89 (*ibid.*, Types C52, 84). 93 (*ibid.*, Type C14). 97 (id. Types C13, 52, 84). 107 (*ibid.*, Types C84, 93: Young 1977a). 109 (*ibid.*, Type C11). 202 (*ibid.*, Types C14, 85: Young 1977a). 209 (*ibid.*, Type C84: Young 1977a). 223 (*ibid.*, Types C11, 52, 63, 84, 93: *ibid.*). 228 (*ibid.*, Types C52, 84: Young 1977a). 240 (*ibid.*, Type C52). Ickham, Kent (*ibid.*, Types C11, 13, 52, 63, 84, 85: Young 1977a).

16B. Oxfordshire white slip. Sites: 63 (Young 1977a, Types WC2, 3). 78 (*ibid.*, Type WC3). 80 (*ibid.*, Type WC3: Young 1977a). 88 (*ibid.*, Type WC3). 89 (*ibid.*, Type WC2). 228 (*ibid.*, Type C75 with white slip: McIsaac *et al.* 1979, 63 note).

16C. Oxfordshire Parchment. Sites: 7 (Young 1977a, Types P24, 34). 9A (*ibid.*, Type P24). 15 (*ibid.*, Types P9, 24, 27, 34: Green forthcoming). 25 (bowl with red paint internally). 49 (*ibid.*, Type P24). 55 (*ibid.*, Type P24). 58 (*ibid.*, Type P24). 63 (*ibid.*, Types P3, 24). 68 (*ibid.*, Type P9, ?Oxford). 69 (*ibid.*, Type P24). 78 (*ibid.*, Type P24). 80 (?Oxford). 82. 88 (*ibid.*, Types P9, 24, 29: Young 1977a; P3, ?Oxford: Bushe-Fox 1928, no. 184, with abundant fine to medium-size quartz, coarser than usual for Oxford Parchment). 97 (*ibid.*, Types P24, 25). 107 (*ibid.*, Type P24: Young 1977a). 108 (*ibid.*, Type P24). 209 (P.

Tyers, unpublished archive: 'bowl rim', Ditch F7). 212 (*ibid.*, Type P24: Young 1977a). 223 (*ibid.*, Types P24, 34: Young 1977a). 228 (*ibid.*, Types P9, 23, 24: Young 1977a). 240 (*ibid.*, Type P24: Young 1977a). Ickham (*ibid.*, Type P24: Young 1977a).

17.   'Pevensey' colour-coat. Sites: 44. 80. 82 (Young 1980). 115. 202 (Green 1977, 158–9). 232 (Green 1978a, no. 34). 236 (Fulford 1978b).

18.   'Pompeian Red' wares. Sites: 15 (Peacock 1977c, Fabrics 3 and 6). 31 (*ibid.*, Fabric 7). 63 (*ibid.*, Fabric 7). 88 (*ibid.*, Fabrics 1, 3, 4, 6, 7 and unclassified: Peacock 1977c). 89 (*ibid.*, Fabric 1). 223 (*ibid.*, Fabrics 1 and 3: Peacock 1977c). 240 (*ibid.*, Fabrics 1 and 3: Bird *et al.* 1978b, nos. 596 and 595).

20A.   South Gaulish samian (pre-Flavian). Sites: 12 (mis-located as 76 on Fig. 19). 15 (e.g. Bird 1981c, forthcoming). 27 (Dickinson, in Pollard forthcoming, b). 38 (Bird, in Pollard forthcoming, c). 63 (Meates 1979, 119). 88 (e.g. Cunliffe 1968). 89. 97. 108. 202 (Bell 1977). 208 (Detsicas 1977a, 29). 209 (Gentry *et al.* 1977). 212 (Meates 1973). 216 (Money 1968, 192). 220 (Piercy-Fox 1955). 223 (e.g. Chapman and Johnson 1973). 240 (Bird and Marsh 1978b). 246 (Whiting 1927a).

20B.   South Gaulish colour-coat. Site: 88 (Greene 1979a, fig. 21.3; Bushe-Fox 1932, Pl.XXVI, no. 7).

21.   Spanish colour-coat. Sites: 88 (Greene 1979a, fig. 31, nos. 4, 5, 8, 10, 12, 13). 223 (*ibid.*, fig. 31, nos. 1, 15).

22.   'Staines' lead-glazed. Sites: 8. 12. 63. 69 (Arthur 1978). 88. 97 (*ibid.*,) 107. 209 (*ibid.*,) 210 (*ibid.*,) 212 (*ibid.*,) 223 (*ibid.*,) 240 (*ibid.*,) Plaxtol, Kent (*ibid.*). Shoebury, Essex (*ibid.*,).

24A.   Butt-beakers and wide-mouth pedestal urns with fine-combed motifs. Sites (Fig. 27): 9C (Anon. 1924). 15 (Pollard 1981b, no. 1). 30A (Dale 1971, no. 1). 83 (Dowker 1893, no. 2). 86 (Couchman 1924, 54, right). 88 (Cunliffe 1968, no. 541). 225 (Whiting 1924, fig. 1, Group B, left).

24C.   Painted 'Upchurch' ware. Sites: 15. 24. 42. 43. 67. 84. 88. 89. 97.

25.   West Kent red burnished. Sites: 17. 78 (e.g. Pearce 1930, 163, nos. D31, D43). 101 (Isolation Hospital site: Godwin 1931, site 2).

26.   Rough-cast wares (excluding pre-Flavian and Lower Rhineland white ware fabrics): this category includes material of possible Colchester and North Gaulish sources, fabrics 4B and 15A. Sites: 9A. 9C. 12. 15. 31. 38. 41. 44. 46. 63. 65. 67. 76. 78. 80. 84. 88. 89. 97. 98. 202 (Green 1977, no. 38d). 209 (P. Tyers unpublished archive, Pit F.43). 223 (Tatton-Brown 1974, no. 144). 226 (Green 1976, 274 Group V, and no. 240). 240 (Bird *et al.* 1978b, no. 237).

II. *Coarse Wares*

1A.   Alice Holt grey ware: first to early second centuries. Sites: 15 (Lyne and Jefferies 1979, Class 4.9). 19 (*ibid.*, Classes 1.6, 4.11/15–17). 49 (*ibid.*, Class 4.9). 210 (*ibid.*). 215 (*ibid.*, Class 1.13, ?Alice Holt: Philp 1973, no. 242). 233 (*ibid.*). 228 (*ibid.*, Class 1.9: McIsaac *et al.*, 1979, fig. 27, no. 1). 240 (*ibid.*, Classes 1.12–23, 4.4–34, 5.1–11: Tyers and Marsh 1978, respectively Classes IIC 2/IID 1–2/IIG 1, IIA 12–13, IVK). 249 (*ibid.*, Classes 1.5, 1.6, 1.13, 1.22, 4.16/24, ?Alice Holt: Philp 1973, respectively nos. 159; 162–163, 175, 177, 179; 178; 176; 170). For other sites on Fig. 37, see Lyne and Jefferies 1979.

1B.   Alice Holt-Farnham grey ware: third century and later. Sites: 1 (Lyne and Jefferies 1979, Classes 3B. 10/14, 5B.4/9). 3 (*ibid.*, Classes 3B.11/13, 6A.12/13, 8.12). 7 (*ibid.*, Classes 3B.13, 3C.3, 4.40/41, 5B.8, 5C.2). 9A (body sherd). 15 (*ibid.*, Classes 1.35, 1C.3/5, 3B11/14, storage jar, 5B.5, 8.10/14; see also Pollard forthcoming, d). 17 (*ibid.*, Classes 1.28/31, 1A.18, 1B.5/6, 3B.8/9, 3B.10/14, 4.40/41, 5B.5/9, 5B 10, 5C.2, 6A.8/10, 6C.1, 8.10/14). 23 (*ibid.*, Classes 1A.16/19, storage jar, 5B.8, 10.1/3). 25 (*ibid.*, Classes 1.32, 3B.10/14, 1.32, 5B.9, 5E.2/3). 35A (*ibid.*, Class 5B.10, ?Alice Holt: Philp 1968, no. 239). 44 (*ibid.*, storage jar, and Class 3B.10). 46 (*ibid.*, storage jar). 53 (*ibid.*, Class 5B.9). 55 (*ibid.*, Class 5C). 58 (*ibid.*, Classes 3B.10/14, 5B.9, 5B.10). 63 (*ibid.*, Classes 1.32, 1.33, 1.36, 1A.15, 1A.20, 1B.2, 1C.2, 1C.6, 3A.19/20, 3B.10/14, 4.44, 4.45, 5B.5/9, 5B.10, 5C.2, 5C.3, 6A.6, 6A.8/10, 6C.1, 6C.2, 8.11/14). 65 (*ibid.*, Classes 1.33, 3B.9, 3B.10/14, storage jar). 69 (*ibid.*, Class 8.12). 74 (*ibid.*, Classes 3B.10/14, 4.42/44: *ibid.*). 76 (*ibid.*, Classes 3B.11, 8.12). 78 (*ibid.*, Classes 3B.11, 5B.9). 80 (*ibid.*, Classes 1.30, 1.34, 1A.16/19, 1C.3/5, 1C.6, 3B.10/14, 4.42/44, 5B.5/9, 6A.8/10, 8.11/14, 8.12, 10.1/3). 82 (*ibid.*, Classes 1A.16/19 or 1B.3, 3B.10/14). 88 (*ibid.*, Classes 1A.16/19, 1C.3/5, 1C.6, 3B.10/14, 4.42/44, 4.45, 5B.9, 5B.10, 6A.9, 8.10, 8.11/14, 8.12). 89 (*ibid.*, Classes 1.33, 1B.4/6?, 1C.6, 3B.8/9, 3C.5, 5B.9, 5B.10, 6A.12, 6C.1, 8.11/14?). 91 (*ibid.*, Class 3B.11/13: *ibid.*). 93 (*ibid.*, Classes 3B.11, 8.12). 96 (*ibid.*, Class 4.42). 97 (*ibid.*, Classes 1.29/30, 1A.11, 1A.16, 1C.5, 3B.8/9, 3B.10/14, 3C.2, 3C.3/7, 3C.8, 4.41/43, 5B.8/9, 5B.10,

6A.8/10). 99 (*ibid.*, Class 8.12). 108 (*ibid.*, Classes 4.44, 5B.9). 110 (*ibid.*, Class 5B.9). 115 (*ibid.*, Classes 1.35, storage jar, 3B.8/13, 5B.8, 6A.12, 8.12). 202 (*ibid.*, Classes 1A.16, 5B.8: Green 1977, nos. 144 and 75–76, respectively). 209 (storage jar: P. Tyers unpublished archive, Ditch F.3). 210 (*ibid.*, Classes 1.26/30, 1A.16/19, 1C.2/4, 1C.6, 3A.1/15, 3B.9/13, 4.42/44, 5A.1/4, 6B.1/3: *ibid.*). 212 (storage jar: Meates 1973, no. 33; other Farningham sites gazetteered in Lyne and Jefferies 1979). 220 (*ibid.*, Classes 1A.16/19, 4.42/44: *ibid.*). 223 (see Orton 1977b; Lyne and Jefferies 1979). 228 (*ibid.*, Classes 1A.14/15, 1A.16/19, 1C.3/5, 1C.6, 3B.8/14, 4.42/44, 8.11/14: *ibid.*; 5C.3, 6A.2: McIsaac *et al.* 1979, nos. 260, 259). 232 (jars: Green 1978a, context 9). 238 (*ibid.*, Class 1C.3/5: *ibid.*). 240 (*ibid.*, Classes 1B.2, 3B.8/9, 4.45, 6A.2/3, 6A.13, 8.11/14, 8.12; Bird *et al.* 1978b, respectively nos. 342, 312, 841, 281, 362, 1373, 1374). For other sites on Fig. 38, see Lyne and Jefferies 1979.

3.   BB1 (i): Hadrianic finds (Fig. 35). Sites: 49 (Gillam 1970, Class 307). 55 (*ibid.*, Classes 121/132, 122/133, 306/314 rim). 63 (*ibid.*, Class 309). 74 (*ibid.*, Class 119/120/125/129/141 rim). 88 (*ibid.*, Classes 132, 221/308: respectively, Bushe-Fox 1932, no. 319, Cunliffe 1968, no. 602). 101 (*ibid.*, Class 221/308). 209 (Tyers and Marsh 1978, Classes IIF.2, IVG.1–3: P. Tyers unpublished archive, and Tyers 1977b, fig. 6, no. 6). 223 (Gillam 1970, Classes 118 – Orton 1977b, no. 64, 120 – Chapman and Johnson 1973, no. 41, 123 – *ibid.*, no. 142, 219 – Tatton-Brown 1974, nos. 369 and 393). 240 (Tyers and Marsh 1978, Classes IIF.1–3, IVG.1–3).

3.   BB1 (ii): Severan and later forms (Fig. 36). Sites: 3 (Gillam 1970, Class 228, plain). 7 (*ibid.*, Classes ?133, 228). 12 (*ibid.*, Classes 329, 330). 15 (*ibid.*, Classes 146, 147/148, 226, 227, 228, 329, 330). 23 (*ibid.*, Class 148). 24 (*ibid.*, Class 314). 25 (*ibid.*, Classes 145/148, 226/227/306/314 rim, 228, 329). 31 (*ibid.*, Classes 130/146, 145, 227, 228, 314, 329, 330). 33 (*ibid.*, Classes 147, 329). 38 (*ibid.*, Classes 130/146 rim, 145, 226/227/306/314 rim, 329, 329/330 rim). 39 (*ibid.*, Classes 146/148, 227, 329). 46 (*ibid.*, Class 228). 55 (*ibid.*, Classes 127/146, 226/227/306/314 rim, 228, 330). 58 (*ibid.*, Class 329/330 rim). 59 (*ibid.*, Classes ?145/146, 228). 63 (*ibid.*, Classes 146, 227, 228, 329). 66 (*ibid.*, Class 130/146 rim). 74 (*ibid.*, Classes 145/148, 228, 329/330). 76 (*ibid.*, Classes 65, 146, 329, 330; Williams 1977, fig. 3, no. 4). 79 (Gillam 1970, Class 228 plain). 80 (*ibid.*, Types 146/148, 228, 330). 82 (*ibid.*, Classes 146, 148, 330). 87 (*ibid.*, Classes 228, plain, 329; probably BB1: *ibid.*, Classes 220, 228, 329: Philp 1957, respectively nos. 27, 7, 30). 88 (*ibid.*, Classes 145, 147). 89 (*ibid.*, Types 228, plain, 330). 94 (*ibid.*, Class 146/147). 97 (*ibid.*, Classes 226/227/306/314 rim, 329, 329/330 rim). 107 (*ibid.*, Class 226/227/306/314 rim). 108 (*ibid.*, Classes 228, 329/330 base). 110 (*ibid.*, Class 228). 113 (*ibid.*, Classes 130/146 rim, 228, 330). 202 (*ibid.*, Classes 118, 146/148, 227, 228 plain, 330: Green 1977, respectively nos. 85, 139, 140, 36 and 141, 52). 209 (Tyers and Marsh 1978, Class IVG.3: P. Tyers unpublished archive, Ditch F.67). 223 (Gillam 1970, Classes 65, 146/148, 147, 228, 329: Orton 1977b e.g. respectively nos. 158, 172, 151, 160, 69; *ibid.*, Class 227: Tatton-Brown 1974, no. 37). 226 (*ibid.*, Classes 146, 306/314 plain: Green 1976, nos. 188, 257). 228 (*ibid.*, Classes 65/118 rim, 146, 330: McIsaac *et al.* 1979, respectively nos. 3, 6, 86; 228, 329: Sheldon 1972, e.g. fig. 7, no. 1; fig. 10, no. 5). 232 (Green 1978a, context 9). 236 (*ibid.*, Types 148, 228, 330: Fulford 1978b, nos. 86, 66 and 76, 70). 237 (*ibid.*, Classes 329, 330: Jessup *et al.* 1954, nos. 2, 4 and 7). 239 (*ibid.*, Class 145: Rodwell 1976b, no. 87). 240 (*ibid.*, Classes 65, 146, 147/148 rim, 227, 228b plain, 329: Bird *et al.* 1979, e.g. respectively nos. 1691, 1683, 266, 1697, 290, 294, 282).

4.   BB2 (i) decorated 'pie-dishes'. Sites: 9B. 12. 15. 16. 17. 19. 23. 25. 27. 30. 31. 33. 36. 38. 40. 41. 46. 47. 49. 53. 55. 63. 65. 69. 70. 77. 84. 88. 89. 91. 97. 98. 108. 113. 203 (Philp 1973, no. 170). 206 (*ibid.*, no. 317). 209 (P. Tyers unpublished archive). 210 (Pemberton 1973). 221 (Eames 1957, fig. 3, nos. 13, 15). 223 (e.g. Orton 1977b, nos. 26–32). 228 (Sheldon 1971, fig. 7, nos. 31–32). 238 (Ocock and Syddell 1967, nos. 15, 26). 240 (Tyers and Marsh 1978, Classes IVH.1–4).

4.   BB2 (ii) plain pie-dishes (pers. exam. only). Sites: 1. 8. 9B. 10. 12. 15. 16. 23. 25. 26. 27. 28. 30. 31. 33. 36. 38. 39. 40. 46. 47. 49. 53. 55. 59. 62. 63. 65. 66. 68. 69. 76. 77. 84. 88. 89. 91. 96. 97. 98. 104. 107. 108. 112. 113. 114.

4.   BB2 (iii) decorated dog-dishes. Sites: 8. 15. 16. 17. 25. 31. 41. 47. 49. 63. 65. 76. 88. 89. 97. 98. 209 (P. Tyers unpublished archive, Pit F43b, Class IVJ.2). 223 (Tatton-Brown 1974, no. 335). 240 (Tyers and Marsh 1978, Class IVJ.2).

4.   BB2 (iv) plain dog-dishes (pers. exam. only). Sites: 1. 7. 8. 9B. 10. 12. 15. 17. 23. 25. 31. 33. 36. 38. 43. 46. 47. 49. 53. 55. 56. 59. 62. 63. 65. 66. 69. 76. 77. 84. 89. 97. 98. 107. 108. 109. 110. 112. 113.

4.   BB2 (v) bead-and-flange dishes (Fig. 46 'flanged bowl'): Sites: 12. 15. 17. 23. 25. 27. 30. 31. 39. 46. 47. 55.

58. 59. 63. 65. 69. 76. 77. 79. 84. 89. 90. 97. 107. 110. 113. 206 (Philp 1973, nos. 329, 368, 372, 412 e.g.; ?BB2). 209 (P. Tyers unpublished archive, Pit F.1, Ditch F.3; ?BB2). 228 (McIsaac *et al.* 1979, nos. 24, 88; ?BB2). 230 (Rodwell 1974, nos. 57–58). 240 (Bird *et al.* 1978b, no. 295; ?BB2).

4. BB2 (vi) bead-rim jars (Fig. 40, no. 114). Sites: 17. 31. 63. 88. 209 (P. Tyers unpublished archive, Pit F.43b, Class IIA 17). 223 (Orton 1977b, nos. 24–25). 240 (Tyers and Marsh 1978, Class IIA 17).

4. BB2 (vii) everted-rim jars: Sites (underlined: those with vessels from second-century levels, Fig. 30): 8. 12. 15. 16. 17. 23. 25. 26. 27. 31. 35A (Philp 1968, nos. 254–255, ?BB2). 38. 40. 41. 46. 47. 53. 55. 58. 59. 62. 63. 65. 69. 70. 76. 77. 78. 84. 88. 89. 97. 98. 107. 108. 112. 113. 206 (Philp 1973, nos. 319, 326 e.g.). 209 (P. Tyers unpublished archive, e.g. Pit F.41, layers 13–14: Class IIF.5; Pit F.64, Classes IIF.5, IIF.7). 210 (Pemberton 1973, no. 6). 223 (Orton 1977b, e.g. nos. 70, 73; Tatton-Brown 1974, no. 138, ?BB2). 228 (McIsaac *et al.* 1979, nos. 96, 117, 123; ?BB2). 230 (Rodwell 1974, nos. 43–45). 238 (Ocock and Syddell 1967, nos. 5, 33). 240 (Tyers and Marsh 1978, Classes IIF.4–10, IIF.12). Acol near Birchington. Canvey Island, Essex (Rodwell 1966a, no. 6).

4. BB2 (viii): Sites mapped on Fig. 48: 12. 15. 38. 41. 63. 89. 97. 223.

5. Brockley Hill-Verulamium buff sandy (i): flagons and jugs. Sites: 9B (flagon?). 10 (flagon?) 11. 15. 19. 24. 25. 40. 41. 52. 55. 63. 69. 70. 74. 77. 84. 85. 89 (flagon?). 91. 97. 101. 104. 105. 209 (P. Tyers unpublished archive, Fabric C.1, Classes IB.2, IB.5, IB.6, IC.1). 223 (e.g. Chapman and Johnson 1973, nos. 16, 36, 45, 110). 228 (McIsaac *et al.* 1979, fig. 4, no. 17). 240 (Tyers and Marsh 1978, Classes IA.2, IB.1–9, IC.1, ID.1). Greenwich Park. N.B. 'Numbers of classes' (Fig. 10) refers to generalised Southwark Classes – Tyers and Marsh 1978 – e.g. IA, IIG.

5. Brockley Hill-Verulamium buff sandy (ii): reed-rim carinated bowls (= 'buff' on Fig. 24). Sites: 55. 88. 99. 209 (Tyers 1977b, nos. 12.15, 13. 5). 210 (Lowther 1946/47; Pemberton 1973). 223 (Orton 1977b, nos. 11–13). 240 (Tyers and Marsh 1978, Classes IVA.2–9). 249A (Philp 1973, nos. 167, 173). N.B. Given its location, 88 (unpublished, from Pit 182) could be an import from the Pas-de-Calais; Seillier and Thoen 1978, nos. 45–46 provide exact parallels in beige ware.

5. Brockley Hill-Verulamium buff sandy (iii): jars, including Tyers and Marsh 1978 Classes IIG.3, IIH, IIJ.2–3, IIK. Sites: 8 (*ibid.*, Class IIJ.3). 19 (*ibid.*, Class IIG.3). 43 (*ibid.*, Classes IIK). 63 (*ibid.*, Class IIG.3). 209 (*ibid.*, Classes IIG.3, IIH, IIK: P. Tyers, unpublished archive, Fabric C.1). 223 (*ibid.*, Class IIG.3: Chapman and Johnson 1973, nos. 141, 181, 251; IIJ.3: Tatton-Brown 1974, no. 215). 240 (Tyers and Marsh 1978, Classes listed above). 249B (*ibid.*, Class IIG.3: Philp 1973, no. 218).

5. Brockley Hill-Verulamium buff sandy (iv): other types (referring to Tyers and Marsh 1978, excluding mortaria). Sites: 19 (*ibid.*, Class IJ.1). 23 (*ibid.*, Class IJ.1). 96 (*ibid.*, Class IJ.1). 209 (*ibid.*, Classes IJ.1 – P. Tyers unpublished archive – and IVA.1 – Tyers 1977b, no. 18). 223 (*ibid.*, Classes IE – Orton 1977b, no. 54, IIJ.1/2 – Tatton-Brown 1974, no. 77; unclassified dish – *ibid.*, no. 53; *tazza* – Chapman and Johnson 1973, no. 256). 240 (Tyers and Marsh 1978, Classes IE.1, IH.1–2, IJ.1–2, IIJ.1, IVA.1, IVB).

6C. 'Canterbury' sandy (i): flagons. Sites: 9B. 9C. 10. 12. 15. 31. 32. 33. 36. 37 (not on Fig. 22). 41. 49. 63. 66. 76. 78. 84. 88. 89. 101. 108. 112. 113. 114. 115. Broadstairs (Broadstairs Library). Ramsgate (Ramsgate Library).

6C. 'Canterbury' sandy (ii): reed-rim carinated bowls (='grey' on Fig. 24, eastern group). Sites: 12. 15. 31. 36. 49. 84. 88. 108. 110. 112. 113. 114. 221 (Eames 1957, fig. 5, no. 11). 238 (Cook 1928, no. 17: ?Canterbury source).

6C. 'Canterbury' sandy (iii): lid-seated bag-shape jars. Sites: 5. 9B. 12. 15. 31. 33. 36. 49. 84. 88. 108. 110. 112. 114. Barham Downs (Canterbury Royal Museum).

8. 'East Sussex Ware'. Sites: 3. 10. 28. 38. 44. 45. 63. 77. 79. 80. 81. 91. 102. 202 (Green 1977, 154–6; Hamilton 1977, Fabric 5). 226 (Green 1976, 258–9). 232 (Green 1978a, 247). 236 (Fulford 1978b, 'hand-made, grog-tempered ware' – see Green 1980, 78).

9. 'Aylesford-Swarling' flint-tempered (i): dishes of 'Gallo-Belgic' derivation (Fig. 17). Sites: 84. 89.

9. 'Aylesford-Swarling' flint-tempered (ii): 'furrowed' jars (Fig. 20), and other jars. Sites: 9A. 9B. 15. 49. 61. 66. 67. 84. 87 (Thompson 1953, no. 2). 89. 103B (Noël Hume 1954, fig. 1, no. 8; fig. 2, nos. 1–5). 112.

11A. 'Aylesford-Swarling' grog-tempered (i): flagons. Sites: 2. 9A. 9B. 9C. 12. 15. 33. 66. 76. 84. 88. 108. 113. Deal (not on Fig. 17) (Deal Castle Museum).

11A. 'Aylesford-Swarling' grog-tempered (ii): dishes of 'Gallo-Belgic' derivation. Sites: 2. 9B. 9C. 12. 15. 33. 49. 66. 88. 89. 108. 110. 112. 205 (Jessup 1939, nos. 3, 4).

11A. 'Aylesford-Swarling' grog-tempered (iii): 'furrowed' jars. Sites: 9A. 9B. 12. 13A (Watson 1963, fig. 14, no. 4). 15. 28. 33. 35A (Philp 1968, e.g. no. 178). 36. 49. 61. 66. 69 (not on Fig. 20: kiln products in shelly ware only mapped). 76. 84. 87 (Thompson 1953, 53–54, ?grogged). 88. 89. 91 (in 'East Sussex Ware': Green 1980). 95. 108. 110. 112. 113. 200 (Philp and Philp 1974, nos. 1–2). 221 (Eames 1957, Plate X, nos. 1–6, ?grogged).

11B. 'Late Roman' grog-tempered, Kent. Sites: 9A. 15. 17. 25. 33. 35. 56. 63. 65. 68. 69. 76. 82. 84. 88. 89. 97. 108. 112. 115. 218 (Jessup 1935, no. 2: ?grogged). 228 (McIsaac *et al*. 1979, no. 174).

12. Mayen ware. Sites: 9A. 15 (Fulford and Bird 1975, Forms 2, 3, 9). 17 (*ibid*., Form 9). 36 (*ibid*., Form 3: *ibid*.). 39. 46 (C. Going, pers. comm.). 55 (*ibid*., Form 3). 63 (*ibid*., Form 8). 69 (*ibid*., Form 3: Fulford and Bird 1975). 78 (*ibid*., Form 3). 80 (*ibid*., Form 3). 82 (*ibid*., Form 3). 87 (*ibid*., Form 3: *ibid*.) 88 (*ibid*., Forms 1, 3, 5, 6, 9/10, 11). 97 (*ibid*., Form 3: Fulford 1977a). 206 (*ibid*., Form 3: Fulford and Bird 1975). 223 (*ibid*., Forms 2, 3, 9: *ibid*., Form 6: Tatton-Brown 1974, no. 269; unclassified form: Orton 1977b, no. 368). 228 (*ibid*., Form 3: Sheldon 1972, fig. 8, no. 39). 240 (*ibid*., Forms 9, 11: Bird *et al*. 1978b, nos. 315, 300). 248 (Huggins 1978, no. 48). Chadwell St. Mary (Essex), Ickham (Kent), West Blatchington (East Sussex) all include Form 3 and Ickham also Form 6/7 (Fulford and Bird 1975).

15. 'Native Coarse Ware'. Sites: 12. 15. 31 (e.g. Willson 1981, no. 738). 36. 76. 87 (including Philp 1957, nos. 22 and 29, probably). 88. 97. 108.

16. 'Arras' North Gaulish grey sandy. Sites: 9B. 15. 31 (Willson 1981, e.g. nos. 512, 515, 646, 661, 667, 669, 694, 853). 36. 48. 88. (see also Richardson and Tyers 1984, '*vases tronconiques*'.)

18. 'Patch Grove' ware. Sites: 4. 6. 10. 15. 17. 19. 25. 29. 29A (Ward-Perkins 1938, fig. 6, no. 6). 30. 30A (Dale 1971, no. 20). 38. 40. 41. 55. 56. 57. 61. 63. 65. 70. 72. 73. 74. 76. 77. 78. 88. 89. 97. 101. 105. 111. 203 (Philp 1973, 103). 206 (*ibid*., 138). 207 (*ibid*., 79). 208 (Detsicas 1966, 156–158). 210 (Ward-Perkins 1944, 175). 211 (Philp 1973, 115). 212 (Meates 1973, 16). 213 (Philp 1963a, 64–65). 215 (Philp 1973, 88). 216 (Money 1968, fig. 16, no. 22). 220 (Philp 1973, nos. 258, 267). 223 (Chapman and Johnson 1973, no. 118; Orton 1977b, 39: ?'Patch Grove'). 229 (Ward-Perkins 1944). 234 (Little 1964, fig. 1, nos. 1–3, 5). 238 (Ocock and Syddell 1967, fig. 3, nos. 19, 29). 240 (Tyers and Marsh 1978, Class IIL). 245 (Philp 1973, 99–100). 249A (*ibid*., 60–61). 249B (*ibid*., 70–71). Tonbridge. From Ward-Perkins 1944, 175 (additional sites within study zone): Banstead, Surrey; Hale, Kent; Limpsfield, Surrey. From Frere 1944, (additional): Beddington, Surrey; Shoeburyness, Essex.

19. 'Portchester "D"'. Sites: 1 (Lyne and Jefferies 1979, Class 3C). 3 (*ibid*., Class 3C). 15 (*ibid*., Classes 3C, 5B, 6A). 18 (*ibid*., Class 6A: Allen 1954, nos. 19, 26; ?'Portchester "D"'). 23 (*ibid*., Class 3C). 25. 31. 51 (jar base). 58 (*ibid*., Class 3C, and lid-seated jar cf. Clark 1949, nos. 5–6). 63 (*ibid*., Classes 3C, 5B, 6A, 7, 8 and lid-seated jar). 65 (jar). 68 (*ibid*., Class 3C). 69 (jar). 74 (*ibid*., Class 3C). 80 (*ibid*., Classes 3C, 6A). 85 (*ibid*., Class 5B). 88 (*ibid*., Classes 3C, 5B, 6A and lid-seated jar). 89 (*ibid*., Classes 3C, 6A). 97 (*ibid*., Classes 3C, 5B, 6A). 115. 202 (*ibid*., Classes 3C, 5B, 6A, 8: Green 1977, respectively nos. 64 + 77a + 93 + 156, 154, 155, 77 + 157). 223 (*ibid*., Classes 3C, 5B: Orton 1977b, 35). 228 (*ibid*., Classes 3C, 5B; Sheldon 1972, fig. 11, no. 17; fig. 7, no. 14). 232 (*ibid*., Classes 3C, 6A: Green 1978a, context 9). 236 (*ibid*., Class 6A: Fulford 1978b). 240 (*ibid*., Class 3C: Bird *et al*. 1978b, nos. 829, 831). 248 (*ibid*., Class 3C: Huggins 1978, no. 43).

22B. 'Lower Thames' sandy ware (i): bead-rim jar (Fig. 29, no. 90). Sites (Fig. 30: Kent examples of this form only): 12. 15 (not mapped). 16. 17. 25. 41. 43. 49. 55. 63. 65. 70. 76. 89. 97. 98. 111. 207 (Philp 1973, no. 230). 213 (Philp 1963a, no. 12). 220 (Philp 1973, no. 264). 238 (Ocock and Syddell 1967, nos. 17, 28).

22B. 'Lower Thames' sandy ware (ii): everted-rim storage jar (cf. Fig. 12, no. 16). Sites (Fig. 31): 25. 63. 97. 223 (Chapman and Johnson 1973, no. 194).

22B. 'Lower Thames' sandy ware (iii): lid-seated jar (Fig. 50, no. 201). Sites (Fig. 45): 1. 8. 17. 23. 39. 46. 47. 55. 59. 63. 65. 69. 77. 89. 90. 96. 97. 107. 206 (Philp 1973, nos. 342, 362). 223 (Tatton-Brown 1974, no. 254). 228 (McIsaac *et al*. 1979, nos. 4, 108, 243). 230 (Rodwell 1974, nos. 28–34). 238 (Ocock and Syddell 1967, no. 9). 240 (Bird *et al*. 1978b, no. 1280). 244 (Drury and Rodwell 1973, no. 105).

22B. 'Lower Thames' sandy ware (iv): 'swan's neck' jar (Fig. 50, no. 203). Sites (Fig. 45): 1. 7. 15. 16. 17. 23. 47. 51. 58. 63. 65. 69. 89. 97. 113. 223 (Chapman and Johnson 1973, nos. 252–253). 228 (Sheldon 1971, fig. 8, nos. 33–35; Sheldon 1972, fig. 8, nos. 30–31, fig. 10, no. 6). 230 (Rodwell 1974, no. 62). 240 (Bird *et al*. 1978b, no. 585). 248 (Huggins 1978, no. 36).

22B. 'Lower Thames' sandy ware (v): necked jar/bowl including slipped examples (Fig. 50, no. 194). Sites

(Fig. 45): 9A. 15. 17. 23. 25. 26. 27. 41. 43 (including Noël Hume 1954, fig. 3, no. 6). 46. 47. 51. 59. 63. 65. 69. 84. 87 (Philp 1957, no. 4). 89. 90. 97. 98. 107. 115. 228 (Sheldon 1972, fig. 8, no. 12; fig. 10, no. 14; McIsaac *et al.* 1978b, nos. 17, 126, 244). 230 (Rodwell 1974, no. 42). 240 (Bird *et al.* 1978b, no. 1679). Canvey Island, Essex (Rodwell 1966a, nos. 28–29). Greenwich Park (Greenwich Museum).

22B. 'Lower Thames' sandy ware (v): necked jar/bowl including slipped examples (Fig. 50, no. 194). Sites (Fig. 45): 9A. 15. 17. 23. 25. 26. 27. 41. 43 (including Noël Hume 1954, fig. 3, no. 6). 46. 47. 51. 59. 63. 65. 69. 84. 87 (Philp 1957, no. 4). 89. 90. 97. 98. 107. 115. 228 (Sheldon 1972, fig. 8, no. 12; fig. 10, no. 14; McIsaac *et al.* 1978b, nos. 17, 126, 244). 230 (Rodwell 1974, no. 42). 240 (Bird *et al.* 1979, no. 1679). Canvey Island, Essex (Rodwell 1966a, nos. 28–29). Greenwich Park (Greenwich Museum).

22B. 'Lower Thames' sandy ware (vi): flasks, including slipped examples. Sites (Fig. 45): 8. 17. 23. 26. 41. 46. 47. 51. 59. 63. 65. 69. 71. 76. 97. 98. 110. 223 (Orton 1977b, no. 212). 228 (Sheldon 1972, fig. 2, no. 1; fig. 9, no. 29: McIsaac *et al.* 1979, no. 170). 230 (Rodwell 1974, nos. 49–50). 240 (Bird *et al.* 1978b, no. 1278 – flask or jar).

22B. 'Lower Thames' sandy ware (vii): folded beakers (Fig. 50, no. 192). Sites (Fig. 45): 17. 23. 25. 26 (possibly not kiln waster). 27. 46. 48. 59. 63. 65. 69. 74. 77. 97. 99. 209 (Tyers 1977b, no. 20.5). 223 (Orton 1977b, no. 205). 228 (McIsaac *et al.* 1979, no. 39). 240 (Bird *et al.* 1978b, no. 560).

23A. Early shelly ware, including sand + shell undesignated. Sites (Fig. 20): 1. 12. 16. 17. 23. 25. 27. 29A (Ward-Perkins 1938, fig. 4, nos. 1–6, 8 10; fig. 5, nos. 1–4, 7–10). 38. 41. 43. 51. 63. 69. 75. 78. 84. 85. 89. 96. 97. 98. 104. 209 (Tyers 1977b, Fabric D). 210 (Lowther 1946/47). 211 (Philp 1973, 115). 213 (Philp 1963a, 64–67; Philp 1973, no. 286). 215 (*ibid.*, 88). 223 (Chapman and Johnson 1973, e.g. nos. 31, 35, 100, 235, 250). 228 (Sheldon 1971, fig. 4, no. 5; fig. 9, nos. 9, 20, 22; McIsaac *et al.* 1979, fig. 4, no. 6; nos. 245–246 and 252, possibly residual). 238 (Ocock and Syddell 1967, no. 8). 239 (Rodwell 1976b, nos. 73, 75). 240 (Tyers and Marsh 1978, Classes IIA.10–11, 16). 244 (Drury and Rodwell 1973). 249A (Philp 1973, 61). 249B (*ibid.*, 71). Canvey Island, Essex (Rodwell 1966a). Limpsfield, Surrey (Ward-Perkins 1944, fig. 14, nos. 18, 19).

23A. 'Cooling' sand + shell ware style. Sites: 15 (Macpherson-Grant 1982, no. 296). 25. 76. 89 (Harrison and Flight 1968, no. 44). 97. 98. 238 (Ocock and Syddell 1967, no. 8). Borden-near-Sittingbourne (Worsfold 1948, no. 10).

23A. Early shelly ware with 'graffito' (Fig. 12, no. 13): see Jones 1972.

23B. 'Thames Estuary' shelly storage jars. Sites: 5. 7A (Caiger 1958, no. 1). 15. 16. 19. 24. 25. 30A (Dale 1971, no. 22). 35A (Philp 1968, no. 273). 40. 41. 42. 47. 49. 55. 63. 67. 76. 78. 88. 89. 97. 98. 209 (P. Tyers unpublished archive, Class IIM, Pit F.48 layer 3). 210 (Pemberton 1973, fig. 8, no. 12). 212 (Meates 1973, no. 1). 223 (Chapman and Johnson 1973, nos. 42, 83, 175, 194–195). 240 (Tyers and Marsh 1978, Class IIM). 244 (Drury and Rodwell 1973, nos. 81, 84). Canvey Island, Essex (Rodwell 1966a, no. 1). Coulsdon, Surrey (Frere 1944, fig. 10, no. 3). Greenwich Park (Greenwich Museum).

23C. Late Roman shelly. Sites: 1. 15. 17. 23. 31. 39. 58. 69. 74. 85. 88. 89. 97. 206 (Philp 1973, nos. 374, 397, 418). 209 (Tyers 1977b, nos. 21.2, 21.3, 21.5, 24.1). 223 (Orton 1977b, 37–9). 228 (Sheldon 1971, fig. 7, no. 36; fig. 8, nos. 8, 14, 22, 26, 31). 233 (Drury 1977, nos. 37–40). 239 (Rodwell 1976b, no. 93). 248 (Huggins 1978, nos. 44–46, 60–61, 93, 105).

26. 'Tilford' coarse grey sandy. Sites: 15. 17. 63. 65. 88. 89. 97. 115. 223 (Orton 1977b, 35, fabric (iii)).

Miscellaneous wares mapped: A. Sand-tempered 'Gallo-Belgic' dishes. Sites (Fig. 17): 23. 25. 43. 60. 67. 89. 90. 97. 110. 209 (P. Tyers unpublished archive, Class VA, Ditch F.25). 211 (Philp 1973, nos. 304–305). 213 (Philp 1963a, no. 15). 223 (Chapman and Johnson 1973, nos. 107–108, 247). 226 (Green 1976, nos. 43, 220). 240 (Tyers and Marsh 1978, Classes VA, VB; Sheldon 1974, no. 15). 244 (Drury and Rodwell 1973, no. 117).

B. Grey sandy reed-rim bowls, undesignated London and Sussex vessels. Sites (Fig. 24): 55. 79. 91. 209 (P. Tyers unpublished archive, Fabric A.3, e.g. Ditch F.4, Class IVA.3). 210 (Lowther 1946/47). 217 (Brown and Sheldon 1974, nos. 46, 66–67, 77, 89). 223 (Chapman and Johnson 1973, nos. 89, 155–156; Marsh and Tyers 1976, nos. 55–56, 61). 226 (Green 1976, nos. 49–50). 240 (Bird *et al.* 1978b, nos. 205, 867). 249A (Philp 1973, no. 174).

C. Grog-tempered third-century jars (excluding 'Native Coarse Ware'). Sites (Fig. 45): 8. 25. 31. 65. 97. 107.

III. *Mortaria*

1. Brockley Hill-Verulamium. Sites: 10. 12. 15. 19. 23. 24. 25. 31A (Hartley 1981, no. 363). 38. 40. 41. 43. 44.
    48. 55. 63. 69. 70. 76. 77. 78. 88. 89. 91. 97. 101. 114. 209 (Tyers 1977b, fig. 26, nos. 3–10, 12–13, 15). 210
    (Lowther 1946/47). 212 (Meates 1973, no. 20). 215 (Philp 1973, nos. 243–244). 223 (Orton 1977b, 35–7).
    228 (McIsaac *et al.* 1979, fig. 4, no. 16). 239 (Rodwell 1976b, no. 94). 240 (Tyers and Marsh 1978, 580–1).
    249A (Philp 1973, nos. 183–184).

2. 'Canterbury' oxidised sandy and similar wares. (i) unstamped. Sites: 10. 12. 15. 17. 33. 36. 38. 40. 42. 43.
    44. 46. 48. 49. 55. 63. 65. 69. 70. 71. 76. 77. 78. 87. 88. 97. 98. 108. 112. 113. 115. 203 (Philp 1973, no. 274).
    (ii) stamped: see Hartley 1968, 1981a, forthcoming. Summarised in Chapters 4 and 5.III herein.

3. 'East Kent' oxidised. Sites: 15. 31. 33. 36. 38. 43. 63. 65. 69. 77. 78. 84. 87 (Philp 1959, no. 7). 88. 89. 108.
    110. 202 (Green 1977, no. 51). 238 (Cook 1928, no. 5; Ocock and Syddell 1967, no. 21).

5. Kent-Essex cream-buff. Sites: 3. 12. 15. 19. 25. 31. 33. 36. 38. 39. 40. 41. 44. 46. 49. 55. 59. 63. 69. 76. 78.
    84. 87. 88. 89. 91. 97. 98. 101. 107. 110. 112. 113. 114. 202 (Green 1977, no. 34). 203 (Philp 1973, no. 277).
    206 (*ibid.*, nos. 345, 353). 209 (Gentry *et al.* 1977, fig. 26, no. 14). 223 (Tatton-Brown 1974, nos. 91, 95;
    Orton 1977b, nos. 143–144). 226 (Green 1976, no. 292). 239 (Rodwell 1976b, no. 95). 240 (Bird *et al.*
    1978b, e.g. nos. 256, 783, 1263, M12).

6. Mancetter-Hartshill. Sites: 15. 23. 63. 80. 82. 88. 209 (Gentry *et al.* 1977, fig. 26, no. 11). 223 (Orton 1977b,
    no. 323).

8. Nene Valley buff. Sites: 1. 9A. 15. 23. 46. 63. 69. 80. 84. 88. 223 (Orton 1977b, no. 362). 228 (Sheldon
    1972, fig. 10, no. 18; McIsaac *et al.* 1979, no. 54). 233 (Drury 1977, no. 71).

9A. Oxfordshire white ware. Sites: 1 (Young 1977a, Class M22). 3. 7. 9A (*ibid.*, Class M20). 10 (*ibid.*,
    Class M17/18). 12 (*ibid.*, Classes M19, 22). 15 (*ibid.*, Classes M17, 18, 22). 17 (*ibid.*, Classes M17, 18, 22).
    23 (*ibid.*, Classes M17, 17/18, 22). 25. 30 (*ibid.*, Class M17). 31 (*ibid.*, Classes M18, 22). 36 (*ibid.*, Classes
    M11 (Oxford or Fabric 11B below), 22). 38. 40 (*ibid.*, Class M22). 44 (*ibid.*, Class M22). 49. 55 (*ibid.*, Class
    M21). 63 (*ibid.*, Classes M6, 10/21, 17, 18, 22). 65 (*ibid.*, Classes M17, 22). 66. 76 (*ibid.*, Class M22). 77
    (*ibid.*, Type M17). 78 (*ibid.*, Classes M17, 22). 80 (*ibid.*, Class M22). 82 (*ibid.*, Classes M18, M22: Young
    1980). 84 (*ibid.*, Class M22). 85 (*ibid.*, Class M22). 87 (*ibid.*, Class M17: Philp 1957, no. 8). 88 (*ibid.*, Class
    M11 (Oxford or Fabric 11B below), 17, 18, 22). 89 (*ibid.*, Class M22). 97 (*ibid.*, Classes M18, 22). 107
    (*ibid.*, Classes M17, 20, 22: Young 1977a.). 108 (*ibid.*, Classes M11/21, 22). 112 (*ibid.*, Class M11 (Oxford
    or Fabric 11B below)). 113. 115 (*ibid.*, Classes M22, 22/23). 202 (*ibid.*, Class M22: Green 1977, no. 166).
    206 (*ibid.*, Class M22: Philp 1973, no. 398). 210 (*ibid.*, Class M3: Pemberton 1973, fig. 12, no. 7). 212 (*ibid.*,
    Class M22: Meates 1973, no. 24). 223 (*ibid.*, Classes M10, 11, 14, 17, 18, 20, 21, 22, 23: Young 1977a). 228
    (*ibid.*, Classes M17, 22: e.g. McIsaac *et al.* 1979, nos. 113 and 114, 176 and 177). 232 (Green 1978a, body
    sherd). 233 (*ibid.*, Class M22: Drury 1977, no. 19). 238 (*ibid.*, Class M22: Ocock and Syddell 1967, no. 22).
    240 (*ibid.*, Classes M17, 21, 22: Bird *et al.* 1978b, e.g. nos. 340, 374, 341, respectively). 248 (*ibid.*, Class
    M22: Huggins 1978, no. 1). Ickham, Kent (*ibid.*, Class M22: Young 1977a.).

9B. (i) Oxfordshire red colour-coated ware. Sites: 1 (Young 1977a, Classes C97, 100). 3 (*ibid.*, Class C100).
    5 (*ibid.*, Class C100). 12. 15 (*ibid.*, Classes C97, 99, 100). 25 (*ibid.*, Class C100). 36 (*ibid.*, Class C100).
    46. 55 (*ibid.*, Class C100). 58. 63 (*ibid.*, Classes C97, 100). 65. 69. (*ibid.*, Classes C97, 100). 76 (*ibid.*,
    Class C97). 78 (*ibid.*, Class C100). 80 (*ibid.*, Classes C97, 100). 82 (*ibid.*, Classes C97, 100: Young 1980).
    84 (*ibid.*, possibly Class C97). 88 (*ibid.*, Classes C97, 98, 99, 100). 89 (*ibid.*, Classes C97, 100). 90 (*ibid.*,
    Class C100). 97 (*ibid.*, Classes C97, 100). 107 (*ibid.*, Classes C97, 98, 100: Young 1977a.). 108. 112 (*ibid.*,
    Class C97). 113 (*ibid.*, Class C97). 115 (*ibid.*, Class C97). 202 (*ibid.*, Classes C97, 100: *ibid.*). 206 (*ibid.*,
    Class C97: *ibid.*). 209 (*ibid.*, Class C97, 100: *ibid.*). 223 (*ibid.*, Classes C97, 98, 100: *ibid.*). 228 (*ibid.*,
    Classes C97, 98: e.g. McIsaac *et al.* 1979, nos. 135 and 136, 78). 233 (*ibid.*, Class C97: Young 1977a). 240
    (*ibid.*, Class C97: *ibid.*). 248 (*ibid.*, Class C100: Huggins 1978, no. 101).

9B. (ii) Oxfordshire white-slip, Young 1977a Class WC7 unless stated otherwise. Sites: 15 (also WC.4/5:
    Jenkins 1952, nos. 28, 29). 17. 36. 46. 63. 65 (base). 69. 76. 80. 88. 89. 97. 107 (Young 1977a.). 202 (Green
    1977, no. 165). 203 (Young 1977a). 223 (*ibid.*). 228 (e.g. McIsaac *et al.* 1979, no. 216). 233 (WC5, 7: Drury
    1977, nos. 66, 69). 240 (Young 1977a). Ickham, Kent (WC6, 7: *ibid.*,).

10. Rhineland. Sites: 15. 31 (Hartley 1981, no. 381). 63. 97. 223 (Chapman and Johnson 1973, no. 261;
    cf. Hartley *ibid.*, but 'flint' trituration grit alleged). 240 (Bird *et al.* 1978b, nos. 1820, 1821).

11A.   (i) Claudio-Neronian iron-free ware 'wall-sided'. Sites: 15. 64. 88. 208 (Detsicas 1977a). 240 (Bird *et al.* 1978b, e.g. nos. 16, 637, 745).

11A.   (ii) Q. Valerius Se-, Q. Valerius Veranius, *et al.* (Hartley 1977): bead-and-flange mortaria of the Neronian-Trajanic period. 1, 3/4 refer to Hartley's rim-types (*ibid.*, fig. 2.1); I, II refer to name stamps of Hartley's Groups 1 and 2 potters (*ibid.*,), published therein.

.   Sites: 9B (3/4; II). 15 (1, 3/4; II). 19 (3/4). 33 (1, 3/4). 38 (1). 63 (1). 65 (II: site not recorded). 77 (1). 84 (1, 3/4). 88 (1, 3/4; I, II). 91 (3/4). 97 (1; I). 113 (3/4). 223 (I, II). 240 (I).

11B.   South Britain/North Gaul white ware, Hartley 1981, nos. 382–385 type. Sites: 12. 15 (Jenkins 1950, no. 56; Jenkins 1952, nos. 24, 26). 31 (Hartley 1981b, nos. 382–385, 387). 36 (or Fabric 9A above). 76. 88 (Bushe-Fox 1949, no. 515). 112 (or Fabric 9A above). 240 (Bird *et al.* 1978b, no. 1260).

12.   'Surrey/Sussex' white 'hammer-head', Gillam 1970, Class 272. Sites: 15. 36. 38. 69. 87 (including Philp 1957, no. 13). 88. 97. 223 (Tatton-Brown 1974, nos. 42, 92, 94). 228 (McIsaac *et al.* 1979, no. 22).

APPENDIX 4

KEY TO SOURCES OF ROMAN POTTERY IN KENT (Figs. 54–68)

I. *Continental Sources* (Figs. 54–61)

 1: Gallia Belgica – fine wares, coarse ware(?), mortaria(?)
 2: Arrezo – Arretine ware
 3: Southern Italy (Latium, Campania) – 'Pompeian Red' ware, wine amphorae, mortaria
 4: Lyon – fine ware
 5: Lezoux (Central Gaul) – samian, other fine wares
 6: Allier valley (Central Gaul – Vichy, Les-Martres-de-Veyre) – samian, other fine wares, micaceous jars (? – *q.v.* Pollard forthcoming, d)
 7: South Gaul (La Graufesenque, Montans, Banassac) – samian, other fine ware
 8: South Spain (Baetica) – olive oil and fish-sauce amphorae, fine ware
 9: Lower Rhineland (including Cologne) – fine wares
 10: Northern France – fine wares(?), coarse ware, mortaria(?)
 11: Lower Rhône Valley – wine amphorae
 12: La Madeleine (East Gaul) – samian
 13: Blickweiler (East Gaul) – samian
 14: Kreis Düren (including Soller) – mortaria, coarse ware(?)
 15: Trier (East Gaul) – samian, other fine wares
 16: Rheinzabern – samian
 17: Argonne (including Lavoye, Les Allieux) – samian, other fine wares
 18: Westerndorf (Raetia) – samian
 19: West Flanders – 'Pompeian Red' ware(?), coarse ware(?), other fine wares(?), mortaria(?)
 20: Loire-Gironde basin – fine ware *'A l'éponge'*
 21: Eastern Mediterranean/Aegean – amphorae(?)
 22: The Eiffel (Mayen, Speicher) – coarse ware

II. *British Sources* (Figs. 62–68)

 1: Colchester – fine wares, samian(?), mortaria, coarse ware (BB2, plus others?)
 2: Brockley Hill region (including Radlett, Bricket Wood) – mortaria, coarse ware, fine ware
 3: Canterbury – coarse wares, mortaria, fine ware (mica-dusted, plus others?)
 4: Eccles – fine wares, mortaria
 5: West Kent/East Surrey – 'Patch Grove' coarse ware (other wares not specific to this region, e.g. shelly wares, also produced hereabouts)
 6: Thames Estuary – coarse wares (including BB2), mortaria(?), fine wares
 7: Upchurch Marshes – fine wares, coarse wares

 8: Southern Essex – coarse wares (including BB2?), mortaria(?)

 9: Otford – flagons

10: Alice Holt, Farnham, Tilford – coarse wares

11: Staines (vicinity) – fine ware

12: Much Hadham – fine ware (including mortaria), coarse ware(?)

13: Highgate Wood (type-site) – fine ware

14: London – fine wares, coarse ware(?)

15: Greenhithe (vicinity) – coarse ware (BB2–derivatives)

16: Richborough (vicinity) – coarse wares

17: Poole Harbour – coarse ware (BB1)

18: Verulamium – mortaria, coarse ware(?)

19: Nene valley – fine wares, mortaria

20: Maidstone (vicinity) – coarse ware

21: The High Weald – coarse wares (including 'East Sussex Ware')

22: West Surrey/West Sussex – mortaria

23: Mancetter-Hartshill – mortaria

24: New Forest – fine wares (including mortaria?)

25: Oxfordshire – fine wares (including mortaria), mortaria

26: Preston-near-Wingham – coarse ware

27: Pevensey (vicinity) – fine ware (including mortaria)

APPENDIX 5

QUANTIFICATION TABLES

I. *Introduction*

These tables present vessel rim equivalents proportions by fabric for a small number of Kent assemblages, calculated by the present author (*q.v.* Chapter 2.IV.3). The fabrics are divided into four groups: fine wares, coarse wares, mortaria and amphorae. These are accorded fabric numbers from Appendix 2, with some additional undesignated ware categories, for example, hand-made and iron-free ('buff') fine wares. The sandy coarse wares are divided into categories in order to facilitate comparison of assemblages and to circumvent the problem of source-allocation. The following in parenthesis codes are employed for sandy wares:

    (B) = iron-free 'buff' (or white, cream)

    (O) = oxidised

    (R) = reduced

    (W) = covered in iron-free 'white' (or buff, cream) slip.

Unless otherwise specified, all sandy wares are wheel-thrown. The 'glauconite' fabric is that of the third to first century B.C. discussed in Chapter 3. 'Flint' covers flint-grog and flint-sand wares, excepting Coarse Ware Fabric 10, which is isolated. Amphorae are given a Dressel type-number where possible.

The tabulated figures are set out as follows. In all groups, the right-hand column contains the figures for the proportion of Fabric X as a part of the total assemblage (summing all four groups), with the first line quoting the total vessel rim equivalence of the assemblage (e.g. 409 per cent). The centre column of Fine Wares, and the left-hand column of other groups, deals with the proportion of Fabric X within its group: thus, for 5.II.1 Springhead (1), 65.2 per cent of the Fine Wares were of Fabric 24A. However, in several instances the samian was not available for study, and in order to allow comparison between assemblages with and without available samian, a third (left-hand) Fine Ware column gives fabric proportions of the Fine Ware assemblage excluding samian. A / in the centre column denotes samian present but not studied. The first line in the centre/left columns quotes the total vessel rim equivalence of the Fabric Group. An x in any column denotes the presence of a fabric as body/base sherds or as rims too small for measurement.

The assemblages studied (dating is the present author's, unless otherwise specified):

Rochester (1) – Chaplin 1962, 50–54 High Street, Trench E2 layer 15. First century B.C. to early/mid-first century A.D.

Rochester (2) – *ibid.*, Trench E2 Pit K. First century A.D. with intrusives. Rochester (1) and (2) studied by kind permission of Mr G.K. Horner.

Springhead (1) – Grid 114, pit layers 7+8+10. Second half first century A.D. Springhead (1)–(4) studied by kind permission of the late Mr S.R. Harker and Mr J. Shepherd.

Brenley Corner (1) – Area 3.3/3.7, Ditch 1. Second half first century A.D.

Wye (1) – Bradshaw 1970, the Ditch. Late first century A.D., possibly extending into early second. Studied by kind permission of Mr J. Bradshaw.

Canterbury (1) – Bennett *et al.* 1982, Pit layers 229+242+249+269+270. Pottery dated to mid-first to mid-second century (*ibid.*). Canterbury (1)–(3), (6)–(9) studied by kind permission of the Canterbury Archaeological Trust.

Canterbury (2) – *ibid.*, occupation in ditch-gutter, layers 177+179+195+196+200+221+226+227+264+273+274+289+303 (layers 195, 273 aceramic, 274 and 289 devoid of rim sherds). Pottery dated to *c.* A.D. 70–180 (*ibid.*).

Springhead (2) – Grid 117, layers 5+6. Late first and first half of second centuries.

Greenhithe (1) – Detsicas 1966, Pit 1. Late first to early second century.

Greenhithe (2) – *ibid.*, layer 17. Early to mid-second century.

Greenhithe (3) – *ibid.*, Oven 1 (layers 14+47). Mid-second century.

Rochester (3) – Pollard 1981a, Romano-British sealed topsoil + Brownsoil (marking-out bank?). Late first to third quarter second centuries. Rochester (3)–(5) studied by kind permission of Mr A.C. Harrison.

Springhead (3) – Grid 114/115/116/117/141/142, layer 3. Mid-second to mid-third century.

Rochester (4) – Pollard 1981a, Rubbish of rampart body. Later second to early/mid-third centuries.

Maidstone – The Mount villa. Trenches Q21, T21, W21, B/1/22, X22: Brown mortary soil and black sooty layer between 26 and 50 in. below modern ground surface, accumulated rubbish in gap between north-east wall of Phase 1 and south-west wall of Phase 2, post-dating construction of latter. *c.* A.D. 180–250. Studied by kind permission of Mr D.B. Kelly, Maidstone Museum, with whom archive is lodged.

Brenley Corner (2) – Pit J6. Late second to mid-third century.

Brenley Corner (3) – Area 3.1, Pit 1. Late second to mid/late third century.

Canterbury (3) – Bennett *et al.* 1982, Well 101. Mid-second to early third century.

Chalk (1) – Johnston 1972, layer 8 (Group A). Third century. The assemblage studied is incomplete, owing to the retention of certain pieces by the excavator: these include *ibid.*, nos. 3, 4, 6 and 7 in Oxfordshire red colour-coat (Young 1977a). No. 11 was stolen from the site and thus not available for examination. The net effect of these absences will be to understate the importance of Oxfordshire wares, and also of grey 'fine' (sandy?) wares, to Chalk in the third century.

Chalk (2) – *ibid.*, layer 7 (Group B). Late third century.

Canterbury (4) – Frere 1970, Trench DII layer 11 + DIII layer 33. Second and third quarters of third century.

Springhead (4) – Grid 105, layers 3 and 5, and Grid 86, layer 2. Late third to early fifth century.

Chalk (3) – Johnston 1972, layers 5 + 6. Late third to late fourth century.

Rochester (5) – Flight and Harrison 1978, late Roman Black earth. Third to early fifth century.

Canterbury (5) – Frere 1970, Trench DII layers 13 and 15 plus DIII layer 39. Late third to early fourth century.

Canterbury (6) – Pollard forthcoming, d, MIIB layer 243. Late third to early fourth century.

Canterbury (7) – *ibid.*, MIIA *caldarium* flood silts. Mid-fourth century.

Canterbury (8) – *ibid.*, MIII layer 429. Late fourth century.

Canterbury (9) – *ibid.*, MIII layer 291. Late fourth to early fifth century.

Wye (2) – Bradshaw 1972; Pollard forthcoming, a. Mid- to late fourth century. Studied by kind permission of Mr J. Bradshaw.

Brenley Corner (4) – Trench 3A, unstratified layers 1–4. Mid-first to mid-third centuries.

Joyden's Wood. Total site assemblage (Tester and Caiger 1954). Late first to mid-fourth century.

In addition to these assemblages, a number of published sites utilising vessel rim equivalence analysis have been consulted. These are: Bishopstone (Green 1977), London, Angel Court, Walbrook (Orton 1977b) and Ranscombe Hill (Green 1978a). The forthcoming report on the Marlowe Car Park excavations at Canterbury (Blockley and Day forthcoming) will also contain data of this kind, in addition to that reproduced here (Canterbury (6)–(9)).

II. First century A.D.

1. *Fine Wares*

	Rochester (1)			Rochester (2)			Springhead (1)		
	0	/	409	123	/	283	87	92	263
20A				–	/	–	–	5.4	1.9
24A				69.1	/	30	69	65.2	22.8
24B				15.4	/	6.7	13.8	13	4.6
24D				15.4	/	6.7	17.2	16.3	5.7
Buff							x	x	x
Hand-made									

	Brenley (1)			Wye (1)		
	105	113	339	131	/	389
20A	–	7.1	2.4	–	/	–
24A	64.8	60.1	20.1	100	/	33.7
24B	18.1	16.8	5.6			
24D						
Buff						
Hand-made	17.1	15.9	5.3			

2. *Coarse Wares*

	Rochester (1)		Rochester (2)		Springhead (1)	
	389	409	160	283	156	263
11A	62.8	59.6			10.9	6.5
Flint	22.6	21.5				
Sand (hand)	1.5	1.5				
18	1.5	1.5			x	x
23A	10	9.5	28.1	15.9	50	29.6
Glauconite	1.5	1.5				
Sand (R)			33.2	18.8	39.1	23.2
4			8.8	5	x	x
Sand (O)						

	Brenley (1)		Wye (1)			
	126	339	250	389		
11A	88.1	32.7	56.4	36.3		
Flint						
Sand (hand)	2.4	0.9				
18						
23A						
Glauconite						
Sand (R)	9.5	3.5	37.2	23.9		
4			4	2.6		
Sand (O)			2.4	1.5		

3. *Mortaria*

	Rochester (1)		Rochester (2)		Springhead (1)	
1 11A	0	409	x x	283 x	30 x 100	263 x 11.4
	Brenley (1)		Wye (1)			
1 11A	0	339	8 100	389 2.1		

4. *Amphorae*

	Rochester (1)		Rochester (2)		Springhead (1)	
Dr 1 Dr 20	20 100	409 4.9	0	283	x x	263 x
	Brenley (1)		Wye (1)			
Dr˙1 Dr 20	100 100	339 29.5	0	389		

III. First to mid-second century A.D.

1. *Fine Wares*

	Canterbury (1)			Canterbury (2)		
	132	262	1224	266	406	1554
1				x	x	x
3D/5C/20A	–	49.6	10.6	–	30	8.6
5B (r-c)				14.1	9.9	2.8
7A	x	x	x	2.2	1.5	0.4
7B	40.9	20.6	4.4	x	x	x
11				x	x	x
4B/15A	12.1	6.1	1.3	x	x	x
16A				x	x	x
24A	41.7	21	4.5	65.4	45.9	13.2
24B				3.4	2.4	0.7
24D	x	x	x	4.3	3	0.9
Buff	5.3	2.7	0.6	6.4	4.5	1.3
Mica-dusted	x	x	x	x	x	x
Grey, black c-c				4	2.8	0.8

2. *Coarse Wares*

	Canterbury (1)		Canterbury (2)	
	934	1224	1109	1554
11A	63.3	48.3	54	37.2
Sand (R)	26.7	20.3	36	24.8
4			2.9	2
1			0.9	0.6
Sand (O)	10.1	7.7	1.8	1.2
Sand (B)			x	x
Sand (W)			4.5	3.1

3. *Mortaria*

	Canterbury (1)		Canterbury (2)	
	28	1224	39	1554
11A			61.5	1.5
Buff wall-sided	100	2.3		
Grey sand pre-Flavian			38.5	0.9
9B red c-c			x	x

IV. Late first to second century A.D.

1. *Fine Wares*

	Springhead (2)		Greenhithe (1)			Greenhithe (2)			
	83	118	385	76	/	444	967	/	5242
3D/5C/20A	–	29.7	9.1	–	/	–	–	/	–
4B									
4B/15A							8.2	/	1.5
5B (r-c)							15.5	/	2.9
5B/13A									
9							3.1	/	0.6
11	x	x	x						
24A	100	70.3	21.6	48.7	/	8.3	49.6	/	9.2
24B	x	x	x	21.1	/	3.6	23.6	/	4.3
24D	x	x	x	30.3	/	5.2	/	/	/
Buff	x	x	x				x	x	x
Mica-dusted	x	x	x						

	Greenhithe (3)			Rochester (3)		
	9	/	407	387	478	1199
3D/5C/20A				–	19	7.6
4B				2.3	1.9	0.8
4B/15A				x	x	x
5B (r-c)				x	x	x
5B/13A				7.2	5.9	2.3
11						
24A	100	/	2.2	54.5	44.1	17.6
24B	x	x	x	28.4	23	9.2
24D				5.7	4.6	1.8
Buff						
Mica-dusted				1.8	1.5	0.6

2. *Coarse Wares*

	Springhead (2)		Greenhithe (1)		Greenhithe (2)	
	239	385	343	444	4229	5242
11A	x	x	x	x		
18	x	x	2.9	2.3	4.2	3.4
23A	22.7	14.1	13.1	10.2	2.2	1.9
23B					2.2	1.9
Glauconite					0.4	0.3
Sand (hand)			22.7	17.6	23	18.5
Sand (R)	28	17.4	47.6	43.7	58.7	47.4
4	8.4	5.2			6.9	5.6
5	41.8	26				
Sand (O)					1.9	1.5
Sand (B)	x	x				
Red sandy, grey c-c					0.2	0.2

	Greenhithe (3)		Rochester (3)	
	389	407	700	1199
11A			x	x
18				
23A	x	x	1.6	0.9
23B			2.3	1.3
Glauconite				
Sand (hand)			7.4	4.3
Sand (R)	23.7	22.6	49.3	28.8
4	76.3	73	41.7	24.4
5				
Sand (O)				
Sand (B)				
Red sandy, grey c-c				

3. *Mortaria*

	Springhead (2)		Greenhithe (1)		Greenhithe (2)	
	x	385	25	444	0	5242
1	x	x	x	x		
3						
5			100	5.6		

	Greenhithe (3)		Rochester (3)	
	9	407	21	1199
1				
3	100	9		
5			100	1.8

4. *Amphorae*

	Springhead (2)		Greenhithe (1)		Greenhithe (2)	
Dr. 20	26	385	0	444	46	5242
	100	6.8			100	0.9

V. Mid-second to mid-third century A.D.

1. *Fine Wares*

	Springhead (3)			Rochester (4)			Maidstone		
	505	1012	5901	171	253	1927	133	133	4431
3D/5C/20A	–	50.1	8.6	–	32.4	4.3	x	x	x
4B				29.2	19.8	2.6	x	x	x
4B/15A	2.6	1.3	0.2	x	x	x			
5B/13A	1	0.5	0.1	8.8	5.9	0.8	x	x	x
7B									
3E	4	2	0.3	x	x	x	12	12	0.4
5D	x	x	x						
16A	x	x	x						
18				x	x	x			
22									
24A	59	29.4	5	52	35.2	4.6	46.6	46.6	1.4
24B	3.8	1.9	0.3	5.3	3.6	0.5	9.8	9.8	0.3
24D	19.8	9.9	1.6	4.7	3.2	0.4	31.6	31.6	0.9
Buff	3.8	1.9	0.3						
Mica-dusted	6.1	3.1	0.5						
9				x	x	x			

	Brenley (2)			Brenley (3)			Canterbury (3)		
	330	402	1264	612	678	1313	375	688	1436
3D/5C/20A	–	17.9	5.7	–	9.7	5	–	45.5	21.8
4B	x	x	x	3.4	3.1	1.6	3.5	1.9	0.9
4B/15A				x	x	x	x	x	x
5B/13A	x	x	x				x	x	x
7B							x	x	x
3E	2.4	2	0.6	2.3	2.1	1.1			
5D	x	x	x				x	x	x
16A	x	x	x	3.4	3.1	1.6			
18									
22	x	x	x						
24A	97.6	80.1	25.5	28.1	25.4	13.1	64	34.9	16.7
24B				7.5	6.8	4	28.8	15.7	7.5
24D	x	x	x	27.6	24.9	12.3	x	x	x
Buff				x	x	x	2.1	1.2	0.6
Mica-dusted				9.3	8.4	4.3	1.6	0.9	0.4
9				2	1.8	0.9			

2. *Coarse Wares*

	Springhead (3)		Rochester (4)		Maidstone	
	4737	5901	1650	1927	4298	4431
11A/B	1.1	0.9	x	x	10.3	10
18	1.2	0.9	x	x	1	1
Flint			x	x	1.3	1.3
23A	0.8	0.7	x	x		
23B	0.2	0.2				
Sand (hand)			0.4	0.4		
Sand (R)	32.3	26	15.9	13.7	54.1	52.5
4	63.8	51.1	80.6	69	33.2	32.2
3	0.2	0.2				
Sand (O)	x	x				
Sand (W)	0.3	0.3	2	1.7		
Sand (B)						
5			x	x		

	Brenley (2)		Brenley (3)		Canterbury (3)	
	857	1264	735	1313	673	1436
11A/B	8.9	6	10.2	5.7	17.8	8.4
18						
Flint						
23A						
23B						
Sand (hand)	2.2	1.5				
Sand (R)	57	38.6	68.2	38.1	42.3	19.9
4	32.3	22	3.1	1.8	34.8	16.3
3	1.5	1				
Sand (O)	x	x	5	2.8	2.7	1.3
Sand (W)					2.4	1.2
Sand (B)	x	x	13.6	7.6		
5						

3. *Mortaria*

	Springhead (3)		Rochester (4)		Maidstone	
	152	5901	24	1927	0	4431
1			33.3	0.4		
2						
5	85.5	2.2	66.7	0.8		
11A						
12	14.5	0.4				
Colchester brown						

	Brenley (2)		Brenley (3)		Canterbury (3)	
	5	1264	0	1313	70	1436
1						
2					64.3	3.1
5	100	0.4			x	x
11A					35.7	1.7
12						
Colchester brown					x	x

VI. Third century A.D.

1. *Fine Wares*

	Chalk (1)			Chalk (2)			Canterbury (4)		
	171	231	1876	156	163	1081	143	/	588
3D/5C	–	26	3.2	–	4.3	0.7		/	
1	x	x	x						
4B	4.4	3.3	0.4						
5B	4.1	3	0.4				x	x	x
5B/13A	4.4	3.3	0.4				8.4	/	2
12A	4.7	3.5	0.4						
16A	7	5.2	0.6	14.7	14.1	2.1			
24A	52	38.5	4.7	15.4	14.7	2.2	91.6	/	22.3
24B	x	x	x				x	x	x
24D				6.4	6.1	0.9	x	x	x
Buff	5.8	4.3	0.5	64.1	61.3	9.3	x	x	x
Mica-dusted				x	x	x			
Pink, black c-c	17.5	13	1.6						

2. *Coarse Wares*

	Chalk (1)		Chalk (2)		Canterbury (4)	
	1609	1876	847	1081	445	588
11A/B/15	27	20.4	x	x		
18			x	x		
23B			0.5	0.4		
Sand (R)	67.3	57.6	67.8	45	35.3	26.7
4	44.5	38.2	42.2	33.1	32.1	24.3
1/2	0.6	0.5	x	x		
25			0.9	0.7		
3			1.3	1		
Sand (O)					5.6	4.3

3. *Mortaria*

	Chalk (1)		Chalk (2)		Canterbury (4)	
	37	1876	65	1081	0	588
2	48.6	1				
9A	51.4	1	100	6		

4. *Amphorae*

	Chalk (1)		Chalk (2)		Canterbury (4)	
	14	1876	0	1081	0	588
Dr. 20	x	x				
Mediterranean	100	0.75				
(Peacock 1977d)						

VII. Third to early fifth century A.D.

1. *Fine Wares*

	Springhead (4)			Chalk (3)			Rochester (5)		
	138	143	816	26	51	710	266	300	1590
3D/5C	–	3.5	0.6	–	49	3.5	–	11.3	2.1
2	x	x	x						
3E									
5B/13A	x	x	x	42.3	21.6	1.5	2.3	2	0.4
5D							x	x	x
12A	8	7.7	1.3	x	x	x	x	x	x
16A	80.4	77.6	13.6	57.7	29.4	2.1	53.8	47.7	9
24A	12.3	11.9	2.1				38.7	34.3	6.5
24B				x	x	x	5.3	4.7	0.9
Buff									
Mica-dusted									

	Canterbury (5)			Canterbury (6)		
	231	/	898	155	155	294
3D/5C		/			–	
2					–	
3E	x	x	x	x	x	x
5B/13A	2.6	/	0.7	27.8	27.8	14.6
5D	8.7	/	2.2	x	x	x
12A						
16A	x	x	x	7.8	7.8	4.1
24A	88.7	/	22.8	62.6	62.6	33
24B				14.8	14.8	7.8
Buff				x	x	x
Mica-dusted	x	x	x			

2. *Coarse Wares*

	Springhead (4)		Chalk (3)		Rochester (5)	
	643	816	635	710	1198	1590
11B/15	33.8	26.7	6.8	6.1	17.6	13.3
18	2.3	1.8				
23B	1.2	1				
23C	x	x			x	x
Sand (hand)						
Sand (R)	33.6	26.5	43.1	38.5	29.6	22.3
4	12.1	9.6	32.9	29.4	32.6	24.5
1/2	12.3	9.7	16.1	14.4	11	8.3
19	5.8	4.5			2.3	1.7
25	x	x	x	x	3.9	3
3			1.1	1	3.4	2.6
Sand (O)			x	x		
Sandy red, grey c-c	x	x				

	Canterbury (5)		Canterbury (6)	
	614	898	139	294
11B/15	7.8	5.3	16.6	7.8
18				
23B				
23C				
Sand (hand)			x	x
Sand (R)	41.9	28.6	36	17
4	36.4	25	14.4	6.8
1/2	1.8	1.2		
19				
25				
3	5.4	3.6	18.7	8.8
Sand (O)	6.7	4.6		
Sandy red, grey c-c				

3. *Mortaria*

	Springhead (4)		Chalk (3)		Rochester (5)	
	30	816	24	710	68	1590
5					10.3	0.4
7	26.7	1			x	x
8						
9A	53.3	2	100	3.4		
9B red c-c					8.8	0.4
9B white c-c	20	0.7			80.9	3.5
12						

	Canterbury (5)		Canterbury (6)	
	18	898	0	294
5				
7				
8	72.2	1.4		
9A				
9B red c-c	27.8	0.6		
9B white c-c				
12	x	x		

4. *Amphorae*

	Canterbury (5)	
Buff undesignated	35 100	898 3.5

VIII. Fourth to early fifth century A.D.

1. *Fine Wares*

	Canterbury (7)			Canterbury (8)			Canterbury (9)			Wye (2)		
	245	/		25	25	173	49	49	185	277	289	2478
3D/5C		/								–	4.2	0.5
2	2.5	/								11.2	10.7	1.3
4B							x	x	x	3.6	3.5	0.4
5B	33.9	/		72	10.4	10.4	x	x	x	18.8	18	2.1
7A	x	x	x									
12A	x	x	x				x	x	x			
16A	34.3	/		28	4.1	4.1	42.9	11.4	11.4	44.4	42.6	5.1
16C	4.5	/								x	x	x
17										5.8	5.5	0.7
5E	x	x	x									
14A	10.2	/										
24A	6.5	/					x	x	x	4.3	4.2	0.5
24B							57.1	15.1	15.1	3.6	3.5	0.4
Buff										x	x	x
Black c-c										8.3	8	0.9

N.B. Final figures for Canterbury 7 not available at time of writing: see Pollard forthcoming, d.

2. *Coarse Wares*

	Canterbury (7)		Canterbury (8)		Canterbury (9)		Wye (2)	
			133	173	136	185	2122	2478
11B/15			74.4	57.2	96.3	70.8	69.3	59.4
10							0.6	0.5
23C			12.8	9.8				
12					x	x		
Sand (hand)								
Sand (R)			6.8	5.2	3.7	2.7	21.6	18.6
4					x	x	0.9	0.8
1/2			x	x	x	x	6.7	5.7
19			6	4.6	x	x	x	x
25							0.3	0.2
3								
Sand (O)			x	x			x	x
Sand (B)	x	x						

3. *Mortaria*

	Canterbury (7)		Canterbury (8)		Canterbury (9)		Wye (2)	
2	61		15	173	x	185	67	2478
5	x	x					x	x
9A	70.5		100	8.7	x	x	89.6	2.4
9B red c-c	29.5		x	x	x	x	10.4	0.3
Nene Valley c-c	x	x						

4. *Amphorae*

	Wye (2)	
	x	2478
Dr. 20	x	x
Undesignated	x	x

IX. Mixed deposits

1. *Fine Wares*

	Brenley (4)			Joyden's Wood		
	237	254	586	684	841	4766
3D/5C/20A	–	6.7	2.9	–	18.7	3.3
3E				x	x	x
4B				8.9	7.3	1.3
5B/13A				1.9	1.6	0.3
9				55.1	44.8	7.9
16C				x	x	x
24A	97	90.6	39.2	22.2	18.1	3.2
24B				6.6	5.4	0.9
24D	x	x	x	5.3	4.3	0.8
Buff	x	x	x			
Hand-made	3	2.8	1.2			

2. *Coarse Wares*

	Brenley (4)		Joyden's Wood	
	332	586	3827	4766
11A/B/15	63.2	35.8	2.9	2.3
18			12.6	10.1
23B			0.4	0.3
Sand (R)	22.6	12.8	38	30.5
4	14.2	8	40.5	32.5
3			0.8	0.7
Sand (O)			x	x
Sand (B)			3.4	2.7
5			3.8	3
12			0.3	0.2

3. *Mortaria*

	Brenley (4)		Joyden's Wood	
	0	586	61	4766
2			x	x
5			26.2	0.3
9A			21.3	0.3
9B red c-c			27.9	0.4
Fine grey			24.6	0.3

4. *Amphorae*

	Brenley (4)		Joyden's Wood	
	0	586	x	4766
Dr. 20			x	x
Undesignated			x	x

GENERAL INDEX

This index lists references to sites within the Main Study Area (Fig. 1) and in East Sussex. Numbers in italics refer to pottery illustrations. Numbers in brackets after the site name are the site numbers listed in Appendix One. References to fabrics are listed in Appendices Two and Three.